THIRD EDITION

Using Samba

Gerald Carter, Jay Ts, and Robert Eckstein

Beijing · Cambridge · Farnham · Köln · Paris · Sebastopol · Taipei · Tokyo

Using Samba, Third Edition
by Gerald Carter, Jay Ts, and Robert Eckstein

Copyright © 2007, 2003, 2000 O'Reilly Media, Inc. All rights reserved.
Printed in the United States of America.

Published by O'Reilly Media, Inc., 1005 Gravenstein Highway North, Sebastopol, CA 95472.

O'Reilly books may be purchased for educational, business, or sales promotional use. Online editions are also available for most titles (*safari.oreilly.com*). For more information, contact our corporate/institutional sales department: (800) 998-9938 or *corporate@oreilly.com*.

Editor: Andy Oram
Executive Editor: Mary T. O'Brien
Production Editor: Lydia Onofrei
Copyeditor: Nancy Kotary
Proofreader: Nancy Reinhardt

Indexer: Julie Hawks
Cover Designer: Karen Montgomery
Interior Designer: David Futato
Illustrators: Robert Romano and Jessamyn Read

Printing History:

January 2000:	First Edition.
February 2003:	Second Edition.
January 2007:	Third Edition.

 This book uses RepKover™, a durable and flexible lay-flat binding.

ISBN-10: 0-596-00769-8
ISBN-13: 978-0-596-00769-0
[M]

Table of Contents

Preface

You are reading a book about Samba, a software suite that connects Windows, Unix, and other operating systems using Windows' native networking protocols. Samba allows Unix servers to offer Windows networking services by matching the filesystem and networking models of Unix to those of Windows. Samba acts as a bridge between the two systems, connecting the corresponding parts of their architectures and providing a translation wherever necessary.

Bridging the gap between systems as dissimilar as Windows and Unix is a complex task—one that Samba handles surprisingly well. To be a good Samba administrator, your abilities must parallel Samba's. For starters, you need to know basic Unix system and network administration and have a good understanding of Windows filesystems and networking fundamentals. In addition, you need to learn how Samba fills in the "gray area" between Unix and Windows; for instance, how a Unix user relates to a corresponding Windows account. Once you know how everything fits together, you'll find it easy to configure a Samba server to provide your network with reliable and high-performance resources.

Our job is to make all of that easier for you. We do this by starting out with a quick but comprehensive tour of Windows networking in Chapter 1, followed by task-oriented Chapters 2 and 3, which tell you how to set up a minimal Samba server and configure Windows clients to work with it. Most likely, you will be surprised how quickly you can complete the required tasks.

We believe that a hands-on approach is the most effective, and you can use the clients and servers you build in Chapters 2 and 3 to test examples that we describe throughout the book. You can jump around from chapter to chapter if you like, but if you continue sequentially from Chapter 4 onward, by the time you finish the book you will have a well-configured production Samba server ready for use. All you have to do is add the appropriate support for your intended purpose as we explain how to use each feature.

Audience for This Book

This book is primarily intended for Unix administrators who need to support Windows clients on their network, as well as anyone who needs to access the resources of a Windows network environment from a Unix client. Although we assume that you are familiar with basic Unix system administration, we do not assume that you are a networking expert. We do our best along the way to help out with unusual definitions and terms.

Furthermore, we don't assume that you are an expert in Microsoft Windows. We carefully explain all the essential concepts related to Windows networking, and we go through the Windows side of the installation task in considerable detail, focusing on the current Microsoft operating system offerings. For the Unix side, we give examples that work with common Unix operating systems, such as Linux, Solaris, FreeBSD, and Mac OS X.

We concentrate on Samba 3.0. However, because Samba releases include a high degree of backward compatibility with older releases, we believe you will find this book largely applicable to other versions as well.

How This Book Is Organized

Here is a quick description of each chapter:

Chapter 1, *An Introduction to Samba*
> Provides an overview of Samba and its capabilities, and then describes the most important concepts of NetBIOS and SMB/CIFS networking. Finally, we give you a quick overview of the daemons and utilities that are included in the Samba distribution.

Chapter 2, *Installing Samba on a Unix System*
> Covers both building Samba from source and using vendor-provided packages. We discuss the pitfalls surrounding upgrading Samba from one release to the next, as well as some basic configuration settings.

Chapter 3, *Configuring Windows Clients*
> Explains how to configure Microsoft Windows 2000 and later clients to participate in an SMB/CIFS network.

Chapter 4, *The Samba Configuration File*
> Gets you up to speed on the structure of the Samba configuration file and shows you how to take control of basic file-sharing services.

Chapter 5, *Accounts, Authentication, and Authorization*
> Gives you all the details about creating and managing users and groups in both local files and LDAP directory services. We'll also explain how to manage user privilege assignments as well security options for protecting shares.

Chapter 6, *Advanced Disk Shares*

Continues the discussion of file-sharing options, and covers more advanced functions such as permissions, access control lists, opportunistic locks, setting up a distributed filesystem tree, and Virtual File Systems plug-ins.

Chapter 7, *Printing*

Discusses how to share Unix printers on SMB/CIFS networks, including how to centrally manage the printer settings and drivers used by Windows clients. We also show you how to access SMB/CIFS printers from Unix clients.

Chapter 8, *Name Resolution and Network Browsing*

Introduces name resolution, which is used to convert NetBIOS computer names into IP addresses, and browsing, the method used in SMB networking to find what resources are being shared on the network.

Chapter 9, *Domain Controllers*

Dives into the world of Samba's domain control features, including domain trusts, support for remote management tools, and migrating from a Windows NT 4.0 domain to Samba.

Chapter 10, *Domain Member Servers*

Answers any questions you have about configuring Samba as a member of either a Samba or Windows domain, including integration with Active Directory. We also explain how Winbind can help ease account management on member servers and provide unified authentication for Unix services such as SSH.

Chapter 11, *Unix Clients*

Supplies you with the information necessary to configure native SMB/CIFS filesystems on Linux, FreeBSD, and OS X to access Samba and Windows server alike. Additionally, we show you how to use *smbclient* to develop portable backup strategies, and how the *net* tool can help you remotely manage SMB/CIFS servers.

Chapter 12, *Troubleshooting Samba*

Explains in detail what to do if you have problems installing Samba. This comparatively large chapter is packed with troubleshooting hints and strategies for identifying what is going wrong.

Appendix A, *Summary of Samba Daemons and Commands*

Is a quick reference that covers each server daemon and tool that make up the Samba suite.

Appendix B, *Downloading Samba with Subversion*

Explains how to download the latest development version of the Samba source code using SVN.

Appendix C, *Configure Options*

Documents each option that can be used with the *configure* command before compiling the Samba source code.

Conventions Used in This Book

The following font conventions are followed throughout this book:

Italic

> Filenames, file extensions, commands, URLs, domain names, new terms, user and group names, and emphasis.

`Constant width`

> Samba configuration options, hostnames, command options, other code that appears in the text, and command-line information that should be typed verbatim on the screen.

`Constant width bold`

> Commands that are entered by the user and new configuration options that we wish to bring to the attention of the reader.

`Constant width italic`

> Replaceable content in code and command-line information.

 This format designates a note, which is an important aside to the nearby text.

 This format designates a warning related to the nearby text.

Using Code Examples

This book is here to help you get your job done. In general, you may use the code in this book in your programs and documentation. You do not need to contact us for permission unless you're reproducing a significant portion of the code. For example, writing a program that uses several chunks of code from this book does not require permission. Selling or distributing a CD-ROM of examples from O'Reilly books *does* require permission. Answering a question by citing this book and quoting example code does not require permission. Incorporating a significant amount of example code from this book into your product's documentation *does* require permission.

We appreciate, but do not require, attribution. An attribution usually includes the title, author, publisher, and ISBN. For example: "*Using Samba*, Third Edition, by Gerald Carter, Jay Ts, and Robert Eckstein. Copyright 2007 O'Reilly Media, Inc., 978-0-596-00769-0."

If you feel your use of code examples falls outside fair use of the permission given above, feel free to contact us at *permissions@oreilly.com*.

How to Contact Us

Please address comments and questions concerning this book to the publisher:

O'Reilly Media, Inc.
1005 Gravenstein Highway North
Sebastopol, CA 95472
800-998-9938 (in the United States or Canada)
707-829-0515 (international/local)
707-829-0104 (fax)

To ask technical questions or comment on the book, send email to:

bookquestions@oreilly.com

We have a web page for this book. You can access this information at:

http://www.oreilly.com/catalog/9780596007690

You can also contact Gerald Carter, the lead author of this edition, at:

jerry@samba.org

Safari® Enabled

 When you see a Safari® Enabled icon on the cover of your favorite technology book, that means the book is available online through the O'Reilly Network Safari Bookshelf.

Safari offers a solution that's better than e-books. It's a virtual library that lets you easily search thousands of top tech books, cut and paste code samples, download chapters, and find quick answers when you need the most accurate, current information. Try it for free at *http://safari.oreilly.com*.

Acknowledgments

We would like to thank our technical reviewers on the third edition, David Collier-Brown, Deryck Hodge, Jim McDonough, Judith Myerson, and Bruno Gomes Pessanha. Their comments, corrections, and advice were invaluable in putting this book together. David Brickner acted as the original editor and helped guide the initial chapters. But the real captain of this ship was Andy Oram, who helped to bring the book to completion (once again).

Gerald Carter

I once described writing a book as an interruption in life. Andy (citing legendary editor Frank Willison) describes them as a kitten that one day grows up into an adult cat and requires constant day-to-day care (perhaps with less of the cuteness factor than the original kitten). I think both analogies point to the immense amount of time required from all parties involved that it takes to bring a book from the initial drafts to the copy you have in your possession now.

I am always amazed to be granted the grace to finish a writing project such as this. I hope that I have fulfilled this statement: "Whatever you do, do it all for the glory of God" (1 Corinthians 10:31).

To my wife, Kristi, who is always my guide back from the land of over-caffeination and sleep deprivation: I can say only thank you once again for your love, support, and understanding. You make me a better person.

To Andy: you have confirmed to me once again why I love writing for O'Reilly.

To the Samba developers I work with on a daily basis: thanks for letting me be a part of something great and for giving me something to write about.

Jay Ts

This book would have been extremely difficult to write if it hadn't been for the copy of VMware Workstation graciously provided by VMware, Inc. I want to thank Rik Farrow for his clarifying comments on security topics related to Samba and Windows, and thank both him and Rose Moon for their supportive friendship. Thanks also go to Mark Watson for his encouragement and advice on the topic of authoring technical books. Additionally, I'd like to express my appreciation to Andy Oram at O'Reilly for being a supportive, friendly, and easygoing editor, and for offering me terms that I could say yes to—something that a few other publishers didn't even approach. SUSE, Inc., generously provided a copy of SUSE Linux 8.1 Professional.

Robert Eckstein

I'd first like to recognize Dave Collier-Brown and Peter Kelly for all their help in the creation of this book. I'd also like to thank each technical reviewer who helped polish this book into shape on such short notice: Matthew Temple, Jeremy Allison, and of course Andrew Tridgell. Andrew and Jeremy deserve special recognition, not only for creating such a wonderful product, but also for providing a tireless amount of support in the final phase of this book—hats off to you, guys! A warm hug goes out to my wife Michelle, who once again put up with a husband loaded down with too much caffeine and a tight schedule. Thanks to Dave Sifry and the people at Linux-Care, San Francisco, for hosting me on such short notice for Andrew Tridgell's visit. And finally, a huge amount of thanks to our editor, Andy Oram, who (very) patiently helped guide this book through its many stages until we got it right.

All

We would especially like to give thanks to Perry Donham and Peter Kelly for helping mold the first draft of this book. Although Perry was unable to contribute to subsequent drafts, his material was essential to getting this book off on the right foot. In addition, some of the browsing material came from text originally written by Dan Shearer for O'Reilly.

## CHAPTER 1

An Introduction to Samba

Samba has been the subject of many cute descriptions in the past, some of which might have included a dancing penguin carrying a Microsoft Windows logo. We have been guilty of these things ourselves at one time or another. Although these pictures and descriptions can make great opening lines for magazine articles, they don't have the substance to sell IT shops on the elegance with which this piece of software can solve the very complex interopability problems faced by environments composed of Macintosh, Microsoft, and Unix (or Unix-like) systems. If we had to come up with a one-line executive summary to justify the existence of Samba, we would say, "Samba is a software suite that allows a Unix-based system to appear and function as a Microsoft Windows server when viewed by other systems on a network."

There are many components to Samba. Each of the pieces operate together to implement both the client and server portion of the Common Internet File System (CIFS) protocol. CIFS is the network protocol used by Microsoft operating systems for remote administration and to access shared resources such as files and printers. Despite the name, CIFS is neither a filesystem nor suitable for the Internet. It is, however, the protocol of choice in Windows networks.

There are several reasons to use Samba instead of Windows Server. As many experienced network administrators can testify, Samba provides day-in and day-out reliability, scalability, and flexibility. In addition, Samba offers freedom in both choice and cost. Samba is freely available from *http://www.samba.org* under the terms of the GNU General Public License (*http://www.fsf.org/licensing/licenses/gpl.html*). And because of Samba's portability, you are free to choose which server platform to use, such as FreeBSD, Linux, Solaris, or OS X.

One of the fascinating things about open source software such as Samba is that it creates a community of people surrounding the project, composed of more than just developers. The community of Samba users varies from IT professionals to teachers, consultants, and dentists. Also, many large companies, such as HP, IBM, Sun, Apple, RedHat, and Novell, distribute and commercially support Samba. If a time arises that you need outside support for your Samba servers, you are free to choose any of these providers for your support.

The remainder of this book is dedicated to helping you use Samba to meet the requirements of your network.

What Is Samba?

Samba is the brainchild of Andrew Tridgell, who started the project in 1991, while working with a Digital Equipment Corporation (DEC) software suite called Pathworks, created for connecting DEC VAX computers to computers made by other companies. Without knowing the significance of what he was doing, Andrew created a fileserver program for an odd protocol that was part of Pathworks. That protocol later turned out to be the Server Message Block (SMB), the predecessor to CIFS. A few years later, he expanded upon his custom-made SMB server and began distributing it as a free product on the Internet under the name "SMB Server." However, Andrew couldn't keep that name—it already belonged to another company's product—so he tried the following Unix renaming approach:

```
$ grep -i '^s.*m.*b.*' /usr/dict/words
```

And the response was:

```
salmonberry
samba
sawtimber
scramble
```

Thus, the name "Samba" was born. Today Samba is actively developed by a team of programmers distributed around the world.

One of the best ways to describe Samba is to explain some of the things that it can do. As previously mentioned, Samba implements the CIFS network protocol. By supporting this protocol, Samba enables computers running Unix-based operating systems to communicate with Microsoft Windows and other CIFS-enabled clients and servers. Some examples of common services offered by Samba are:

- Share one or more directory trees
- Provide a Distributed Filesystem (MS-DFS) namespace
- Centrally manage printers, print settings, and their associated drivers for access from Windows clients
- Assist clients with network browsing
- Authenticate clients logging onto a Windows domain
- Provide or assist with Windows Internet Name Service (WINS) name-server resolution

The Samba suite also includes client tools that allow users on a Unix system to access folders and printers that Windows systems and Samba servers offer on the network.

Samba's current stable release, version 3.0, revolves around three Unix daemons:

smbd

This daemon handles file and printer sharing and provides authentication and authorization for SMB clients.

nmbd

This daemon handles Samba's NetBIOS name registration, implements a Microsoft-compatible NetBIOS Name Server (NBNS) service, also referred to a WINS server, and partcipates in browsing elections.

winbindd

This daemon communicates with domain controllers for providing information such as the groups to which a user belongs. It also provides an interface to Windows' LanManager authentication schemes, commonly referred to as NTLM authentication, for Unix services other than Samba.

What Can Samba Do for Me?

As explained earlier, Samba can help Windows and Unix computers coexist in the same network.* However, there are some specific reasons why you might want to set up a Samba server on your network:

- You do not need—or wish to pay for—a full-fledged Windows server, yet you need the file and print functionality that one provides.

- You want to provide a common area for data or user directories to transition from a Windows server to a Unix one, or vice versa.

- You want to share printers among Windows and Unix workstations.

- You are supporting a group of computer users who have a mixture of Windows and Unix computers.

- You want to integrate Unix and Windows authentication, maintaining a single database of user accounts that works with both systems.

- You want to network Unix, Windows, Macintosh (OS X), and other systems using a single protocol.

Let's take a quick tour of Samba in action. Imagine the following basic network configuration: a Samba-enabled Unix system, to which we will assign the name RAIN, and a pair of Windows clients, to which we will assign the names LETTUCE and TOMATO, all connected via a local area network (LAN). The server RAIN has a local inkjet printer connected to it, inkprint, and a disk share named documents—both of

---

* The name Unix will be used throughout this book to mean Unix and Unix-like variants such as BSD, Linux, SysV, and Mac OS X.

which it can offer to the other two computers. A graphic of this network is shown in Figure 1-1.

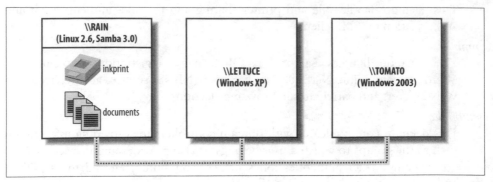

Figure 1-1. A simple network set up with a Samba server

In this network, each computer listed shares the same *workgroup*. A workgroup is a group name tag that identifies an arbitrary collection of computers and their resources on an SMB/CIFS network. Several workgroups can be on the network at any time, but for our basic network example, we'll have only one: the GARDEN workgroup.

Sharing Files

If everything is properly configured, we should be able to see the Samba server, RAIN, through the My Network Places directory on the Windows desktop, as shown in Figure 1-2. In fact, you should also be able to see each host that belongs to the GARDEN workgroup. Note the Microsoft Windows Network icon in the lefthand toolbar. As we just mentioned, more than one workgroup can exist on a network at any given time. A user who clicks this icon will see a list of all the workgroups that currently exist on the network.

We can take a closer look at the RAIN server by double-clicking its icon. This action causes the client to contact the server and request a list of its *shares*—the file and printer resources—that the computer provides. In this case, a printer named inkprint and a disk share named documents are on the server, as shown in Figure 1-3. Thanks to Samba, Windows sees the Unix server as a valid CIFS server and clients are able to access the documents folder as if it were just another directory on a local disk. Note that Windows displays the names of machines in mixed case (Rain). Case is irrelevant in NetBIOS and DNS names, so you might see rain, Rain, and RAIN in various displays or command output, but they all refer to a single system.

One popular Windows feature is the capability to map a drive letter (such as *H:*) to a remote shared directory. To create a path that points to a remote directory or printer, combine the server (*RAIN*) and share name (*documents*) to form a Universal

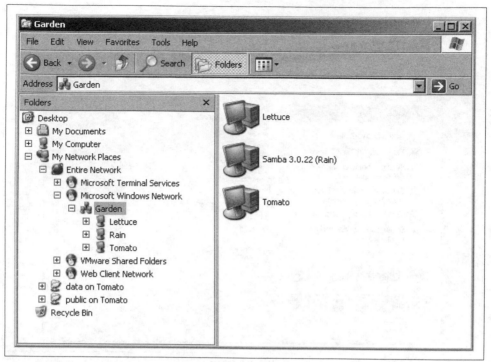

Figure 1-2. Viewing the members of a workgroup using My Network Places on a Windows client

Naming Convention (UNC) path (*\\RAIN\documents*). There are several methods of creating such a connection. One that works across almost all Windows operating systems versions is the *net.exe* command. The following command connects the *P:* driver letter to the documents share on RAIN:

```
C:\> net use p: \\rain\documents
```

Once this drive mapping is established, applications can access the files in the documents folder across the network as if it were an additional local hard disk mounted at *P:*. You can store data on it, install and run programs from it, and even restrict access to prevent unwanted visitors. If you have any applications that support multiuser functionality on a network, you can install those programs on the network drive.* Figure 1-4 shows the resulting network drive as it would appear with other storage devices in the Windows XP client. Note the pipeline attachment in the icon for the *P:* drive; this indicates that it is a network drive rather than a fixed drive.

---

* Be warned that many end-user license agreements forbid installing a program on a network so that multiple clients can access it. Check the legal agreements that accompany the product to be absolutely sure.

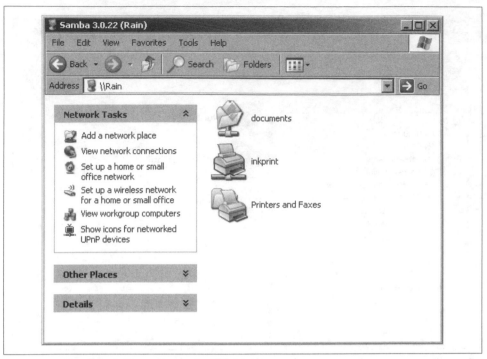

Figure 1-3. Shares available on the Samba host \\RAIN

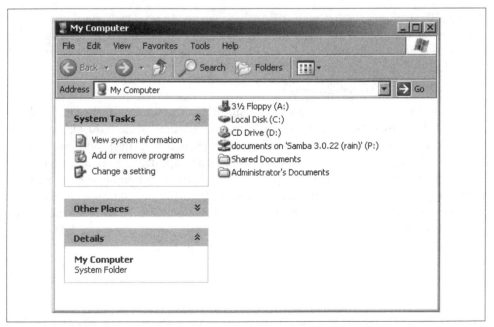

Figure 1-4. Displaying local and network drives in My Computer

Sharing a Printer

You probably noticed that the printer inkprint appeared under the available shares for RAIN in Figure 1-3, indicating that the Unix server has a printer that can be accessed by various clients. Data sent to the printer from any of the clients will be spooled on the Unix server and printed in the order in which it is received.

Connecting to a Samba printer from a Windows client is even easier than creating a mapping to a disk share. Windows systems support a system called *Point and Print* by which clients can automatically download the correct driver for a shared printer, and this system works with Samba shared printers just as easily as with Windows Server shared printers. Merely by double-clicking on the printer, the client downloads the necessary files from the server and creates a usable printer connection. An application can then access the print share using the same mechanisms as it would for a local printer. Figure 1-5 display a printer connection to *\\RAIN\inkprint* along with a local printer named HP LaserJet. Again, note the pipeline attachment below the printer, which identifies it as being on a network. More information on configuring Samba's printer and driver management features is provided in Chapter 7.

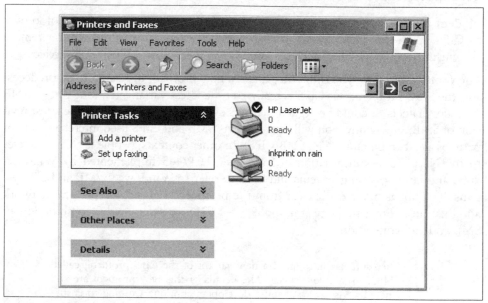

Figure 1-5. A client connection to the printer Q1 on the server RAIN

Seeing Things from the Unix Side

As mentioned earlier, Samba appears in Unix as a set of daemon programs. You can view them with the Unix *ps* command, you can read any messages they generate through custom debug files or the Unix *syslog* service (depending on how Samba is set up), and you can configure them from a single Samba configuration file: *smb.conf*. Additionally, if you want to get an idea of what the daemons are doing, Samba has a program called *smbstatus*, which displays the current state of the server's open client connections and file locks. Here's an example that shows that the user *lizard* has a connection to the documents share from the machine lettuce.

```
$ smbstatus

Samba version 3.0.22
PID     Username    Group    Machine
------------------------------------------------------------
19889   lizard      users    lettuce (192.168.1.143)


Service     pid     machine     Connected at
------------------------------------------------------------
documents   19889   lettuce     Fri Jun  3 01:34:46 2006

No locked files
```

The Common Internet File System

Modern Microsoft operating systems rely upon a resource-sharing protocol known as CIFS. CIFS provides APIs for manipulating files and for implementing remote administration functionality such as user password changes and printing services.

Microsoft would have you think that this is a new protocol unrelated to its predecessor, the SMB protocol, but CIFS is really just the latest variant in a long line of SMB protocol dialects. It could be argued that it is even just a new name for the latest revision of SMB. Frequently, you will see the terms SMB and CIFS used interchangably or perhaps as a combination (e.g., SMB/CIFS). In other contexts, people use CIFS to refer to the NetBIOS-less incarnation of SMB over TCP/445 implemented by Windows 2000 and later operating systems and SMB to refer to Windows 9x/ME and NT systems. The line is never really clear from the perspective of a developer or a network administrator. For simplicity, this book uses CIFS to refer to the combination of SMB and CIFS operations.

 Microsoft has introduced a new variant of the CIFS protocol, called SMB2, in Windows Vista. The details of this new protocol are still emerging. As always, Samba developers continue working to ensure compatibility with the most recent OS releases from Redmond.

CIFS is a connection-oriented, stateful protocol that relies upon three supporting network services:

- A name service
- A means of sending datagrams to a single or group of hosts
- A means of establishing a long-term connection between a client and server

Both Samba 3.0 and Windows 2000/XP/2003 support using standard IP services to meet these requirements. For example, the Domain Name Service (DNS) translates names to addresses, UDP packets provide the datagram service, and the TCP protocol provides the support needed for CIFS sessions. More on TCP/IP and DNS can be found in *TCP/IP Network Administration*, by Craig Hunt, and *DNS and BIND*, by Paul Albitz and Cricket Liu, both published by O'Reilly.

Prior to Windows 2000, Microsoft clients relied upon a layer called NetBIOS to provide this supporting infrastructure. Although modern CIFS clients and servers, including Samba, can function without utilizing NetBIOS services, most usually provide a legacy mode of operation for communicating with older CIFS implementations. Figure 1-6 illustrates the relationship between CIFS, hosts on a network, and core network services. The NetBIOS protocol is generally unfamiliar to Unix sysadmins and therefore deserves a little more attention.

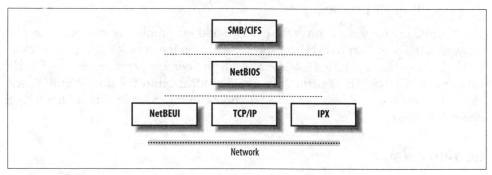

Figure 1-6. CIFS and its required support services

Understanding NetBIOS

To begin, let's step back in time. In 1984, IBM authored a simple application programming interface (API) for networking its computers, called the Network Basic Input/Output System (NetBIOS). The NetBIOS API provided a rudimentary design for an application to connect and share data with other computers.

It's helpful to think of the NetBIOS API as networking extensions to the standard BIOS API calls. The BIOS contains low-level code for performing filesystem operations on the local computer. NetBIOS originally had to exchange instructions with computers across IBM PC or Token Ring networks. It therefore required a low-level transport protocol to carry its requests from one computer to the next.

In late 1985, IBM released one such protocol, which it merged with the NetBIOS API to become the NetBIOS Extended User Interface (NetBEUI). NetBEUI was designed for small LANs, and let each computer claim a name (up to 15 characters in length) that wasn't already in use on the network. By "small LANs," we mean those with fewer than 255 nodes on the network—which was considered a generous number in 1985!

The NetBEUI protocol was very popular with networking applications, including those running under Windows for Workgroups. Later, implementations of NetBIOS over Novell's IPX networking protocols also emerged and competed with NetBEUI. However, the network stack of choice for the burgeoning Internet community was TCP/IP, and implementing the NetBIOS APIs over this protocol suite soon became a necessity.

Recall that TCP/IP uses numbers to represent computer addresses (192.168.220.100, for instance), and that NetBIOS uses only names. This difference was a point of contention when trying to integrate the two protocols together. In 1987, the IETF published standardization documents, titled RFC 1001 and 1002, that outlined how NetBIOS would work over a TCP/IP network. This set of documents still governs each implementation that exists today, including those provided by Microsoft with its Windows operating systems, as well as the Samba suite.

Since then, the standard that this document governs has become known as NetBIOS over TCP/IP, or NBT for short.

The NetBIOS name service solves the name-to-address problem mentioned earlier by allowing each computer to declare a specific name on the network that can be translated to a machine-readable IP address. With the current pervasiveness of TCP/IP networks and DNS, which performs a function identical to the three NetBIOS services, it is understandable why Microsoft choose to migrate away from NetBIOS in newer OS releases.

Getting a Name

In the NetBIOS world, when each computer comes online, it attempts to claim a name for itself; this process is called *name registration*. However, no two computers in the same namespace should be able to claim the same name; this state would cause endless confusion for any computer that wanted to communicate with either of them. There are two different approaches to ensure that this doesn't happen:

- Allow each computer on the network to defend its name in the event that another computer attempts to use it. Names are claimed through broadcast packets on local network segments.
- Use a WINS server to keep track of which hosts have registered a NetBIOS name. This approach is required when the hosts exist on different network segments that are not reachable via standard broadcast means.

Figure 1-7 illustrates a (failed) name registration, with and without WINS.

As mentioned earlier, there must be a way to resolve a NetBIOS name to a specific IP address; this process is known as *name resolution*. There are two different approaches with NBT here as well:

- Have each computer report back its IP address when it "hears" a broadcast request for its NetBIOS name.
- Use WINS to help resolve NetBIOS names to IP addresses.

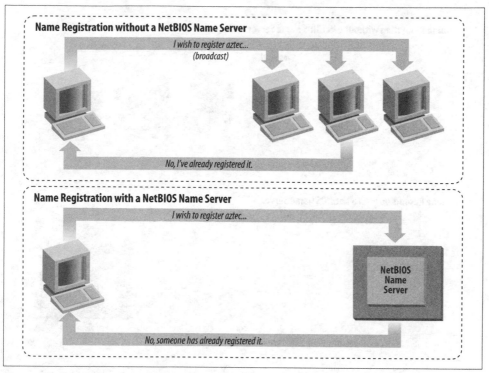

Name Registration without a NetBIOS Name Server

I wish to register aztec...
(broadcast)

No, I've already registered it.

Name Registration with a NetBIOS Name Server

I wish to register aztec...

NetBIOS
Name
Server

No, someone has already registered it.

Figure 1-7. Broadcast versus WINS name registration

Figure 1-8 illustrates the two types of name resolution.

As you might expect, having a WINS server on your network can help out tremendously. To see exactly why, let's look at the broadcast method.

When a client computer boots, it broadcasts a message declaring that it wishes to register a specified NetBIOS name as its own. If nobody objects to the use of the name, it keeps the name. On the other hand, if another computer on the local subnet is currently using the requested name, it sends a message back to the requesting client that the name is already taken. This is known as *defending* the name. This type of system comes in handy when one client has unexpectedly dropped off the network—another can take its name unchallenged—but it does incur an inordinate amount of traffic on the network for something as simple as name registration.

With WINS, the same thing occurs, except that the communication is confined to the requesting computer, the defending host, and the WINS server. No broadcasting occurs when the computer wishes to register the name; the registration message is simply sent directly from the client to the WINS server, which asks the defending host whether it wishes to continue to use the name. The WINS server reply to the name registration request is determined by the defending host's reply. This system is known as *point-to-point communication*, and it is often beneficial on networks with

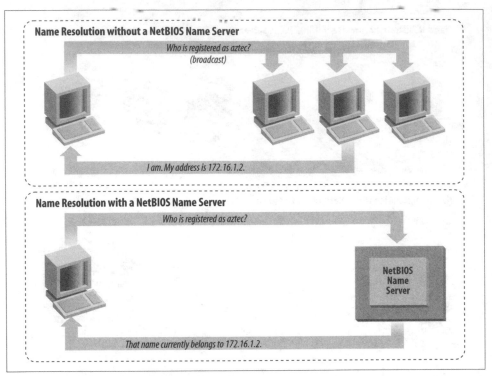

Figure 1-8. Broadcast versus WINS name resolution

more than one subnet, because routers are generally configured to block incoming packets that are broadcast to all computers in the subnet.

The same principles apply to name resolution. Without WINS, NetBIOS name resolution would also be done with a broadcast mechanism. All request packets would be sent to each computer in the network, with the hope that one computer that might be affected will respond directly back to the computer that asked. Using WINS and point-to-point communication for this purpose is far less taxing on the network than flooding the network with broadcasts for every name-resolution request.

It can be argued that broadcast packets do not cause significant problems in modern, high-bandwidth networks of hosts with fast CPUs, if only a small number of hosts are on the network, or if the demand for bandwidth is low. There are certainly cases where this argument is correct; however, the assumption does not hold in environments that support more than one broadcast segment connected together by routers. Therefore, the advice throughout this book is to avoid relying on broadcasts as much as possible. This rule is good for large, busy networks, and if you follow this advice when configuring a small network, your network will be able to grow without encountering problems later on that might be difficult to diagnose.

Node Types

Each computer on an NBT network earns one of the following designations, depending on how it handles name registration and resolution: b-node, p-node, m-node, and h-node. The behaviors of each type of node are summarized in Table 1-1.

Table 1-1. NetBIOS node types

Role	Value
b-node	Uses broadcast registration and resolution only.
p-node	Uses point-to-point registration and resolution only.
m-node (mixed)	Uses broadcast for registration. If successful, it notifies the NBNS of the result. Uses broadcast for resolution; uses the NBNS if broadcast is unsuccessful.
h-node (hybrid)	Uses the NBNS for registration and resolution; uses broadcast if the NBNS is unresponsive or inoperative.

Windows clients are usually h-nodes. The first three node types appear in RFC 1001/1002. H-nodes were invented later by Microsoft, as a more fault-tolerant method.

You can find the node type of a Windows 95/98/Me computer by running the winipcfg.exe command from the Start → Run dialog box (or from an MS-DOS prompt) and clicking the More Info button. On operating systems based on Windows NT, such as Windows 2000, Windows XP, and Windows 2003, you can use the ipconfig /all command in a command-prompt window, as shown in the next example. In either case, search for the line that says Node Type.

```
C:\> ipconfig /all
Windows IP Configuration

        Host Name . . . . . . . . . . . . : lettuce
        Primary Dns Suffix  . . . . . . . :
        Node Type . . . . . . . . . . . . : Hybrid
        IP Routing Enabled. . . . . . . . : No
        WINS Proxy Enabled. . . . . . . . : No
        DNS Suffix Search List. . . . . . : localdomain

Ethernet adapter Local Area Connection 2:

        Connection-specific DNS Suffix  . : localdomain
        Description . . . . . . . . . . . : AMD PCNFT Family PCI Ethernet Adapter #2
        Physical Address. . . . . . . . . : 00-0C-29-82-92-98
        Dhcp Fnabled. . . . . . . . . . . : Yes
        Autoconfiguration Enabled . . . . : Yes
        IP Address. . . . . . . . . . . . : 192.168.56.129
        Subnet Mask . . . . . . . . . . . : 255.255.255.0
        Default Gateway . . . . . . . . . :
        DHCP Server . . . . . . . . . . . : 192.168.56.254
        DNS Servers . . . . . . . . . . . : 192.168.56.1
        Lease Obtained. . . . . . . . . . : Tuesday, June 07, 2005 10:36:24 AM
        Lease Expires . . . . . . . . . . : Tuesday, June 07, 2005 11:06:24 AM
```

What's in a Name?

The names that NetBIOS uses are quite different from the DNS hostnames with which you might be familiar. First, NetBIOS names exist in a flat namespace. In other words, there are no hierarchical levels, such as in *oreilly.com* (two levels) or *ftp.samba.org* (three levels). NetBIOS names consist of a single unique string such as RAIN or SLEET within each WINS server or broadcast segment. Second, NetBIOS names may be no longer than 15 characters in length and can consist only of standard alphanumeric characters (a–z, A–Z, 0–9) plus the following:

```
! @ # $ % ^ & ( ) - ' { } . ~
```

Any name with fewer than 15 characters is padded with spaces at the end to reach the 15-character length.

Although you are allowed to use a period (.) in a NetBIOS name, it is a very bad idea. A NetBIOS name containing a period is very hard to distinguish from a valid DNS name. Even worse is something like the valid NetBIOS name 192.168.1.100.

It's not a coincidence that all valid hostnames are also valid NetBIOS names. In fact, the hostname for a Samba server is often reused as its NetBIOS name. For example, if you had a system with a fully qualified DNS name of sleet.plainjoe.org, its NetBIOS name would default to SLEET (followed by 9 spaces).

Resource names and types

With NetBIOS, a computer not only advertises its presence, but also tells others what types of services it offers. For example, SLEET can indicate that it's not just a workstation, but that it's also a file server and can receive Windows Messenger messages. This is done by adding a sixteenth byte to the end of the machine name, called the *resource type* (or *resource byte*), and registering the name multiple times, once for each service that it offers. See Figure 1-9.

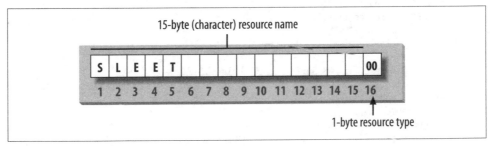

Figure 1-9. The structure of a NetBIOS name

The one-byte resource type indicates a unique service that the named computer provides. In this book, you will often see the resource type shown in angle brackets (<>) after the NetBIOS name, such as SLEET<0x00> or SLEET<00>. Note that Samba documentation and tools often use the hash mark in place of angle brackets (SLEET#00).

It is possible to see which names are registered for a particular NBT computer using the Windows command-line *nbtstat* utility. Because these services are unique (i.e., there cannot be more than one registered), you will see them listed as type UNIQUE in the output. For example, the following partial output describes the SLEET server:

```
C:\> nbtstat -a sleet

        NetBIOS Remote Machine Name Table
    Name                Type        Status
---------------------------------------------
    SLEET        <00>  UNIQUE      Registered
    SLEET        <03>  UNIQUE      Registered
    SLEET        <20>  UNIQUE      Registered
    ...
```

This output indicates that the server has registered the NetBIOS name SLEET as a machine (computer) name, as a recipient of messages from the Windows Messenger service, and as a file server. Some of the attributes a name can have are listed in Table 1-2.

Table 1-2. NetBIOS unique resource types

Named resource	Hexadecimal byte value
Standard Workstation Service	00
Messenger Service	03
RAS Server Service	06
Domain Master Browser Service (associated with primary domain controller)	1B
Master Browser name	1D
NetDDE Service	1F
Fileserver (including printer server)	20
RAS Client Service	21
Network Monitor Agent	BE
Network Monitor Utility	BF

Group names and types

NetBIOS also uses the concept of *groups* with which computers can register themselves. Earlier, we mentioned that the computers in our example belonged to a *workgroup*, which is a partition of computers on the same network. For example, a business might very easily have an ACCOUNTING and a SALES workgroup, each with different servers and printers. In the Windows world, a workgroup and a NetBIOS group are the same thing.

Continuing our *nbtstat* example, the SLEET Samba server is also a member of the GARDEN workgroup (the GROUP attribute hex 00) and will participate in elections for the browse master (GROUP attribute 1E). Here is the remainder of the *nbtstat* output:

```
         NetBIOS Remote Machine Name Table
   Name                 Type      Status
   ---------------------------------------------
   GARDEN      <00>     GROUP     Registered
   GARDEN      <1E>     GROUP     Registered
   ..__MSBROWSE__.<01>  GROUP      Registered
```

The possible group attributes a computer can have are listed in Table 1-3. An excellent reference to the internals of NetBIOS names and services can be found in Chris Hertel's book, *Implementing CIFS: The Common Internet File System* (Prentice Hall), available online at *http://www.ubiqx.org/cifs*.

Table 1-3. NetBIOS group resource types

Named resource	Hexadecimal byte value
Standard Workstation group	00
Logon server	1C
Master Browser name	1D
Normal Group name (used in browser elections)	1E
Internet Group name (administrative)	20
<01><02>__MSBROWSE__<02>	01

The final entry, __MSBROWSE__, is used to announce a group to other master browsers. The nonprinting characters in the name show up as dots in an *nbtstat* printout. Don't worry if you don't understand all of the resource or group types. Some of them you will not need with Samba, and others you will pick up as you move through the rest of the chapter. The important thing to remember here is the logistics of the naming mechanism.

Scope ID

In the dark ages of SMB networking, before NetBIOS groups were introduced, you could use a very primitive method to isolate groups of computers from the rest of the network. Each SMB packet contains a field called the *scope ID*, based on the idea that systems on the network could be configured to accept only packets with a scope ID matching that of their configuration. This feature was hardly ever used and unfortunately lingers in modern implementations. Some of the utilities included in the Samba distribution allow the scope ID to be set. Setting the scope ID in a network is likely to cause problems, and we are mentioning scope ID only so that you are not confused by it when you later encounter it in various places.

Datagrams and Sessions

NBT offers two transport services: the *session service* and the *datagram service*. Understanding how these two services work is not essential to using Samba, but it does give you an idea of how NBT works and how to troubleshoot Samba when it doesn't work.

The datagram service has no stable connection between computers. Packets of data are simply sent or broadcast from one computer to another, without regard to the order in which they arrive at the destination, or even if they arrive at all. The use of datagrams requires less processing overhead than sessions, although the reliability of the connection can suffer. Datagrams, therefore, are used for quickly sending nonvital blocks of data to one or more computers. The datagram service communicates using the simple primitives shown in Table 1-4.

Table 1-4. Datagram primitives

Primitive	Description
Send datagram	Send datagram packet to computer or groups of computers.
Send Broadcast datagram	Broadcast datagram to any computer waiting with a Receive Broadcast datagram.
Receive datagram	Receive a datagram from a computer.
Receive Broadcast datagram	Wait for a Broadcast datagram.

The session service is more complex. Sessions are a communication method that can, in theory, detect problematic or inoperable connections between two NetBIOS applications. It helps to think of an NBT session as being similar to a telephone call. Once a connection is made on a session, it remains open throughout the duration of the conversation; each side knows who the caller and the called computer are; and each can communicate using the simple primitives shown in Table 1-5.

Table 1-5. Session primitives

Primitive	Description
Call	Initiate a session with a computer listening under a specified name.
Listen	Wait for a call from a known caller or any caller.
Hang-up	Exit a call.
Send	Send data to the other computer.
Receive	Receive data from the other computer.
Session status	Get information on requested sessions.

Sessions are the backbone of resource sharing on an NBT network. They are typically used for establishing stable connections from client computers to disk or printer shares on a server. The client "calls" the server and starts trading information such as which files it wishes to open, which data it wishes to exchange, and so on. These calls can last a long time—hours, even days—and all of this occurs within the context of a single connection. If there is an error, the session software (TCP) retransmits until the data is received properly, unlike the "punt-and-pray" approach of the datagram service (UDP).

In truth, although sessions are supposed to handle problematic communications, they sometimes don't. If the connection is interrupted, session information that is open between the two computers becomes invalid. If this happens, the only way to regain the session information is for the same two computers to call each other again and start over.

If you want more information on each service, the best place to look is RFC 1001/1002. Just make sure to keep these two points in mind:

- Sessions are always point-to-point, taking place between two NetBIOS computers. If a session service is interrupted, the client is supposed to store sufficient state information for it to reestablish the connection.
- Datagrams can be sent to individual computers or broadcast to multiple computers, but they are unreliable. In other words, there is no way for the source to know that the datagrams it sent have indeed arrived at their destinations.

Connecting to a CIFS File Share

So, what happens when a user types net use p: \\rain\documents? To simplify the answer, let's assume the presence of a name service, a datagram service, and a session service, and ignore the details of whether the underlying network uses the NetBIOS interface or TCP/IP. In Chapter 5, we discuss how a CIFS server such as Samba handles operations such as authentication and authorization when connecting to file and printer shares; for now, let's just assume that these things are working.

Figure 1-10 shows the basic steps that a client will go through in order to access a remote share such as \\RAIN\documents. The diagram assumes that the client, named CATHY, has already resolved the server's name, SAM, to an IP address using either DNS or the NetBIOS mechanisms discussed earlier. Be aware that the steps to connect to a file or printer share are not always the same, because CIFS supports multiple authentication types and models. For now however, just focus on the scenario of an individual connecting to a share using a login name and password for the session credentials. This is by far the most common and intuitive case.

The first step in establishing the CIFS connection is to negotiate the protocol dialect that the client and server will use. The client transmits a list of dialects that it understands and the server selects the one that it prefers (supposedly the one with the most supported features). Table 1-6 lists the CIFS dialects supported by Samba 3.0.

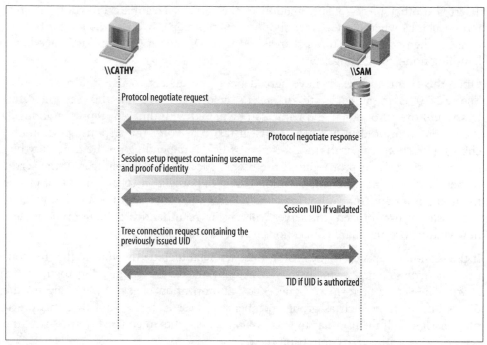

Figure 1-10. Examining what happens when a user types net use p: \\server\share

 Developers plan to enhance the POSIX 2 dialect in a future version of Samba so that the client can take more advantage of the Unix CIFS Extensions for file operations. More details on these extensions are covered in Chapter 11.

Table 1-6. CIFS protocol dialects

Protocol name	smb.conf name	Example clients
NT LANMAN 1.0	NT1	Windows 95, NT 4.0, and later
NT LM 0.12		smbclient
POSIX 2		Linux CIFS FS
LANMAN2.1	LANMAN2	
LM1.2X002		
Samba		
DOS LM1.2X002		
LANMAN1.0	LANMAN1	MS DOS network client
MICROSOFT NETWORKS 3.0		
MICROSOFT NETWORKS 1.03	COREPLUS	
PC NETWORK PROGRAM 1.0	CORE	

There are other pieces of information in the server's Negotiate Protocol (*negprot*) reply, such as whether the server supports encrypted passwords, what security level is used when connecting to its shares, and whether the server supports Unicode for handling non-ASCII strings.

Once the client and server have agreed upon the dialect to use, the next step in Figure 1-10 is to authenticate the user's credentials. During this session setup (*sesssetup*) operation, the login name can be paired with different representations of the user's proof of identify, such as a clear-text password, the response portion of a challenge/response algorithm, or a Kerberos ticket, depending on the capability bits set in the server's negprot reply. If the user is successfully authenticated, the server responds by sending the client a session virtual uid or *vuid*, a 16-bit token that proves the user's prior authentication. It has no relation to a Unix uid or a Windows SID. If the session is ever broken, the server will have to reauthenticate the user and issue a new vuid before any share connections can be reestablished.

If the session setup step is successful, the client can include the vuid in the tree connection (*tcon*) request, which is what actually makes the connection to the CIFS share. The server performs any necessary authorization checks by looking up the user's information, such as group membership, based on the vuid that was previously assigned. If the user has the necessary access rights to connect to the share, the server replies with a tree connection ID (*tid*).

Now the client is able to open and save files on the share just as if it were a local disk. When issuing the open file call in Figure 1-10, the client sends the previously issued tid to point to the root of the directory tree and the vuid for use in the server's file authorization checks.

Browsing

Browsing is the process of finding the other computers and shared resources in the Windows network. Note that this is unrelated to web browsing on the Internet, apart from the general idea of "discovering what's there." On the other hand, browsing the Windows network is like the Web in one way: what's out there can change without warning. Also be aware that browsing is not the same thing as searching Active Directory (AD) for hosts or resources. Although the NetBIOS browse service and AD are each a type of directory service, the implementation details are completely different. The comments in this section apply to browsing NetBIOS networks, not AD.

Before browsing existed, users had to know the name of the computer they wanted to connect to on the network and then manually enter a UNC such as \\rain\ *documents* to an application or file manager to access resources. Browsing is much

---

more convenient, making it possible to examine the contents of a network by using the point-and-click My Network Places GUI interface on a Windows client.[*]

You will encounter two types of browsing in an SMB network:

- Browsing a list of computers and shared resources
- Browsing the shared resource of a specific computer

Let's look at the first type. On each LAN (or subnet) with a workgroup or domain, one computer has the responsibility of maintaining a list of the computers that are currently accessible through the network. This computer is called the *local master browser*, and the list it maintains is called the *browse list*. Computers on a subnet use the browse list to cut down on the amount of network traffic generated while browsing. Instead of each computer dynamically polling to determine a list of the currently available computers, the computer can simply query the local master browser to obtain a complete, up-to-date list.

To browse the resources on a computer, a user must connect to the specific computer; this information cannot be obtained from the browse list. Browsing the list of resources on a computer can be done by double-clicking the computer's icon when it is presented in My Network Places. As you saw at the opening of the chapter, the computer responds with a list of shared resources that can be accessed after the user is successfully authenticated.

Each server in a Windows workgroup is required to announce its presence to the local master browser after it has registered a NetBIOS name, and (theoretically) announce that it is leaving the workgroup when it is shut down. It is the local master browser's responsibility to record what the servers have announced.

 The My Network Places application can behave oddly, until you select a particular computer to browse. You might see a list of computers that is not quite up-to-date, including hosts that are not longer on the network or new ones that have not been been noticed yet. Put succinctly, once you've selected a server and connected to it, you can be a lot more confident that the shares and printers really exist on the network.

Unlike the roles you've seen earlier, almost any Windows system can act as a local master browser. The local subnet can also have one or more backup browsers that will take over in the event that the local master browser fails or becomes inaccessible. The local master browser creates one backup browser for each group of 32 Windows NT based hosts on the subnet,[†] or each group of 16 Windows 95/98/ME hosts

---

[*] This was originally called Network Neighborhood in Windows 95/98/NT. Microsoft has changed the name to My Network Places in the more recent Windows Me/2000/XP.

[†] Windows 2000 and later operating systems are all based on Windows NT technology.

on the subnet (or a fraction of such a group). To ensure fluid operation, the local backup browsers synchronize their browse list frequently with the local master browser. There is currently no upper limit on the number of backup browsers that can be allocated by the local master browser.

Browsing Elections

Browsing is a critical aspect of any Windows workgroup. However, this can go wrong on any network. For example, let's say that a computer running Windows on the desk of a small company's office manager is the local master browser—that is, until she switches it off to plug in a fax machine. At this point, the Windows XP Workstation in the spare parts department might agree to take over the job. However, that computer is currently running a large, poorly written program that has brought its processor to its knees. The moral: browsing has to be very tolerant of servers coming and going. Because nearly every Windows system can serve as a browser, there has to be a way of deciding at any time who will take on the job. This decision-making process is called an *election*.

An election algorithm is built into all Windows operating systems so that they can agree who is going to be a local master browser and who will be local backup browsers. An election can be forced at any time. For example, let's assume that the office manager has finished using the fax machine and reboots her desktop PC. As the server comes online, it announces its presence, and an election takes place to see whether the PC in the spare parts department should still be the master browser.

When an election is performed, each computer broadcasts information about itself via datagrams. This information includes the following:

- The version of the election protocol used
- The operating system on the computer
- The amount of time the client has been on the network
- The name of the client

These values determine which operating system has seniority and will fulfill the role of the local master browser. (Chapter 8 describes the election process in more detail.) The architecture developed to achieve this is inelegant, and has no built-in security to prevent rogue machines from taking over. Thus it is possible for any computer running a browser service to register itself as participating in the browsing election and (after winning) being able to change the browse list. Nevertheless, browsing is a key feature in many Windows networks, and backward-compatibility requirements will ensure that it is in use for years to come.

Authentication: Peer-to-Peer Versus Domains

Peer-to-peer networks (not to be confused with P2P file sharing) were originally designed to allow users to share resources from their desktop computer with other users across a network. Network browsing was also originally designed to support this type of ad hoc networking in which no central management of disks or printers was needed. Users could turn their PCs on or off at will without fear of disrupting other users or network services (except those people who were accessing files or printers on the now-offline host).

When a request to access a file share or printer was received, the local computer was responsible for handling the authentication request as part of the connection process. Thus, any user account information or passwords had to be stored on the CIFS "server." If a user required access to shares on six remote machines, the user had to either remember six passwords or keep her account information synchronized across all six servers. Both solutions faced a scalability issue.

The peer-to-peer networking model of local authentication functions fairly well, as long as the number of computers on the network is small and there is a close-knit community of users. However, in larger networks, the simplicity of workgroups becomes a limiting factor. To support the needs of larger networks, such as those found in departmental computing environments, Microsoft introduced *domains* with Windows NT 3.51. A Windows NT domain is essentially a browsing group of CIFS-enabled computers with one addition: a server acting as a domain controller (see Figure 1-11).

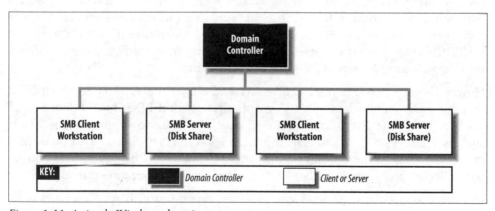

Figure 1-11. A simple Windows domain

A *domain controller* in a Windows domain performs a role similar to a Network Information Service (NIS) server or LDAP directory service in a Unix network, maintaining a domain-wide database of user and group information, as well as performing related services. The responsibilities of a domain controller are mainly related to security, including verifying user credentials (*authentication*) and granting or denying a user access to the resources of the domain (*authorization*). These tasks are typically done through the use of a username and password. The service that maintains the database on the domain controllers is called the Security Account Manager (SAM).

The Windows security model revolves around security identifiers (SIDs) and access control lists (ACLs). Security identifiers are used to represent objects in the domain, which include (but are not limited to) users, groups, and computers. SIDs are commonly written in ASCII form as hyphen-separated fields, like this:

```
S-1-5-21-1638239387-7675610646-9254035128-1000
```

The part of the SID starting with the "S" and leading up to the rightmost hyphen identifies a domain. The number after the rightmost hyphen is called a *relative identifier* (RID) and is a unique number within the domain that identifies the user, group, computer, or other object. The RID is the analog of a user ID (uid) or group ID (gid) on a Unix system or within an NIS domain.

Because domains centralize the management of account information, users are now able to use just one login name/password combination. However, the downside of this setup is that if the domain controller is unavailable, servers can no longer authenticate user requests. Therefore, Microsoft developed the concept of multiple domain controllers that maintain duplicate copies of the domain's SAM. For example, Windows NT domains utilize a primary domain controller (PDC) and one or more backup domain controllers (BDCs). A server in a Windows domain can use the SAM of any PDC or BDC to authenticate a user who attempts to access its resources and log on to the domain. If the PDC fails or becomes inaccessible, its duties can be taken over by one of the BDCs. BDCs frequently synchronize their SAM data with the PDC so that if the need arises, any one of them can immediately begin performing domain-controller services without affecting the clients.

However, note that Windows NT BDCs have read-only copies of the SAM database; they can update their data only by synchronizing with a PDC. In AD domains, all domain controllers (DCs) are considered equal. In order to support legacy clients such as Windows NT, one AD DC is designated as the PDC, but all DCs maintain a modifiable copy of the domain's authentication database. Changes on one domain controller are propagated to other DCs via a multimaster replication protocol.

Domain *trust relationships* allow clients within one domain to access the resources within another without having to possess a separate account in the second domain. The user's credentials are passed from the client system in the first domain to the server in the second domain, which consults a domain controller in its own domain. This DC then contacts a DC in the first (trusted) domain to check whether the user is valid before instructing the server to grant access to the resource.

Samba 3.0 can perform the role of a Windows NT domain controller. It is possible to have a Samba PDC and Samba BDCs in the same domain. Samba can even participate in trust relationships with other domains. However, at the current time of writing, you cannot mix Windows DCs and Samba DCs in the same domain. This rule may change in a future release. Make sure to check the Samba web site for the latest release and updates.

Samba can also function as a *domain member server* in either a Windows or Samba controlled domain, meaning that it has a computer account in the DC's account database and is therefore recognized as being part of the domain. A domain member server does not authenticate users logging on to the domain, but still handles security functions (such as file permissions) for domain users accessing its resources.

What's in Samba 3.0?

Samba 3.0 includes many features designed at better integration with Active Directory domains. Additionally, Samba's implementation of a Windows NT domain controller has become richer, although it is still missing a few features. Samba developers have also continued to improve functionality introduced in earlier releases, such as printing support for Windows 2000/XP clients, filesystem ACLs, and Winbind.

Windows NT Domain Controller Support

Samba 3.0 includes support for several newer security additions to the CIFS protocol, such as packet integrity checks known as SMB signing, secure channel communication, and the NTLMv2 authentication algorithm. Thus, it is possible to have a Samba server support domain logons for a network of Windows clients, including the most recent releases from Microsoft. This setup can result in a very stable, high-performance, and more secure network; it also provides the benefit of not having to purchase per-seat Windows Client Acccess Licenses (CALs) from Microsoft. The current release also supports migration of user and group information from a Windows NT 4.0 domain to a Samba domain, so that you are able to continue to upgrade your network without the costs of purchasing Windows 2000 Server or newer in order to use Active Directory.

Active Directory Domain Member Servers

In addition to the NT4 domain mode security provided by Samba 2.x, 3.0 introduces a new ADS domain mode security that allows a Samba host to join an Active Directory domain and authenticate individual connection requests from clients using Kerberos tickets. The *winbindd* daemon also supports obtaining user and group information via more effecient LDAP searches instead of Remote Procedure Calls (RPC).

Local Nested Groups

Windows has always supported the concept of adding groups as members of other groups. Current Samba releases also support this capability, by using Winbind to define a group that is local to the server and can contain Windows domain groups. Upon receiving a request for the list of users in the local group, Winbind expands the membership of any nested domain groups that it contains. This feature can be useful, such as when you want to set the group ownership of a file that must be accessible by multiple domain groups. You define on the Samba host a local group that contains all of the appropriate domain groups. Of course, it is possible to perform an equivalent function if the filesystem supports access control lists. However, local groups have the advantage of requiring you to deal with only one group instead of many. More on Winbind's support for local groups is in Chapter 10.

Unicode and Internationalization

Unicode is the pervasive means of representing non-English character sets on Windows NT-based computers. The older DOS codepage methods used by Windows 9x and Samba prior to 3.0 could support extended character sets, but not in multiple combinations. You could support English and Spanish clients, but not English, Spanish, and French. The UCS2 encoding represents each character using 16 bits, providing more than enough combinations to handle more languages that any of us have to manage on our network. Building Samba to include Unicode support is covered in Chapter 2.

User and Group Account Storage Plug-in Modules

Libraries knows as *passdb* modules allow an administrator to choose the persistent storage backend for user and group information. Prior versions of Samba supported this feature in a limited fashion and required the storage interface—for example, a flat text file (*smbpasswd*) or an LDAP directory service—to be defined at compile time. Samba 3.0 supports multiple passdb backends, which can be defined in its configuration file at runtime. This approach allows for easy migration from one storage format to another and to have one Samba package that supports the needs of multiple installations. Users and groups and how they are stored are discussed in Chapter 5.

Stackable Virtual File System (VFS) Modules

Samba's VFS layer allows programmers to write a plug-in that handles all of the disk I/O operations for a particular share. Good examples of current VFS modules are the network recycle bin, virus scanners, and filesystem snapshot tools. Samba 2.2 only allowed one plugin to be used on given file share at any given time. Samba 3.0 allows multiple VFS modules to be chained together in series so that, for example, you could log when a user deleted a file and move it to a trash can rather than actually removing it. Chapter 6 will explore Samba's VFS.

User Privileges

Recent releases of Samba introduced the ability to grant certain rights, such as the ability to join Windows clients to a Samba domain, to a nonroot user. Prior versions of Samba required the use of a user account with a uid of 0 (that is, the superuser). Being able to delegate such security-sensitive operations goes a long way when managing Samba domains with multiple administrators. Privileges are discussed in the context of users and groups in Chapter 5.

Windows Automatic Driver Downloads

Samba 2.2 began support for the Windows Point and Print model. Samba 3.0 extends this support, with the latest releases able to back up and restore print queues and drivers in bulk as well as migrate printers from a Windows server to a Samba host using Microsoft's Print Migrator application. Samba's printing support and the details of Point and Print are explained in Chapter 7.

But Wait, There's More

And of course, Samba developers have include numerous bug fixes, performance improvements, and added support for newer CIFS protocol operations. There's really no reason to be running an older version of Samba.

Future Research in Samba 4.0

Samba 4.0 is an ambitous research project, taken up by Samba developers around the time that Samba 3.0.0 was released (in late 2003), to address a desire for newer features that were believed to be extremely hard to achieve in the Samba 3.0 code base. Examples of these projects of these items include:

- Support for non-POSIX filesystems
- Full NTFS semantics
- Active Directory domain control support

At the time of writing, a proof-of-concept AD implementation has been completed, with the exception of the directory replication protocol.

There has been a great deal of confusion about the relationship between Samba 3.0 and Samba 4. Both source code repositories are part of the Samba project. Samba 3.0 is the current production branch, and Samba 4 is the research branch, which is focused on new functionality that will be integrated into production releases once it has matured.

The current question system administrators ask most often is "When will Samba 4 be released?" In our opinion, it is helpful to view Samba 4 as a blueprint of what project leaders want Samba to be. Of course, blueprints often require a prototype, so developers will release technical previews of the Samba 4 branch from time to time as a way to expose designs to a wider audience. Some prototypes succeed; others are thrown away. At some point, the production releases of Samba will look like the working prototypes. Whether this occurs gradually or all at once is yet to be seen.

Pieces of Samba 4 have already been released as production quality services. For example, the *samba4wins* project (*http://enterprisesamba.org*) provides a WINS server that supports the Microsoft WINS replication protocol. Other pieces, such as Samba 4's memory management library, are shipping in Samba 3.0 today. It's likely that Samba 4 in whole or in part will continue to coexist with Samba 3.0 for several years to come. No one can accurately predict which release will contain the combined features of Samba 3.0 and technology of Samba 4.

For the latest in development and release news, check the Samba news site (*http://news.samba.org*), available mailing lists hosted at *https://lists.samba.org*, and community topics at *http://wiki.samba.org*.

What Can Samba Do?

We'll wrap up by showing how Samba can currently help out and how it is limited. Table 1-7 summarizes the roles that Samba can and cannot play in a Windows NT or Active Directory domain or a Windows workgroup. The Windows domain protocols are proprietary and have not been documented by Microsoft, and therefore must be analyzed by developers before Samba can support them.

Table 1-7. Samba roles (as of version 3.0.22)

Role	Can perform?
File server	Yes
Printer server	Yes
Microsoft DFS server	Yes
Windows NT 4 domain controller	Yes
Interact with Windows DCs in the same domain	No
Active Directory DC	No
Windows 95/98/Me authentication	Yes
Windows NT/2000/XP/2003 authentication	Yes
Local master browser	Yes
Domain master browser	Yes
Primary WINS server	Yes
Secondary WINS server	No

An Overview of the Samba Distribution

As mentioned earlier, Samba actually contains several programs that serve different but related purposes. Here we introduce each of them briefly and describe how they work together. These programs are documented fully in Appendix A.

The majority of the programs that come with Samba center on its three major daemons and one management service application. Let's take a high-level look at the responsibilities of each:

nmbd

> The *nmbd* daemon is a simple name server that supplies WINS functionality. This daemon listens for name-server requests and provides the appropriate IP addresses when called upon. It also provides browse lists for the My Network Places application and participates in browsing elections.

smbd

> The *smbd* daemon manages the shared resources between the Samba server and its clients. It provides file and print services to SMB/CIFS clients across one or more networks and handles all notifications between the Samba server and the network clients. In addition, it is responsible for user authentication, resource locking, and data sharing through the SMB/CIFS protocol.

swat

> The Samba Web Administration Tool (SWAT) is a HTTP-based application for managing Samba. In essence, SWAT offers a graphical interface to functions performed by the included command-line tools.

winbindd

> This daemon is used along with the name service switch to get information on users and groups from a Windows domain controller, and allows Samba to authenticate users from a Windows domain.

The Samba distribution also comes with a small set of Unix command-line tools:

findsmb

> A program that searches the local network for computers that respond to SMB protocol and prints information on them. It is written in Perl and is a good example of how scripts can utilize Samba command-line tools to extend functionality.

net

> This new program distributed with Samba 3.0 can be used to perform remote administration of servers. It also includes some local Samba administration functions.

nmblookup

This program provides NBT name lookups to translate NetBIOS names to network addresses, and vice versa.

ntlm_auth

This tool provides a command-line interface to Winbind's NTLM authentication interface. This tool allows third-party applications such as *pppd* and the *squid* web proxy server to support NTLM authentication by leveraging Samba's existing functionality.

pdbedit

This tool is the replacement program for many of the functions performed by the *smbpasswd* utility in previous releases. It is the command-line management tool for user account information stored in a passdb backend.

rpcclient

This program can be used to run MS-RPC functions on Windows clients. Although it can be useful, it is primarily a developer testing tool, and so has a tendency to change frequently. The *net* command is promoted as the stable, administrative tool for performing similar functions.

smbcacls

This program is used to set or show ACLs on Windows NT filesystems.

smbcquotas

This program is used to set or show filesystem quotas on Windows servers.

smbclient

This *ftp*-like Unix client connects to SMB shares and operates on them.

smbcontrol

This simple administrative utility sends messages to *nmbd* or *smbd*.

smbmnt, smbmount, smbumount, mount.cifs, umount.cifs

These helper utilities for the Linux *smbfs* and *cifs* filesystems allow Linux systems to access shares offered over SMB/CIFS.

smbpasswd

This program allows an administrator to change the passwords used by Samba. It also provides a means for a user to remotely change his password on a SMB/CIFS server.

smbspool

This print-spooling program is used by the Common Unix Printing System (CUPS) to send files to remote printers that are shared on the SMB network.

smbstatus

This program reports the current network connections to the shares on a Samba server.

smbtar

> This program, similar to the Unix tar command, backs up data in SMB shares. This is another example of a script written around an existing Samba command-line utility.

smbtree

> This program is similar to the *findsmb* Perl script, but was written using the *libsmbclient* library.

smbget

> This utility is the SMB equivalent of the GNU *wget* utility for retreiving files.

tdbbackup, tdbdump, tdbtool

> These tools manipulate Samba's trivial database (*tdb*) files.

testparm

> This simple program checks the Samba configuration file.

wbinfo

> This utility queries the *winbindd* daemon.

Each major release of Samba goes through an exposure test before it's announced and is quickly updated afterward if problems or unwanted side effects are found. The latest stable distribution as of this writing is Samba 3.0.22, and this book focuses mainly on the functionality supported in this release, as opposed to older versions of Samba.

How Can I Get Samba?

Source and binary distributions of Samba are available from mirror sites across the Internet. The primary web site for Samba is located at *http://www.samba.org*. From there, you can select a mirror site that is geographically near you. Most Linux and many Unix vendors provide binary packages. These can be more convenient to install and maintain than the Samba team's source or binary packages, due to the vendor's efforts to supply a package that matches its specific products. The next chapter focuses on all the details necessary to get Samba up and running on your server.

CHAPTER 2
Installing Samba on a Unix System

It would be unwise to purchase a car or a house on appearance alone or from a description in a brochure. It is similarly unwise to talk about a piece of software without hands-on experience. Systems administration is a hands-on job. In this chapter, we are dedicated to helping you test drive your own server so that you can see for yourself how Samba behaves. Because open source projects (and software packages in general) evolve over time, the remainder of this book is based on the current production Samba release at the time of writing, version 3.0.22. We start with the necessary steps to install Samba both from the source release available on the official Samba web site and from vendor or community packages. By the end of the chapter, you will have a working server with a simple disk share.

Binary Packages

Samba is so popular with Unix/Linux administrators that many vendors include pre-packaged versions in their operating system distributions. There are advantages to using software packages, one of which is that you do not have to bother with the details of compiling the software itself. The main drawback is that you are dependent on the options the vendor chose when building Samba. It is also likely that the server will be slightly behind the current production Samba release, because vendors tend to upgrade packages only when there is a strong reason, such as a widely experienced bug or security issue. On the other hand, you can be fairly sure that a bundled version has been installed properly, and perhaps it will take only a few simple modifications to your *smb.conf* file for you to be up and running. Samba is mature enough that you probably don't need the latest release to meet your basic needs, so you might be perfectly happy running a bundled version.

If you choose this option, be aware that your Samba files, including the very important *smb.conf*, will likely be stored somewhere other than the default locations used by Samba when it has been built from source. For example, with most Linux distributions, *smb.conf* and some other Samba-related files are in the */etc/samba* directory. The default location when building from source is */usr/local/samba/lib*.

If Samba is already installed on your system, you can check which version you have by using the command:

```
$ smbd -V
Version 3.0.12
```

If you receive a message back similar to "command not found," either Samba is not installed or *smbd* is not in your shell's search path. In the latter case, use the *find* command to locate the *smbd* executable.

```
$ find / -name smbd -print
/opt/samba/sbin/smbd
```

You might also be able to use a system-specific tool to query a software-package maintenance utility for the location of the Samba programs. On RPM-based systems such as Red Hat Enterprise Linux and Novell's SUSE Linux, you can use the *rpm* command to query the installed packages for Samba. In this example, Samba has been split between multiple packages.

```
$ rpm -qa | grep samba
samba-3.0.12-5
samba-client-3.0.12-5
samba-common-3.0.12-5
```

Other platforms will most likely have similar toolsets for querying installed software packages. For example, Solaris includes the *pkginfo* application and Debian Linux provides *dpkg*. If you are unsure which tools are available, check your server's operating system documentation.

It is possible to determine certain information about Samba's build using the -b option. This option instructs *smbd* to print its list of compile-time values for items such as directory search paths. The -b option can produce several screens of data. So unless you can read extremely fast, it is best to pipe the output to a file, page through it with a pager utility such as *less* or *more*, or simply *grep* the information you need. The following example shows that *smbd* expects its configuration file to be found in the */etc/samba* directory.

```
$ smbd -b | grep CONFIGFILE
    CONFIGFILE: /etc/samba/smb.conf
```

Even if a vendor does not include Samba with the operating system, precompiled binary packages are available for a large number of platforms. These packages are often maintained by members of the Samba community for the purpose of saving you a fair amount of time and trouble. The best place to begin when looking for installable Samba packages is *http://www.samba.org/samba/ftp/Binary_Packages*. Here you will find either the packages themselves or links to sites that do provide them.

When using a package from a third party, it is vital to ensure that the correct libraries required by the executables are also installed. If your system does not already have the required version of a library, you might have to install a new version.

Package managers such as RPM provide dependencies checks to ensure that all of the necessary libraries for a piece of software are available before the software can be installed. If your software packaging system does not support this feature, many systems with shared libraries do come with a tool called *ldd*. This tool tells you which libraries a specific binary requires and which libraries on the system satisfy that requirement. For example, checking the *smbd* program on our test machine gave us:

```
$ ldd /usr/local/samba/sbin/smbd
linux-gate.so.1 => (0xffffe000)
libldap-2.2.so.7 => /usr/lib/libldap-2.2.so.7 (0x40019000)
liblber-2.2.so.7 => /usr/lib/liblber-2.2.so.7 (0x4004b000)
libgssapi_krb5.so.2 => /usr/lib/libgssapi_krb5.so.2 (0x40058000)
libkrb5.so.3 => /usr/lib/libkrb5.so.3 (0x4006f000)
libk5crypto.so.3 => /usr/lib/libk5crypto.so.3 (0x400e2000)
libcom_err.so.2 => /lib/libcom_err.so.2 (0x40120000)
libcups.so.2 => /usr/lib/libcups.so.2 (0x40124000)
libssl.so.0.9.7 => /usr/lib/libssl.so.0.9.7 (0x40141000)
libcrypto.so.0.9.7 => /usr/lib/libcrypto.so.0.9.7 (0x40171000)
libnsl.so.1 => /lib/libnsl.so.1 (0x40264000)
libcrypt.so.1 => /lib/libcrypt.so.1 (0x40279000)
libpam.so.0 => /lib/libpam.so.0 (0x402ab000)
libresolv.so.2 => /lib/libresolv.so.2 (0x402b4000)
libdl.so.2 => /lib/libdl.so.2 (0x402c7000)
libpopt.so.0 => not found
libc.so.6 => /lib/tls/libc.so.6 (0x402d3000)
libsasl2.so.2 => /usr/lib/libsasl2.so.2 (0x403ec000)
libkrb5support.so.0 => /usr/lib/libkrb5support.so.0 (0x40401000)
/lib/ld-linux.so.2 (0x40000000)
```

If there are any incompatible (or missing) libraries at this stage, the distribution-specific documentation should highlight them. In this example, the *popt* library cannot be found. This type of problem usually occurs for one of two reasons: either the library is not present on the system or the library is present but is stored in a location outside the runtime library search path. The solution to the first problem is simple: install the missing library. The solution to the second issue is platform-dependent. For example, on Linux, you can edit */etc/ld.so.conf* to add directories to the search path for the run time linker, and on Solaris, you can use the *crle* tool to perform a similar function.

Compiling from Source

A typical Samba installation takes about an hour to complete, including downloading the source files and compiling them, setting up the configuration files, and testing the server. Conventionally installing from source is called the *./configure &&make && make install* process. Here is a complete list of the individual steps:

1. Download the source or binary files.
2. Read the installation documentation.
3. Run the *autoconf* script that generates the Makefile appropriate for your system.

4. Compile the server and utility programs.

5. Install the server files.

6. Create a Samba configuration file.

7. Test the configuration file.

8. Start the Samba daemons.

9. Test the Samba daemons.

Downloading the Source Distribution

If you would like to download the latest version of the Samba software, the primary web site is *http://www.samba.org*. Once you connect to this page, you should see a drop-down list of world-wide mirrors. Choose a site that is closest to your own geographic location. The link to the download area is located on the lefthand tool bar that appears on every page on the Samba web site.

The Samba site includes online documentation, links to mailing list archives, and the latest Samba news,[*] as well as source and binary distributions of Samba. Unless you specifically want an older version of the Samba server or are going to install a binary distribution, download the latest source distribution from the closest mirror site. This distribution is always named *samba-latest.tar.gz*, which for the 3.0.22 release is a 16 MB file.

It is also a good idea to verify the digital signature on the uncompressed tarball to ensure that the version you are downloading is one actually released by the Samba Team. To do this you will need either GnuPG (*http://www.gnupg.org*) or some other *pgp*-compatible utility installed on a system. You can verify the tarball's signature on any machine. It does not have to be done on the server used for compiling Samba.

First, download the current Samba public GPG key. Look for a file named *samba-pubkey.asc* residing in the same directory as the Samba source release tarball. This key should be imported into your *pgp* keyring by executing:

```
$ gpg --import samba-pubkey.asc
gpg: key F17F9772: public key "Samba Distribution Verification Key <samba-bugs@samba.
org>" imported
gpg: Total number processed: 1
gpg:               imported: 1
...
```

The key ID (F17F9772) will change from year to year as the old key expires and a new one is issued by the Samba developers. The latest key will always be available at *http://www.samba.org/samba/ftp/samba-pubkey.asc*.

---

[*] A recent addition to the Samba web site is a news portal (*http://news.samba.org*). This site is a collection of all things Samba, from release announcements to advocacy stories and new developer announcements.

Now you can verify the integrity of the source tarball by uncompressing it and asking *gpg* to verify the signature file (*samba-latest.tar.asc*).

```
$ gunzip samba-latest.tar.gz
$ gpg --verify samba-latest.tar.asc
gpg: Signature made Thu 14 Apr 2005 01:23:58 AM CDT using DSA key ID F17F9772
gpg: Good signature from "Samba Distribution Verification Key <samba-bugs@samba.org>"
```

Now you are ready to extract the files from the tar archive. While the following *tar* command runs, it prints out a list of the files it installs:

```
$ tar xvf samba-latest.tar
```

The archive creates a single directory named *samba-VERSION* (where *VERSION* is the current release number, such as 3.0.22). This directory contains all of the source files, documentation, packaging files, and examples included in the distribution.

Read the Documentation

In the top-level directory that you just created, a file named *WHATSNEW.txt* contains the latest news about the release. If you are upgrading, you can find important information in this file about bug fixes or configuration parameters that have been added or are no longer supported.

With both source and binary packages, you'll find a large number of documents in the *docs* directory, in a variety of formats. Samba documentation has improved substancially over the years. There are currently three full-length books, one of which is the one you are currently reading, included in this directory. You'll have plenty of time to browse this collection while Samba is compiling.

Configuring Samba

The source distribution of Samba 3.0 doesn't initially have a makefile. Instead, one is generated through a GNU Autoconf script, which is located in the *samba-3.0.x/source/* directory. The *configure* script takes care of the machine-specific issues of building Samba, such as which libraries are needed, what's the maximum value that can be stored in a integer, and how to automatically determine the available network interfaces on a system. The *configure* script also allows you to enable or disable specific features in Samba (more on this task shortly).

When *configure* runs, it prints messages telling what it is doing, and error messages might be mixed in. To make sure that you see those very important error messages, it is helpful to run *configure* with its standard output passed through some filter to capture the output and keep it from scrolling out of sight. For example:

```
$ ./configure | more
```

Although executing *configure* with no options generates a working set of binaries, you might want to add support for extra features by passing options on the command line. Each option enables or disables various features. You typically enable a feature by specifying the --with-*feature* option, which causes the feature to be compiled and installed. Likewise, if you specify a --without-*feature* option, the feature will be disabled. Note that options to the *configure* script start with two hyphens.

The following command instructs *configure* to test for Pluggable Authentication Module (PAM) support on the build host:

```
$ ./configure --with-pam
```

We'll discuss Samba PAM integration when we examine users and passwords in Chapter 5.

If you would like a complete list of options, type the following:

```
$ ./configure --help
```

The full list of configuration options is reproduced in Appendix C. Here is a brief list of some of the most popular features, which are covered later in this book:

--with-acl-support
> Include support for integrating with filesystem POSIX ACLs. Samba acts as a thin layer of glue for many features by mapping what a Windows client requests to what a Unix/Linux server can provide. Samba does not implement filesystem ACLs internally, but instead provides an interface to the ACL implementation provided by the host's filesystem. ACLs will be discussed in more detail in Chapter 6.

--with-ads
> Include support for integration with Active Directory services using the Kerberos 5 and LDAP protocols. This is one of the major advances in Samba 3.0, but it also introduces dependencies on third-party software components. Compiling Samba to include ADS support is covered in more detail later in this chapter, while the steps for configuring Samba as a domain member server will be presented in Chapter 10.

--enable-cups
> Require that Samba enable its support for the CUPS. If the necessary CUPS development files are not found, the *configure* script will fail. See Chapter 7 for more information on integrating Samba and CUPS.

--with-syslog
> Integrate Samba's debug logs with the system logs via the *syslogd* service. Logging and syslog are covered in Chapter 4.

--with-smbmount
> Include the userspace tools for managing the *smbfs* filesystem on Linux clients. Be aware that *smbfs* is different from the newer CIFS filesystem included in the Linux 2.6 kernel. Both Linux filesystem modules are discussed in Chapter 11.

--enable-debug
> Instruct the compiler to enable debug symbols in the resulting binaries for use by a symbolic debugger such as *gdb*. Troubleshooting and debugging Samba are covered in Chapter 12.

Each option is set to a default that is appropriate for most systems, and none of the features are essential to basic Samba installations. However, you may want to include them in your configuration (as we will in our example) at least to be able to try out the options in later chapters.

In addition, Table 2-1 shows some other parameters that you can give the *configure* script if you wish to store parts of the Samba distribution in different places, perhaps to make use of multiple disks or partitions. Note that the defaults sometimes refer to a prefix specified earlier in the table. In other words, if you set the --prefix option to */opt/samba*, the default bindir becomes */opt/samb/bin*.

Table 2-1. Additional configure options

Option	Meaning	Default
--prefix=*directory*	Install architecture-independent files at the base directory specified.	*/usr/local/samba*
--bindir=*directory*	Install user executables in the directory specified.	*${prefix}/bin*
--sbindir=*directory*	Install administrator executables in the directory specified.	*${prefix}/sbin*
--datadir=*directory*	Install read-only architecture-independent data in the directory specified.	*${prefix}/share*
--libdir=*directory*	Install program libraries in the directory specified.	*${prefix}/lib*
--localstatedir=*directory*	Runtime state information.	*${prefix}/var*
--mandir=*directory*	Install manual pages in the directory specified.	*${prefix}/man*
--with-privatedir=*directory*	Directory to use for Samba's private files, such as *smbpasswd* and *secrets.tdb*	*${prefix}/private*
--with-piddir=*directory*	Directory that Samba daemons will use for storing the main parent pid files.	*${localstatedir}/var/locks*
--with-configdir=*directory*	Directory that Samba daemons will use for locating configuration files.	*${libdir}*
--with-lockdir=*directory*	Directory that Samba will use for storing database and runtime state files.	*${localstatedir}/var/locks*
--with-logfilebase=*directory*	Directory that Samba daemons will use for storing logfiles.	*${localstatedir}*
--with-fhs	Use a directory structure below *${prefix}* that adheres to the Linux Filesystem Hierarchy Standard.	

Here is one example of a possible directory layout when building Samba from scratch:

```
$ ./configure --prefix=/opt/samba \
        --localstatedir=/var/lib/samba \
        --with-piddir=/var/run \
        --with-logfilebase=/var/log/samba \
        --with-privatedir=/etc/samba/private \
        --with-configdir=/etc/samba \
        --with-lockdir=/var/lib/samba
```

This layout results in the following set of directories after installing the binaries and files created from the compilation process:

/opt/samba
> The base installation directory for Samba client and server binaries, manpages and other documentation, libraries and header files

/etc/samba
> Samba configuration files

/etc/samba/private
> User accounts and other security-sensitive data

/var/log/samba
> Logfiles created by Samba daemons

/var/lib/samba
> Samba's repository of Trivial Database (*tdb*) files used to maintain configuration and state information, such as open file locks held by clients and printer attributes

/var/run
> Pid files created by *smbd*, *nmbd*, and *winbindd*

This type of installation makes it easy to share a build via NFS while storing the local configuration information on a local filesystem. Feel free to add on any additional feature flags (e.g., --with-acl-support) that you think would be useful.

 Samba *tdb* files must always reside on a filesystem that provides locking and a coherent *mmap()* implementation. For most systems, this rule implies that you must use a local native filesystem.

Here is a sample execution of the *configure* script, which creates a Samba 3.0.22 makefile for the Linux platform:

```
$ cd samba-3.0.22/source/
$ ./configure --prefix=/usr/samba --with-smbmount \
    --with-syslog 2>&1 | more
SAMBA VERSION: 3.0.22
checking for gcc... gcc
checking for C compiler default output file name... a.out
checking whether the C compiler works... yes
checking whether we are cross compiling... no
checking for suffix of executables...
checking for suffix of object files... o
checking whether we are using the GNU C compiler... yes
checking whether gcc accepts -g... yes
...(content omitted)...
Using libraries:
    LIBS = -lcrypt -lresolv -lnsl -ldl
    KRB5_LIBS = -lgssapi_krb5 -lkrb5 -lk5crypto -lcom_err
    LDAP_LIBS = -lldap -llber
    AUTH_LIBS = -lcrypt
```

In general, any message from *configure* that doesn't begin with the words checking or creating is an error. If there was an error during configuration, more detailed information about it can be found in the *config.log* file, which is written to the local directory by the *configure* script. If the configuration works, you'll see a checking configure summary message in the output on the screen followed by a yes message and four or five file-creation messages:

```
checking configure summary... yes
configure: creating ./config.status
config.status: creating include/stamp-h
config.status: creating Makefile
config.status: creating script/findsmb
config.status: creating smbadduser
config.status: creating script/gen-8bit-gap.sh
config.status: creating include/config.h
```

So far, so good.

Kerberos and LDAP

In order to integrate with Active Directory using the Kerberos and LDAP protocols, Samba relies upon third-party libraries such as those provided by MIT, Heimdal, and OpenLDAP. However, the introduction of these build dependencies can complicate the previous simple *./configure && make && make install* steps.

Microsoft introduced a new Kerberos encryption type when initially creating Active Directory. The reason for this new algorithm (RC4-HMAC-MD5) was to enable smooth upgrades from Windows NT 4.0 domains by using existing account passwords as the basis for generating the new long-term secrets keys in the AD Kerberos realm. However, earlier versions of both the MIT and Heimdal Kerberos libraries did not support this new encryption type (type 23) and were forced to rely on DES keys.

Things have since improved, and both the major open source Kerberos players have RC4-HMAC (sometimes called ARCFOUR-HMAC) support now. Samba's *configure* script will attempt to locate a working set of Kerberos client libraries. Be aware that just because Kerberos is included with the operating system (e.g., Solaris) does not necessarily mean it is a usable installation. The script will ignore any unusable Kerberos libraries. Thus, unless you are paying attention, it is quite possible to end up with a set of binaries that don't allow you to run the Samba's newer ADS security mode.

To decide whether you have to install a Kerberos client distribution, consider the following to be the bare minimum for interoperating with Active Directory:

- MIT Kerberos 1.3 (*http://web.mit.edu/kerberos/www*)
- Heimdal Kerberos 0.6.1 (*http://www.pdc.kth.se/heimdal*)

It is possible to use releases older than these, but things get slightly more complicated when it comes time to configure Samba (as you will see in Chapter 10). A good source of information (compilation, installation, and management) covering both Kerberos distributions as well as Active Directory is *Kerberos: The Definitive Guide*, by Jason Garman (O'Reilly).

Once the Kerberos piece is set, we have to deal with the LDAP dependency as well. Currently, Samba supports only the OpenLDAP distribution for AD integration. Any OpenLDAP 2.x release should work, but experience has shown that the latest stable release is generally best. Note that Samba requires only the client libraries, so there is no need to compile or install the OpenLDAP server or server related tools. More information on OpenLDAP can be found at *http://www.openldap.org* or in *LDAP System Administration*, by Gerald Carter (O'Reilly).

One final note is that when using third-party libraries such as the Kerberos or LDAP ones mentioned here, you should also ensure that once installed, the libraries can be located by dependent applications such as Samba. There are two primary means of achieving this.

One method is to add the directory (e.g., */opt/openldap/lib*) to the global library search path. On some platforms, this can be done at run time by appending the new directory to the LD_LIBRARY_PATH search list.

```
# export LD_LIBRARY_PATH=$LD_LIBRARY_PATH:/opt/openldap/lib
```

Other, more permanent solutions, differ from platform to platform. For example, Linux's */etc/ld.so.conf* file and Solaris' *crle* tool have already been mentioned.

The other solution is to encode the library search path in the binary itself during the compilation process, usually done by instructing the compiler to pass additional flags onto the linker. The following script shows how this would be done if Heimdal Kerberos were installed in */opt/heimdal* and OpenLDAP were installed in */opt/openldap*:

```
#!/bin/sh

CC="gcc"
CFLAGS=""
CPPFLAGS=""
LDFLAGS=""

DIRPATH="/opt/heimdal /opt/openldap"
for dir in $DIRPATH ; do
        CPPFLAGS="$CPPFLAGS -I$dir/include"
        CFLAGS="$CFLAGS -Wl,-rpath,$dir/lib"
        LDFLAGS="$LDFLAGS -L$dir/lib"
done

export CPPFLAGS CFLAGS LDFLAGS CC
```

The resulting $CPPFLAGS variable (used by the C preprocessor) would be:

```
-I/opt/heimdal/include -I/opt/openldap/include
```

The $CFLAGS variable (used by the compiler) would appear as:

```
-Wl,-rpath,/opt/heimdal/lib -Wl,-rpath,/opt/openldap/lib
```

and the linker flags ($LDFLAGS) would be:

```
-L/opt/heimdal/lib -L/opt/openldap/lib
```

Other compilers and linkers besides *gcc* (e.g., the Sun C compiler), may use the -R*dir* flag for encoding library search paths rather than -Wl,-rpath,*dir*. Check the compiler documention to be sure.

Once these variables are set, we can run *configure* followed by *make* and we should end up with an AD-enabled version of Samba. If you want to verify that the resulting *smbd* binary does in fact include AD support, use the -b flag again and this time *grep* for WITH_ADS :

```
$ smbd -b | grep ADS
   WITH_ADS
```

Unicode and the iconv Library

Internally, Samba uses Unicode when communicating with Unicode-aware clients such as Windows NT and later clients. There are times when these Unicode strings must be converted to a locale encoding (a non-Unicode collection of language, country, and cultural information), such as when writing a filename to disk or displaying a username. When possible, Samba utilizes the GNU *iconv* library, available from *http://www.gnu.org/software/libiconv*, to handle these translations.

Some Unix variants, such as FreeBSD and Linux, come with a suitable *iconv* library installed. But some variants—Solaris being the most notable—do not have sufficient support in the included *iconv* implementation for Samba's purposes. There are two codepages that can be handled independently of *iconv*: the European CP850 and CP437 character sets. Therefore, these character sets work on systems that lack the necessary *iconv*.

However, if your server will be supporting characters outside the standard English ASCII character set, it is best to verify that your server has a working *iconv* installation.

Compiling and Installing Samba

At this point you should be ready to build the Samba executables. Compiling is even easier than configuration: in the *source* directory, type *make* on the command line. The *make* utility will produce a stream of explanatory and success messages, beginning with:

```
Using FLAGS = -O -Iinclude ...
```

This build includes all the mentioned Samba client and server binaries. If you encounter a problem when compiling, first check the Samba documentation to see whether it is easily fixable. Another possibility is to search or post to the Samba mailing lists, links to which are given at the end of Chapter 12 and on the Samba home page. Most compilation issues are system-specific and almost always easy to overcome.

Now that the files have been compiled, you can install them in the directories you identified. Make sure to change to the root user before running the following command:

```
$ make install
```

If you configured Samba to use the default locations for files, the new files will be installed in the directories listed in Table 2-2.

Table 2-2. Samba installation directories

Directory	Description
/usr/local/samba	Main tree
/usr/local/samba/bin	Client binaries and administartive tools
/usr/local/samba/sbin	Server binaries
/usr/local/samba/lib	smb.conf, lmhosts, configuration files, and so on
/usr/local/samba/man	Samba documentation
/usr/local/samba/private	Samba-encrypted password file
/usr/local/samba/swat	SWAT files
/usr/local/samba/var	Samba logfiles, lock files, tdb files, browse list info, shared memory files, process ID files

The remainder of the book assumes a default install location of */usr/local/samba*. Beware that this can vary from system to system. Many vendors install Samba either to */opt* or to */usr* by default. If you are using a prepackaged version of Samba or have inherited a Samba server from a past administrator, be sure that you find out where the various tools, daemons, and configuration data were installed.

If you happen to be upgrading into the same directory tree as a previous Samba installation, the preexisting client tools and server binaries are saved with the extension *.old*, and you can go back to that previous version with the command make revert. After issuing make install, you should copy the *.old* files (if they exist) to a new location or name. Otherwise, the next time you install Samba (or even run make install a second time), the original *.old* will be overwritten without warning and you could lose your earlier version.

Congratulations! You now have Samba on your system!

Upgrading Your Installation

Eventually a new version of Samba will be released, and you will want to upgrade. Just repeat the same steps you used to install your current version. Download the source distribution from the Samba web site, unpack it, and then run the *./configure*, *make*, and *make install* commands as before. If you've forgotten which options you used with the *configure* script, either take a look at the *source/config.status* file in your previous version's source distribution or examine the output of *smbd -b* to determine which features and directories were used. The *config.status* file is similar to a cache file. Its first few lines will show the options used the last time *configure* was run.

When upgrading, it is a good idea to back up a few important files in case something goes wrong. Samba developers support upgrades of Samba databases from one version to the next. However, downgrading is not supported. So keep a copy of the files listed in Table 2-3.*

Table 2-3. Important Samba configuration files

Filename	Description
${configdir}/smb.conf	Main configuration file.
${privatedir}/*	This directory contains sensitive data about such things as user passwords and important state information, such as the local machine security identifier (SID).
${lockdir}/nt*tdb	These database files contain information about printers, queues, and installed print drivers on the system.
${lockdir}/share_info.tdb	Contains the security descriptors assigned to file shares.
${lockdir}/group_mapping.tdb	Contains the table of Windows groups SID to Unix group IDs.
${lockdir}/account_policy.tdb	Local account policy data, such as password expiration time and account lockout settings.
${lockdir}/winbindd_idmap.tdb	Maintains the mappings between Windows users and groups and the allocated Unix uids and gids. Important only if you are running the *winbindd* daemon.

Table 2-4 gives a brief description of the remaining *tdb* files. These files either maintain runtime state information, and are therefore recreated by the Samba daemons on startup, or store cache information that can be rebuilt as necessary.

Table 2-4. Samba's volatile tdb and datafiles

Filename	Description
${lockdir}/brlock.tdb	Maintains information about open byte range file locks.
${lockdir}/locking.tdb	Contains data about open files, granted oplocks, and share mode entries on files.
${lockdir}/deferred_open.tdb	Maintains data necessary to implement Samba deferred file open semantics in conjunction with file locks.
${lockdir}/sessionid.tdb	Stores the list of active CIFS session UIDs.
${lockdir}/connections.tdb	Information regarding open share connections.
${lockdir}/printing/*tdb	Caches the queue listing of each available printer in *smb.conf*.
${lockdir}/permon/*tdb	Performance counters (if configured) to be returned to clients querying the HKPD registry hive.
${lockdir}/eventlog/*tdb	Eventlogs (if configured).
${lockdir}/gencache.tdb	Generic caching database used for such things as failed name resolution.
${lockdir}/login_cache.tdb	Cache of the failed login attempts used to enforce the password lockout policy setting.
${lockdir}/netsamlogon_cache.tdb	Cache of user and group information obtained in replies from domain controllers when authenticating via NTLM.

---

* The list of *tdb* files might change in future releases, so be sure to check the *WHATSNEW.txt* file for updates.

Table 2-4. Samba's volatile tdb and datafiles (continued)

Filename	Description
${lockdir}/registry.tdb	Implementation of the Windows registry for Samba servers. Currently, the file is rebuilt at startup and contains no sensitive or critical data.
${lockdir}/unexpected.tdb	List of unhandled packets returned from Windows clients on port 137 or 138.
${lockdir}/winbindd_cache.tdb	Cache file used by the *winbindd* daemon to improve performance when handling requests such as enumerating domain users and groups and mapping names to Windows sids.
${lockdir}/browse.dat	State information maintained by *nmbd* in relation to network browsing elections.
${lockdir}/wins.dat* *${lockdir}/wins.tdb	Contains the most recent dump of *nmbd*'s internal WINS database. This file is applicable only when the *wins support* parameter has been enabled in *smb.conf*.

Reconfiguring Samba

If you have already compiled Samba and wish to recompile the same source code with different *configure* options, run the following command in the *source* directory before rerunning the *configure* script:

```
$ make distclean
```

This ensures that you are starting with a clean slate and that your previous *configure* command does not leave any files laying around that can affect your new build. From here, you can rerun *./configure* and then *make* and *make install*.

Setting Search Paths

You will probably want to run commands included in the Samba distribution without having to specify their full directory paths. For that to work, the directory in which the Samba executables are located, */usr/local/samba/{bin,sbin}* by default, must be added to your shell's PATH environment variable. This environment variable is usually set in one or more of the shell's startup files, which in the case of *bash* are */etc/profile* (systemwide) and the *.profile*, *.bash_profile*, and *.bashrc* files in each user's home directory.

To be able to read the Samba manual pages using the *man* command, the directory where Samba's manual pages reside, */usr/local/samba/man* by default, must be in your MANPATH environment variable. On SUSE Linux, this can be accomplished by adding the following two lines to */etc/manpath.config*:

```
MANPATH      /usr/local/samba/man
MANPATH_MAP  /usr/local/samba/bin /usr/local/samba/man
```

Other systems might just require a line such as the following in your shell's initialization file:

```
export MANPATH=$MANPATH:/usr/local/samba/man
```

Enabling the Samba Web Administration Tool (SWAT)

The Samba Web Administration Tool (SWAT) provides a forms-based editor in your web browser for creating and modifying Samba's configuration file. It runs as a daemon under *inetd* or *xinetd*. For SWAT to work, entries must be added for it in the */etc/services* and */etc/inetd.conf* (or */etc/xinetd.d/swat*) configuration files. To add the entries, follow these three steps:

1. Check your */etc/services* file, and add the following line to the end if a line like it does not already appear.

   ```
   swat    901/tcp
   ```

2. If an entry exists and has assigned port 901 to a service other than SWAT, you can select any unused port. However, you will need to adapt any references to port 901 in our examples to your local configuration.

3. Make sure that an *inetd*-style daemon is running. *inetd* and *xinetd* are "Internet super daemons" that handle starting daemons on demand, instead of letting them sit around in memory consuming system resources. Most Unix systems use *inetd*, but some utilize the more secure *xinetd* service. Most Linux distribution now use *xinetd* by default. You can use the *ps* command to see which of the two your system is running.

For *inetd*, add a line to the */etc/inetd.conf* file. (Check your *inetd.conf* manual page to see the exact format of the *inetd.conf* file whether it differs from the following example.) Don't forget to change the path to the SWAT binary if you installed it in a different location from the default */usr/local/samba*:

```
swat   stream  tcp  nowait  root  /usr/local/samba/sbin/swat  swat
```

Then force *inetd* to reread its configuration file by sending it a SIGHUP (hangup) signal:

```
$ kill -HUP -a inetd
```

Notice that we are using a version of the *kill* command that supports the -a option, so as to allow us to specify the process by name. On FreeBSD and Linux (but not Solaris), you can use the *killall* command as follows:

```
$ killall -HUP inetd
```

On Solaris up to and including Solaris 9, use the *pkill* command.

```
$ pkill -HUP inetd
```

On Solaris 10 and later, *inetd* is not used, but there is an automatic conversion program. Enter the configureation details into *inetd.conf* and then run the following command.

```
$ inetconv
```

If you are not running one of the previously mentioned operating systems and your version of *kill* doesn't have the -a option, you will need to use the *ps* command to find the process ID and then supply that to *kill*:

```
$ ps ax | grep inetd
  780 ?         S        0:00 inetd
 1981 pts/4     S        0:00 grep inetd
$ kill -HUP 780
```

If your system is using *xinetd*, add a file named *swat* in your */etc/xinetd.d* directory and make sure it is readable by the account used to run the *xinetd* metadaemon (usually *root*). The file should contain the following:

```
# description: swat is the Samba Web Administration Tool, which
#        allows an administrator to configure Samba using a web
#        browser interface, with the URL http://localhost:901
service swat
{
        socket_type            = stream
        wait                   = no
        protocol               = tcp
        only_from              = localhost
        user                   = root
        log_on_failure         += USERID
        server                 = /usr/local/samba/sbin/swat
        port                   = 901
        disable                = no
}
```

Then *xinetd* needs to be sent a signal* to make it reread its configuration files:

```
$ kill -HUP -a xinetd
```

SWAT has its advantages and its disadvantages. On the plus side:

- SWAT prevents typos in parameter names by writing *smb.conf* based on your input.
- SWAT makes it easy to determine the default value for parameters.
- Samba's Online documentation is linked from SWAT's front page.
- Online help for each parameter is linked beside each input field.

On the minus side:

- To utilize SWAT's full functionality, you must log in as the root user. This is the reason why SWAT is usually restricted by administrators to run over the loop-back interface rather than remotely across a network.
- SWAT supports only HTTP (no HTTPS), allowing snoopers to see what you are doing. It is possible to use a tool such as Stunnel (*http://www.stunnel.org*) to add secure communication outside of SWAT.
- SWAT strips out all comments and rewrites *smb.conf* upon committing changes to disk. This is a problem only if you swap back and forth between editing the file in an external editor and editing *smb.conf* in SWAT.

---

* Depending on the version of *xinetd* you have and how it was compiled, you might need to send a USR1 or some other signal rather than the HUP signal. Check the manual page for *xinetd_ (8)* on your system for details.

That's pretty much it for the installation. Before starting Samba, however, you need to create a configuration file for it.

A Basic Samba Configuration File

The key to configuring Samba is its configuration file, *smb.conf*. This configuration file can be very simple or extremely complex, and the rest of this book is devoted to helping you get deeply personal with this file. For now, however, we'll show you how to set up a single file service, which will allow you to fire up the Samba daemons and see that everything is running as it should be. In later chapters, you will see how to configure Samba for more complicated and interesting tasks.

The installation process does not automatically create an *smb.conf* configuration file, although several example files are included in the Samba distribution in the *samba-3.0.x/examples/* directory. To test the server software, we'll use the following file, which you can create in a text editor of your choosing. It should be named *smb.conf* and placed in the */usr/local/samba/lib* directory:*

```
[global]
    workgroup = GARDEN
[test]
    comment = For testing only, please
    path = /export/tmp
    read only = no
```

This brief configuration file tells the Samba server to offer the */export/tmp* directory on the server as an SMB share called *test*. Parameters in *smb.conf* are case-insensitive—*path* is the same option as *PATH*. They are also whitespace-insensitive so that *read only* and *ReadOnly* are interpreted as the same parameter. Values, however, may or may not be case-insensitive, depending on their use. For example, a username or a directory path should be considered to be case-sensitive, yet Samba interprets Boolean value such as yes or no as case-insensitive strings.

Our server will operate as part of the GARDEN workgroup, of which each client should also be a part. If you have already chosen a name for your own workgroup, use the existing name instead of GARDEN in the previous example. In case you are connecting your server to an existing network and need to know the workgroup name, ask another system administrator or go to a Windows system in the workgroup and follow these instructions for Windows 2000/XP/2003:

- Right click on My Computer icon and select Properties.
- The workgroup or domain name should be listed in the windows after selecting the Network Identification (or Computer Name) tab.

---

* If you did not compile Samba, but instead downloaded a binary, check with the documentation for the package to find out where it expects the *smb.conf* file to be. Or, check the output from *smbd -b* and locate the value of the CONFIGFILE variable. If Samba came preinstalled with your Unix system, an *smb.conf* file is probably already somewhere on your system.

We'll use the [test] share in the next chapter to set up the Windows clients. For now, you can complete the setup by performing the following commands as root on your Unix server:

```
# mkdir -p /export/tmp
# chmod 1777 /export/tmp
```

If the version of *mkdir* included on your system doesn't support creating a full directory path (-p), just create each directory one by one. You might also want to put a file or two in the */export/tmp* directory, so that after the Windows clients are initially configured, it will be easier to verify that that everything works.

Encrypted Passwords

Password encryption is one of those areas where interoperability between Windows and Unix/Linux systems gets extremely messy. Both sides of the fence use a different nonreversible encryption algorithm, which means that you cannot generically convert Unix passwords to the LanMan or NT password hashes or vice versa.

There is even widespread misunderstanding about Windows support for password encryption and the associated NTLM challenge/response authentication protocol. The myth is that Microsoft added support for encrypted passwords only with the release of the Windows 95 network redirector update and Windows NT 4 Service Pack 3. The truth is that all Microsoft operating systems (including the DOS LanMan client) support NTLM authentication and therefore support at least one of these password encryption algorithms, either the LanManager or the NT password hashes. The misunderstanding stems from the fact that prior to these operating system updates, Windows clients would downgrade to sending the clear text of a password if the remote SMB/CIFS server did not support password encryption. Of course, there are ways to exploit this behavior and gain access to users' passwords. Therefore, Microsoft decided that it was a good idea to disable the capability to automatically fall back to clear text authentication. It can still be done, even on Windows 2003, but requires a registry setting change and a client reboot.

Samba 3.0 follows this same path to interoperability. Because Windows clients no longer send clear text passwords without explicit configuration changes, Samba defaults to requiring that you, as the administrator, create LanMan and NT password hashes for all the users who will be accessing your server. But as there is no way to convert the existing */etc/passwd* entries to Samba's password format, you have to start from scratch.

Samba does support authenticating users against the system's */etc/passwd* file, NIS *passwd* map, and PAM stack, but you must ensure that all clients have clear text authentication for CIFS connections enabled. As previously noted, this is not the default behavior in modern Microsoft clients. Additional mechanisms for authenticating users are presented in Chapter 5.

By default, Samba 3.0 enables the *encrypt passwords* option. For the sake of clarity, and because you may not be familiar with all of Samba's default settings, we add the following line to our *smb.conf* in the [global] section.

```
encrypt passwords = yes
```

The *smbpasswd* program (typically located in the directory */usr/local/samba/bin/*) can be used to enter the username/password combinations of the Samba users into Samba's encrypted password database. For example, to allow Unix user *lizard* to access shares from a client system, use this command:

```
# smbpasswd -a lizard
New SMB password: <enter password for lizard>
Retype new SMB password: <re-enter password for lizard>
Added user lizard.
```

 Samba requires that all users accessing the system be mapped to a valid Unix uid. This includes guest users, who are mapped to the specified *guest acount*.

When the first user is added, the program may output a message saying that the encrypted password database does not exist. Don't worry: it will then create the database for you. Make sure that the username/password combinations you add to the encrypted database match the usernames and passwords that you intend to use on the Windows client side. You must run *smbpasswd* for each client user that will authenticated access to the server. There are simpler ways to configure a server to allow guest access, which we explore in Chapter 5.

Using SWAT to Create an smb.conf File

Creating a configuration file with SWAT is even easier than writing a configuration file by hand. To invoke SWAT, use your web browser to connect to *http://localhost:901/*, and log on as root with the root password, as shown in Figure 2-1.

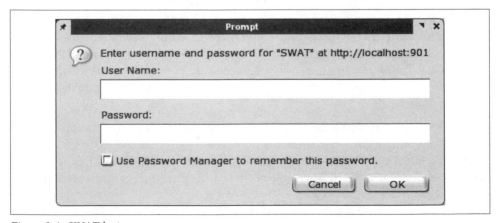

Figure 2-1. SWAT login

After logging in, click the GLOBALS icon at the top of the screen. You should see the Global Parameters page shown in Figure 2-2.

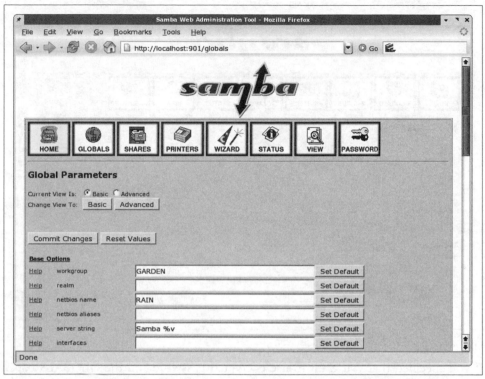

Figure 2-2. SWAT Global Parameters page

In this example, notice that SWAT retrieved the workgroup name from the *smb.conf* file that you created. (If it didn't, go back and perform that step correctly.) Make sure that the security field is set to USER (the default).

The only other option you need to change from the menu is one determining which system on the LAN resolves NetBIOS addresses; this system is called the *WINS server*. At the very bottom of the page, set the wins support field to Yes, unless you already have a WINS server on your network. If you do, put the WINS server's IP address in the wins server field instead. Then return to the top of the screen, and press the Commit Changes button to write the changes out to the *smb.conf* file. If your Samba server and clients are all on a single broadcast subnet (i.e., if they all have the same broadcast address), you can ignore the WINS settings for now.

Next, click the SHARES icon. Select test (to the right of the Choose Share button), and click the Choose Share button. You will see the Share Parameters screen, as shown in Figure 2-3, with the comment and path fields filled in from your *smb.conf* file.

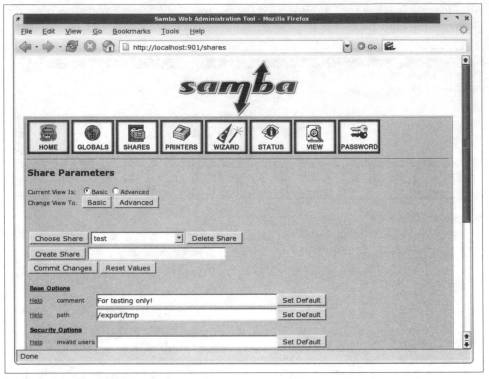

Figure 2-3. SWAT Share Parameters screen

If you specified that you want to use encrypted passwords on the GLOBALS page, click the PASSWORD icon. Near the top of the screen is the Server Password Management section. Enter your Unix username and password in the spaces, and click the Add New User button. This step functions the same as the *smbpasswd* utility and creates an entry in the */usr/local/samba/private/smbpasswd* file to allow you to authenticate from a Windows client.

Now click the VIEW icon at the top; SWAT then shows you the following *smb.conf* file:

```
# Samba config file created using SWAT
# from localhost (127.0.0.1)
# Date: 2005/06/27 09:56:43

# Global parameters
[global]
        workgroup = GARDEN

[test]
        comment = For testing only!
        path = /export/tmp
        read only = No
```

Notice that the encrypt passwords option is not listed, because SWAT does not write parameters with default settings to the configuration file. Once this configuration file is completed, you can skip the "Testing the Configuration File" step, because the output of SWAT is guaranteed to be syntactically correct.

Testing the Configuration File

If you didn't use SWAT to create your configuration file, you should probably test it to ensure that it does not contain any syntax errors. It might seem silly to run a test program against a six-line configuration file, but it's good practice for the longer, more complex ones that we'll be writing later on.

The parser, *testparm*, examines an *smb.conf* file for syntax errors and reports any it finds along with a list of the services enabled on your machine. An example follows; you'll notice that in our haste to get the server running, we mistyped workgroup as workgrp (the output can be lengthy, so again it is best to use some type of filter or pager):

```
$ testparm -s /usr/local/samba/lib/smb.conf | more
Load smb config files from /usr/local/samba/lib/smb.conf
Unknown parameter encountered: "workgrp"
Ignoring unknown parameter "workgrp"
Processing section "[test]"
Loaded services file OK.

# Global parameters
[global]

[test]
    comment = For testing only!
    path = /usr/local/samba/tmp
    read only = No
```

Samba 3.0 displays a brief listing of the configuration file. In fact, this is identical to how SWAT will strip the file and display it.

 The *testparm* tool has a verbose output mode (-v) that dumps the default values for all unset variables. Beginning with the 3.0.20 release, it is also possible to query for a specific parameter (--parameter-name=*STRING*) or a particular share (--section-name=*SHARE*).

Firewall Configuration

As with any services that run on TCP/IP, the SMB networking services offered by Samba can be accessed from across the Internet unless your organization's firewall is configured to prevent it.

The following ports are used by Samba for SMB networking and SWAT:

137/udp
Used for NetBIOS network browsing (*nmbd*).

138/udp
Used for NetBIOS name service (*nmbd*).

139/tcp
Used for file and printer sharing and other operations (*smbd*).

445/tcp
The so called NetBIOS-less CIFS port, which is used by Windows 2000 and later clients (*smbd*).

901/tcp
Used by SWAT. Unless you have configured complementary *stunnel* support, it is best to limit access to this port to the loopback interface only.

As stated in Chapter 1, SMB/CIFS is really not Internet-ready. There have been many security improvements in CIFS recently, including the use of Kerberos for authentication, packet integrity check (SMB signing), and Secure Channel communication. However, other than passwords, most data in CIFS networks travels in the clear. If your users require external access to Samba or Windows file servers, it is best to use some type of a Virtual Private Network to secure data in transit. See the O'Reilly book *Virtual Private Networks*, by Charlie Scott et al., for more information on this subject.

Outside of a VPN solution, it is strongly advised that you block the appropriate ports from access by clients external to your network. In addition, you might wish to configure a firewall on the Samba host system to keep SMB packets from traveling further than necessary within your organization's network. For example, port 901 can be shut down for remote accesses so that SWAT can be run only on the Samba host system. If you are using Samba to serve only a fraction of the client systems within your organization, consider allowing SMB packets (i.e., packets on ports 137–139 and 445) to go to or come from only those clients. For more information on configuring firewalls, see *Building Internet Firewalls*, by Elizabeth D. Zwicky et al. (O'Reilly).

Starting the Samba Daemons

Two Samba processes, *smbd* and *nmbd*, need to be running for Samba to work correctly.* There are three ways to start them:

- Manually
- Automatically, during system boot
- From *inetd* or *xinetd*

---

* You will see in Chapter 10 that *nmbd* is not always needed, but for now just consider it to be a required daemon.

Starting the Daemons Manually

If you're in a hurry, you can start the Samba daemons by hand. As *root*, enter the following commands:

```
$ /usr/local/samba/sbin/smbd -D
$ /usr/local/samba/sbin/nmbd -D
```

Samba will now be running on your system and is ready to accept connections. However, keep in mind that if either of the daemons exit for any reason (including system reboots), they must be restarted manually.

Automatic Startup

To have the Samba daemons started automatically when the system boots, add the commands listed in the previous section to your standard Unix startup scripts. The exact method varies depending on the flavor of Unix you're using.

BSD Unix

With a BSD-style Unix variant, append the following code to the *rc.local* file, which is typically found in the */etc* or */etc/rc.d* directories:

```
if [ -x /usr/local/samba/bin/smbd]; then
    echo "Starting smbd..."
    /usr/local/samba/bin/smbd -D
    echo "Starting nmbd..."
    /usr/local/samba/bin/nmbd -D
fi
```

This code is very simple: it checks to see whether the *smbd* file exists and has execute permissions, and if so, starts up both of the Samba daemons.

System V Unix and most Linux distributions

With System V, things can get a little more complex. Depending on your Unix version, you might be able to get away with making a simple change to an *rc.local* file as with BSD Unix, but System V typically uses directories containing links to scripts that control daemons on the system. Hence, you need to instruct the system how to start and stop the Samba daemons. The first step to implement this is to modify the contents of the */etc/rc.d/init.d* directory by adding an init script. The *samba-3.0.x/packaging/sysv* directory contains an example init script that should work on most System V based hosts. It is at least a place to begin making any local tweaks necessary for your system.

Assuming that we have installed this script using the name *smb* and set the execute permissions on it, we can now start and stop *smbd* and *nmbd* like this:

```
# /etc/rc.d/init.d/smb start
Starting SMB services:
Starting NMB services:
```

```
# ps ax | grep mbd
 1268 ?          S          0:00 smbd -D
 1269 ?          S          0:00 smbd -D
 1270 ?          S          0:00 nmbd -D
 1465 pts/2      S          0:00 grep mbd
# /etc/rc.d/init.d/smb stop
Shutting down SMB services:
Shutting down NMB services:
```

If you are having trouble modifying the existing SysV init script or are unable to write your own, check to see whether there is a packaged release of Samba (available from your Unix vendor or the Samba FTP site). If so, you might be able to extract a startup script from it to use as a starting point. Typically, this script doesn't change much (if at all) from release to release, so using a script from an older Samba version should not be a problem.

Finally, we need to add symbolic links to the *smb* script in the */etc/rc.d/rcn.d* directories:

```
# for i in 3 5; do
> ln -s /etc/rc.d/init.d/smb /etc/rc.d/rc$i.d/S35smb
> done

# for i in 0 1 2 4 6; do
> ln -s /etc/rc.d/init.d/smb /etc/rc.d/rc$i.d/K35smb
> done
```

The first for loop, with a link name starting with an S (*S35smb*), causes Samba to be started when entering runlevels 3 or 5, which are the runlevels in which network file sharing (NFS) is normally enabled. The next for loop, with a link name starting with a K, causes Samba to be shut down when entering any of the other runlevels (0, 1, 2, 4, or 6).

The links starting with S are used to start the daemons, and the links starting with K are used for killing them. When the runlevel is changed, the links starting with K in the corresponding directory (e.g., the *rc3.d* directory for runlevel 3) are executed, followed by the links starting with S. If we wanted, we could have Samba restarted when switching between runlevels 3 and 5 by adding a *K35smb* link to each *rc3.d* and *rc5.d* directory.

The number after the K or S in the link names is used to set the order in which all the daemons with links in the directory are started or killed off. Get a long listing of the *rc3.d* or *rc5.d* directories to see how this is set up on your system. We use 35 to match the behavior of Red Hat's Samba RPM package. The important thing is to make sure that when starting Samba, all services that it requires are started before it. When shutting down, it is a good idea to shut down Samba before services it requires, to avoid excess error messages in the logfiles, but the shut down order is not as crucial.

Mac OS X

An installation of Samba is bundled with Mac OS X.* In true Apple style, all of the startup and shutdown details have been hidden beneath the System Preferences → Sharing applet. Selecting the Services sheet displays a list of network services that are installed (although all may not be currently running). See Figure 2-4 for a screenshot of this window. Under the Services tab, turn on Windows File Sharing. In technical terms, enabling Windows File Sharing launches *nmbd* as a daemon and enables *smbd* to be run via the *xinetd* meta-server. The OS X included *smb.conf* file is located in the */etc* directory.

Figure 2-4. Mac OS X sharing preferences

If you decide to install Samba yourself on Mac OS X, it's best not to stomp on the installation provided with the operating system. Use the procedures detailed earlier in this chapter to install the software into */usr/local/samba* or some other area unaffected by operating system upgrades. You can then rename the original *smbd* and *nmbd* binaries and create soft links from */usr/sbin/smbd* and */usr/sbin/nmbd* to your newly installed ones.

---

* The coverage in this book pertains to OS X version 10.3.

If you install Samba yourself and you're using encrypted passwords, remember to set up users with *smbpasswd*, as described earlier in this chapter. This step is handled automatically if you're using the built-in server on Mac OS X.

Testing automatic startup

If you can afford a few minutes of downtime, reboot your system and again use the *ps* command to confirm that the *smbd* and *nmbd* daemons are running. And if you are managing a 24/7 server, we highly recommend that you find some downtime in which to reboot and perform this check. Otherwise, your next unscheduled downtime might surprise you with a mysterious absence of SMB networking services when the system comes up again!

Starting from inetd/xinetd

These days, memory and disk space tend to be very cheap. This is probably one of the reasons why running the Samba daemons from the *inetd* meta-server has fallen into disuse. The other is that *nmbd* needs to maintain state when participating in network browsing elections. The *inetd* server is not really geared towards this type of long-term service. The best advice is to simply run *smbd* and *nmbd* as daemons using the methods previously discussed.

However, if you wish to start from *inetd*, first open */etc/services* in your text editor. Add the following two lines if you don't already have them defined:

```
netbios-ns      137/udp
netbios-ssn     139/tcp
```

Next, edit */etc/inetd.conf*. Look for the following two lines and add them if they don't exist. If you already have smbd and nmbd lines in the file, edit them to point at the new *smbd* and *nmbd* you've installed. Your brand of Unix might use a slightly different syntax in this file; use the existing entries and the *inetd.conf* manual page as a guide:

```
netbios-ssn stream tcp nowait root /usr/local/samba/sbin/smbd smbd
netbios-ns  dgram  udp wait   root /usr/local/samba/sbin/nmbd nmbd
```

Finally, kill any *smbd* or *nmbd* processes and send the *inetd* process a hangup (HUP) signal to tell it to reread its configuration file:

```
$ kill -TERM -a smbd
$ kill -TERM -a nmbd
$ kill -HUP -a inetd
```

After that, *inetd* should be listening on the two NetBIOS ports and will spawn the appropriate Samba daemon when it receives a packet destined for either port.

As we've pointed out before, modern Linux distributions and perhaps other Unix vendors supply *xinetd* rather than *inetd*. If you need to use *xinetd*, you must supply configuration files in the */etc/xinetd.d* directory for both *smbd* and *nmbd*, as shown here:

```
## configuration file for smbd
## save as /etc/xinetd.d/netbios-ssn
service netbios-ssn
{
        disable         = no
        socket_type     = stream
        protocol        = tcp
        wait            = no
        user            = root
        server          = /usr/local/samba/sbin/smbd
}

## configuration file for nmbd
## save as /etc/xinetd.d/netbios-ns
service netbios-ns
{
        disable         = no
        socket_type     = dgram
        protocol        = udp
        wait            = yes
        user            = root
        server          = /usr/local/samba/sbin/nmbd
}
```

Testing the Samba Daemons

We're nearly done with the Samba server setup. All that's left to do is to make sure
that everything is working as we think it should. A convenient way to do this is to
use the *smbclient* program to examine what the server is offering to the network. If
everything is set up properly, you should be able to do the following:

```
$ smbclient -L localhost -N

Anonymous login successful
Domain=[GARDEN] OS=[Unix] Server=[Samba 3.0.22]

        Sharename       Type        Comment
        ---------       ----        -------
        test            Disk        For testing only, please
        IPC$            IPC         IPC Service (Samba 3.0.22)
        ADMIN$          Disk        IPC Service (Samba 3.0.22)

        Server                      Comment
        ---------                   -------
        RAIN                        Samba 3.0.22

        Workgroup                   Master
        ---------                   -------
        GARDEN                      RAIN
```

This example used an anonymous connection. But because we've already added a Samba account for *lizard*, we can also connect to and browse a specific share. Being greeted by the smb: \> is an indication of success.

```
$ smbclient //localhost/test -U lizard
Password: <enter password>
Domain=[GARDEN] OS=[Unix] Server=[Samba 3.0.22]
smb: \>
```

If there is a problem, don't panic! Try to start the daemons manually, and check the system output or the debug files at */usr/local/samba/var/log.smbd* to see if you can determine what happened. If you think it might be a more serious problem, skip to Chapter 12 for help on troubleshooting the Samba daemons.

If it worked, congratulations! You now have successfully set up the Samba server with a disk share. It's a simple one, but we can use it to set up and test the Windows clients in the next chapter. Then we will start making it more interesting by adding services such as home directories, printers, and security, and by seeing how to integrate the server into a larger Windows domain.

## CHAPTER 3

Configuring Windows Clients

Samba's main philosophy is that it is better to teach the server to speak the client's language than the other way around. Past experiences with client software such as PC-NFS have led many network administrators to share this belief. SMB/CIFS is the protocol of choice for resource sharing in Windows networks. The advantage of using the Windows' native CIFS support is that it is no longer your responsibility to verify that third-party client networking software is compatible with the latest hotfix or service pack from Microsoft. The CIFS client software updates are included with the OS upgrades.

The dominance of CIFS in Microsoft networks means that the components necessary for connecting to a Samba host are usually present in default Windows installations. There was a time many Windows releases ago (such as with Windows for Workgroups) when TCP/IP network stacks were hard to find and install. Such instances still exist, but are thankfully rare.

This chapter is devoted to helping you understand the pieces necessary for the latest Microsoft operating systems to communicate with Samba servers. Its intent is not to act as a Windows troubleshooting guide or to provide an in-depth look at Windows networking. By the end of our discussion, however, you will be comfortable verifying that the necessary networking protocols and services are installed and functioning properly. If you are already comfortable with configuring Windows clients to access Microsoft servers, it is safe to skim this chapter and move on to the next.

The dialog boxes and screenshots that you will see throughout this chapter are taken from a Windows XP client. All of the concepts and terminology, however, apply to Windows 2000, Windows XP, and Windows Server 2003 hosts. Microsoft has come a long way in consolidating the user interface between releases. but each one does possess a few nuances, which are highlighted as we continue our discussion.

Windows Networking Concepts

Windows is different from Unix in many ways, including how it supports network-ing. Before we get into the hands-on task of clicking our way through the configura-tion dialog boxes, it is best to establish a common foundation of networking technologies and concepts that apply to the entire family of Windows operating systems.

These are the main client issues with which we will be dealing:

- Ensuring that the required networking components are installed and bound to a working network adapter
- Configuring TCP/IP networking with a valid IP address, netmask, and gateway, and with any appropriate WINS and DNS name servers
- Assigning workgroup and computer names
- Creating user accounts

One can spend a lifetime understanding the ways in which Unix is different from Windows (in fact, Samba developers do just this), or the ways in which members of the Windows family are different from each other in underlying technology, behav-ior, or appearance. For now let's just focus on their similarities and determine any common ground.

Networking Components

Unix systems historically have been monolithic in nature, requiring recompilation or relinking to create a kernel with a customized feature set. Modern versions, how-ever, have the ability to load or unload device drivers or various other operating-system features as modules while the system is running, without requiring a reboot. Windows allows for such configuration by installing or uninstalling *components*. Networking components can be one of three things:[*]

- Protocols
- Clients
- Services

Figure 3-1 illustrates how these components work in conjunction with each other. The client and server components are distinct pieces that communicate with each other in the same fashion whether both exist on the same machine or reside on dif-ferent machines in a network. Practically, the distinction is not so clean-cut, but in the abstract, this model still holds.

---

[*] Device drivers are explicitly omitted from this list, because they are hardware-specific and therefore difficult to address in a generic sense. Our discussion assumes that you have received installation directions from the card's manufacturer if you have installed your own network card.

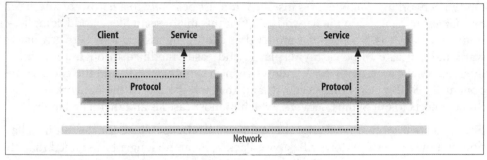

Figure 3-1. An overview of the Microsoft networking puzzle

Chapter 1 described how SMB/CIFS rests on top of a set of network services and explained that these services have been historically provided by a variety of protocols, such as NetBEUI, IPX/SPX, and NBT. Samba, however, supports only TCP/IP services, even through it does implement a NetBIOS layer internally. Field experience has proven that Windows clients accessing SMB/CIFS servers perform better when only one network protocol is installed.

Older Windows releases such as Windows 95 and Windows NT 4.0 did not install TCP/IP by default, but rather included support for the NetBEUI protocol. Having NetBEUI running at the same time as NetBIOS over TCP/IP caused the system to look for services under two different protocols, only one of which was likely to be in use. Delays of up to 30 seconds resulted as Windows tried to communicate with the unused protocol. Eventually, the client timed out and attempted to use the next protocol in the list. This process continued until the desired service was located. This fruitless searching resulted in terrible performance. The moral of this story is to remove any unnecessary protocols and use only TCP/IP, if at all possible.

The other two items in the list, client and service components, are pretty much what their names imply. Client components perform tasks related to connecting with network servers, and service components make the local system into a server of resources on the network. Microsoft has traditionally depended upon the presence of a working server service on Windows NT-based clients to perform management tasks such as remotely adding shares or creating users and groups. Even the MS-RPC-based printing implementation expects to be able to connect back to the client in order to report asynchronous change notification events, such as when a job has finished being printed. Therefore, it is extremely common for both the client and server component to be installed by default.

The names for these items has evolved in various Windows releases. Windows NT 4.0 referred to the client component as the *Workstation* service and creatively named the server component the *Server* service. Windows 9x and Windows 2000 have standardized on the name *Client for Microsoft Networks* for the client piece and *File and Printer Sharing for Microsoft Networks* for the server piece.

Once a networking component is installed, it must be *bound* to a hardware interface, or *adapter*, to be used on the network. At first this might seem like an odd complication; however, it is a conceptual model that allows the associations between hardware and software to be clearly displayed and easily modified through a graphical interface. Make sure that your Windows client has both TCP/IP and the client component for SMB networking installed, and that it is bound to the network adapter that connects to our Samba network, which in most cases is an Ethernet adapter.

Firewalls are beginning to change the Windows landscape. With the default installation of a firewall in Windows XP Service Pack 2, it can no longer be assumed that all remote management tools work as you would expect them to work. For example, after installing SP2, it is probable that you will not even be able to ping the Windows XP host, although from the client's point of view, networking functions are operating correctly. You can view and modify the client's firewall settings by running *control firewall.cpl* from *cmd.exe* or the Run... option of the Start menu.

 Windows XP SP2 changed quite a few things. Its initial release broke the print change notification mechanism previously described. There are various theories as to whether this was intentional. At the time of writing, no hotfix has been released by Microsoft to address this problem.

IP Address

Just like any Unix system (or any other system that is using TCP/IP), your Windows systems needs an IP address. If you have a DHCP server on your network, you can configure Windows to obtain its IP address automatically. Otherwise, you must assign a static IP address manually, along with a netmask. Make sure to use the same netmask as all other systems on the network. You can determine the netmask in use by checking with Unix or Windows systems that have already been configured.

If you are on a private network where you have the authority to assign your own IP addresses, you can select from addresses in one of three ranges:

- 10.0.0.1 through 10.255.255.254
- 172.16.0.1 through 172.31.255.254
- 192.168.0.1 through 192.168.255.254

These address ranges are reserved for private networks that are not directly connected to the Internet. Keep in mind that IP addresses ending in .0 are reserved for network addresses and that ones ending in .255 are for broadcast addresses. These should never be assigned to any system on the network. For more information on using these private network addresses, see RFC 1918.

If you're not maintaining your own separate network, see your system administrator for some available addresses on your network, as well as for the proper netmask to use.

You should also be prepared to enter the IP address of the default gateway for the network. In some networks, the default gateway is the system or router that connects the LAN to the Internet. In other cases, the default gateway connects a subnet into a larger departmental or enterprise network.

In the absence of a DHCP server and manual configuration, many clients support the so-called "dynamic" configuration addresses outlined by RFC 3927. These addresses exist within the 169.254.0.0/255.255.0.0 space and can be used only to communicate with other clients in the same broadcast space (also known as *link local space*). Dynamic configuration addresses are similar to the private addresses of RFC 1918, except that 169.254.0.0/16 addresses should not be routed at all, even within a private network.

Unless a Windows client requires a static IP address, such as for doubling as a database or web server, the simplest solution is to install and configure a DHCP server for your network. The two most popular choices for this service are currently the Internet Systems Consortium's implementation (*http://www.isc.org*) or the DHCP server that ships with Windows 2000 and Windows Server 2003. Either solution is fine, as both support the basic TCP/IP network parameters and the additional data, such as WINS server addresses, required by Windows clients.

Name Resolution

Name resolution is the function of translating human-friendly hostnames, such as *lettuce*, or fully qualified domain names (FQDNs), such as *lettuce.garden.plainjoe.org*, into IP addresses, such as 192.168.1.154 or 192.168.1.10.

Unix systems perform name resolution using an */etc/hosts* file at the minimum, and more commonly rely upon the DNS to perform this function.* The name resolution interface on Unix hosts is managed by the *Name Service Switch* (NSS) layer, which is often implemented as as part of the standard C library. The NSS configuration file, */etc/nsswitch.conf*, controls the order in which services (DNS, */etc/hosts*, and so on) are queried to resolve a name to an address.

Although the specific implementation is different, name resolution in Windows is also performed by querying a number of resources. For example, when you attempt to ping a host using its name, Windows uses all possible mechanisms at its disposal to resolve the name. Some of these resolution functions are similar (or even identical) to their Unix counterparts, and others are very foreign to Unix systems.

In the past, DNS was considered unimportant for functioning Windows networks. Of course, it was still necessary for locating services on the Internet, but DNS was a

---

* Although DNS is the dominant name resolution service on TCP/IP networks, you may also encounter other directory services, such as NIS domains or LDAP directories, performing a similar role.

nonissue in regard to finding and accessing file, print, and authentication services within the internal network. Things changed with the introduction of Windows 2000 and Active Directory. Now most services on a Windows network can be located by querying DNS server resource (SRV) records. (More about AD and DNS is provided in the context of Samba's domain membership capabilities in Chapter 10.) Chances are good that you need DNS for other services besides Windows and Samba and that it is already available on your network. If you don't know the IP addresses of the local DNS servers, check with another administrator or look them up in the */etc/ resolv.conf* file on one of your Unix servers.

For those of us who still have NetBIOS services on our networks, WINS is usually a requirement. The basic operation of WINS was covered in Chapter 1. If you require a WINS server for your network, Samba can happily perform that function if you specify the following line in the [global] section of the server's *smb.conf*:

```
wins support = yes
```

One caveat about using Samba as a WINS server is that Samba (up to vbooleaner-sion 3.0.22, at least) cannot synchronize with other WINS servers. So if you specify a Samba server as your Windows system's WINS server, you must be careful not to specify any additional (i.e., secondary) WINS servers. If you do, you are likely to run into problems, because the servers will not be able to synchronize their databases with each other. In Samba's defense, if you are using a Samba WINS server (running on a typically reliable Unix host), you probably have little need for a secondary WINS server anyway. The scarcity of requests for WINS replication could be consi-derd a testimony to Samba's stability.*

If a Windows workstation has NetBIOS support enabled and has no WINS server address defined, it defaults to using the broadcast method of name resolution, as described in Chapter 1, probably resulting in a very busy network. This effect in itself makes Samba's WINS support more attractive. Beyond this however, it is impracti-cal (if not impossible) to configure a working NetBIOS network with client and serv-ers on different subnets without a working WINS infrastructure.

Windows' LMHOSTS and HOSTS

Flat text files that contain name-to-address mappings are a relic of days gone by, when networks were small and central name services were unnecessary. Today, DNS and WINS services are more common than web or email servers. However, text files such as */etc/hosts* are still in use to bootstrap a system before the networking service has been successfully started or as a backup means of locating vital services when name servers are unavailable.

---

* A WINS Replication service, under the name *samba4wins*, has been developed using the Samba 4 research tree.

All Windows versions support using a pair of local files for name resolution. The two files, *HOSTS* and *LMHOSTS*, are stored in *%Systemroot%\System32\drivers\etc*.* As a general rule, it is better to avoid these files, due to the dynamic nature of Windows networks. But creative administrators can always come up with interesting scenarios that require bending the rules a bit.

The Windows *HOSTS* file is identical in syntax and function to its */etc/hosts* cousin. At first glance, the *LMHOSTS* file appears to be identical as well. However, the scope of the *LMHOSTS* file is limited to handling NetBIOS name resolution queries from the local machine, and the file's syntax has been extended to handle certain NetBIOS features that were originally outside the scope of DNS, such as defining addresses for domain controllers.

In its most basic form, each line in the *LMHOSTS* file is a single IP address and case-insensitive name:

```
192.168.1.154              LETTUCE
```

More advanced Windows *LMHOSTS* files can be written using the following extensions:

#PRE
> Preload the name in the NetBIOS name cache upon startup.

#DOM:*domain*
> Specify a host as a domain controller for *domain*.

#INCLUDE *filename*
> Read and parse the IP addresses and names from *filename*.

#BEGIN_ALTERNATE, #END_ALTERNATE
> Beginning and ending tags for grouping sets of #INCLUDE lines together into one logical group. Only one included file is required to succeed from the block, allowing a file to be copied to multiple network locations in case one server is unreachable.

\0x*nn*
> Define nonprintable characters, such as specific NetBIOS resource bytes for a given name.

For example, we could define the DC for the VALE domain by specifying:

```
192.168.1.154              LETTUCE   #PRE #DOMAIN:VALE
```

We could also use a centralized *LMHOSTS* file by making use of the #INCLUDE directive and a guest accessible file share name *config*:

```
192.168.1.11              MEL #PRE
#INCLUDE \\MEL\config\lmhosts
```

---

* The *%Systemroot%* environment variable expands to the operating system's installation directory (e.g., *C:\Winnt* or *C:\Windows*).

But even given this advanced functionality, it is really hard to come up with a good technical reason to use *LMHOSTS* files when a stable WINS server is easily within your grasp.

Windows Setup

Before a Windows client can connect to a Samba server or other any CIFS server, a few network components must be configured. Despite a few cosmetic differences, the Windows networking management interface is much more consistent these days than in times past. The terms and information in the remainder of this chapter apply to Windows 2000 and later. However, the screenshots are taken from a Windows XP client.

Before beginning to configure the Windows system, ensure that you are logged onto the client using an account that has the level of privilege necessary to make any networking changes. The built-in Administrator account will work fine, but any member of the Administrators group should have sufficient authority to update the client's configuration.

Networking Components

First locate the Control Panel. Depending on what version of Windows or what desktop theme is currently selected, this item may or may not be found in the Start menu (or Settings submenu). If you cannot find an icon for the Control Panel, you can start the application by running *control.exe* from a shell window or from the Run subcommand in the Start menu. Launching the Control Panel displays a window similar to the one shown Figure 3-2. If you see a headline in the screen that asks you to "Pick a category," select the Classic View option from the lefthand side of the window to convert to the layout shown here.

Next, find and click the Network Connections icon. Windows 2000 refers to this as "Network and Dial-Up Connections." The resulting dialog box lists all of the available network interfaces (LAN cards, modems, and so on). Figure 3-3 illustrates a client with a single Ethernet adapter installed. By right-clicking the icon for the appropriate network connection and selecting the Properties context menu option, you can view the list of installed networking components, as shown in Figure 3-4.

 If you ever get tired of navigating the Windows Start Menu looking for the Control Panel and networking applet, run *control ncpa.cpl* from a command shell or the Run… option on the Start Menu.

This is a quick method of launching the networking configuration screen. In fact, any of the control panel applets (*%Systemroot%\ system32*.cpl*) can be started in this fashion.

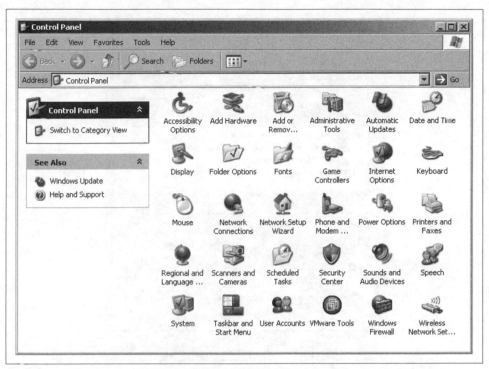

Figure 3-2. The Windows XP Control Panel application in Classic View

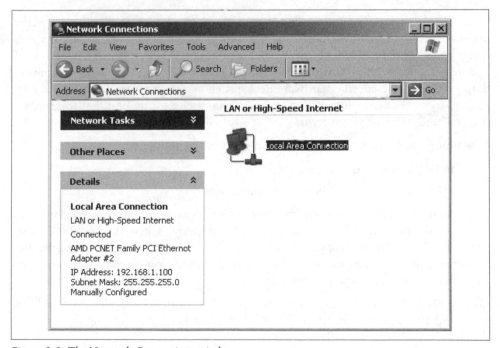

Figure 3-3. The Network Connections window

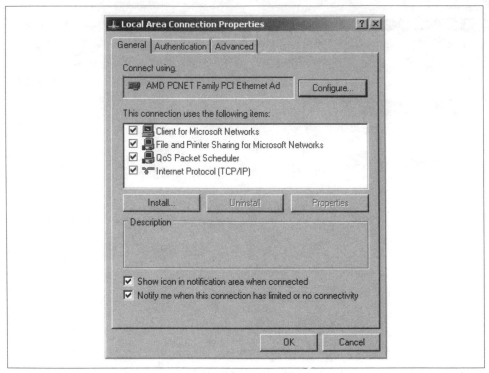

Figure 3-4. List of installed network components for the local area connection

Older clients maintained the notion of binding protocols and services to a specific network card, and therefore presented a complicated configuration dialog for specifying which interface would use which component. Windows 2000 and later updated this setup step with the concept of *connections*. When viewing a connection, you will see a specific hardware device such as the Ethernet card (Figure 3-4). Each entry in the list of installed components has a check box beside it to enable it (that is, bind it) for this connection.

At a minimum, we need the following two software components:

- The TCP/IP network protocol stack
- The Client for Microsoft Networks component

We assume a working network interface, although it is probably a good idea to check for the message "This device is working properly" when clicking the Configure button beside the network card icon. There is no way to navigate back to the previous window, so you must reopen the network connection property window once you exit the network adapter configuration dialog.

Add the TCP/IP protocol if it is not present. When you click Install..., you will be prompted to select a service from the three categories. After selecting the *Protocol*

---

category, and continuing by clicking Add…, you will be presented with a list of available network stacks. TCP/IP will appear in the list of available choices (unless it has already been installed). If the client has any additional network protocols installed, such as NetBEUI, NWLink, or IPX/SPX, remove them now unless they are necessary for accessing other resources on your network. If you are unsure whether the extra protocol stacks are required, check with another network administrator. To remove a component, select the component in the list, click Uninstall, and then choose Yes in the dialog box that pops up. In some cases, the change might not take effect until Windows has been rebooted.

You can follow similar steps for installing the "Client for Microsoft Networks." Select the Client category from the Install window instead of the Protocol category, as we did previously.

Configuring TCP/IP

Now click Internet Protocol (TCP/IP), and then Properties to open the Internet Protocol (TCP/IP) Properties dialog box, shown in Figure 3-5.

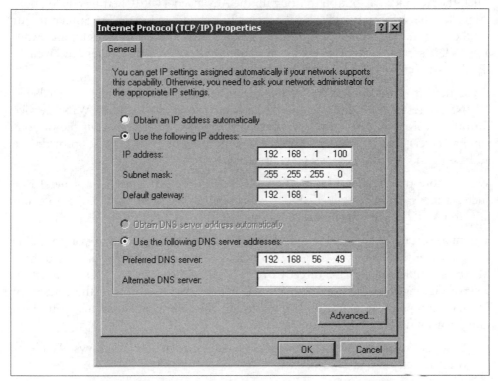

Figure 3-5. The Internet Protocol (TCP/IP) Properties dialog box

IP address and DNS servers

If you are using DHCP on your network to assign IP addresses dynamically, choose "Obtain IP address automatically" (the default setting). Otherwise, select "Use the following address" and fill in the computer's IP address and netmask in the spaces provided. It is easiest, when you first start, to use a client and server on the same subnet (the same network address and netmask), but this is not required. For example, if the server's address is 192.168.1.2 and its network mask is 255.255.255.0, you might use the address 192.168.1.100 (if it is available), along with the same netmask. You can also fill in the IP address of the default gateway.

If the client is not using DHCP to obtain an address, you probably must fill in the DNS information manually. In the lower part of the dialog box, select "Use the following DNS server addresses," and fill in the IP address of your DNS server. If you are using a DHCP network for assigning this information, leave the default "Obtain DNS Server Address Automatically" radio button selected.

WINS server

Click the Advanced... button to bring up the Advanced TCP/IP Settings dialog box, then click the WINS tab to display the dialog box shown in Figure 3-6. Similar to our DNS configuration, if your client is using a DHCP server, the addresses for any available WINS servers were probably assigned automatically when the client received its IP address, even though none are shown on this screen.

If you need to manually specify a WINS server, enter its address in the space labeled "WINS addresses, in order of use." If your Samba server is providing WINS service (in other words, you have the line wins support = yes in the *smb.conf* file of your Samba server), specify the Samba server's IP address here. Otherwise, provide the address of another WINS server on your network.

We'll ignore the "Enable LMHOST lookup" check box, because as a general rule such static files should be avoided. If at some point in the future you choose to maintain an *LMHOSTS* file on clients, check this box.

The final section of this dialog box, located near the bottom, allows you to define whether NetBIOS support should be enabled. We have briefly discussed how Microsoft implemented CIFS directly over TCP/IP without the NetBIOS abstraction layer beginning in Windows 2000. We haven't yet discussed this in the context of Samba's complete set of features, however. In the following situations, you absolutely must have NetBIOS support enabled on the client:

- You plan to access pre-Windows 2000 computers, such as Windows NT file or print servers or Windows 9x clients.
- You plan to use Samba as a domain controller.
- You require support for network browsing.

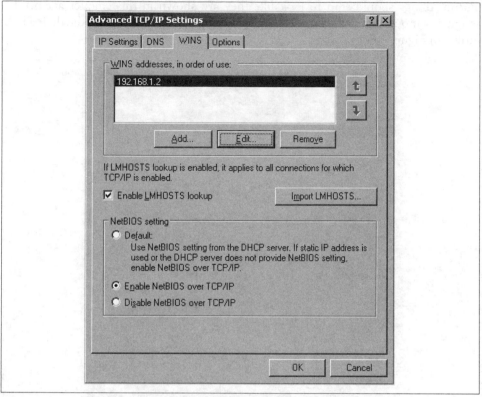

Figure 3-6. The WINS tab of the Advanced TCP/IP Settings dialog box

If you are using a workgroup environment, network browsing can be useful. It is not a required feature, however, so the choice is up to you. When in doubt, it is best to leave the setting enabled. At worst, it causes a few extra log messages on Samba servers or a few extra packets on your network.

When you are satisfied with your settings for IP Address, WINS Address, and DNS server, click OK in each open dialog box and close the Local Area Connection Properties dialog box to complete the configuration. The client may need to load some files from the Windows distribution CD-ROM, and you might need to reboot for your changes to take effect.

Computer and Workgroup Names

From the Control Panel, double-click the System icon to open the System Properties dialog box (or run *control.exe sysdm.cpl*). Click the Computer Name tab, and the resulting System Properties dialog box will look similar to Figure 3-7. (Here, Windows 2000 diverges slightly. The Computer Name is called the Network Identification tab, and instead of Change, you will see a Properties button. After clicking this button, things should start to look like they are shown in this chapter again.) To assign a computer name and workgroup name, click Change to access the dialog box shown in Figure 3-8.

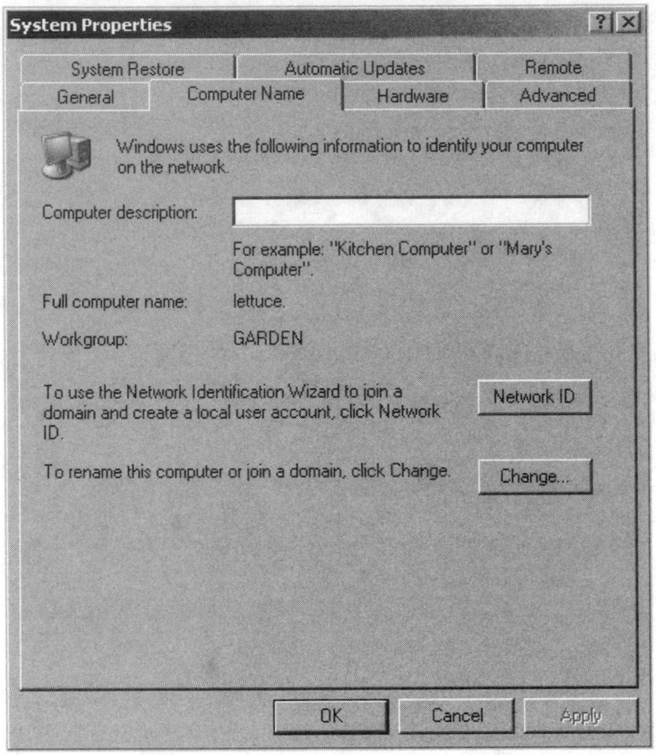

Figure 3-7. *The System Properties dialog box, showing the Computer Name tab*

Choosing a name for machines is probably one of the most fun but geekiest things we do as administrators. Select a name. We'll stick with the vegetable theme and choose lettuce. Now define the workgroup name to match the workgroup parameter value in *smb.conf* (we used GARDEN in our example in Chapter 2). Case is irrelevant when defining either of these two configuration values on the client. Click OK and, when requested, and reboot to put your configuration changes into effect. Once again, log in using an administrative account for the next activity.

Connecting to the Samba Server

Assume that we have a Unix user account named rose and that we have previously created a Samba account for this user by running:

```
root# smbpasswd -a rose
New SMB password: fiddle
Retype new SMB password: fiddle
Added user rose.
```

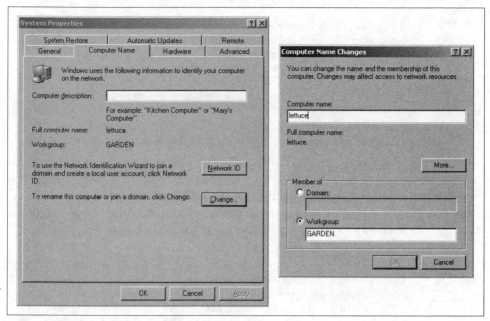

Figure 3-8. The Computer Name Changes dialog box

We should now be able to map to the [test] share that we created on the server rain during the last chapter. Open a command shell window (*cmd.exe*) on your Windows client and run:

```
C:\> net use t: \\rain\test /user:rose fiddle
```

You should be greeted with the following line:

```
The command completed successfully.
```

If instead you see an error stating that the "network path was not found," try connecting using the IP address of the Samba server instead. If this fails also and you know from the tests in the previous chapter that the server is running, there is most likely a problem with network connectivity. Go directly to the section "The Fault Tree" in Chapter 12 for instructions on troubleshooting.

Creating Local Users on Window Clients

Extra steps, such as specifying a username and password when connecting to a server, can be error-prone. If you try to connect without any credentials, Windows automatically attempts to use the username and password that you used to initially log on and prompts you if the connection attempt fails with a logon error. So far, you have logged into your Windows XP system as a user in the Administrators group. To access resources on the Samba server transparently, it is best to have your account credentials on the Samba server synchronized with your username and password on the local client.

All of this direction assumes that the client and server are participating in a workgroup. If your client is part of a domain, it is best to enter your domain account information at the Windows logon dialog box. Windows then automatically tries to use these credentials when connecting to other servers. Chapters 9 and 10 provide more information on Samba's role in controlling a domain and acting as a member of a domain.

You've already seen how to create Samba accounts on the server. Here is a quick tour of creating local accounts on the Windows client. The fastest way to bring up the user management console is to run the *lusrmgr.msc* application. This application is a plug-in for the Microsoft Management Console (MMC). After you launch the Local Users and Groups utility, either from the Run option of the Start menu or from a command shell window, a screen similar to the one shown in Figure 3-9 is displayed.

Windows XP Home is Microsoft's variant designed for home and personal use, much like the earlier Windows 95/98/Me variants, and Windows XP Professional is advertised as the upgrade for Windows 2000 installations. In most circumstances, the Home and Professional version operate similarly. There are two notable limitations in the Home edition that apply to our discussion. The first is that XP Home is unable to join a Windows domain; this limitation is applicable to our discussion in Chapter 9. The second, which is of immediate interest, is that local user accounts can be created only from the User Accounts applet in the Control Panel (which you can also bring up through the command *control.exe nusrmgr.cpl*).

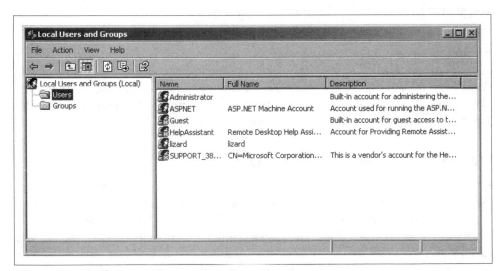

Figure 3-9. The Local Users and Group MMC plug-in

Selecting the Users folder in the lefthand panel enables the New User… option in the Action menu. Figure 3-10 shows the process of creating a local user account for our existing Unix/Samba account named *rose*. Make sure to enter the same password used when creating the Samba account. After creating the account, you can add the user to any local group by selecting the group folder from the left side, highlighting a group, and modifying its properties. Group membership on the local client does not affect the Unix user's group membership on the server.

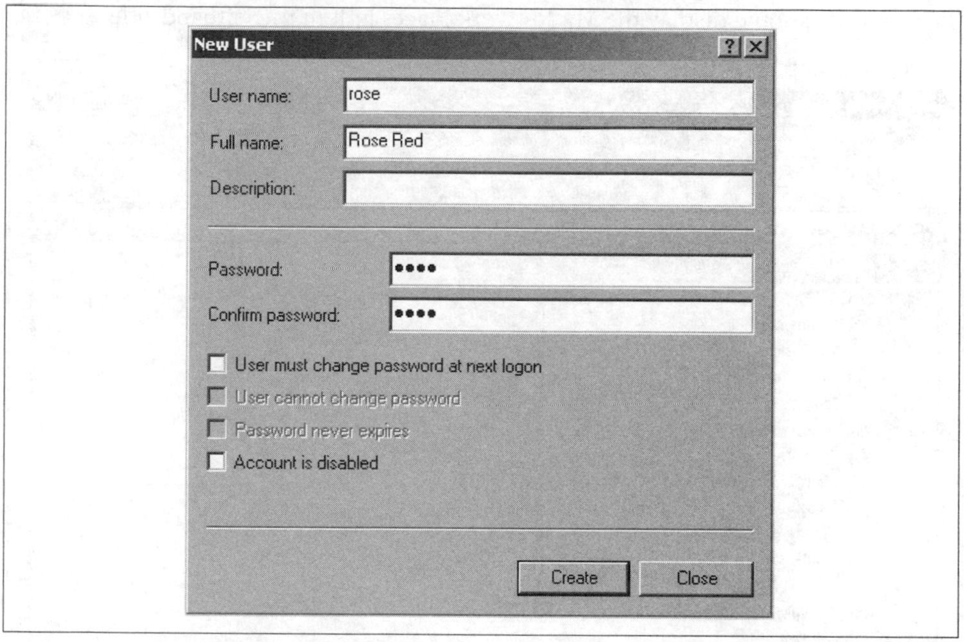

New User	?	X
User name:	rose	
Full name:	Rose Red	
Description:		
Password:	••••	
Confirm password:	••••	

☐ User must change password at next logon
☐ User cannot change password
☐ Password never expires
☐ Account is disabled

| Create | Close |

Figure 3-10. Creating a user account for rose

You can now log out of the client and back on again as the user *rose*. Usually this means selecting Log Off from the Start Menu and entering the new username and password in the resulting dialog box. Now you can connect to the Samba host without specifying any extra information:

```
C:\> net use t: \\rain\test
The command completed successfully.
```

 Default installations of Windows NT-based hosts will remember any file or printer connections that you have as part of your user profile and attempt to automatically reestablish those connections for you the next time you log onto the client.

Browsing the Samba Server

We've connected to the server, so we can be sure that authentication is working correctly. Now for the big moment—seeing Samba in the My Network Places window. As with so many things in Windows and in the Perl programming language, there is more than one way to do it. The most consistent way to browse the network across all recent Microsoft operating system releases is to use the Windows Explorer application. Go to Start → Run and enter *explorer.exe*. The window that results (Figure 3-11) should display the My Network Places link in the lefthand side.

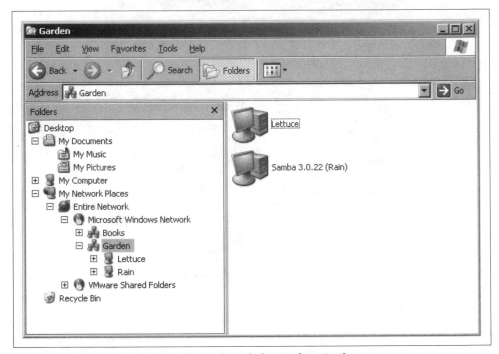

Figure 3-11. Viewing My Network Places through the Windows Explorer

The next thing to do is drill down through the entire network to your workgroup and expand the list of servers. You should see the server named Rain. You will also see the client (Lettuce) appear, if the "File and Printer Sharing for Microsoft Networks" component is installed locally.

Now select Rain from the list of servers and view the available shares. Figure 3-12 shows that we currently have only one file share, which is named test. There is also an empty Printers and Faxes folder. If we had any shared printers on the server, they would show up in the share list beside the test file share and inside of Printers and Faxes. Printing is covered in Chapter 7.

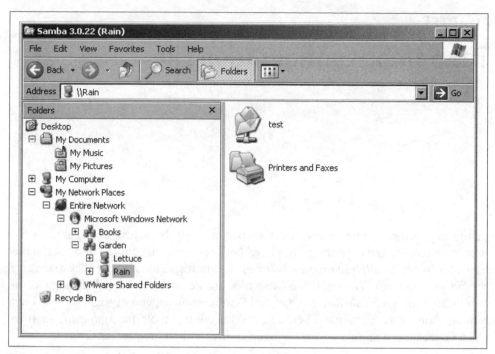

Figure 3-12. Viewing the list of shares on the server \\RAIN

Congratulations! You have a working Windows client from which you can test the Samba configurations that are explored in the upcoming chapters.

## CHAPTER 4

The Samba Configuration File

In the beginning, Samba servers were managed solely by a text configuration file named *smb.conf*. Today settings are mixed between the *smb.conf* file and local database files in */usr/local/samba/var/locks* (or the location specified by the lock directory setting in *smb.conf*). The database (*tdb*) files are normally managed through command-line tools such as *pdbedit* or *net* and Windows management tools such as User Manager or MMC plug-ins. There are several editing tools for *smb.conf*, such as SWAT, but most administrators still prefer to fire up their favorite text editor.

In previous chapters, we introduced some of the basic *smb.conf* settings, yet we have so far barely scratched the surface. At last count, there are more than 360 configuration options defined in the Samba source code. Though this sounds intimidating, approximately 90 percent of installations require less than one-quarter of the available options (or parameters; we use these terms interchangeably). Consider how much functionality we were able to obtain with fewer than a dozen in Chapter 2. For this reason, we do not discuss every option. Rather, our approach is present the common and necessary parameters in the context of a working server. If you require a full reference, the *smb.conf* manpage, available both in the documentation and on the Samba web site, contains an alphabetical index of all the configuration options and their meanings.

In this chapter, we introduce the structure of the Samba configuration file and show you how to use options to create and modify disk shares. In subsequent chapters, we discuss browsing, how to configure users, security, printing, and other topics related to implementing Samba on your network.

Basic Syntax and Rules

The Samba configuration file, called *smb.conf* by default, uses the same format as the Windows *ini* files. If you have ever worked with such a file on a Microsoft client, you will find *smb.conf* easy to create and modify. And even if you haven't, you will find the format to be simple and easy to learn. Here is an example of a Samba configuration file:

```
[global]
    ## core networking options
    netbios name      = RAIN
    workgroup         = GARDEN
    encrypt passwords = yes

    ## netbios name service settings
    wins support      = yes

    ## logging
    log level         = 1
    max log size      = 1000

    ## default service options
    read only         = no

[homes]
    browseable        = no

[test]
    comment           = For testing only, please
    path              = /export/tmp
```

This configuration file, based on the one we created in Chapter 2, sets up a workgroup in which Samba authenticates users using encrypted passwords and the default user-level security method. WINS server support is enabled and to be provided by the *nmbd* daemon. We've configured very basic event logging to use a logfile not to exceed 1 MB in size and added the [homes] share to allow Samba to export the home directory of each user who has a Unix account on the server.

Configuration File Structure

Let's take another look at this configuration file, this time from a higher level:

```
[global]
    ...
[homes]
    ...
[test]
    ...
```

The names inside the square brackets delineate unique *sections* of the *smb.conf* file; the section name corresponds to the name of each share (or service) as viewed by CIFS clients. For example, the [test] and [homes] sections are unique disk shares; they contain options that map to specific directories on the Samba server. All the sections defined in the *smb.conf* file, with the exception of the [global] section, are available as a file or printer share to clients connecting to the Samba server.

These sections help to group settings together by defining the scope of a parameter. There are two types of parameter scope:

Global

> Global options must appear in the [global] section and nowhere else. These options apply to the behavior of the Samba server itself and not to any of its shares.

Share or service

> Share options can appear in share definitions, the [global] section, or both. If they appear in the [global] section, they define a default behavior for all services, unless a specific share overrides the option with a value of its own.

The remaining lines of our *smb.conf* example are individual configuration options for each section. An option's specific scope continues until a new section is encountered or until the end of the file is reached. Because parameters are parsed in a top-down fashion, if you set the same option more than once in the same section, the last value specified is the only one that will be applied. Each configuration option follows a simple format:

```
option = value
```

Options in the *smb.conf* file are set by assigning a value to them. Some of the option names are self-explanatory. Others might require consulting the *smb.conf* manpage. For example, read only is self-explanatory and is typical of many recent Samba options. In many cases, the common settings are easily understood.

Parameter values in *smb.conf* fall into five categories:

Boolean

> Yes/No, True/False, 1/0.

Integer

> The maximum value of the integer depends on the use of the parameter. Note that some options accept a range of valid integers such as a minimum and maximum uid. Certain values, such as 0, may have special meanings—in this case, to not apply the option at all.

Character string or list

> Aside from boolean, this is the most common parameter type. Strings are often free-form, such as comment fields, lists of users and groups, or directory paths.

Enumerated types

> Some parameters accept a value from discrete list of possibilities. The most common option of this type is the security parameter, which accepts values of share, user, server, domain, or ads. Anything other than the values in this list are reported as syntax errors and the parameter reverts to its default value.

Plug-ins

> These are predominately new to Samba 3.0. Several *smb.conf* settings accept the name of an internal or external module. For example, user account information can be stored in an *smbpasswd* file or in an LDAP directory. The storage location is controlled by the plug-in value for the passdb backend parameter.

The *testparm* utility verifies only the syntax of parameter names and Boolean parameter values. It is not smart enough to know whether values such as an arbitrary string or a director path are valid.

Whitespace, delimiters, and capitalization

Parameter names are case- and whitespace-insensitive. For example, READONLY is the same as Read Only or read only. For consistency, option names in this book are usually lowercase and usually follow the spacing conventions as they appear in the *smb.conf* manpage.

The rules are a little less clear when dealing with parameter values. Generally, the whitespace and capitalization rules are defined by the use of the value. For example, case does not matter for Boolean values: YES is the same as Yes. But string or list values might be case-sensitive, and at a minimum should be assumed to be case-preserving.

Consider the case of a directory path on disk. Common Unix filesystems honor case in file and directory names. This means that */EXPORT* is not the same path as */export*. However, what if Samba were sharing a FAT filesystem in which case does not matter? What about user or group names? Should they be considered case-sensitive in *smb.conf*? Normally Unix does treat account names as case-sensitive strings. The bottom line is that string values are case-sensitive when the underlying system that makes use of them is case-sensitve.

When a string is used by Samba itself or as a value transmitted to Windows clients, it can generally be considered as case-preserving but case-insensitive. The comment option for a share is a good example here. The [test] in our *smb.conf* specifies:

```
comment = For testing only, please
```

Samba strips away the spaces up to the first F in For. The remainder of the string is seen as it is by Windows clients. The character case here is only cosmetic.

If an option accepts multiple strings such as a list of usernames or groups, there are two issues of which you must be aware. The first is knowing which characters Samba will interpret as entry delimiters.

The standard delimiting characters in *smb.conf* are:

- Whitespace
- Comma (,)
- Semicolon (;)
- New line (\n)
- Carriage return (\r)

You haven't been introduced to a parameter that accepts a list of values yet, but imagine a list of users. All of the following lists of three items are semantically the same:

```
rose, smitty, foo
rose smitty, foo
rose; smitty foo
```

So this brings us to to the second question: how can we define a list entry that contains one of these delimiting characters? The most common example is a username that contains a space. The answer is that we explicitly group the tokens in an entry together by surrounding the string with double quotes.

```
"Alex Rose", smitty, foo
```

However, never use quotation marks around an option name; Samba will treat this as an error.

smb.conf section names are case-insensitive, but the whitespace does matter when a client attempts to access the share. For this reason, many admins find it easier to avoid share names with whitespace in them.

 Some older Windows clients, such as Windows 9x, cannot access shares with names longer than 12 characters.

Line continuation

You can continue a line in the Samba configuration file using the backslash, like this:

```
comment = The first share that has the primary copies \
          of the new Teamworks software product.
```

Because of the backslash, these two lines will be treated as one line by Samba. The second line begins at the first nonwhitespace character that Samba encounters; in this case, the o in of.

Comments

You can insert single-line comments in the *smb.conf* configuration file (not to be confused with the comment parameter) by starting a line with either a hash (#) or a semicolon (;). For example, the first three lines in the following example would be considered comments:

```
#  Export the home directory for a each user
; Pulls the home directory path via the getpwnam( ) call
; (e.g. a lookup in /etc/passwd)

[homes]
    browseable       = no
```

Samba ignores all comment lines in its configuration file; there are no limitations to what can be placed on a comment line after the initial hash mark or semicolon. Note that the line continuation character (\) is *not* honored on a commented line. Like the rest of the line, it is ignored.

Samba does not allow mixing of comment lines and parameters. Be careful not to put comments on the same line as anything else, such as:

```
path = /data # server's data partition
```

Errors such as this, where the parameter value is defined with a string, can be tricky to notice. The *testparm* program won't complain. The only clues you'll receive from *testparm* are that it reports the value of the path parameter as /data # server's data partition. Failures result when clients attempt to access the share.

Updating a Live System

You can modify the *smb.conf* configuration file and any of its options at any time while the Samba daemons are running. The question when they will take effect on the server (and be seen by clients) requires a detailed response.

When changing core NetBIOS or networking settings, such as modifying the name of the server or joining a domain, it is best to assume that a restart of all Samba daemons is necessary. For other global parameters and most changes to shares, apply these rules:

- When a new connection is received, the main *smbd* process spawns a child process to handle the incoming request. The new child rereads *smb.conf* upon startup, and therefore sees the change.

- Once started, Samba daemons check every three minutes to determine whether any configuration files have been modified, and if so, reload and act on the parameters.

- An administrator can force an immediate reload of *smb.conf* by sending the *smbd* process the Hangup (HUP) signal or by sending a reload-config message via the *smbcontrol* utility.

- Scanning for new printers in the underlying printing system (e.g., CUPS or */etc/printcap*) is controlled by the printcap cache time parameter, which specifies the monitoring interval in seconds.

Be wary of editing *smb.conf* on a live system. This is an easy way to introduce syntax errors in *smb.conf* that are unintentionally propagated to client connections. A good practice is to update a copy of the server's *smb.conf* and then move it to the existing configuration only after you have verified that it has no syntax errors or unintended changes. It is also a good idea to apply some type of version control to server configuration files such as *smb.conf*.

The next question that should be asked is what happens to active client connections when you restart Samba. The daemon that directly handles client connections is *smbd*. *smbd*'s architecture uses a fork-on-connect model of handling incoming TCP connections. If you kill the main *smbd* process, all child processes continue until the client disconnects, and each *smbd* exits normally. However, until the parent is restarted, the host machine does not allow additional incoming CIFS connections.

If an *smbd* child that is handling an active connection is killed, all files and shares that the client had open become invalid. Windows clients will automatically reconnect to the server as soon as the user attempts to access one of these previously valid resources. In many instances, the user will never know that the connection was dropped and reestablished. There are a few exceptions:

- If the server does not support encrypted passwords, current releases of Windows cannot reauthenticate the user, because they cache only the hash of the user's password and not the clear text.

- Many applications, when stored on a remote system and run from a network drive, crash when the connection is dropped. However, local applications simply accessing datafiles or documents on a network drive frequently experience no problems during the reconnection.

Variables

Because a new copy of the *smbd* daemon is created for each connecting client, each client can have its own customized configuration file. Samba allows a limited yet useful form of variable substitution in the configuration file to allow information about the Samba server and the client to be included in the configuration at the time the client connects. A variable in the configuration file consists of a percent sign (%), followed by a single upper- or lowercase letter. Variables can be used only on the right side of a configuration option (i.e., after the equal sign). An example is:

```
[pub]
    path = /home/ftp/pub/%a
```

The %a stands for the client system's architecture and is replaced according to Table 4-1.

Table 4-1. %a substitution

Client operating system ("architecture")	Replacement string
Windows for Workgroups	WfWg
Windows 95, 98 and Millenium	Win95
Windows NT	WinNT
Windows 2000	Win2K
Windows XP	WinXP

Table 4-1. %a substitution (continued)

Client operating system ("architecture")	Replacement string
Windows Server 2003	Win2K3
OS/2	OS2
Samba	Samba
Linux CIFS filesystem client	CIFSFS
All other clients	UNKNOWN

In this example, Samba assigns a unique path for the [pub] share to client systems based on what operating system they are running. The path that each client would see as its share differ according to the client's architecture:

```
/home/ftp/pub/WinNT
/home/ftp/pub/Win2K
/home/ftp/pub/Samba
...
/home/ftp/pub/UNKNOWN
```

Using variables in this manner comes in handy if you wish to have different users run custom configurations based on their own unique characteristics or conditions. Samba has more than 20 variables, shown in Table 4-2.

Table 4-2. Samba variables

Variable	Definition
Client variables	
%a	Client's architecture (see Table 4-1)
%i	IP address of the interface on the server to which the client connected
%I	Client's IP address (e.g., 172.16.1.2)
%m	Client's NetBIOS name
%M	Client's DNS name (defaults to the value of %I if hostname lookups = no)
User variables	
%u	Current Unix username (requires a connection to a share)
%U	Username transmitted by the client in the initial authentication request
%D	User's domain (e.g., the string DOM-A in DOM-A\user)
%H	Home directory of %u
%g	Primary group of %u
%G	Primary group of %U
Share variables	
%S	Current share's name
%P	Current share's root directory
%p	Automounter's path to the share's root directory, if different from %P

Table 4-2. Samba variables (continued)

Variable	Definition
Server variables	
%d	Current server process ID
%h	Samba server's DNS hostname
%L	Samba server's NetBIOS name sent by the client in the NetBIOS session request
%N	Home directory server, from the automount map
%v	Samba version
Miscellaneous variables	
%R	The SMB protocol level that was negotiated
%T	The current date and time
%$(*var*)	The value of environment variable *var*

Here's another example of using variables: suppose that you do not want to share the user's Unix home directory, but prefer instead to keep a separate set of home directories specifically for SMB/CIFS clients. You can do this by defining a path in the [homes] service that includes the %U variable.

```
[homes]
    path = /export/smb/home/%U
    ...
```

People often wonder what the difference is between %U and %u. The value of %U is derived from the username sent during the CIFS session setup request covered in Chapter 1. This occurs before a connection to any share. The %u variable is expanded from the uid assigned to a user in the context of a file share. This can change depending on the share. More about this issue is explained in Chapter 6, when we discuss the force user option.

When user rose connects to the UNC path *RAIN\homes*, the path statement expands to */export/smb/home/rose*. Samba does not automatically create this directory if it does not already exist. One way to solve this this problem is to instruct Samba to run an external program or script when a user connects to a specific share. More about this technique is discussed in Chapter 6.

Special Sections

Now that you've gotten your feet wet with variables, we will talk about a few special sections of the Samba configuration file. Again, don't worry if you don't understand every configuration option listed here; we go over each of them in the upcoming chapters.[*]

---

[*] The [IPC$] share is another specialized service used by CIFS clients for interprocess communication. Samba provides this built-in share regardless of the services listed in *smb.conf*.

The [global] Section

The [global] section appears in virtually every Samba configuration file, even though it is not mandatory. If the section is not present, Samba uses the default values for all global settings. Any option that appears before the first marked section is assumed to be a global option. This means that the [global] section heading is not absolutely required; however, following the rule that it is better to explicitly state what you mean, include it for clarity and to protect your server against changes in default behavior in any future Samba releases.

There are two purposes for the [global] section. Server-wide settings are defined here, and any options that apply to shares will be used as a default in all share definitions, unless overridden within the share definition.

To illustrate this, let's again look at the example at the beginning of the chapter:

```
[global]
    ## core networking options
    netbios name     = RAIN
    workgroup        = GARDEN
    encrypt passwords = yes

    ## netbios name service settings
    wins support     = yes

    ## logging
    log level        = 1
    max log size     = 1000

    ## default service options
    read only        = no

[homes]
    browseable       = no

[test]
    comment          = For testing only, please
    path             = /export/tmp
```

When Samba reads its config file, it creates a special internal service that contains the default values of all parameters. Any service parameters that you define in the [global] section are assigned to this list. When a client connects to the [test] share, Samba first consults the explicit parameter list for that share. Then it looks in the default settings for implicit option assignments. Explicit settings take precedence over any compile-time or [global] defaults. In other words, if the [test] service contained a line that said read only = yes, the share would be marked as read-only regardless of the default or global value the parameter had been assigned.

The [homes] Section

If a client attempts to connect to a share that doesn't appear in the *smb.conf* file, Samba searches for a [homes] share in the configuration file. If a [homes] share exists, *smbd* begins a search to validate the share name as a Unix username. If that username appears in the password database (e.g., */etc/passwd*) on the server, Samba creates a temporary share bearing the specified username and all the attributes of the [homes] share.

For example, assume that a client system is connecting to the Samba server RAIN for the first time and tries to connect to a share named [alice]. After verifying the user's credentials, *smbd* searches *smb.conf* for a share named [alice], but fails to locate one. There is however, a [homes] share, so Samba then attempts to validate the username alice in the server's */etc/passwd* (or other account database). If the validation is successful, Samba then creates a share called [alice] for use during the client's session. From this point on, the share [alice] is treated as a normal file share. Any variables are expanded according to the standard rules.

The [printers] Section

We will delay a detailed explanation of Samba's printing features until we get to Chapter 7. For the sake of completeness, however, we will introduce a third built-in section. This section, named [printers], performs a service for system printers analagous to what the [homes] share does for user home directories. If a client attempts to connect to a share that isn't in the *smb.conf* file and the [homes] check fails (or [homes] is not defined), Samba will check to see whether it is a printer share (assuming that the [printers] has been included). Samba does this by querying the operating system's printing system database to see whether the share name appears there. If it does, Samba creates a share named after the printer.

This behavior means that as with [homes], you don't have to maintain a share for each printer available on the system in your *smb.conf* file. Instead, Samba honors the Unix printer registry if you ask it to, and provides these printers to the client systems. However, there is a potential difficulty: if you have an account named fred and a printer named fred, Samba will always find the user account first and ignore the existence of the printer, even if the client really needed to connect to the printer, assuming that both [homes] and [printers] sections are defined. We revisit the [printers] section again in Chapter 7.

Configuration File Options

When one of the Samba daemons is launched, it looks first at any configuration file specified with the -s option or in the default compile-time-defined location (e.g., */usr/local/samba/lib/smb.conf*). There are two *smb.conf* options that allow you either to replace or to extend the current configuration at runtime. These two options, along with the copy directive, which allows you to clone one share in *smb.conf* into another, are described in Table 4-3.

Table 4-3. Configuration file options

Parameter	Value	Description	Default	Scope
config file	string	Sets the location of a configuration file to use instead of the current one.	None	Global
include	string	Specifies an absolute path to a file that should be read and parsed into the current configuration file.	None	Global
copy	string	Allows you to clone the configuration options of another share in the current share.	None	Share

config file

The global config file option specifies a replacement configuration file that will be loaded when the option is encountered. If the target file exists, the remainder of the current configuration file, as well as the options encountered so far, will be discarded, and Samba configures itself entirely with the options in the new file. Variables can be used with the config file option, which is useful in the event that you want to use a special configuration file based on the NetBIOS machine name or user of the client that is connecting.

For example, the following line instructs Samba to use a configuration file specified by the NetBIOS name of the client connecting, if such a file exists. If it does, options specified in the original configuration file are ignored:

```
[global]
    config file = /etc/samba/smb.conf.%m
```

If the configuration file specified does not exist, the option is ignored, and Samba continues to configure itself based on the current file. This behavior allows a default configuration file to serve most clients, while providing for exceptions with customized configuration files.

include

The fundamental difference between the config file option and the include parameter is that the former completely replaces all existing configuration settings, yet the latter does just as its name implies: it inserts settings from an additional file in the current configuration. Figure 4-1 illustrates how all three options override their previous values. This option also can be used with variables for such purposes as including additional settings that differ for each client machine.

```
[global]
    include = /usr/local/samba/lib/smb.conf.%m
```

If the configuration file specified does not exist, the option is ignored. Options in the include file override any option specified previously, but not options that are specified later. Because the included file is inserted into the main file, beware of including global options into the section for a file or printer share as this will generate an error in the Samba logfiles.

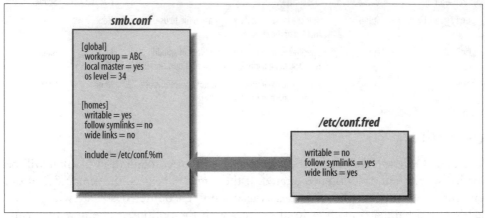

Figure 4-1. The include option in a Samba configuration file

The majority of parameters can be overridden in an included file, but a few cannot. The workgroup and the server string directives are two examples of parameters that cannot be redefined.

copy

The copy configuration option allows you to clone the configuration options of the share name that you specify in the current share. The template share must appear earlier in the configuration file than the share that is performing the copy. For example:

```
[basic]
    read only    = no
    browseable   = yes
    available    = no

[data]
    copy         = basic
    available    = yes
    path         = /data
```

Note that any options in the [data] share defined prior to the copy directive are overridden by those from the [basic] share. However, the top-down parsing of *smb.conf* allows us to reset these copied values by specifying more options after the copy parameter.

Basic Server Configuration

We now start from scratch and build a configuration file for a new Samba server. Our goal is to create a working server and to examine the options that are important for basic functionality. The server will export a single share named [data].

First, we'll introduce three configuration options that should appear in the [global] section of our *smb.conf* file:

```
[global]
    #  Server configuration parameters
    netbios name = PIGEON

    workgroup = GARDEN
    server string = Engr Dept Server (Samba %v)
    encrypt passwords = yes
    security = user
```

This configuration file is pretty simple; it advertises the Samba server under the Net-BIOS name PIGEON. In addition, it places the system in the GARDEN workgroup and displays a description to clients that includes the Samba version number. The last two parameters explicitly relate to how Samba is to validate user credentials in connect requests. You've already been briefly introduced to encrypted password support in Chapter 2. The security parameter value of user was not been explicitly mentioned. However, we relied upon it as Samba's default authentication model in Chapter 2 when creating user accounts with *smbpasswd* and connecting to the server using *smbclient*. Both parameters are covered in depth in Chapter 5 in the context of users and groups. Until then, the information you previously learned is sufficient for your current needs.

Because this is a perfectly valid configuration file, it is possible to test it out. Create a file named *smb.conf* under the */usr/local/samba/lib* directory and enter the displayed parameters and values. It might also be a good idea to test the new configuration using the same steps that you followed in Chapter 2. Be sure that your Windows clients are in the GARDEN workgroup as well. After double-clicking the My Network Places icon on a Windows client, you should see a window similar to that in Figure 4-2.

You can verify the server string by either viewing the properties of the Samba host (right-clicking the server icon to launch the context menu and selecting the Properties option), or enabling the details listing of hosts in the workgroup from the View menu. PIGEON's properties are displayed in Figure 4-3.

If you were to click the PIGEON icon, a window would appear that shows the services that it provides. In this case, with the exception of the built-in Printers and Faxes icon, the window would be completely empty, because there are no shares defined on the server yet.

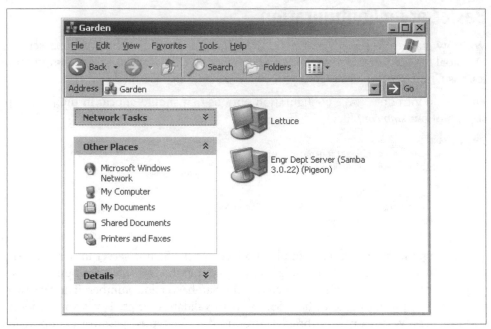

Figure 4-2. Browsing the GARDEN workgroup and viewing the Samba server PIGEON

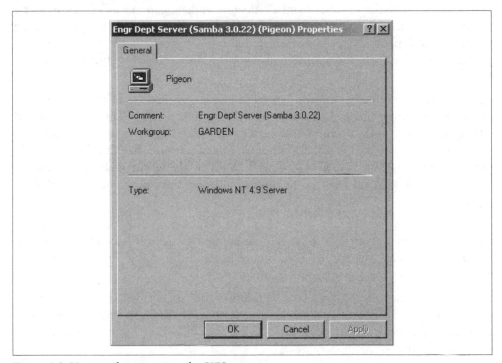

Figure 4-3. Viewing the properties of a CIFS server

Server Configuration Options

Table 4-4 summarizes the server configuration options previously used. All three of these options are global in scope, so they must appear in the [global] section of the configuration file.

Table 4-4. General server options

Parameter	Value	Description	Default	Scope
netbios name	string	NetBIOS name of the Samba server.	Server's unqualified hostname	Global
workgroup	string	NetBIOS group to which the server belongs.	WORKGROUP	Global
server string	string	Descriptive string for the Samba server.	Samba %v	Global

netbios name

The netbios name option allows you to set the NetBIOS name of the server. For example:

```
netbios name = YORKVM1
```

The default value for this configuration option is the server's hostname—that is, the first part of its fully qualified domain name. For example, a system with the DNS name *public.example.com* would be given the NetBIOS name PUBLIC by default. Although you can use this option to restate the system's NetBIOS name in the configuration file (as we did previously), it is more commonly used to assign the Samba server a NetBIOS name other than its current DNS name. Remember that the name given must follow the rules for valid NetBIOS machine names as outlined in Chapter 1.

Changing the NetBIOS name of the server is not recommended without a good reason. One such reason might be if the hostname of the system is not unique because the LAN is divided over two or more DNS domains. For example, YORKVM1 is a good NetBIOS candidate for *vm1.york.example.com* to differentiate it from *vm1.falkirk.example.com*, which has the same hostname but resides in a different DNS domain.

Another use of this option is to relocate SMB services from a dead or retired system. For example, if SALES is the SMB server for the department and it suddenly dies, you could immediately reset netbios name = SALES on a backup Samba server that's taking over for it. Users won't have to change their drive mappings to a different server; new connections to SALES will simply go to the new server.

workgroup

The workgroup parameter sets the current workgroup (or domain, as you will see in Chapters 9 and 10) in which the Samba server will advertise itself. Clients that wish to access shares on the Samba server should be in the same NetBIOS group. Remember that workgroups are really just NetBIOS group names and must follow the standard NetBIOS naming conventions outlined in Chapter 1.

The default option for this parameter is set at compile time to WORKGROUP. Because this is the default workgroup name of every unconfigured Samba system, we recommend that you always set your workgroup name in the *smb.conf* file. When choosing your workgroup name, make sure to avoid duplicating a name of an existing server or user.[*]

server string

The server string parameter defines a descriptive comment string that will be associated with the server. You can use variables to provide information in the description. For example, our previous example entry was:

```
[global]
    server string = Engr Dept Server (Samba %v)
```

The default for this option simply presents the current version of Samba and is equivalent to:

```
server string = Samba %v
```

Disk Share Configuration

So far we have not defined the [data] share on our server. So the next step is to create the directory tree on disk that will be exported, as well as the share section in *smb.conf* to make it accessible to clients.

Samba requires that the directory path being shared actually exist in order for clients to connect it. Otherwise the client will receive an error message about a "bad network path." So if this is a new share with no preexisting files, we must create the path first. The second of the following commands sets the permissions to allow anyone to create files and directories, but the sticky bit prevents a user from deleting another user's files.

```
root# mkdir -p /export/smb/data
root# chmod 1777 /export/smb/data
```

The service details in *smb.conf* resemble the [test] share we created in Chapter 2:

```
[data]
    path = /export/smb/data
    comment = Data Drive
    read only = no
```

The [data] share is typical for a Samba disk share. The share maps to the directory */export/smb/data* on the Samba server. We've also provided a comment that describes the share as a Data Drive.

---

[*] The tools presented in Chapter 8 can help you to scan the network to determine whether a particular NetBIOS name is currently in use.

Samba's default is to create a read-only share. As a result, the read only option must be explicitly disabled for each disk share that is intended to be writable. Of course, we could define read only = no in the [global] section as the runtime default.

Now, if we connect to the PIGEON server again by double-clicking its icon in the Windows Network Neighborhood, we will see a single file share entitled data, as shown in Figure 4-4. This share has read/write access, so files can be copied to or from it.

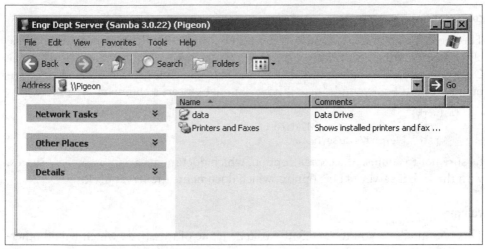

Figure 4-4. The initial data share on PIGEON

Disk Share Configuration Options

Table 4-5 lists the basic Samba configuration options previously introduced for disk shares.

Table 4-5. Basic share configuration options

Parameter	Value	Description	Default	Scope
path (directory)	string	Specifies the Unix directory that will be provided for a disk share or used for spooling by a printer share.	/tmp	Share
comment	string	Sets the comment that appears with the share.	None	Share
volume	string	Sets the MS-DOS volume name for the share.	None	Share
read only	boolean	Controls whether clients should be allowed to write the share.	yes	Share
writable (write ok, writeable)	boolean	Inverse of read only. That is, read only = no is the same as writable = yes.	no	Share

path

This option, which has the synonym directory, indicates the absolute pathname for the root of the shared directory or printer. You can choose any directory on the Samba server. If the connected user is unable to change to the directory due to a lack of appropriate permissions or because it does not exist, Samba refuses the user's connection request.

comment

The comment option allows you to enter a free-form string that is transmitted to the client when it attempts to browse the share. A user can see the comment by using the Details view on the share folder or with the *net view* command at a Windows command prompt. For example, here is how you might insert a comment for a share:

```
[network]
    comment = Software installation drive (I:)
    path = /export/smb/software
```

Be sure not to confuse the comment option, which documents a Samba server's shares, with the global server string option, which documents the server itself.

volume

This option allows you to specify the volume name of the share, which would otherwise default to the name of the share given in the *smb.conf* file.

Some software installation programs check the volume name of the distribution CD-ROM to make sure that the correct CD-ROM is in the drive before attempting to install from it. If you copy the contents of the CD-ROM into a network share and wish to install from there, you can use this option to make sure the installation program sees the correct volume name:

```
[software]
    comment = Software installation drive (I:)
    path - /cxport/smb/software
    volume = ASVP-102-RTYUIKA
```

read only, writable

The options read only and writable (also called writeable or write ok) are inverse Boolean options. Both default to enforcing read-only behavior on a file share but in a logically opposite fashion. If you want to be able to write data to a share, you must explicitly specify *one* of the following options in the configuration file for each share:

```
read only = no
writable = yes
```

Samba treats both parameters as the same feature. If you specify more than one occurrence of either or both options, Samba adheres to the last value it encounters for the share.

Networking Options with Samba

By default, both *smbd* and *nmbd* bind to all available broadcast-capable network interfaces on a system. There are times when you may wish to restrict this behavior, such as on a multihomed host that acts as a gateway from the internal network to the Internet, or perhaps on a laptop that has both a local network connection and a dial-up VPN connection.

Here's a simple example. Assume that our Samba server can access two subnets. The device eth0 is is bound to the 192.168.1.0/24 network and 192.168.2.0/24 is available on eth1. If Samba is not supposed to advertise itself on the 192.168.1.0/24 network, we must instruct it to use a subset of available network interfaces and bind only to those listed:

```
[global]
    interfaces = eth1
    bind interfaces only = yes
```

These two parameters, which are always used together, work in combination to restrict *smbd* and *nmbd* to the specified networks. The interfaces parameter can accept a device name (eth1), an IP address or hostname, a network/netmask pair (192.168.2.0/24), or a broadcast/netmask (192.168.2.255/255.255.255.0). The bind interfaces only option limits the behavior of *smbd* and *nmbd* to the subnets represented by the interfaces list. *nmbd* does not accept any broadcast messages that originate outside these subnets and *smbd* binds to only the specified interfaces.

It is important to realize, however, that if packets can be routed between the two networks in our example, a client on the 192.168.1.0/24 network can still access the Samba server using its 192.168.2.0/24 address.

A second alternative to restricting traffic is the hosts allow and hosts deny options. Unlike the previous two global parameters, these new options can be used on a per-service basis. If these options sound familiar, you're probably thinking of the *hosts.allow* and *hosts.deny* files found in the */etc* directories of many Unix systems. The purpose of these options is identical to those files; they provide security by allowing or denying the connections of other hosts based on their IP addresses. However, Samba includes its own internal implementation of the TCP Wrappers functionality, so there is no need for additional external libraries or configuration files.

Here's a simple example that allows a portion of the hosts on the 192.168.1.0/24 network to connect to our server. Notice that we have removed the interfaces and bind interfaces only lines to ensure that *smbd* and *nmbd* bind to both eth0 and eth1:

```
[global]
    hosts allow = 192.168.2. 192.168.1.100
    hosts deny  = 192.168.1.
```

With the hosts allow option, we've specified a 192.168.2. IP address, which is equivalent to saying: "All hosts on the 192.168.2.0/24 subnet." The trailing period is very important. Without this ending punctuation, Samba does not correctly interpret the address as a network. We have also added a single host from the 192.168.1.0/24 network to the access list. However, we've explicitly specified in a hosts deny line that hosts on the 192.168.1.0/24 network cannot connect.

It is important to understand how Samba sorts out the rules specified by hosts allow and hosts deny:

1. If no allow or deny options are defined anywhere in *smb.conf*, Samba allows connections from any system.

2. If hosts allow or hosts deny options are defined in the [global] section of *smb.conf*, they determine general access to the server, even if either option is defined in one or more of the shares.

3. If only a hosts allow option is defined for a share, only the hosts listed are allowed to use the share. All others are denied.

4. If only a hosts deny option is defined for a share, any client that is not on the list can use the share.

5. If both a hosts allow option and a hosts deny option are defined, the allow list takes precedence. But if a host does not match the allow list or the deny list, it is granted implicit access.

 Take care that you don't explicitly allow a host to access a share, but then deny access to the entire subnet of which the host is part.

Let's look at another example of that final item. Consider the following options:

```
hosts allow = 111.222.
hosts deny = 111.222.333.
```

In this case, hosts that belong to the subnet 111.222.*.* will be allowed access to the Samba shares. The deny list in the case is completely disregarded because it is a subset of the allow list. To allow all hosts in the 111.222.0.0/16 network except those on the 111.222.333.0/24 network, we can specify the following hosts allow shorthand notation:

```
hosts allow = 111.222. EXCEPT 111.222.333.
```

Networking Options

The networking options introduced earlier are summarized in Table 4-6.

Table 4-6. Networking configuration options

Parameter	Value	Description	Default	Scope
hosts allow (allow hosts)	string	Client systems that can connect to Samba.	none	Share
hosts deny (deny hosts)	string	Client systems that cannot connect to Samba.	none	Share
interfaces	string	Network interfaces Samba will respond to. Allows changes to defaults.	All available interfaces capable of broadcasts	Global
bind interfaces only	boolean	When enabled, Samba will bind only to those interfaces specified by the interfaces option.	no	Global

hosts allow

The hosts allow option (sometimes written as allow hosts) specifies the clients that have permission to access shares on the Samba server, written as a comma- or space-separated list of hostnames of systems or their IP addresses. You can gain quite a bit of security simply by placing your LAN's subnet address in this option.

You can specify any of the following formats for the option:

- Hostnames, such as ftp.example.com.
- IP addresses, such as 130.63.9.252.
- Domain names, which can be differentiated from individual hostnames because they start with a dot. For example, .ora.com represents all systems within the *ora.com* domain.
- Netgroups, which start with an at sign (@), such as @printerhosts. Netgroups are usually available only on systems running NIS or NIS+. If netgroups are supported on your system, there should be a netgroups manual page that describes them in more detail.
- Subnets, which end with a dot. For example, 130.63.9. means all the systems whose IP addresses begin with 130.63.9.
- Network/netmask pairs such as 192.168.1.0/24 or 192.168.2.0/255.255.255.0.
- The keyword ALL, which allows any client access.
- The keyword EXCEPT followed by one or more names, IP addresses, domain names, netgroups, or subnets. For example, you could specify that Samba allow all hosts except those on the 192.168.110.0/24 subnet with hosts allow = ALL EXCEPT 192.168.110. (remember to include the trailing dot).

The hostname localhost, for the loopback address 127.0.0.1, is included in the hosts allow list by default and does not need to be listed explicitly unless you have specified it in the hosts deny list (probably as part of a subnet). This address is required for Samba to work properly.

Other than that, there is no default value for the hosts allow configuration option. The default course of action, in the event that neither the hosts allow or hosts deny option is specified in *smb.conf*, is to allow access from all sources.

 If you specify hosts allow or hosts deny in the [global] section, that definition applies to all connections to the server. In a sense, this definition overrides any hosts allow lines in the share definitions, which is the opposite of the usual behavior. In actuality, the service level definition applies to the tree connection requests described in Chapter 1 and the [global] defaults apply to all packets prior to that request (i.e., protocol negotiation and authentication).

hosts deny

The hosts deny option (synonymous with deny hosts) specifies client systems that do not have permission to access a share, written as a comma- or space-separated list of hostnames or their IP addresses. Use the same format for specifying clients as the hosts allow option earlier. For example, to restrict access to the server from everywhere but the subnet *example.com*, you could write:

```
hosts deny = ALL EXCEPT .example.com
```

There is no default value for the hosts deny configuration option, although the default course of action in the event that neither option is specified is to allow access from all sources.

 Never include the loopback address (localhost at IP address 127.0.0.1) in the hosts deny list. The *smbpasswd* program needs to connect through the loopback address to the Samba server as a client to change a user's encrypted password. If the loopback address is disabled, the locally generated packets requesting the change of the encrypted password are discarded by Samba.

In addition, both local browsing propagation and some functions of SWAT require access to the Samba server through the loopback address and do not work correctly if this address is disabled.

interfaces

The interfaces option specifies the networks that you want the Samba server to recognize and respond to. This option is handy if you have a computer that resides on more than one network subnet and want to restrict the networks that Samba will serve. If this option is not set, Samba searches out and utilizes all broadcast-capable network interfaces on the server, including loopback devices. The loopback interface (lo) is automatically added to this list.

The value of this option is specified as one or more sets of IP address/netmask pairs, device names, or broadcast/netmask pairs, as in the following example:

```
interfaces = eth0 192.168.2.30
```

You can optionally specify a numeric bitmask, like this:

```
interfaces = 192.168.220.100/24 192.168.210.30/24
```

Make sure to specify the device name in the `interfaces` list if your Samba host is configured to use DHCP, because the server's IP address and netmask may change.

bind interfaces only

The `bind interfaces only` option can be used to force the *smbd* and *nmbd* processes to respond only to those addresses specified by the `interfaces` option and to loopback network devices. To prevent Samba from processing any packets (including broadcast packets) whose source address does not correspond to any of the network interfaces specified by the `interfaces` option, define the following line in addition to a list of `interfaces`:

```
bind interfaces only = yes
```

Virtual Servers

Virtualization has become a hot topic in recent years. Unix administrators have a longer history managing virtual services. Samba's capability to provide multiple virtual servers comes with a twist. Originally Samba relied upon the name sent by the client in the NetBIOS session setup request to fill in the %L variable (Table 4-2).* An administrator could then include alternative configuration files based on the destination name that the client used in the connection. However, with the introduction of NetBIOS-less CIFS in Windows 2000 and later clients, this name is no longer available. In fact, nothing but the standard TCP and IP headers are available in the initial connection request packet.

There are two solutions to this problem. One is to force the client to use the NetBIOS session transport layer. By default, *smbd* binds to TCP ports 139 and 445. Clients running Windows 2000 or a later Microsoft OS prefer to conect to port 445 and thus bypass the overhead of NetBIOS. However, the *smb ports* option allows administrators to restrict *smbd* solely to TCP port 139 and thus force the clients to use NetBIOS services for locating and accessing a Samba host.

Once you have restricted clients to using NetBIOS sessions, you can again use the name passed by the client to fill in the %L configuration variable and therefore conditionally include various configuration files. The only piece of information yet presented is the option for defining additional NetBIOS names to which the server will respond.†

---

* NetBIOS session services were covered in Chapter 1.

† Samba really doesn't care what name is used in the NetBIOS session request. The `netbios aliases` parameter relates more to name registration.

Now to put all the pieces together. This example builds a server named PIGEON, which registers the additional names of SEAGULL and PELICAN. *smbd* binds solely to port 139 and uses the destination name used by the client in the connection request to include the configuration files for the various virtual hosts:

```
[global]
    netbios name    = PIGEON
    netbios aliases = SEAGULL PELICAN
    server string   = Engr Dept Server (Samba %v)
    workgroup       = GARDEN
    smb ports       = 139
    include         = /usr/local/samba/lib/%L.conf
```

Figure 4-5 illlustrates how the virtual servers would appear when browsing the network. Notice that all three hosts, PIGEON, SEAGULL, and PELICAN, have the same comment string when a user views the server details.

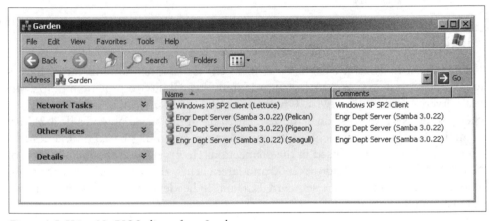

Figure 4-5. Using NetBIOS aliases for a Samba server

To support virtual configurations over port 445, the server must possess multiple network interfaces, although they do not necessarily have to be real interfaces; virtual interfaces work also. In this case, the destination IP address transmitted in the connection request determines what role the Samba server should play. When a client contacts Samba, *smbd* fills in the %i variable with the IP address to which the client connected. In this case, the configuration can drop the netbios aliases option and add the new names to the domain name service.

If the server has three IP addresses, 192.168.1.10 (*pigeon*), 192.168.1.11 (*seagull*), and 192.168.1.12 (*pelican*), we can update the configuration file to appear as follows:

```
[global]
    netbios name = PIGEON
    workgroup = GARDEN
    include = /usr/local/samba/lib/%i.conf
```

Notice that we have removed the `smb ports` line, so the parameter reverts to the default of both 139 and 445. Having removed the `netbios aliases` option, we enter the hostnames into our DNS server:

```
; Bind 9 address entries
pigeon      IN      A       192.168.1.10
seagull     IN      A       192.168.1.11
pelican     IN      A       192.168.1.12
```

Any legacy clients such as Windows NT or Windows 9x/Me will continue to be able to access the server. But Windows 9x/Me clients are unable to use DNS names or IP addresses of CIFS/SMB connections and therefore are unable to access any virtual server other than PIGEON. None of the Windows NT-based operating systems are subject to this limitation.

Virtual Server Configuration Options

Table 4-7 summaries the new parameters necessary for configuring virtual Samba hosts.

Table 4-7. Virtual server configuration options

Parameter	Value	Function	Default	Scope
netbios aliases	string	Additional NetBIOS names to respond to, for use with multiple virtual Samba servers.	None	Global
smb ports	integer list	List of port numbers to which *smbd* should listen for incoming CIFS requests.	139, 445	Global

netbios aliases

The `netbios aliases` option can give the Samba server more than one NetBIOS name. Each NetBIOS name listed as a value is displayed in the My Network Places of Windows clients. When a connection is requested to any of the servers, it connects to the same Samba server.

```
[global]
    netbios name    = BOSS
    netbios aliases = SALES ACCOUNTING ADMIN
```

nmbd registers each additional NetBIOS name with the list of addresses provided by configured network interfaces. But only the server's primary name (the value of `netbios name`) is used for network browsing (Chapter 8), domain control (Chapter 9), and domain membership (Chapter 10).

smb ports

The `smb ports` parameter controls the TCP ports on which *smbd* listens. The default list, ports 139 and 445, matches Windows 2000 and later servers. It is possible to bind *smbd* to a nonstandard CIFS/SMB port, but only non-Microsoft clients that are flexible enough to connect to alternative ports will be able to access the server. A more common use is to restrict *smbd* to only one of the default ports, such as forcing clients to use NetBIOS transport services:

```
[global]
    smb ports = 139
```

Logging Configuration Options

Occasionally, you'll need to find out what Samba is up to, such as when Samba is performing an unexpected action or is not performing at all. To find out why Samba did what it did, check the logfiles.

Samba logfiles can be as brief or verbose as you like. Here is an example of what a Samba logfile at level 3 looks like:

```
[2005/07/21 13:23:25, 3] smbd/service.c:close_cnum(514)
  cabbage (192.168.1.100) closed connection to service IPC$
[2005/07/21 13:23:25, 3] smbd/connection.c:yield_connection(40)
  Yielding connection to IPC$
[2005/07/21 13:23:25, 3] smbd/process.c:process_smb(615)
  Transaction 923 of length 49
[2005/07/21 13:23:25, 3] smbd/process.c:switch_message 4-8)
  switch message SMBread (pid 467)
[2005/07/21 13:23:25, 3] lib/doscalls.c:dos_ChDir(336)
  dos_ChDir to /home/samba
[2005/07/21 13:23:25, 3] smbd/reply.c:reply_read(2199)
  read fnum=4207 num=2820 nread=2820
[2005/07/21 13:23:25, 3] smbd/process.c:process_smb(615)
  Transaction 924 of length 55
```

Much of this information is of use only to Samba programmers. However, we go over the meaning of some of these entries in more detail in Chapter 12.

Samba includes several options that allow administrators to define the granularity, verbosity, and location of logfiles. Each of these are global options and cannot appear inside a share definition. Here are some of the more common logging options that you might use on a production server:

```
[global]
    log level = 1
    log file = /var/log/samba/log.%m
    max log size = 50
```

Here, we've added a custom logfile that reports information up to debug level 1. This is a relatively light debugging level. The logging level ranges from 0 to 10; level 0 provides only critical error messages and level 10 provides a plethora of low-level information.* A log level of 1 provides some information about connections, and levels 2

---

* The log levels used in the Samba source code are at the discretion of individual developers. For example, level 100 can be used to debug password changes. Generally, 10 is the highest debug level used when debugging (even by developers).

or 3 can provide useful debugging information without wasting disk space on the server. In practice, avoid using log levels greater than 3 unless you are working on the Samba source code or temporaily debugging a specific problem.

The logging file is in the */var/log/samba* directory, thanks to the log file configuration option. You can use variable substitution to create logfiles specifically for individual users or clients, as with the %m variable. Isolating the log messages can be invaluable in tracking down a network error if you know the problem is coming from a specific client system or user.

 A common question is why two logfiles are created for each client machine when the logfile is defined as *log.%m*. The reason is the use of port 445 by newer Windows operating systems. When a new connection is received on port 445, the %m can be expanded only to the client's IP address. After the client transmits its name as part of the authentication process (SMBsessetup&X), Samba can resubstitute the %m variable with the real machine name and reopen the expected log filename.

We've added a precaution to the logfiles: no one logfile can exceed 50 KB in size, as specified by the max log size option. If a logfile exceeds this size, the contents are moved to a file with the same name but with the suffix *.old* appended. If the *.old* file already exists, it is overwritten and its contents are lost. The original file is cleared, waiting to receive new logging information. This precaution prevents the hard drive from being overwhelmed with Samba logfiles during the life of the Samba daemons.

Using syslog

It is possible to use the system logger (*syslog*, implemented by the *syslogd* daemon) in addition to or in place of the standard Samba logging file. However, in order to use syslog, you must first make sure that Samba was built with the --with-syslog configure option. See Chapter 2 for more information on configuring and compiling Samba. See the *smb.conf* manpage for more information about the --with-syslog option.

Next, configure your */etc/syslog.conf* file to accept logging information from Samba. If there is not already a daemon.* entry in the */etc/syslog. conf* file, add the following:[*]

```
daemon.*          /var/log/daemon.log
```

This line specifies that any logging information from system daemons is stored in the */var/log/daemon.log* file, where the Samba information will be stored as well. From there, you can set a value for the syslog parameter in your Samba configuration file

---

[*] Many *syslogd* implementations require that you send a HUP signal to force it to reread its configuration file. Others may require that any new logfiles exist prior to writing to log entries.

to specify which logging messages are to be sent to syslog. Only messages that have debug levels lower than the value of the `syslog` parameter are sent to syslog. This parameter only defines the threshold below which messages are sent to *syslogd*. The `log level` parameter still controls which messages are logged in the first place. For example, setting the following:

```
syslog = 3
```

specifies that any logging messages with a level of 2 or below is to be sent to both syslog and the Samba logging files. (The mappings to syslog priorities are described in the upcoming section "syslog.") To continue the example, let's assume that we have set the `log level` option to 4. Logging messages with levels of 0 through 2 are sent to both syslog and the Samba logging files, and messages with a level of 3 or 4 are sent to the Samba logging files, but not to syslog.

If you want to specify that messages be sent only to syslog—and not to the standard Samba logging files—you can enable the `syslog only` option.

```
syslog only = yes
```

If this is set, any logging information at or above the number specified in the `syslog` option is discarded.

Logging Configuration Options

Table 4-8 lists each logging configuration option that Samba can use.

Table 4-8. Logging configuration options

Parameter	Value	Description	Default	Scope
log file	string	Name of the logfile that Samba is to use.	Specified in Samba makefile	Global
log level(debug level)	integer	Number of messages that are sent to the logfile.	0	Global
max log size	integer	Maximum size of a logfile, in kilobytes.	5000	Global
debug timestamp (timestamp logs)	boolean	Controls whether Samba includes timestamped headers for log entries.	yes	Global
debug pid	boolean	Specifies whether Samba should include the process ID in the log header.	no	Global
debug uid	boolean	Specifies whether Samba should include the real and effective uid in the log header.	no	Global
syslog	integer	The threshold below which messages are sent to *syslogd*.	1	Global
syslog only	boolean	If yes, uses *syslogd* entirely and sends no output to the Samba logfiles.	no	Global

log file

By default, Samba writes log information to text files in the *${prefix}/var* directory defined at compile time (for example, */usr/local/samba/var*). The `log file` option can be used to set the name of the logfile to another location. For example, to put the Samba log information in */var/log/samba.log*, you could use the following:

```
[global]
    log file = /var/log/samba.log
```

Variable substitution allows you to create logfiles specifically for individual users or clients.

You can override the default logfile location using the -1 command-line switch when either daemon is started. However, this switch does not override the `log file` option. If you do specify this parameter, initial logging information is sent to the file specified after -1 (or the default specified in the Samba makefile) until the daemons have processed the *smb.conf* file and know to redirect it to a new logfile.

log level

The `log level` option sets the amount of data to be logged. Normally this option is set to 0 (the default, which logs only critical messages) or 1. However, if you have a specific problem, you might want to set it to 2 or 3, either of which provides the most useful debugging information you would need to track down a problem. Levels above 5 provide information primarily for the developers to use for chasing internal bugs, and slow down the server considerably. For normal day-to-day operation, the recommended setting is 0, unless you are tracking specific information.

max log size

The `max log size` option sets the maximum size, in kilobytes, of the debugging logfile that Samba keeps. When the logfile exceeds this size, the current logfile is renamed to add a *.old* extension (erasing any previous file with that name) and a new debugging logfile is started with the original name. For example:

```
[global]
    log file = /var/log/samba.log
    max log size = 1000
```

Here, if the size of any logfile exceeds 1 MB, Samba renames the logfile *samba.log.old*, and a new logfile is generated. If there is already a file with the *.old* extension, Samba deletes it. Using this option protects unwary administrators from suddenly discovering that most of the space on a disk or partition has been swallowed up by a single Samba logfile.

It is generally a good idea to use some type of log rotation strategy, either by leveraging internal functionality or by using external tools such as *logrotate*.

debug timestamp

By default, Samba includes a timestamp header with each log entry. This can be very useful when running at level 0 or 1, due to the infrequency at which messages are logged. If you happen to be debugging a network problem and you find that the timestamp information within the Samba log lines gets in the way, you can turn it off by disabling the debug timestamp (also known as timestamp logs). For example, a normal Samba logfile presents its output in the following form:

```
[2005/10/04 13:55:12, 1] smbd/service.c:make_connection_snum(666)
    rain (127.0.0.1) connect to service lizard initially as user lizard (uid=780,
gid=100) (pid 28317)
```

With a no value for this option, the output would appear without the timestamp, giving no indication of when the event occurred.

debug pid, debug uid

These two options provide a means of separating log messages for different users that are interwoven into a single logfile. When enabled, the debug pid parameter includes a pid=PROCESSID field in the header information. The debug uid option fills in the real and effective uid and group values in the header. The following is an example of a message written by an *smbd* with a pid of 28554, a uid of 780, and a gid of 100:

```
[2005/10/04 14:05:38, 1, pid=28554, effective(780, 100), real(780, 0)] smbd/service.
c:make_connection_snum(605)
```

Both options require that the debug timestamp parameter be enabled to have any effect.

syslog

The syslog option causes Samba log messages to be sent to the Unix system logger and is available only when Samba has been compiled to include --with-syslog when running the configure script at build time. The presence of the string WITH_SYSLOG in the output of smbd -b confirms that compile-time support for syslog has been enabled. The amount of log information to be sent is specified as a numeric value; syslog can accept any valid log level. Logging information with a level lower than the number specified is sent to the system logger. Debug logs greater than or equal to the syslog level, but less than the log level, are still sent to the standard Samba logfiles. For example:

```
[global]
    log level = 3
    syslog = 2
```

In this instance, all logging information with a level of 0 and 1 is sent to the standard Samba logs and the system logger, and information at levels 2 and 3 is sent only to the standard Samba logs. Levels above 3 are not logged at all. All messages sent to the system logger are mapped to a priority level that the *syslogd* daemon understands, as shown in Table 4-9. The default level is 1.

Table 4-9. syslog priority conversion

Log level	syslog priority
0	LOG_ERR
1	LOG_WARNING
2	LOG_NOTICE
3	LOG_INFO
4 and above	LOG_DEBUG

syslog only

The `syslog only` option instructs Samba not to use its own logging files at all and to use only the system logger. To enable this behavior, specify the option in the global section of the Samba configuration file, as in the following example:

```
[global]
    log level   = 2
    syslog      = 3
    syslog only = yes
```

This option has no effect if Samba has not been compiled to include the `--with-syslog` feature.

## CHAPTER 5

Accounts, Authentication, and Authorization

Authentication is proving that you are who you say you are. You do this every day, during such activities as printing a document or saving a file to a network drive. When things are working correctly, the steps taken by a server to authenticate a request are often taken for granted. You enter a password, and it is used whenever the client machine needs to access a network resource on your behalf. Authentication is a prerequiste to *authorization*. Authorization is what the server does to verify that the authenticated user should (or should not) gain access to the requested resource (such as the printer or file share).

Chapter 1 described the basic steps necessary to connect to a share. The second step, after negotiating the protocol dialect, is the session setup, a packet exchange in which the client sends some proof of identify. This proof must be validated somehow. In this chapter, you will see how Samba can be configured to verify this request using a set of local user accounts. More advanced authentication environments involving domain controllers are covered in Chapters 9 and 10.

Security Modes

The SMB/CIFS protocol has two *security levels*: user and share. Samba implements these levels across five *security modes* defined by the global security parameter in *smb.conf*.* Only three of these values are relevant to modern Samba servers, all of which are variations of SMB/CIFS user-level authentication. In this chapter, we cover the details of security = user and local accounts. Chapter 10 presents the domain member server modes security = domain and security = ads. Table 5-1 lists the valid security modes as well as their current level of support from Samba developers.

---

* The term *security level* refers to the capabilities of the SMB/CIFS protocol and the term *security mode* describes Samba's various implementations of the SMB/CIFS security levels.

Table 5-1. Samba's security modes

Parameter	Value	Description	Default	Scope
security	user (Chapter 5)	Authentication model used to validate incoming requests.	user	Global
	ads (Chapter 10)			
	domain (Chapter 10)			
	share (deprecated)			
	server (deprecated)			

What About the Other Two Security Modes?

The remaining two security modes, security = share and security = server, are historical artifacts from past releases. Both of these implementations are remnants of authentication models primarily used by Windows 9x and earlier hosts. Neither security mode offers functionality beyond that provided by the three recommended security values covered in this chapter. Furthermore, in many instances, the deprecated modes suffer from severe protocol limitations. For this and other reasons, there is a high chance that both will be removed from Samba at some future time. It is strongly suggested that you avoid these two values when building new servers.

Guest Access with security = user

We already talked about user-level security in Chapter 1, so we won't repeat the protocol background here. Rather, we are currently interested in how the server determines whether to respond to a session setup request with success or failure. Let's consider a very simple case in which a server must provide open access to users without requiring creation of individual accounts. This example might seem a little counterintuitive, given the previous discussion of authentication, but it has its purpose and its uses.

Assume for a minute that Samba receives an authentication request in the form of a session setup packet and that the user cannot be authenticated. This might happen in a small office network where all clients and servers are operating in standalone configurations. This type of setup was described in Chapter 1 as peer-to-peer networking. If there is a user named *susan* logged into her local Windows workstation trying to access the share public on the Samba server named OAK (*OAK\public*), *smbd* will be responsible for looking in its own list of accounts (e.g., a *smbpasswd* file) to validate *susan*'s credentials. But what should Samba do when *susan* has no account on the server? The default behavior is to reject the connection attempt and indicate a logon failure.

The response to a failed logon is controlled by the map to guest parameter. To implement open sharing in this example, the parameter should be set to the value bad user. When *susan* cannot be authenticated (because she has no account), *smbd* evaluates the reason for the failure. A bad user is one whose name cannot be found in the the password storage system denoted by the passdb backend option. The concept of a backend is explored more in the upcoming section "Account Storage"; the default backend is an *smbpasswd* file. When the reason for the authentication is determined to be a bad username, *smbd* then honors *susan*'s request, but requires all authorization requests to be done using the guest account defined in *smb.conf*. The guest account value is a normal Unix account that *smbd* can use for this one purpose. The *smb.conf* for our guest server appears as follows:

```
[global]
    netbios name = OAK
    workgroup = GARDEN
    server string = Public access file server
    security = user
    map to guest = bad user
    guest account = smbguest

[public]
    path = /export/public
    guest ok = yes
    read only = no
```

Here is one file share named [public], which makes the */data/public* directory available for users. The permissions on this directory should allow anyone to create files (i.e., permission set to 1777). The guest ok option is needed to tell *smbd* that users mapped to the guest account should be allowed access to the share, assuming that the guest user, *smbguest* in this example, is allowed access by the filesystem permissions. The read only parameter operates as it has in past examples.

One disadvantage of a public server such as this one is that when a connection is mapped to the guest user, you lose all ability to audit any changes made by that connection. Any files created by this user are owned by the guest user. Other tasks, such as printer page accounting, also become impossible, as all knowledge of the original user is essentially lost.

Table 5-2 lists the various guest-related *smb.conf* parameters, and Table 5-3 lists the complete set of map to guest values.

Table 5-2. Guest-related parameters

Parameter	Value	Description	Default	Scope
guest account	username	The Unix account *smbd* uses this parameter when a connection is allowed guest access.	nobody	Global
guest ok	boolean	Specifies whether a user mapped to the guest account is allowed access to this share.	no	Share

Table 5-2. Guest-related parameters (continued)

Parameter	Value	Description	Default	Scope
guest only	boolean	Automatically maps the user to the guest account for access to this share.	no	Share
map to guest	never, bad password, bad user, bad uid	Determine whether a failed authentication request should be treated as the guest user and allowed access. The complete list of values and their description is in Table 5-3.	never	Global

Table 5-3. Values for the map to guest parameter

Value	Description
never	Reply with a logon failure error. This is the default behavior.
bad password	Use the guest account if the username exists in Samba's list of accounts but the client transmitted the wrong password. This value is not recommended in most circumstances, due to the confusion that it may cause when a user is allowed access but does not have the expected access.
bad uid	Valid only when used on member servers (security = ads or security = domain). Use the guest account if the domain mode authentication succeeded but a local uid for the username cannot be found.
bad user	Use the guest account if the username is unknown to Samba's list of accounts.

The only real word of caution when you configure guest servers is to remember that the map to guest parameter is a global setting. A client may wish to access multiple file or printer shares on the same server. However, when providing user-level security, there is only one authenticated session per user for all share connections. It is not possible for a client to access the server as a guest for one share and then to provide a valid set of credentials to access another share. One way around this limitation is to use the virtual server technique described in Chapter 4. One server identity would be dedicated to providing guest access and another would be used for non-guest access. The map to guest option can have different values in each virtual server configuration.

Passwords and Authentication

The proof of identity in the session setup request can take several forms. We group the mechanisms supported by Samba into three categories:

- Clear-text passwords
- NTLM and related challenge/response exchanges
- Kerberos tickets

The first two areas are covered here. Kerberos authentication will be covered in the context of Active Directory domain membership in Chapter 10.

Dispelling the Myth of Windows and Encrypted Password Support

Much of Samba is surrounded by urban legends and common misunderstandings. One such myth is that older versions of Windows did not support password encryption or the NTLM challenge/response authentication mechanism. The confusion arises from the behavior of pre-Windows NT 4.0 SP3 clients and the original versions of Windows 95. These clients would happily transmit the password's clear text to a server if the neg-prot response indicated that password encryption was not supported. Such behavior is open to abuse, as you can imagine.

The result was that Microsoft decided that Windows clients must refuse to downgrade to sending clear-text passwords to servers that report lack of support for NTLM. This move was valid, as all Microsoft servers have long supported NTLM. Samba has also supported NTLM for many years, but it was not the default password setting until the 3.0.0 release.

All recent Microsoft clients, including the MS-DOS LanMan client, Windows for Workgroups, and the original Windows 95 releases, prefer to use encrypted passwords if supported by the server. Therefore, if you change a Samba host from encrypt passwords = no to yes, Windows clients automatically begin to use the NTLM authentication algorithm. You might want to configure the clients to never downgrade to clear-text authentication at this point, just to prevent clever attackers masquerading as SMB/CIFS servers. But no client-side changes are required to have the new server functionality utilized.

Clear-text passwords

Using clear-text passwords has many disadvantages in modern networks. The lack of security is the most serious of these; plus, no current CIFS clients support this in their default configurations. But clear-text authentication has one alluring feature that still entices some systems administrators even today: having *smbd* authenticate users against an NIS map or local */etc/passwd* file.

 Samba's domain controller functionality cannot be used with encrypt passwords = no.

If you choose this route, the first requirement is to configure the Windows clients to send the clear-text password, which can be done by importing the appropriate file from the *docs/registry/* directory of the Samba source distribution into the client's local registry. The operating system name is part of the filename. So for a Windows XP client, use the file called *WinXP_PlainPassword.reg*. After you import the correct file, a reboot of the client is required to make the change effective.

The second step is to set encrypt passwords = no in the [global] section of *smb.conf*. This setting instructs Samba to ignore any *smb.conf* passdb backend directives when authenticating users, and instead to validate each user by hashing the transmitted password and comparing it against the entry returned from the system account list.

There are a few subtleties of which you should be aware. Although Windows NT-based clients send the clear text password as it was typed by the user, Windows 9x/Me hosts do not. These clients transmit the clear-text password in all uppercase. You must inform Samba as to how many permutations of that password it should attempt to validate before giving up and reporting failure. The password level option accepts a positive numeric value that represents the maximum number of uppercase letters in password test cases. For example, if the client transmitted a password of "cow," a password level of 1 would result in the follow variations being tested: COW, cow, Cow, cOw, and coW. The first two combinations shown are tried irrespective of the password level. Samba always tries the password as transmitted first, followed by an all-lowercase version and an all-uppercase version of the string (assuming the originally transmitted password had mixed case). The password level option defaults to 0, because as the number of combinations to be tested increases, a proportional amount of CPU and time is needed for the authentication process.

 If your server's operating system uses DES password hashes, setting a password level of 8 characters effectively makes the passwords case-insensitive, because DES limits the password to 8 characters.

Here is a basic *smb.conf* that allows users to authenticate against */etc/passwd*, as long as passwords contain at most four uppercase characters. If there are no users with Windows 9x/Me clients that will require access to the server, the password level option can be removed altogether.

```
[global]
    encrypt passwords = no
    password level = 4
```

In some extreme cases, it may be necessary to have Samba perform the same type of case permutations to a user's login name, because Windows 9x/Me clients also convert the login name to uppercase before sending to the server. Unix platforms have historically presented usernames as case-sensitive. This is yet another point of contention between Windows and Unix hosts. Internally, Samba first looks for the name in all lowercase, as this is the most common case on Unix hosts, followed by string as transmitted from the client, and finally in all uppercase. If no user by any of the names can be found, Samba then attempts a round of upper- and lowercase combinations controlled by the value of username level. Only when a user's name is stored in mixed case in the server's list of accounts should you even consider changing the username level from its default of 0.

The username and password level options are summarized in Table 5-4.

Table 5-4. Username- and password-level parameters

Parameter	Value	Description	Default	Scope
password level	integer	Number of case permutations to test when validating a clear text password.	0	Global
username level	integer	Number of case permutations to test when searching for the login name sent in a connection request.	0	Global

Pluggable Authentication Modules (PAM)

Pluggable Authentication Modules (PAM) are shared libraries that can be used in combination to allow an administrator to enforce a specific authentication security policy. For a complete discussion of PAM, first try searching your server's operating system documentation. Another good source of information is the Linux PAM web site at *http://www.kernel.org/pub/linux/libs/pam*.

Each PAM module implements one or more of the following functions:

auth
> User authentication requests

account
> User account handling, such as password expiration and denying locked accounts

session
> User management related to this specific session, such as logging user activity to the system's *utmp* file

password
> User password change requests

Samba is able to use PAM to authenticate users and enforce certain authorization controls based on the the configuration of the *samba* PAM service. On some platforms, such as Solaris, all services are configured in a single configuration file named */etc/pam.conf*. On Linux hosts, these settings will be stored in */etc/pam.d/samba*. The following configuration instructs the PAM library to verify that the server is not rejecting logins (i.e., the */etc/nologin* file does not exist) and then validate the user against */etc/passwd*:

```
## /etc/pam.d/samba
auth    requisite    pam_nologin.so
auth    require       pam_unix.so
```

Our focus is not on PAM configuration specifics, but rather on how Samba, and *smbd* in particular, interacts with PAM. First it is necessary to verify that Samba was compiled to include the --with-pam configure option. The build output from smbd -b should include the WITH_PAM string if this is the case.

```
$ smbd -b | grep WITH_PAM
   WITH_PAM
```

If this check fails, return to Chapter 2 and rebuild Samba to include PAM support. You may also need to install additional software to get the PAM development files (e.g., the *pam-devel* package).

Once you have a PAM-aware version of *smbd*, it will require a properly configured */etc/pam.d/samba* file. Samba makes use of the auth settings in its PAM configuration file only if clients use clear-text passwords. If the encrypt passwords parameter has been enabled, the auth PAM module lines are ignored completely. However, it is possible to still make use of the remaining three PAM functions. The account and session settings are respected if the obey pam restrictions options is enabled in *smb.conf*. Any user password change requests that must be synchronized between Samba's and the operating system's list of users will pass through the PAM stack if pam password change = yes. Password synchronization is covered later in this chapter, so we will delay the complete discussion until then. Table 5-5 summarizes these two options and their default settings.

Table 5-5. PAM-related parameters

Parameter	Value	Description	Default	Scope
obey pam restrictions	boolean	Controls whether *smbd* respects the account and session PAM configuration settings.	no	Global
pam password change	boolean	If enabled, *smbd* will, upon receiving a password change request, use PAM for synchronizing a user's Unix credentials.	no	Global

NTLMv1

NTLM is the challenge/response authentication algorithm developed by Microsoft and utilized by Windows and other CIFS clients and servers. In the original implementations of NTLM, the client uses a hashed version of the user's password to generate a 24-byte response to a challenge returned by the server in the negotiate protocol reply. The actual details of the algorithm are not important from the point of view of a systems administrator.[*] The key facts to remember are:

- The hashed password is never sent over the wire.
- The user's password hash is a shared secret used to calculate the response. If the client's and the server's calculated response match, it proves that both knew the same initial password hash.
- Both the LanManager and NT password hashing algorithms do not use any salt. Therefore a string always produces the same LanMan and NT hashes.

---

[*] Details of NTLM and other authentication protocols used by CIFS can be found at Chris Hertel's site *http://ubiqx.org/cifs*.

The last point is important to remember, because it implies that the password hash is a plain-text equivalent. If an attacker were to uncover a user's password hash, he could impersonate that user without deriving the original clear-text string. Even so, many users reuse a single password for multiple services (email, banking accounts, and so on). Given that the LanMan password is limited to 14 uppercase characters and possesses a very weak hashing algorithm, protecting Samba's account database becomes extremely important.

Enabling NTLMv1 authentication in Samba is as simple as setting encrypt passwords = yes in the [global] section of *smb.conf* and then creating user accounts using either *smbpasswd* or the *pdbedit* utility, introduced in Chapter 2. When adding a new user, if the password is less than or equal to 14 characters in length, Samba stores two password hashes. Following is an entry from an *smbpasswd* file for a user named *lizard* with a password of *test*. The first string of hexadecimal digits is the LanMan hash followed by the NT password hash. Each field is separated by a colon. The line has been wrapped due to space limitations and appears as one line in your *smbpasswd* file.

```
lizard:1004:01FC5A6BE7BC6929AAD3B435B51404EE:
   0CB6948805F797BF2A82807973B89537:[U        ]:LCT-44528BD2:
```

If the user's password is longer than 14 characters, the LanMan hash is disabled so that the security value of the password is not degraded by storing a truncated version. A disabled password is represented by a string of Xs. This is what *lizard*'s smbpasswd entry would look like with a password of *somepasswordstringlongerthanfourteen*:

```
lizard:1009:XXXXXXXXXXXXXXXXXXXXXXXXXXXXXXXX:
   0FF1DFDA18B63EC50E1FD9ECFCDFDE05:[U        ]:LCT-44528C6B:
```

It is possible to disable a Samba server's use of LanManager passwords altogether by setting the lanman auth option to no in the [global] service.

Table 5-6 summarizes the *smb.conf* parameters related to NTLMv1 authentication.

Table 5-6. NTLMv1-related parameters

Parameter	Value	Description	Default	Scope
encrypt passwords	boolean	Controls whether Samba advertises support for NTLM authentication.	yes	Global
lanman auth	boolean	Determines whether *smbd* should attempt to validate NTLM responses using the LanManager password hash.	yes	Global

NTLMv2

NTLMv2 is a variant of the original NTLM authentication scheme, and was introduced in Windows NT 4.0 SP4. However, it has seemed to gain any semblance of widespread adoption only in conjunction with Active Directory deployments. Its main advantage over NTLMv1 is protection against man-in-the-middle and replay attacks. As with NTLMv1, the actual protocol details are unimportant for day-to-day system administration duties.

Supporting NTLMv2 on Samba servers is a process of disabling support for the older authentication protocols. The following [global] section snippet illustrates the use of the lanman auth and ntlm auth parameters:

```
[global]
    ## Enable support for only NTLMv2 on the server
    encrypt passwords = yes
    lanman auth = no
    ntlm auth = no
```

Unlike many other client and server capabilities, support for NLTMv2 cannot be negotiated. If a client sends an NTLMv2 response, Samba always uses that. However, unless the older, less secure authentication schemes are disabled on the clients as well, NTLMv2 does very little to help improve the overall security of a system, primarily because both the NTLMv1 and NTLMv2 client responses are created using the NT password hash. The situation is comparable to restricting 9 out of your 10 hosts to SSH access but allowing Telnet access to the remaining tenth host. Security is only as strong as its weakest link.

Table 5-7 summarizes the parameters needed to restrict access to using NTLMv2 authentication only.

Table 5-7. NTLMv2-related parameters

Parameter	Value	Description	Default	Scope
ntlm auth	boolean	Controls whether Samba should validating using the NTLMv1 24-byte response. This parameter should be disabled, along with the lanman auth option, to enforce use of NTLMv2.	yes	Global

User Management

Any discussion about authentication is fruitless without including the topic of users. After all, the users are the ones being authenticated. As early as Chapter 2 we have seen some basic utilities that can be used to create a user account (i.e., the *smbpasswd* tool). However, we have not really talked about what the *smbpasswd* and similar utilities actually do. Here we break the discussion into two parts. We cover the various ways that user account information can be stored, followed by a explanation of the user management tools provided by Samba. First, we expand upon the discussion of Windows SIDs that we started in Chapter 1.

Security Identifiers

A *Windows security identifier* (SID) is a collection of numbers combined into a binary blob that uniquely identifies an object such as a user, group, or computer. The common string representations of a SID is written as:

```
S-1-5-21-3489264249-1556752242-1837584028-1003
```

It is impossible to determine what type of object the SID represents by its value alone. It could be a user or a group or something else. Windows (and Samba) provide calls to convert this SID to a name and to obtain its type.

The structure of a SID can be broken down into four parts:

- The revision (S-1)
- The number of authorities and subauthorities (5)
- The top-level authority (21)
- One or more subauthorities (3489264249-1556752242-1837584028-1003)

The last 32-bit number in the list of subauthorities is referred to as a *relative identifier* (RID). To be completely accurate, each 32-bit number of the subauthority list is a RID, but generally people use the term only to refer to the last number in the list. In this example, the RID is 1003.

Removing the RID from the original SID leaves us with an identifier that represents the SID's security domain. A security domain is not necessarily the same thing as an authentication domain (as discussed in Chapter 1), although there is a relationship between the two. In our example, the security domain would be S-1-5-21-3489264249-1556752242-1837584028. Each Windows host has a machine SID that defines its local domain. On domain controllers, the domain SID is identical to the local machine SID.

You can view Samba's local machine SID by logging on as *root* and running the *net* command from a shell prompt.

```
root# net getlocalsid
SID for domain RAIN is: S-1-5-21-3489264249-1556752242-1837584028
```

The concepts of local and foreign security domains do not neatly match up to Unix hosts, which have one authentication domain, based on an entry in */etc/passwd*. Even when a network of hosts is configured to be part of an NIS domain (which should not be confused with a Microsoft domain), there is no distinction between users within the NIS map and those existing in the local */etc/passwd* file.

From the Windows GUI, the distinction between local and remote domains can be seen from the initial logon box. Figure 5-1 shows the drop-down list of domains available when logging onto a Windows XP client. The local Administrator account is distinguished from the Administrator account in a foreign domain by prefacing the username with either the local machine's name (*LETTUCE\Administrator*) or the name of the foreign domain (*AD\Administrator*). These are two different user accounts with different SIDs, even though they share the same login name of Administrator.

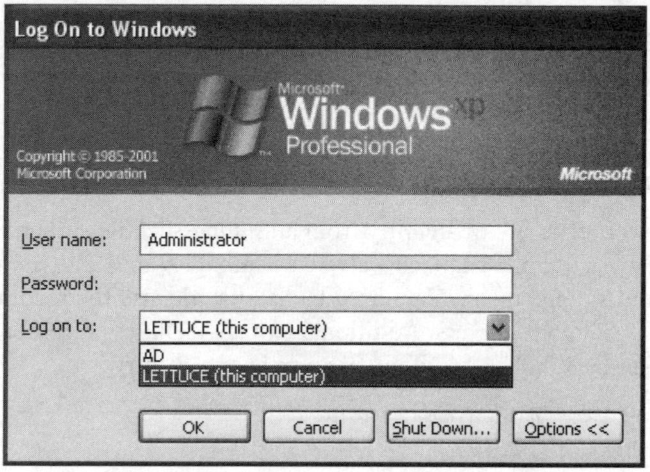

Figure 5-1. Selecting the domain when logging onto a Windows XP client

In addition to the local machine security domain, all Windows and Samba hosts are expected to support the S-1-5-32 domain, which is called BUILTIN. Groups existing within this domain have predefined RIDs. For example, the *BUILTIN\Administrators* group has a SID of S-1-5-32-544 and the *BUILTIN\Users* group's SID is S-1-5-32-545.

More information on SIDs and authentication domains is presented in Chapters 9 and 10.

Account Storage

Samba exposes Unix objects—files, printers, users and groups—in a way that Windows clients understand. It is necessary, however, for Samba to store some additional attributes for users beyond the information in */etc/passwd*. These attributes, such as the LanMan and NT password hashes, the user's SID, and a home directory UNC path, are maintained in what is referred to as a passdb backend. This storage facility can currently take one of three forms:

- A flat text file
- A trivial database (*tdb*) file
- An LDAP directory service

The passdb backend parameter is a global option whose value is in the form *name*: *argument*[,*argument*]. The Samba code for passdb is written such that new storage modules can be written by the community. However, in this chapter, we concern ourselves with only three, which are distributed as part of the core Samba source code: smbpasswd, tdbsam, and ldapsam. Because each passdb module has its own list of supported options, we discuss possible argument values later, after we have covered each backend in depth. Frequently, arguments can be omitted in order to rely on the passdb module's default behavior. If no backend is specified in *smb.conf*, Samba defaults to using an *smbpasswd* file.

passdb backend = smbpasswd

We have seen the structure of an entry from an *smbpasswd* file earlier in this chapter. Although the file's format changed between Samba 1.9 and 2.0, *smbpasswd* is the original account storage mechanism used by Samba and still the recommended solution for most standalone servers. Additional storage facilities were not officially supported until Samba 3.0.* The structure of an *smbpasswd* entry is:

    username:uid:lanman_hash:nt_hash:flags:pw_lct

The fields are defined as follows:

username
> The user's login name.

uid
> The Unix numeric uid of the user. This field is currently ignored by Samba, because the value is obtained by querying the operating system instead.

lanman_hash
nt_hash
> The user's password hashes, represented as 32-character hexadecimal strings. A string of 32 Xs indicates an invalid password. A value of the string "NO PASS-WORD" followed by 21 Xs in the *lanman_hash* indicates that no password has been associated with this account. Accounts with no passwords are allowed access only if the null passwords option (Table 5-8) is enabled in the [global] section of *smb.conf*.

flags
> Various single-character flags representing the type and state of the user's account. The complete list of account flags is in Table 5-9.

pw_lct
> The Unix timestamp of the user's last successful password change, encoded as a hexadecimal string.

---

* Samba 2.2 did support both the LDAP and TDB storage backends. But it was only with the Samba 3.0 releases that developers considered these to be first-class citizens when managing user accounts.

Table 5-8. Null passwords option

Parameter	Value	Description	Default	Scope
`null passwords`	boolean	Determines whether Samba allows connections using accounts with no associated password hash and possessing the N account flag.	no	Global

Table 5-9. User account flags supported by Samba

Flags	Description
D	Account is disabled.
I	Interdomain trust account.
L	The account has been autolocked due to bad login attempts.
N	No password is required by this account. This flag is honored only if the `null passwords` global parameter is enabled.
S	Backup domain controller trust account.
U	User account.
W	Workstation trust account.
X	The associated password will not expire, regardless of the server's password policy settings.

The following example configures Samba to use an *smbpasswd* text file for account storage:

```
[global]
    security = user
    encrypt passwords = yes
    passdb backend = smbpasswd
```

The file's default location is set at compile time and can be determined by entering `smbd -b | grep SMB_PASSWD_FILE`. If you wish to assign a different location, append a colon and the desired absolute path to the `smbpasswd` module name:

```
    passdb backend = smbpasswd:/etc/smbpasswd
```

passdb backend = tdbsam

The TDB `passdb` backend, named `tdbsam`, expands upon the list of user attributes supported by the `smbpasswd` backend. `tdbsam` is the recommended method for storing accounts for a single Samba primary domain controller that does not share its users and groups with any Samba backup domain controllers. The full discussion of Samba domains is provided in Chapter 9. For now, it is sufficient to understand that a `tdbsam` is a database variant of `smbpasswd` with support for a richer set of attributes.

The default `tdbsam` database filename is *passdb.tdb* and is located in the */usr/local/samba/private* directory. For custom Samba installations, you can determine this location by running `smbd -b | grep PRIVATE_DIR`. If you wish to change that location at runtime, `tdbsam` accepts, as its only argument, the absolute path to a *tdb* file:

```
    passdb backend = tdbsam:/etc/passdb.tdb
```

passdb backend = ldapsam

The third officially supported `passdb` module is the `ldapsam` backend. A complete discussion of LDAP is beyond the scope of this book. If you are interested in LDAP and directory services, a recommended resource is *LDAP System Administration*, by Gerald Carter (O'Reilly). The remainder of this section assumes a basic level of comfort with LDAP directories and the OpenLDAP software in particular. If you are using a directory server from a different vendor, the examples should prove easy to adapt.

When you consider the `ldapsam` backend, the first thing to do is to become familiar with the schema. There are two auxiliary classes and one structural object class that will be encountered in relation to users and groups:

sambaDomain

> This structural object class is used to store information that is intended to be shared between Samba domain controllers in the same domain. We examine this more in Chapter 9.

sambaSamAccount

> This auxiliary object class represents normal user and computer accounts and is commonly used to extend a user's `posixAccount` entry in the directory. If a user (or computer) does not have a preexisting entry in the directory service, Samba attempts to use the account object as the structural class to instantiate a user. We haven't discussed how machine and domain trust accounts are implemented yet, but we return to this subject in Chapter 9.

sambaGroupMapping

> This auxiliary object class contains the attributes necessary for Samba's group mapping functionality and is designed to use the `posixGroup` class as its structural basis.* Group mapping is covered later in this chapter.

All the necessary attributes and object classes are defined in an OpenLDAP 2.x compatible schema file named *samba.schema* located in the *examples/LDAP* directory of the Samba source distribution. In this same location are schema files for other directory services as well, although these may not be up to date. Make sure that you include or import the appropriate schema file into your LDAP server's configuration. Be aware that Samba's OpenLDAP schema file requires you include the *nis.schema*, *inetorgperson.schema*, and *cosine.schema* files first.

Remember that the LanMan (`sambaLMPassword`) and NT (`sambaNTPassword`) password hashes stored in the `sambaSamAccount` object are plain-text equivalents and should never be made readable to users. Access control rules should restrict these attributes to administrative users only, such as Samba's `ldap admin dn` distinguished name (discussed a few paragraphs ahead). The following ACLs in OpenLDAP's *slapd.conf* file

---

* This is the `posixGroup` from the original RFC2307 schema and not the auxiliary version defined in the RFC2307bis extensions.

protect the passwords from normal users but allow them to be read and modified by Samba:

```
## protect the samba password hashes
access to attr=sambaNTPassword,sambaLMPassword
  by cn=smbadmin,ou=people,dc=example,dc=com write
  by * none
```

For performance reasons, the directory service should support fast equality searches on the uid, cn, sambaSID, gidNumber, uidNumber, and displayName attributes. Newer Samba releases (beginning with 3.0.23) also use a substring matching rule on the sambaSID attribute. To effect this performance enhancement, add the following indexes (or their equivalents) to the server's database section, if any are missing.

```
## Samba's index settings for OpenLDAP's slapd.conf
index   uid,cn,displayName,memberUid  eq
index   uidNumber,gidNumber           eq
index   sambaSID                      eq,sub
```

Finally, it may be necessary to restart your directory server and/or rerun indexing tools to get it to recognize the changes.

Begin configuring *smb.conf* by setting up the connection parameters, starting with the LDAP server's URI in the passdb backend value.

```
[global]
    passdb backend = ldapsam:ldap://localhost/
```

By default, all LDAP requests are sent to the directory in an unencrypted form. Unless the master LDAP server and Samba are running on the same machine, it is highly recommended that you take steps to secure the LDAP traffic from eavesdropping. Even when an LDAP replica is running locally on the Samba host, any referrals going back to the master LDAP server must still be encrypted.

Use the ldaps:// URI in the passdb backend option if you wish to connect using LDAP over SSL. However, using StartTLS is the recommended method for configuring data privacy when communicating with an LDAP directory. In this case, the ldap:// URI suffices. To enable StartTLS support, add the following setting to the [global] section:

```
    ldap ssl = start_tls
```

It is possible to include multiple LDAP URIs in a single-quoted string for purposes of fault tolerance or load balancing. If there are two servers, *ldap1* and *ldap2*, which are replicas of the directory, we can configure Samba to use one in case the other is unavailable. The list of servers is passed on to the underlying LDAP client libraries, which handle the actual network connection details and any failover behavior. The ldap ssl parameter is included here to reiterate the need to secure all communication with the directory service; its value, however, specifies the use of StartTLS instead of SSL:

```
    passdb backend = ldapsam:"ldap://ldap1/ ldap://ldap2/"
    ldap_ssl = start_tls
```

Samba treats LDAP as another storage facility for users and groups. Thus all of the user's attributes are retrieved from the directory when a SMB/CIFS connection request must be authenticated. When configuring the directory service access control settings, we restricted the password hashes to be readable only by Samba itself when using its `ldap admin dn` distinguished name to bind to the server:

```
ldap admin dn = cn=smbadmin,ou=people,dc=example,dc=com
```

The password associated with this privileged DN is stored in clear text separately in *secrets.tdb*. The *smbpasswd* command can store these credentials interactively (-W option) or on a command line (-w option). Here we have chosen to enter it interactively so that the password will not be displayed in the output of *ps*:

```
root# smbpasswd  -W
Setting stored password for "cn=smbadmin,ou=people,dc=example,dc=com" in secrets.tdb
New SMB password: <enter password>
Retype new SMB password: <re-enter password>
```

The final bit of information that Samba requires for `ldapsam` is the set of base suffixes used to query and store users and groups. The top-level suffix is specified by the `ldap suffix` option. This DN should be the parent of the other *smb.conf* search suffixes, which are specified by the following options:

`ldap user suffix`
  The search base for locating and storing user accounts

`ldap machine suffix`
  The search base for locating and storing computer and domain trust accounts

`ldap group suffix`
  The search base for locating and storing group mapping entries

`ldap idmap suffix`
  The search base for mapping *winbindd*'s SIDs to the Samba host's uid/gid entries; additional information on *winbindd* is provided in Chapter 10

The `ldap suffix` should be specified first in *smb.conf* and should be a full DN. The remaining search suffixes should be defined relative to the `ldap suffix` value. In order to support a directory name space such as the directory information tree (DIT) shown in Figure 5-2, we would add the following parameters to Samba's configuration:

```
[global]
    ldap suffix         = dc=example,dc=com
    ldap user suffix    = ou=people
    ldap machine suffix = ou=people
    ldap group suffix   = ou=group
    ldap idmap suffix   = ou=idmap
```

It is possible to define different machine and user suffixes. If you do so, the server's LDAP NSS module must search both bases when querying for a `posixAccount`. As one of the Samba developers has said, "Machines are people too." The *nss_ldap* library from PADL software (*http://www.padl.com*) supports this by enabling the

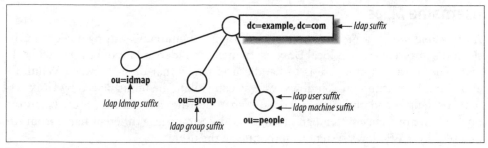

Figure 5-2. Samba's DIT

library's RFC2307bis extensions (pass the `--enable-rfc2307bis` option to the *nss_ldap* configure script when compiling) and then defining multiple nss_base_passwd directives in its configuration file (usually */etc/ldap.conf*). The complete details of PADL's *nss_ldap* configuration is beyond the scope of this discussion. For more information, please refer to PADL's web site and the documentation included with its software.

To finish off the section, Table 5-10 lists the LDAP-related parameters supported in *smb.conf*. Samba and LDAP integration are revisited in Chapters 9 and 10.

Table 5-10. LDAP-related parameters

Parameter	Value	Description	Default	Scope
ldap admin dn	DN	The user DN entry with administrative access to read and modify all Samba attributes and entries in the directory.	""	Global
ldap replication sleep	integer (in milliseconds)	The period to delay queries to an LDAP replica after updating the master directory server.	1000	Global
ldap ssl	off start_tls	Transport layer encryption settings when not using LDAPS in the ldapsam server URI.	off	Global
ldap suffix	DN	The parent search suffix that establishes the base suffix for LDAP queries.	""	Global
ldap group suffix	DN	The suffix relative to the ldap suffix that stores group mapping information.	""	Global
ldap idmap suffix	DN	The suffix relative to the ldap suffix that stores *winbindd*'s identity mapping information.	""	Global
ldap machine suffix	DN	The suffix relative to the ldap suffix that stores computer and domain trust account information.	""	Global
ldap user suffix	DN	The suffix relative to the ldap suffix that stores user account information.	""	Global
ldap timeout	integer (in seconds)	The maximum time in seconds to wait for a response to an LDAP query.	15	Global

Username Maps

A *username map* is a mechanism for translating a login name sent by a client in the session setup request to a local Unix username. It's independent of any `passdb` back-end. The most common use is to handle usernames that differ between Windows and Unix. Usernames on Windows systems can violate the limits placed by Unix systems on length and characters used, so sometimes the user account must be stored on the Unix or Linux system, and recognized by Samba as a different name from the one sent by a Windows system to authenticate the user.

This mapping feature comes in two forms: `username map` uses a file lookup, whereas `username map script` relies upon an external command to perform the search. Both *smb.conf* parameters are summarized in Table 5-11.

Table 5-11. Username mapping

Parameter	Value	Description	Default	Scope
`username map`	string	Absolute path of the username map file.	""	Global
`username map script`	string	Absolute path to a script or tool that accepts the requested username as a parameter and prints the mapped username (if any) to standard output. This script is mutually exclusive with, and takes precedence over, the `username map` parameter.	""	Global

The `username map` option requires the absolute path to a map file on the server. Frequently this file is named *smbusers* and is stored in the same location as *smb.conf*. No default mapping file is distributed with Samba, although some vendors may choose to do so. The `username map` option must be explicitly set as shown here:

```
[global]
    username map = /usr/local/samba/lib/smbusers
```

This map file contains entries in the form of:

```
map_to = map_from
```

The *map_to* value is a single Unix username. The *map_from* value may be a list of values that include:

- A single username. Login names containing whitespace must be surrounded by double quotes (e.g., "Lee Zard").
- A Unix or NIS netgroup name prefaced by a &, @, or +. This same syntax is reused for other *smb.conf* parameters and so is discussed in the final section of this chapter, where it is most applicable.
- A single wildcard character, *, that matches everything.

Processing of the username map file continues until either the complete map has been parsed or until an entry prefixed by an exclamation point (!) matches successfully. Any lines beginning with a hash (#) or semicolon (;) character are ignored as comments. If no match is found at all, the original username is unchanged.

As an example, to map a Windows user of *Lee.Zard* to a Unix login name of *lizard*, we could use a single entry such as:

```
!lizard = Lee.Zard
```

The righthand values are compared in a case-insensitive fashion, so this example would succeed regardless of whether the user logs on with *Lee.Zard* or *LEE.ZARD*. The beginning ! prevents *smbd* from continuing to look for additional matches for *lizard* after this entry is parsed.

The username map script allows an administrator to define an external command that will be invoked, rather than reading a map file directly. It provides the flexibility to store the maps in directory services such as LDAP. The mapping command must accept a username as its sole parameter (provided by *smbd*) and must return a single login name to standard output if any mapping is necessary. Without getting into too many details, the following example uses the OpenLDAP *ldapsearch* tool to query a directory service based on the common name (cn) attribute and maps the user to the login name provided by the uid attribute.

```
#!/bin/sh
ldapsearch -x -LLL -h ldapsrv1 -b "dc=example,dc=com" \
  -s sub "(&(cn=$1)(objectclass=posixAccount))" \|
  grep uid: | cut -d: -f 2 | sed 's/^\s*//'
```

Assuming that this script is named *ldapmapuser.sh*, we can instruct *smbd* to make use of it by adding the following line to *smb.conf*:

```
[global]
    username map script = /usr/local/bin/ldapmapuser.sh
```

In this way, it is possible to integrate the username map functionality with the ldapsam passdb backend.

The point at which the mapping occurs is dependent on the value of the security parameter. In the context of our current discussion around security = user, the map is queried before the user is authenticated. To illustrate the consequence, assume that we have the following entry in a username map file:

```
root = administrator
```

If a user attempts to connect to our standalone server with a login name of *Administrator*, the password supplied must match the one for *root* in Samba's configured passdb backend.

When Samba is configured as a domain member server (security = domain or security = ads), the map is applied after a user has been authenticated by a domain controller. The means that when a user connects as *DOMAIN\administrator*, she must provide the actual password for that account even though the account may be eventually mapped to the local superuser account. The process becomes even more complicated with the presence of *winbindd*. Therefore the remainder of the discussion of username maps and member servers is saved until Chapter 10.

Account Utilities

Samba provides a set of tools for manipulating user accounts stored in its passdb. The Samba developers have designed these tools to work in the same manner, regardless of which passdb module is used. For this reason, our discussion can focus on the tool without worrying about where or how the information is stored.

 Many administrators, particularly LDAP administrators, have a tendency to manage the user attributes (e.g., password hashes or SIDs) manually. It is possible in many instances to do this. However, it is not recommended for most installations. If you understand how to manipulate these attributes directly without breaking your server, it is probably okay. But consider this the sticker that voids your warranty if removed. If you can get away with it, congratulations. Such tactics are not covered here.

The two main user management tools are *smbpasswd* and *pdbedit*. The former is the original tool for setting user passwords in an *smbpasswd* file. During the Samba 3.0 development cycle, it was thought that this tool would be superseded by *pdbedit*. However, this has not yet happened, and *pdbedit* is considered by some as the example of how not to build a command-line interface. In Chapter 9, we explore how to use MS-RPC tools such as the Windows NT 4.0 User Manager for Domains and MMC plug-ins to manage users and group from Windows clients. At the moment, these two command-line utilities are what we have to work with.

The *smbpasswd* tool has two basic categories of functions:

- When run as *root*, the command can be used to manipulate Samba's local user accounts.
- Normal users can use the tool to perform password changes against remote Samba and Windows servers.

Local user management breaks down further into:

- Adding or deleting a user from Samba's list of accounts
- Setting user passwords
- Enabling or disabling user accounts

In previous chapters, you've seen examples of adding a new user by passing a login name to the -a argument. It is also possible to feed the new password to the tool on standard input using the -s option, which can be very useful for shell scripts. Here is an example that adds a user named *smitty* and assigns a password of "cat." The reason for the complicated syntax is to answer both prompts output by the *smbpasswd* command to request the password. Remember that the Unix user *smitty* must already exist.

```
root# (echo "cat"; echo "cat" ) | smbpasswd -s -a smitty
Added user smitty.
```

To later manually change this user's password, run the *smbpasswd* command again, but this time without the -a option. In this example, we enter the new password interactively rather than using the -s option again:

```
root# smbpasswd smitty
New SMB password: <enter new password>
Retype new SMB password: <re-enter new password>
```

The password is verified by comparing both input strings. If both match, the new password is set. Otherwise you will see an error message stating, Mismatch - password unchanged.

An account can be disabled to prevent the user from logging on. Disabling a user's account sets the D flag in the account control flags. (Refer to Table 5-9 in the earlier section on the *smbpasswd* file format for an overview of these flags.) The following lines disable *smitty*'s account (-d option) and then reenable it (-e option):

```
root# smbpasswd -d smitty
Disabled user smitty.
root# smbpasswd -e smitty
Enabled user smitty.
```

When the account is no longer necessary, we can delete this user from our passdb using the -x option and passing it the account name. This command has no effect on the user's Unix account in */etc/passwd*.

```
root# smbpasswd -x smitty
Deleted user smitty.
```

Table 5-12 summarizes the command-line options available to *root* when running *smbpasswd*.

Table 5-12. Command-line options for smbpasswd when run as root

Argument	Description
-a *name*	Add a user account.
-c *smb.conf*	Specify an alternative configuration file.
-d *name*	Disable a user account.
-e *name*	Enable a user account.
-h	Print the command usage.
-n *name*	Set a null password for a user.
-x *name*	Delete a user account.

If *smbpasswd* is a tool for day-to-day administrative tasks, *pdbedit* is more akin to a low-level database editor. Overall, its syntax can be cryptic at times, but it does provide three major functions not supported by the *smbpasswd* command:

- Editing of account policy settings, such as maximum password age and bad login attempts before locking an account.
- Editing the full set of supported user attributes, such as the login script, the user's SID, and roaming user profile location.
- Converting from one passdb backend to another.

The first two features are more related to Samba domain controller functionality, and so are discussed in full detail in Chapter 9. The last is covered here, because without the translation support between passdb storage formats, tasks such as converting from an *smbpasswd* file to tdbsam would be time-consuming and extremely error-prone.

pdbedit's option naming is a bit confusing at first. The import option (-i) reads in from one backend, whereas the export option (-e) writes to another. Each command-line switch accepts a passdb backend value as its argument. So to convert from smbpasswd to a tdbsam backend, you would run the following command as *root*:

```
root# pdbedit -ismbpasswd:/tmp/smbpasswd -etdbsam:/tmp/passdb.tdb
Importing account for root...ok
Importing account for kong...ok
<remaining output deleted>
```

 It is a good idea to copy your current passdb file or database to a temporary location, rather than working on the live version.

Synchronizing Passwords

The complaint with Samba in regard to user accounts is that its user passwords must be maintained separately from the from the Unix or Linux system passwords. To help alleviate the pain of managing multiple passwords for each user, Samba provides a mechanism to synchronize the user's Unix password entry when a CIFS client requests that the LanMan and NT password hashes be changed. Of course, this solution does not help when the user changes the password by means other than the SMB/CIFS protocol, such as using the *passwd* command or writing to the passdb storage directly using *pdbedit*.

The only prerequisite of using this feature is for the *root* user to able to reset a user's password without knowing the old password. The reason for this requirement is that the client encrypts the new password with the old password hash as the key. The clear text of the old password is never sent. Password hashes are one-way, so there is no way to derive the clear text of the password from the old password hash.

It is extremely difficult to make generalities about Windows clients because there are so many different versions. In fact, Windows 9x/Me clients do send the clear text of the old password, in uppercase of course, when the the *net.exe* command is used to change a password. But this approach is hardly useful, because it is impossible to determine the case of the new password.

The *smbd* daemon currently supports three mechanisms for changing a user's Unix password:

- Communicating with an external password program
- Utilizing the PAM password change API
- Requesting that the LDAP Directory service do the work on its behalf

The simplest option of the three, the ldap password sync option (sometimes called ldap passwd sync), instructs *smbd* to send a ModifyPassword extended request to the directory service, which then updates the userPassword attribute on behalf of the user. This option currently works only when Samba is using the ldapsam passdb module and when the LDAP directory service is running a recent version of OpenLDAP. To enable password synchronization, with all these prerequisites in place, add ldap password sync = yes to the [global] section of *smb.conf*.

If you can't make use of this optimal solution, the next option is to enable the unix password sync option and then choose which of the first two mutually exclusive password change mechanisms you wish to use. Relying on an external program is the older method. In this case, you must define a value for the passwd program parameter and then specify a passwd chat conversation string.*

The chat value is a special string generally called an "expect string" or "chat string"; it lists pairs of strings in which the first of each pair is the text that you expect the external program to output, and the second is the text that the external program expects the user to enter. With an expect string, an automated system can interact with a program that was designed for a human user. In this case, Samba is pretending to be the *root* user and is interacting with a password change program. The Samba expect string is case-insensitive and can contain wildcards (*) to eat a variable number of characters when evaluating the output from the program in the passwd program parameter. Remember that the passwd program executable is run as *root*, so be sure to pass the Unix user name (%u) as a command-line argument, or else you will be stuck just changing *root*'s credentials.

---

* In any discussion of Unix utilities, it is admittedly hard to remember which password-related options and files are called "password" and which are called "passwd."

The following example works on most recent versions of Linux from Novell or Red Hat:

```
[global]
    encrypt passwords = yes
    unix password sync = yes
    passwd program = /usr/bin/passwd %u
    passwd chat = *New*password* %n\n\
                   *Reenter*new*password* %n\n\
                   *Passwd*changed*
```

Deriving passwd chat values is not extremely difficult. This one was developed by examining the output from running */usr/bin/passwd* from a shell prompt, as shown here:

```
root# passwd lizard
Changing password for lizard.
New Password:
Reenter New Password:
Password changed.
```

Notice that the expect string collapses the first line of output to a single * character.

The pam password change Boolean parameter replaces the invocation of an external command with a series of calls to the system's PAM library. The passwd chat parameters plays the same role as before, providing a means by which *smbd* is able to interact with the PAM password change interface. This requires that the Samba PAM service has been correctly configured in either */etc/pam.conf* or */etc/pam.d/samba*. The following is a basic PAM password change stack that performs strengths checks on the new password, and finally hands it off to the *pam_unix.so* library to actually update the user's credentials:

```
password required  pam_pwcheck.so  nullok
password required  pam_unix2.so    nullok use_first_pass use_authtok
```

Next, we can update the previous example to make use of the new PAM configuration file:

```
[global]
    encrypt passwords = yes
    unix password sync = yes
    pam password change = yes
    passwd chat = *New*password* %n\n\
                   *Reenter*new*password* %n\n\
                   *Passwd*changed*
```

If desired, password strength checking can be performed using an external utility specified by the check password script parameter. This directive should point to a tool or script that accepts the new password as its single argument and returns 0 for valid passwords and a nonzero value if the strength check fails.

Table 5-13 summarizes all of the password synchronization options we have discussed in this section.

Table 5-13. Password synchronization parameters

Parameter	Value	Description	Default	Scope
check password script	string	Defines an external script that is used to verify the strength of a new password. The script must return 0 to indicate a valid password.	""	Global
ldap password sync	boolean	If enabled, *smbd* sends a Modify Password extended operation (currently supported only by OpenLDAP servers) to request that the user's directory service password attribute be updated.	no	Global
pam password change	boolean	Controls whether *smbd* uses PAM to change a user's Unix password.	no	Global
passwd program	string	External program to change a user's Unix credentials.	""	Global
passwd chat	string	An expect string that *smbd* uses to interact and evaluate the password change conversation.	*new*password* %n\n *new*password* %n\n *changed*	Global
passwd chat debug	boolean	Samba dumps the passwd chat conversation to its logfiles when this option is enabled, the DEBUG_PASSWORD macro was enabled at compile time, and the debug level is set to 100 or greater.	no	Global
passwd chat timeout	integer	The maximum number of seconds that *smbd* should wait for a passwd chat to complete.	2	Global
unix password sync	boolean	Defines whether Samba should attempt to synchronize a user's Unix password upon receiving a password change request from a CIFS client.	no	Global

Group Mapping

Remember that Samba exports Unix objects in a means that is palatable to Windows clients. In keeping with this philosophy, Unix groups are handled in a very similar fashion to Unix users. The underlying Unix group must already exist. Samba then associates a SID and name with that group and displays it to Windows. This operation is referred to as *group mapping*. The additional attributes can be manipulated using the *net groupmap* command.

The group mapping functionality is provided as part of Samba's passdb API and therefore shares the same storage mechanisms as user accounts. Both the smbpasswd and tdbsam passdb modules use the *group_mapping.tdb* file (stored in */usr/local/samba/var/locks* by default). The ldapsam backend stores mapping entries by adding the sambaGroupMapping auxiliary object class to an existing posixGroup entry in the directory service. For all three backends, the actual table entries can be managed using the same Samba command-line tools (as was the case with user accounts).

The group mapping interfaces and internal design have been given a new look starting with the 3.0.23 release. However, the basic concept is the same as in previous releases. Only the tools have changed. The new interface is a command set named *net sam*, which provides an interface to users, groups, and password policies. At the time of writing, the toolset is not yet complete.

A group mapping entry is primarily an association from a SID to a Unix gid. A current entry can be viewed using the *net groupmap list* command. Be aware that all of the *net groupmap* commands must be run as *root*, because they operate on the passdb storage service directly.

```
root# net groupmap list verbose ntgroup="Printer Admins"
Printer Admins
    SID       : S-1-5-21-391507597-2097566357-2340928898-3091
    Unix group: prtadmin
    Group type: Domain Group
    Comment   : Domain Unix group
```

Printer Admins is the name that will be displayed to Windows clients. The membership of this group is handled by managing the *prtadmin* Unix group membership. Only those Unix groups that posses a valid group mapping entry are displayed, as illustrated by Figure 5-3. The same is true for users: only those users who have an account in the current passdb backend are displayed in the Windows object picker UI.

You can view a complete list of current group mappings by omitting the group name when entering *net groupmap list*. But groups mapped to a value of –1 are placeholder entries created by *smbd* and are ignored.

```
root# net groupmap list
Printer Admins (S-1-5-21-391507597-2097566357-2340928898-3091) -> prtadmin
Administrators (S-1-5-32-544) -> -1
Domain Admins (S-1-5-21-391507597-2097566357-2340928898-512) -> -1
Users (S-1-5-32-545) -> -1
Domain Guests (S-1-5-21-391507597-2097566357-2340928898-514) -> -1
Domain Users (S-1-5-21-391507597-2097566357-2340928898-513) -> -1
remaining output deleted
```

The placeholder entries are not present when using an ldapsam passdb backend. Future versions of Samba will remove them from the remaining backends for the sake of consistency.

New maps can be added by executing *net groupmap add* and including the Unix group name and either a SID or simply a Windows group map. It is better to define the ntgroup name value and allow Samba to allocate a SID unless you have a specific group (e.g., Domain Admins) that you require.

```
root# net groupmap add ntgroup="System Managers" unixgroup=sysadmin
No rid or sid specified, choosing algorithmic mapping
Successfully added group Systems Managers to the mapping db
```

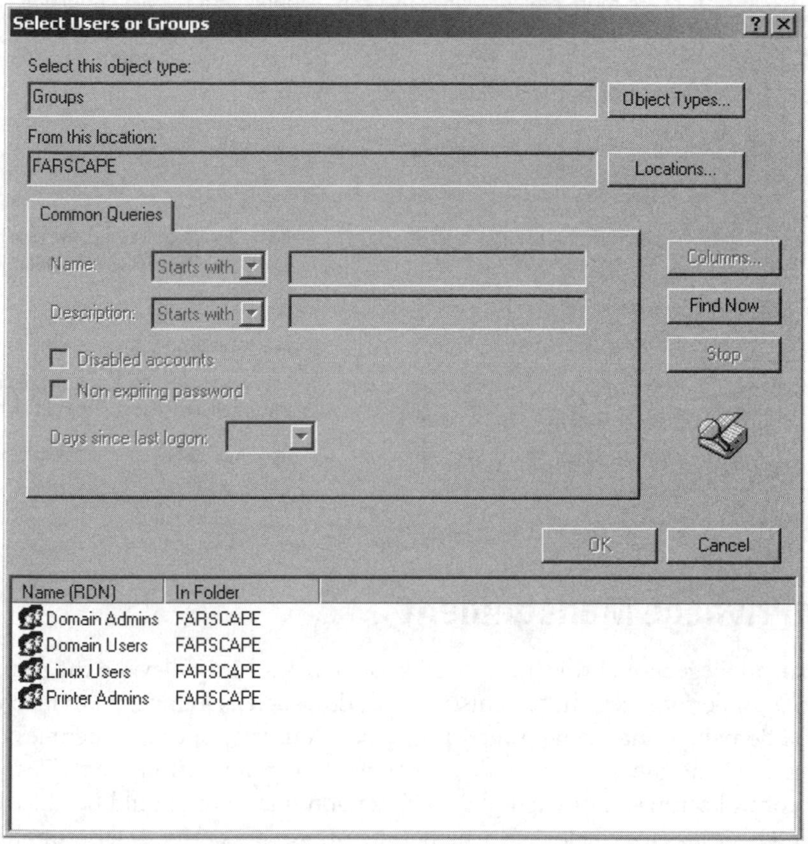

Figure 5-3. Displaying users and groups in the Windows object picker

The associated Unix group and group description can be changed with the `modify` subcommand:

```
root# net groupmap modify ntgroup="System Managers" unixgroup=sysops comment="Server
administrators group"
Updated mapping entry for System Managers
```

The Unix gid is not stored in the map entry and is therefore unaffected by renaming a group in */etc/group*. In this example, the *sysops* and *sysadmins* groups are entirely different groups on the Unix server.

Finally, you can remove entries using *net groupmap delete*:

```
root# net groupmap delete ntgroup="Systems Managers"
Successfully removed Systems Managers from the mapping db
```

Table 5-14 gives a brief overview of the *net groupmap* command-line arguments.

There are more esoteric things that can be done with the *net groupmap* tool. Most of these are prone to error and are not recommend for normal use. The options covered in this section are the most common and the least likely to change in a future Samba release.

Table 5-14. *net groupmap command-line options*

Command	Arguments	Description
add	{*ntgroup=name,sid=sid_string*} *unixgroup=name* [*comment=string*]	Add a new group mapping between a Unix group and a Windows group name or SID.
delete	{*ntgroup=name,sid=sid_string*}	Remove an existing group mapping entry.
list	[*verbose*] [*ntgroup=name,sid=sid_string*]	List all or a specific group mapping record. The verbose option includes all map attributes.
modify	{*ntgroup=name,sid=sid_string*} [*unixgroup=name*] [*comment=string*]	Update an existing group mapping record.

User Privilege Management

The user privilege model was introduced in Samba 3.0.11 to alleviate the need to log on as *root* to perform certain administrative duties, such as joining client machines to a Samba domain or managing printer properties. A user privilege, sometimes called a user right, is the inherent capability to perform certain actions regardless of the access control settings. For example, a printer administrator should be able to manage printer settings irrespective of whether the printer's security descriptor allows his user account administrative access. Currently Samba supports eight different privileges, which are described in Table 5-15, along with references to the chapter that fully covers each one.

Table 5-15. *Samba user privileges*

Privilege	Description
SeAddUsersPrivilege	Add, modify, and delete users, as well as group membership (Chapter 9).
SeBackupPrivilege	Not currently used.
SeDiskOperatorPrivilege	Create, modify, and remove file shares, as well as modify share ACLs (Chapter 9).
SePrintOperatorPrivilege	Create, modify, and remove printers, print drivers, and forms (Chapter 7).
SeMachineAccountPrivilege	Add and remove client machines from a Samba domain (Chapter 9).
SeRemoteShutdownPrivilege	Issues requests to initiate and abort a shutdown of the Samba server (Chapter 9).
SeRestorePrivilege	Set the ownership of a file or directory to an arbitrary user (Chapter 6).
SeTakeOwnershipPrivilege	Take possession of a file or directory (Chapter 6).

The first thing that must be done to take advantage of this administration delegation model is to enable the feature in *smb.conf*:

```
[global]
    enable privileges = yes
```

Table 5-16 provides a short description of the enable privileges parameter, as well as its current default value.

Table 5-16. User-privilege-related parameters

Parameter	Value	Description	Default	Scope
enable privileges	boolean	Controls whether *smbd* supports the assignment and honoring of user rights assignments.	no[a]	Global

a Future versions of Samba will enable this feature by default. Be sure to check the current *smb.conf(5)* manpage for your version.

Once this feature is enabled, the primary means of managing privilege assignments on a Samba server is the *rpc rights* subcommand of the *net* utility.

 It is possible to manipulate user rights assignments with the Windows NT 4.0 User Manager for Domains utility, but only when run from a Windows NT 4.0 client. This specific functionality in *usrmgr.exe* does not work correctly when run from a Windows 2000 or later client, due to a bug in the application.

The net Tool

The *net* tool began as a variation of the *net.exe* command on Windows. The motivation was to be able to perform simple remote administration tasks, such as adding a user or enumerating the open files on a server. To that end, the tool initially supported three main subcommands: *RAP*, *RPC*, and *ADS*. Each of these network commands has a myriad of additional subcommands. This list has grown to include nonnetwork related activities, as is the case with the *groupmap* subcommand. Chapter 11 expands on the *net* command, as we examine some simple scripts that make use of Samba tools. All three of these remote administration protocols share a set of common command-line arguments specifying the server and connection credentials.

When using the commands, first ensure that Samba is running, because the *net rpc* commands make use of the network to communicate rather than directly accessing any local configuration files.

You can anonymously enumerate the available user privileges on a server by running:

```
$ net -S localhost -U% rpc rights list
SeMachineAccountPrivilege  Add machines to domain
 SeTakeOwnershipPrivilege  Take ownership of files or other objects
<remaining output deleted>
```

The -S option specifies the server to query and the -U option specifies the username to use when making the connection. Like most Samba tools, these tools let you specify the full connection credentials in the -U option: a username followed by a % character and then the password. In this example, both the username and password are left empty.

It may be necessary in some circumstances, such as connecting to a server belonging to Active Directory, to define the domain for a username as well. This can be accomplished using the -W command-line flag. The following example connects to a server as the user *AD\Administrator*. If no % character is found in the username, *net* and other Samba client tools prompt for a password.

```
$ net -S localhost -U Administrator -W AD rpc rights list
Password: <enter password>
```

Once you are able to successfully enumerate available privileges, it is time to grant specific privileges to users. The capability to manage user rights assignments is implicitly granted to the *root* user. It is also implicitly granted to members of the Domain Admins group if the server is participating in a domain either as a domain controller or a member server. For now, this example relies on the presence of a *root* account that can connect to the server.

In this example, assume that there is a Unix user named *lizard* and that the server's name is RAIN. We can grant this user the SeDiskOperatorPrivilege by running:

```
$ net -S localhost -U root -W RAIN rpc rights \
      grant 'RAIN\lizard' SeDiskOperatorPrivilege
Password: <enter password for root>
Successfully granted rights.
```

 If you receive an error indicating that the named privilege does not exist, ensure that you have spelled the privilege name correctly and that enable privileges = yes is correctly specified in *smb.conf*.

Privileges can be assigned to any name that can be resolved to a SID. This means that the account being granted a right need not be a local user or group. In fact, a common configuration is grant domain groups certain rights on the Samba host in order to leverage the existing domain infrastructure rather than duplicating it locally. (Future chapters expand on this idea.)

It is possible to view specific privilege assignments by using a variant of the *net rpc rights list* that was discussed earlier. The following command enumerates all accounts stored in Samba's privilege database (*account_policy.tdb*) and any rights associated with that user or group:

```
$ net -S localhost -U% rpc rights list accounts
BUILTIN\Print Operators
No privileges assigned
....
RAIN\lizard
SeDiskOperatorPrivilege
```

This command lists all users and groups stored in Samba's privilege database. If you prefer to list only the rights assigned to a specific name, you can alternatively run this command:

```
$ net -S localhost -U% rpc rights list accounts 'RAIN\lizard'
SeDiskOperatorPrivilege
```

Or, if you wish to find all owners of a particular privilege, run:

```
$ net -S localhost -U% rpc rights list privileges SeDiskOperatorPrivilege
SeDiskOperatorPrivilege:
  RAIN\lizard
```

At times it is necessary to remove a privilege assignment from a user or group. The *net rpc rights revoke* command performs the inverse function to the *grant* subcommand. Here the SeDiskOperatorPrivilege previously assigned to *lizard* is removed:

```
$ net -S localhost -U root -W RAIN rpc rights revoke 'RAIN\lizard' \
SeDiskOperatorPrivilege
Password: <enter password for root>
Successfully revoked rights.
```

In all of these examples, it is possible to list multiple privilege names when listing, granting, or revoking rights. Table 5-17 collects the various options to the *net rpc rights* command covered in this section.

Table 5-17. net rpc rights commands

Command	Description
list [{*accounts,privileges*} [*name*]]	Enumerate supported privileges or assigned rights.
grant *name right* [*right*]	Assign a list of user privileges to a user or group.
revoke *name right* [*right*]	Remove a list of assigned privileges from a user or group.

Controlling Authorization for File Shares

We began this chapter discussing authentication, and we now end it with a discussion about authorization. Authorization under Unix relies upon the user's uid and a list of group gids. Samba can use this same information to perform preliminary access checks to to control whether the user or group should be allowed to modify any files within a share. For example, perhaps you would like to export a set of files as read-only to students but allow modification by teachers. There are several ways to accomplish this goal. The final access granted to a file or directory for a user is the most restrictive permission set allowed after passing the user credentials through the share's:

- Security descriptor
- Access controls in the share's definition in *smb.conf*
- Filesystem permissions

The initial access check is performed by comparing against the share's security descriptor. These share permissions are maintained separately from the server's configuration file and are stored by default in */usr/local/samba/var/locks/share_info.tdb*. All shares initially have a neutral ACL that grants *Everyone* full control of the share.

Figure 5-4 shows the share permissions for [public] viewed from the Computer Management MMC plug-in connected to a Samba host. Expand the Systems Tools → Share Folders → Share hierarchy to list the available file shares. Finally, select an individual share and right-click to navigate to the Properties menu option. The security tab in the dialog box that appears provides access to the share ACL settings. Note that you will not be able to modify the security descriptor unless you are connected as *root* or possess the SeDiskOperatorPrivilege.

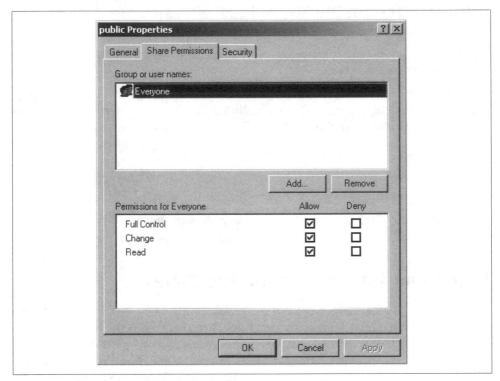

Figure 5-4. Share permissions for \\RAIN\public

Next, we focus on the category of *smb.conf* authorization options that make use of a list of names. Consider the admin users option as a first example. This option accepts a list of users or group members that should be mapped to the *root* account when they access resources on a given share. Assume that we want to allow the users *rose* and *lily* to be able to manipulate files regardless of the filesystem permissions. A basic way to achieve this is to add the *admin users* list to the share definition in *smb.conf*:

```
[documents]
    path = /data/docs
    read only = no
    admin users = rose, lily
```

When a user connects, Samba determines whether that user is a contained within the list *rose, lily*. Evaluating user names is straightforward. A single string comparison returns success or failure depending on whether the login names match.

Authorization lists such as *admin users* can accept group names as well. The next example expands the [documents] share to add the Unix group named *staff* as a member of the admin users list:

```
[documents]
    path = /data/docs
    read only = no
    admin users = rose, lily, +staff
```

When a name is prefixed by the plus sign (+), Samba resolves that name as a Unix group by querying the operating system for its membership. Once the list of user names is expanded, the login name comparison continues until a match is found or until all the members in the list have been checked.

 Any files or directories created by a user contained in the *admin users* list will be owned by *root*, not the actual user.

In most cases, the + character is all that is needed. There are two other available characters to inform Samba of the properties of a name:

@   Attempt to resolve the name as an NIS netgroup, and fall back to evaluating it as a Unix group in case of failure.

&   Attempt to resolve the name as an NIS netgroup, with no fallback mechanism in the case of failure.

It is very likely that Samba's support for NIS will be deprecated at some point, so don't rely upon the @ and & characters unless you actually use netgroups. Doing so prevents you from having to update your *smb.conf*, should support for descriptive characters other than + be removed.

Other parameters that make use of the user and group list syntax are frequently found in pairs. For example, the valid users and invalid users options allow and restrict specific users or groups from accessing a specific share. Although these parameters are not mutually exclusive, the configuration is much easier to understand when only one is present. If one parameter is defined—for example, valid users = +staff—everyone who does not belong to that list is considered to be invalid and is not allowed access to that share. This is a simple method to either disallow everyone and specify a few exceptions (valid users), or to authorize all users and then reject a few particular ones (invalid users). If both parameters are defined, a user must not appear in the invalid users list, but must match the valid users list.

Similarly, the read list and write list options provide a means of deviating from the read only setting for a user or group. A share may be marked as read only with the exception of a few users or groups. The following [administration] share is read only for those who do not belong to the *pcadmins* Unix group:

```
[administration]
    path = /data/administration
    read only = yes
    write list = +pcadmins
```

In a complementary fashion, a share named [documents] is defined here to be modifiable by all users except those in the guest group:

```
[documents]
    path = /data/documents
    read only = no
    read list = +guest
```

Finally, a share can be restricted to a maximum number of simultaneous connections across all user sessions by specifying a nonzero max connections parameter. This approach provides a crude mechanism for metering network software installations. For instance, if you have only 10 licenses for an application, you can install it in a dedicated Samba file share and have the clients run the software from there. To help illustrate the use of the option, the following example configures a share named [cad] that allows only 10 connections at any given time:

```
[cad]
    comment = CAD software for Engineering Department
    path = /data/applications/cad
    read only = yes
    max connections = 10
```

Note that this example restricts only the number of connections to the share. It does not track how many users are currently running an application. A user who has the share open in a Windows Explorer window is consuming one of the connections, even without accessing any files contained in the share.

Table 5-18 concludes this chapter with an overview of the authorization parameters discussed in this section. In the next chapter, we examine many more configuration options and advanced capabilities of Samba's file serving functionality.

Table 5-18. File share authorization-related parameters

Parameter	Value	Description	Default	Scope
admin users	user/group list	List of users or members of a group who are mapped to the root user for all access to this share.	""	Share
invalid users	user/group list	List of users or members of a group who are denied access this share.	""	Share
max connections	integer	Defines the maximum number of concurrent connections to this share across all user sessions. A value of 0 indicates that access should not be restricted.	0	Share
read list	user/group list	List of users or members of a group who are restricted to read only access to this share.	""	Share
valid users	user/group list	List of users or members of a group who are granted access to this share, if permitted by the other authorization checks as well.	""	Share
write list	user/group list	List of users or members of a group who are granted write access to this share, if permitted by the other access checks on the share and filesystem permissions as well.	""	Share

CHAPTER 6
Advanced Disk Shares

So far, the configurations we've discussed have been rudimentary and useful primarily for testing an initial server installation. In this chapter, you will see exactly why so many network administrators have chosen Samba as their interoperable file serving solution. Adding features such as Virtual File System (VFS) plug-ins and support for Microsoft Distributed File Systems (MS-DFS) to Samba's already flexible and powerful file serving capabilities builds a solid foundation that is able to compete with and outperform many commercial CIFS implementations. By the end of this chapter, you will be well-versed in navigating tasks such as bridging the differences between Unix filesystems and Windows clients, configuring group shares, and managing ACLs on file and directories.

Special Share Names

In Chapter 4, we introduced three special section names: [global], [homes], and [printers]. These built-in section names have special meaning to Samba. There is a fourth special service that we have mentioned when listing shares using *smbclient*. This share, [IPC$], is provided by all CIFS servers, not just Samba, and is used for certain network operations such as listing file and printer shares. Other service names can have special meanings to clients. Consider this list of shares on a Windows Server 2003 host:

```
$ smbclient -L trinity -U Administrator%test
Domain=[COLOR] OS=[Windows Server 2003 3790 Service Pack 1] Server=[Windows Server
2003 5.2]

        Sharename      Type      Comment
        ---------      ----      -------
        print$         Disk      Printer Drivers
        C$             Disk      Default share
        IPC$           IPC       Remote IPC
        ADMIN$         Disk      Remote Admin
        public         Disk
        SYSVOL         Disk      Logon server share
        NETLOGON       Disk      Logon server share
```

Now examine the same server's list of shares displayed by a Windows XP client using the *net.exe* command:

```
C:\> net view \\trinity /user:COLOR\Administrator test
Shared resources at \\trinity

Share name   Type   Used as   Comment
-------------------------------------------------------------
NETLOGON     Disk             Logon server share
public       Disk
SYSVOL       Disk             Logon server share
The command completed successfully.
```

Notice that the XP client does not list the four shares whose names end in a $ character, a trait specific to Microsoft clients. There is nothing special about the file shares C$, PRINT$, or ADMIN$, other than the last character of their name. Windows recognizes any share whose name ends with a $ as a hidden share, because such shares are primarily used for remote administration within Microsoft networks. Because these names are filtered from the share listing by the client and not the server, any file share defined *smb.conf* as ending in a $ is hidden from users by the Windows Explorer interface. The following list shows the purpose of each standard hidden share:

C$

This share represents the full contents of the server's *C:* drive. There will be one such share for each hard disk mounted on the server using the traditional alphabetic naming scheme (*C:*, *D:*, etc.). Only administrators are able to connect to this share.

ADMIN$

This share exports the Windows OS directory, pointed to by the %SYSTEMROOT% environment variable. Only administrators are able to connect to this share.

PRINT$

This share provides access to the server's repository of print drivers needed to support point-and-print functionality. This share is covered in more detail in the next chapter, when we explore Samba's own printing support. All authenticated users are able to copy files from this share, but only administrator accounts may add or modify files.

These three shares point to overlapping portions of the same directory tree, as shown in Figure 6-1. For example, the root of the \\SERVER\PRINT$ share is the same directory as \\SERVER\ADMIN$\System32\spool\drivers.

Samba 3.0 includes a built-in [ADMIN$] share as a synonym for the the [IPC$] share. This share was originally implemented (including some other special cases in the Samba server code) for interoperability with the now defunct *Advanced Server for Unix* product. Until the 3.0.20 release, there was no way to disable this feature, which meant that you could not define your own [ADMIN$] file share short of modifying the Samba source code. However, it can be important to define an [ADMIN$]

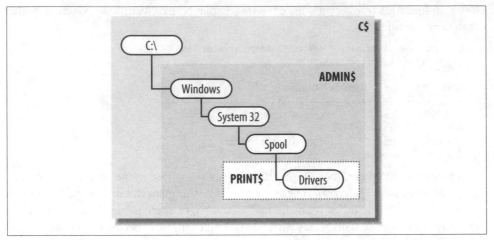

Figure 6-1. The directory hierarchy shared by the C$, ADMIN$, and PRINT$ file shares

share, because some Windows tools rely upon its existence (as well as the other standard administrative shares) and even make assumptions about the directory tree that are found at the [ADMIN$] share.

For this reason, newer Samba releases include the global enable asu support Boolean parameter, so you can disable the internal [ADMIN$] IPC share and define your own file share in *smb.conf*. In this section, we assume that you have version 3.0.20 or later, and show you how to create the standard administrative shares. In order to create all three of the file shares, we will mirror a portion of the Windows operating system directory hierarchy.

The following command creates the full path from */data* to the *drivers* subdirectory. If your *mkdir* command doesn't support the -p option to create the full path all at once, create each subdirectory one at a time.

```
$ mkdir -p /data/windows/system32/spool/drivers
```

Next, define each share in *smb.conf*, taking care to ensure that the directory paths mirror the common directory trees shown in Figure 6-1. Remember to disable the enable asu support option so that you can create an [ADMIN$] in the first place.

```
[global]
    enable asu support = no

[C$]
    path = /data
    read only = no
    valid users = +admins

[ADMIN$]
    path = /data/windows
    read only = no
    valid users = +admins
```

```
[PRINT$]
    path = /data/windows/system32/spool/drivers
    read only = yes
    write list = +admins
```

You have already seen that these administrative shares are hidden only by the Windows user interfaces such as *cmd.exe* and *explorer.exe*. However, *smbclient* happily enumerates all of a server's shares, regardless of the names. If you prefer to have *smbd* not advertise a share at all, disable the browseable parameter in the share's definition. Be aware that hiding a share has no effect on the security of the share. A user who knows the UNC path to the share can still attempt to connect to it.

A frequent trick is to mark the [homes] share as unbrowsable in order to prevent both a share named *homes* and one matching the currently connected user's login name from appearing in the list of available shares. Many administrators also restrict the set of valid users in [homes] to the %S variable. Remember from Chapter 4 that [homes] is copied in memory and renamed to match the user's login name, and that %S is expanded to the name of the current share. Therefore, %S expands in this case to the user's name, preventing users from connecting to home directories other than their own. Here's a short example:

```
[homes]
    comment = Home directory for %U
    read only = no
    browseable = no
    valid users = %S
```

If the name *zulu* is a valid user on the system, Samba internally allocates the following share when that user connects to her home directory:

```
[zulu]
    comment = Home directory for zulu
    read only = no
    browseable = yes
    valid users = zulu
```

Filesystem Differences

The list of differences between Windows filesystems such as FAT and NTFS and those hosted by Unix servers (too numerous themselves to mention) generally fall into the following five categories:

Valid filename characters
> Windows restricts such characters as colons (:) and trailing whitespace; Unix is happy to create files and directories with names such as *"Where I was: or at least thought."* The other major point of contention is the path separation character. Windows breaks directories paths into individual components using the backslash (\), and Unix employs the forward slash (/).

Filename length

Originally DOS and Windows clients only supported filenames that are at most eight characters in length plus a file extension of at most three characters. Today, long filenames are widely supported on Unix and Windows hosts. There are times, however, when a long filename may need to be mangled into a shorter one, as you will see when we discuss valid filename characters.

Case sensitivity

Windows preserves case in the names that users create for folders and files, but allows them to be requested in a case-insensitive manner. That is, you can refer to *My Documents* as *MY DOCUMENTS*. Unix filesystems are traditionally case-sensitive.

File locking and caching

In modern networks, the byte range-locking semantics expected by Windows clients are those provided by the Windows kernel. Thankfully, as an administrator, you don't have much to worry about here. Samba does the heavy lifting to ensure that Windows clients are kept happy. It may be necessary, however, to configure how Samba responds to caching requests by Windows clients.

Permissions and attributes

In Windows, support for permissions and attributes ranges from the FAT filesystem, which possesses no permissions, to NTFS and its elaborate ACLs. In contrast, nine simple bits (read/write/execute for user/group/other) are historically supported by Unix.

This is not a complete list of differences, but does cover about 90 percent of the issues. Examining a few common scenarios faced by administrators will help to illustrate how Samba is able to bridge this gap.

Name Mangling and Filename Lengths

Name mangling is the term given to the process of translating the name of a file (or directory) as it is stored on the server to a form acceptable by the client. There are many reasons why a filename acceptable to the server would be unacceptable to the client. Older SMB clients, such as DOS and some 16-bit applications running on Windows 9x/Me, can make use of only 8.3 filenames, also referred to as short filenames. The name "8.3" is derived from the maximum length of the filename (eight characters), which is followed by a period and up to a three-character extension (such as *NOTES.TXT*). The 8.3 filename convention is used for many applications, even though current operating system requirements are much more flexible. (This is why HTML files are often represented with *.htm* extensions, JPEG files with *.jpg* extensions, and executable files with *.exe* extensions). True 8.3 filenames are uppercase (*WINWORD.EXE*), as they would be appear on an MS-DOS system.

A simple way to view the mapping from long filenames to short ones is to use the Windows XP *cmd.exe* shell and the *dir* command. The default method for displaying files shows the long filename on the lefthand side of the output. To display the short filename as well, specify the /x argument. The following listing shows the contents of a Samba share named [public] mounted on the client at *P:*. Notice that filename *Samba Notes.html* has been mapped to the valid 8.3 filename *SM0EEH~V*.

```
P:\> dir /x
 Volume in drive P is public
 Volume Serial Number is 0200-0882

 Directory of P:\

05/23/2006  05:58 PM    <DIR>                     .
05/23/2006  05:57 PM    <DIR>                     ..
05/23/2006  05:57 PM           0 SM0EEH~V   Samba Notes.html
               1 File(s)            0 bytes
               2 Dir(s)   2,502,819,840 bytes free
```

The algorithm used to determine the derived 8.3 filename is controlled by Samba's mangling method global parameter. This parameter currently accepts either of two values: hash or hash2. The hash method was used in Samba 2.2, and hash2 is the default for Samba 3.0 servers. It is recommended that you do not alter the parameter from its default value unless you explicitly require backward compatibility with the Samba 2.2 installations. This would be the case if you had applications that relied upon the generated 8.3 names (a bad idea to begin with).

 Any filename containing an character that is invalid on Windows, such as *, \, or :, is automatically mangled, even if the client supports long filenames.

One question that often appears on Samba-related mailing lists is how to make the server generate short files names in the same manner as Windows, for example having *Program Files* appear as *PROGRA~1*. It is not possible to configure Samba to do this, because neither the hash nor hash2 method store the generated the short filename for long term use. Unlike FAT32 and NTFS, Unix filesystems do not care about 8.3 filenames and therefore do not allocate any room in the file's metadata record for remembering the shorter variation. Therefore, Samba has to regenerate short filenames every time the server starts up.

Table 6-1 gives a short overview of the mangling method parameter and its possible values.

Table 6-1. The mangling method parameter

Parameter	Value	Description	Default	Scope
mangling method	hash or hash2	Determines the internal hashing function used for generating an 8.3 filename in place of its long filename counterpart. It is recommended to leave this option set to its default value.	hash2	Global

Case Sensitivity and Preservation

Windows filesystems are case-preserving and case-insensitive. Native Unix filesystems are almost always case-preserving and case-sensitive. Case preservation is no problem. Samba simply creates the file or directory using the name specified by the client. But what should the server do if the client creates a file named *Foo.txt* and later tries to open *foo.txt*? Both names should map to the same file.

The way Samba solves this problem is very similar to how it attempts to solve the problems concerning login names and clear-text passwords presented by Windows 9x/Me clients (discussed in the previous chapter). When receiving a request containing a filename (open, remove, rename, etc.), *smbd* first attempts to locate the file using the name transmitted by the client. If this lookup fails, the daemon then continues to try various case permutations of the file name until a match is located or until all string variations fail. A successful lookup is stored in *smbd*'s internal cache. Sometimes it may be necessary to limit the size of this stat cache to prevent *smbd* from allocating large amounts of memory. On a busy server, small amounts of extra memory allocated by many Samba processes can add up quickly.

The max stat cache size accepts an integer value that restricts the amount of memory in kilobytes that the stat cache can consume in an *smbd* process. The default is to allow as much memory as needed. In most cases this behavior is acceptable, because clients activity tends to be pretty localized to a portion of the server's filesystem. Exceptions to this rule might occur when a client's virus software is scanning a large directory tree on the server for infected files. In a worst case scenario, the stat cache parameter can be disabled altogether, although at a high cost in performance. When in doubt, it is best to make use of the default stat cache-related settings (summarized in Table 6-2).

Table 6-2. Stat-cache-related parameters

Parameter	Value	Description	Default	Scope
max stat cache size	integer	Restricts the maximum amount of memory in kilobytes that will be allocated to stat cache in each *smbd* process.	0	Global
stat cache	boolean	If yes, *smbd* caches successful case-insensitive filename lookups.	yes	Global

By default, *smbd* honors the case-preserving semantics expected by Windows clients. However, at times, this functionality must be sacrificed; Samba should adopt a single convention for representing case in file and directory names to provide better service. Historically, Unix filesystems have suffered badly when serving thousands of files from a single directory. Combine this with multiple case-insensitive lookups in Samba and you have a recipe for unhappy users impatiently waiting for their spreadsheet to open.

Beginning with Samba 3.0.12, Samba developers introduced a mechanism by which a Unix filesystem could provide case insensitivity through *smbd*. The trick is to convert all file and directory names into a common case format and then instruct Samba to perform a case-sensitive lookup after converting the name requested by the client to the same default case used by the share. The only downside is that you lose case preservation when creating new files.

Let's look at an example that takes an existing share named [drawings] and converts it to use case-sensitive filename lookups. The initial share definition defines a path and allows write access to its contents:

```
[drawings]
    path = /data/drawings
    read only = no
```

First, the example converts all files and directories in the share to a default case, either upper- or lowercase. This example uses lowercase. Make sure to block out client connections to the share during the conversion, either by taking Samba offline or by setting available = no in the share definition.

The *NormalizePath* bash function listed in the following shell script accepts a path name as its single argument and renames the last component of the path to its lower case variant. The path *Foo/Bar* would be renamed to *Foo/bar*.

```
#!/bin/bash
## normalize.sh - Shell script to convert a directory
## tree beginning at the current working directory to
## lower case file and directory names

## Normalize the last component of a path to lower case
function NormalizePath {
    PARENT=`dirname $1`
    BASE=`basename $1`
    NEWBASE=`echo ${BASE} | tr [:upper:] [:lower:]`
    if [ "${BASE}" != "${NEWBASE}" ]; then
        echo ${PARENT}/${NEWBASE}
        (cd ${PARENT} && /bin/mv ${BASE} ${NEWBASE} )
    fi
}
```

Next, call *NormalizePath* for each file in the directory tree. The reverse sort (sort -r) ensures that work progresses from the bottom of the tree and towards the current directory, walking the directory tree in one pass. Processing the tree in the order returned by *find* or from the shortest paths first (a normal sort order) invalidates some paths, as parent directories are renamed before their subfolders and files have been processed.

```
## traverse the entire directory tree
for file in `find . -print | sort -r `; do
    NormalizePath $file
done
```

Invoking *normalize.sh* products output similar to the following:

```
$ ./normalize.sh
./xml/xmlhosed.xsl
./xml/xmlaffected.xsl
./xml/xmlaffecteduninstall.xsl
./xml/spssdk_info.xml
...remaining output deleted...
```

Now, reconfigure the [drawings] share to take advantage of the normalized directory tree. The preserve case and short preserve case parameters instruct *smbd* as to whether it should maintain the case of new file and directory names for long and short names, respectively. These per-share Boolean options default to the case-preserving semantics to which Windows clients are accustomed. Disable them both and define the share's default case to match the directory tree. Finally, configure Samba to perform a case-sensitive lookup on the normalized name. If the file or directory exists, the name must match. There is no need to retry different case combinations, and therefore the performance appears to increase from the end user's perspective. The modified [drawings] share appears as follows:

```
[drawings]
    path = /data/drawings
    read only = no

    ## Speed up filename lookups after normalizing the
    ## share contents
    case-sensitive = yes
    default case = lower
    preserve case = no
    short preserve case = no
```

Table 6-3 lists the case-related *smb.conf* parameters covered in this section. Each can be used by itself in a share, but we recommend not enabling case sensitivity without first normalizing the share's contents.

Table 6-3. Case sensitivity and preservation parameters

Parameter	Value	Description	Default	Scope
case-sensitive	boolean	Should Samba assume that the client sent the file or directory name in the correct case?	no	Share
default case	upper or lower	The alphabetic case used when not preserving the file's original name.	lower	Share
preserve case	boolean	Should Samba create the long filename as transmitted by the client?	yes	Share
short preserve case	boolean	Should Samba maintain the original format of an 8.3 filename?	yes	Share

Symbolic Links

Symbolic links (symlinks) on the servers appear as normal files or directories by Windows clients. But as the administrator, you should ask:

- Should the Samba server support following symbolic links at all?
- Should Samba follow links outside of the share?

By default, Samba follows all symlinks, as long as the user has appropriate permission to the link target. However, under some circumstances, you may wish to restrict this behavior. If users are able to access shares only from Windows clients, the entire discussion is moot, because Windows cannot create symlinks on remote CIFS shares.[*]

However, users with shell accounts on the Samba server can present a problem. The most common case is when home directories are accessible both by NFS and by Samba. A user could log on to a Unix workstation that mounts his home directory via NFS and create a symbolic link to */etc/passwd*. When accessing that symbolic link from a Windows client, Samba returns the link target, which is */etc/passwd* on the server. Whether this is a security hole is debatable. At the very least, it can be surprising.

To remedy this unintended access, disable wide links. This step causes Samba to refuse to follow links outside the share.

```
[homes]
    comment = home directory for %U
    read only = no
    wide links = no
```

Or if you prefer, disable support for symbolic links altogether by setting follow symlinks = no. Note that there will be a small negative impact on performance when you disable symlinks, as *smbd* must then perform extra checks on every attempt to open a file on a client's behalf. Table 6-4 lists the link-related options supported by Samba.

Table 6-4. Symbolic link options

Parameter	Value	Description	Default	Scope
follow symlinks	boolean	Should Samba follow any symbolic links?	yes	Share
wide links	boolean	Should Samba follow a symbolic link if it leads outside of the root of the current share?	yes	Share

---

[*] The Linux CIFS FS client and the Unix Extensions to the CIFS protocol covered in Chapter 11 do support the creation of symlinks on remote servers.

Hiding Files

Sharing disks between Unix and Windows frequently exposes files that are needed on only one operating system or the other. A prime example is the shell initialization files that exist in a user's Unix home directory (frequently referred to by Windows users as "those pesky dot files"). Preceding a filename with a period is the standard mechanism on Unix for hiding the file from normal directory listing tools. Windows uses the hidden DOS attribute bit (described in more detail later in the section "DOS Attributes) for the same purpose. By default, Samba sets the hidden bit for all dot files when returning the files DOS attributes to a client, but this behavior can be disabled by setting `hide dot files = no`.

The `hide files` option provides additional flexibility to allow you to specify a set of patterns that, if matched, cause a file or directory to be marked as hidden. The filename patterns use the Windows globbing syntax, which is a simple subset of Unix shell metacharacters: a * character matches one more more characters, and a ? character consumes a single character. Multiple patterns can be concatenated using the forward slash (/) character as the delimiter. The following example hides *.ini files and *.log files:

```
[homes]
    read only = no
    hide files = /*.ini/*.log/
```

There are other Boolean parameters for hiding certain types of files. For the following options, it's important to understand that *hiding* does not mean merely setting the Windows filesystem's hidden attribute on a file, but goes much further. It means Samba does not list the file or directory at all.[*] Files matched by the following options are not accessible to a user on a client system, even if she specifies the file by name on the command line or sets her folder to display hidden files. It is as though the file did not exist.

`hide unreadable` *and* `hide unwriteable`
    Excludes files that can not be read or written by the user, respectively.

`hide special files`
    Prevent a user from seeing any objects except regular files, directories, and symbolic links. Thus, it excludes named pipes and other unusual objects in Unix filesystems.

`veto files`
    This option allows the same flexible syntax option as the `hide files` parameter, with the more restrictive sort of hiding.

---

[*] This ambiguity of parameter names is a personal gripe of these authors and one that will hopefully improve in future releases.

Under some circumstances, dropping files into a virtual black hole can be useful. One Samba administrator devised the following pattern to prevent the Nimba worm from using Samba hosts to propagate itself. Placing this in the [global] section insured that the veto files setting was inherited by all file shares, and that no user could download files matching the forbidden names.

```
[global]
    veto files = /*.eml/*.nws/riched20.dll/
```

Vetoing files can lead to a problem. Directories can be removed only after all files they contain have been deleted. If a user drops a file that matches the veto files patterns into a Samba folder, he will never be able to access that file again through Samba. You can understand the confusion when a user tries to remove a directory and it fails because the folder claims to not be empty, and yet no files can be seen. To work around this issue, Samba provides the delete veto files Boolean parameter, which instructs Samba to remove all vetoed files contained by a directory that a user is deleting (assuming there are no visible files there).

Table 6-5 finishes up this section with a short summary of the parameters covered in relation to hiding and excluding files from clients.

Table 6-5. Options for hiding and excluding files

Parameter	Value	Description	Default	Scope
delete veto files	boolean	Can Samba remove vetoed files when removing a directory, if there are no nonvetoed files remaining?	no	Share
hide dot files	boolean	When enabled, Samba sets the hidden attribute on files that begin with a period.	yes	Share
hide files	filename pattern	Specifies a set of filename patterns defining files that should have the DOS hidden attribute enabled.	None	Share
hide special files	boolean	Should Samba exclude from directory listings files such as sockets, named pipes, and device files?	no	Share
hide unreadable files	boolean	Should Samba exclude from directory listings files that cannot be read by the user?	no	Share
hide unwriteable files	boolean	Should Samba exclude from directory listings files that cannot be modified by the user?	no	Share
veto files	filename pattern	Specifies a set of filename patterns defining files that should be excluded from directory listings.	None	Share

Locks and Leases

File and byte range locking is one of those topics that is often better left alone. Generally, the only people that understand how things are supposed to work are the developers themselves. For this reason, it is recommended that you do not modify the majority of locking-related parameter values in *smb.conf*. Samba programmers work extremely hard to ensure that *smbd*'s locking implementation provides exactly what CIFS clients require. In fact, think of the majority of *smb.conf* parameters like values in the Windows registry, with the standard disclaimer: Tweaking too many things could render your Samba server inefficient or even cause it to fail.

With that in mind, there is one parameter that may be of use if you are exporting read-only filesystems, such as CD-ROMs. In this case, there is a possibility of gaining some performance benefit by faking byte range lock support. Disabling the locking parameter allows Samba to grants locks without worrying about keeping track of who has what. Because the share is marked as read-only, all clients can freely believe that they have locked whatever region of the file they desired without fear that someone else will change it out from underneath them. Before you disable the locking option, make sure that no clients can modify the contents of the share via another protocol (e.g., NFS) or the local filesystem.

Samba's byte range-locking options are designed to work well using the default settings. Sometimes, you need to tweak the oplock settings on a share. Oplock is short for *opportunistic locking*. The name is unfortunate, because this feature has little to do with file locking. Oplocks are an aggressive caching mechanism used by Windows clients to boost performance when accessing remote files. When an oplock is granted, the client is able to cache the entire file locally. If the oplock type allows the client to modify the file locally, these changes are flushed back to the server when the file is closed or the client receives a request from the server to break the oplock.

The major hurdle with oplocks is that on most platforms running Samba, the feature is implemented only internally, by *smbd*. A few operating system kernels, such as IRIX and Linux 2.4 and later, support file leases, which are the Unix equivalent of oplocks. By using the kernel to coordinate with other Unix process on these systems, Samba is able process oplock break messages when a file is accessed via another means such as NFS. Otherwise, the non-Samba process may not have a consistent view of the data as it is seen by Windows clients. If users are accessing files concurrently via Samba and another file-sharing protocol, it is probably best to disable oplocks to avoid the risk of corrupting file contents.

The Samba build procedure automatically determines at compile time whether the host operating system supports file leases. If it does, *smbd* is built with support for kernel oplocks, a feature that can be controlled at runtime using the kernel oplocks global parameter. Both the compile-time support and the runtime configuration file parameter are necessary for the kernel oplock feature.

There are three types of oplocks:

Exclusive
> Allows the client to have sole access to the file and to perform local modifications that are flushed back to the server when the oplock is revoked or the client closes the file.

Batch
> Identical to exclusive oplocks, but allows an application to open and close a file repeatedly without relinquishing the lease. Batch file processing tends to follow this multiple open-and-close pattern; hence the name.

Level 2
> Allows a client to perform read caching on a file, which is particularly useful for executables run from a network file share. Only Windows NT-based clients support level 2 oplocks.

Certain application files have historically had problems with oplocks. PC database files, such as FoxPro and Microsoft Access, are among the most fragile. With such files, it is better to disable oplocks on the share or to exclude the relevant set of files from being granted an oplock. The veto oplock files parameter accepts a list of file-name patterns using the same syntax as the hide files and veto files parameters covered in the previous section. The following example shows two file shares: [nooplocks] disables oplocks for all files in a share, and [access-db] oplock support only for MS Access (*.mdb*) files:

```
[nooplocks]
    path = /data/share1
    read only = yes
    oplocks = no

[access-db]
    path = /data/share2
    read only = no
    veto oplock files = /*.mdb/
```

The oplocks option applies to both exclusive and batch oplocks and is a prerequisite to enabling level 2 oplocks. Very rarely does a case warrant disabling level 2 oplocks while leaving exclusive and batch oplocks enabled.

Similar to the locking parameter for byte range locks, Samba also provides fake oplocks. As mentioned earlier for the locking parameter, consider using fake oplocks only for read-only directory trees. When enabled, all requests for any oplock type will succeed and performance may increase.

Table 6-6 concludes this section by listing the byte range locking and oplock related parameters.

Table 6-6. Locking and leasing options

Parameter	Value	Description	Default	Scope
fake oplocks	boolean	If enabled, Samba honors all oplock requests. This option should be considered only for a read-only filesystem.	no	Share
kernel oplocks	boolean	If enabled, and if the operating system's kernel provides support for file leases, Samba coordinates all oplock requests via the kernel lease mechanism.	yes	Share
level 2 oplocks	boolean	Should Samba honor requests for level 2 oplocks if possible?	yes	Share
locking	boolean	If disabled, Samba honors all byte range lock requests without enforcement. This option should be considered only for a read-only filesystem.	yes	Share
oplocks	boolean	Should Samba honor requests for exclusive and batch oplocks if possible?	yes	Share
veto oplock files	filename pattern	Defines a list of filename patterns that should be prevented from being granted exclusive or batch oplocks.	None	Share

DOS Attributes

All Microsoft clients make use of four DOS attributes: archive, hidden, system, and read-only. Newer releases of Windows support additional attributes, such as whether the file is compressed. Currently, Samba provides only support for the original four attributes, so we'll start with a simple explanation of what each one means:

Archive
> Automatically set by the Windows filesystem when a file is modified. This attribute is useful primarily to back up applications, which rely upon it to determine which files have changed since the last run. Unfortunately, Unix filesystems do not set this on Samba's behalf, and Samba does not update it on its own.

Hidden
> Hides files or directories from application interfaces such as the Windows Explorer. A user may choose to view these objects by enabling the appropriate folder settings in Windows.

System
> Indicate items used for operating system purposes, such as a memory swap files.

ReadOnly
> Similar to the immutable bit supported by Unix. The read-only setting is separate from any ACL that may deny read access to a specific user.

DOS attributes still have an impact on servers today. For example, a Windows XP client refuses to load a registry hive from a file marked as ReadOnly. This includes user profiles (*ntuser.dat*) and NT4 system policies (*ntconfig.pol*). Samba provides two mutually exclusive mechanisms for storing DOS attributes, one based on file permissions and the other utilizing the filesystem's *extended attributes* (EAs).

DOS attributes and Unix permissions bits

Because Unix provided only the standard nine bits of read/write/execute permission, Samba originally kept track of the attributes by mapping each one onto a bit in the Unix permission set as follows:

ReadOnly
> The inverse of the owner write bit

Archive
> The user execute bit

System
> The group execute bit

Hidden
> The world execute bit

The main limitation with this approach is that due to the semantics of the execute bits regarding directories, developers decided to apply the mapping only to files. There is no way to represent DOS attributes on folders using this permission mapping method, which is a major deficiency.

The attribute/permission mapping model is controlled by three Boolean parameters and one semiboolean option that can be enabled or disabled on each share: map archive, map hidden, map readonly, and map system. The archive, hidden, and system mapping options accept a yes or no value, which specifies whether *smbd* should examine the execute bits when calculating the attribute set for a file.

The map readonly parameter accepts yes, no, or permissions. The permissions value indicates that *smbd* should analyze the file ACL to determine whether the connected user has write permission and therefore whether to report the ReadOnly attribute. This behavior is different from specifying the option's value as yes, which examines only the owner's write bit to determine the ReadOnly attribute for all users. The map readonly parameter was added in Samba 3.0.21. Prior releases always examined the owner write bit when calculating the ReadOnly property. ACLs are covered in the next section.

 The ReadOnly DOS attribute is independent of the read only share parameter.

Let's look at particular file share and permission set to see how the DOS attributes are displayed. Start with a definition of [data] from *smb.conf*:

```
[data]
    path = /data
    read only = no
    map readonly = yes
    map archive = yes
    map hidden = yes
    map system = yes
```

Now imagine a file named *notes.txt* with the following Unix permissions:

```
-rwxr--r-x 1 lizard users 0 2006-05-24 13:47 notes.txt
```

View its DOS attributes using *smbclient*:

```
$ smbclient //rain/data -U lizard%test -c 'dir notes.txt'
Domain=[GARDEN] OS=[Unix] Server=[Samba 3.0.22]
  notes.txt       AH       0  Wed May 24 13:47:08 2006

      56578 blocks of size 65536. 38189 blocks available
```

The Archive (A) and Hidden (H) attributes are displayed due to the owner execute and world execute permissions. Removing the owner write bit (*chmod u-w notes.txt*) displays the ReadOnly (R) bit as well:

```
$ smbclient //rain/data -U lizard -c 'dir notes.txt'
Domain=[GARDEN] OS=[Unix] Server=[Samba 3.0.22]
  notes.txt       AHR      0  Wed May 24 13:47:08 2006

      56578 blocks of size 65536. 38189 blocks available
```

DOS attributes and Unix extended attributes

Samba 3.0.3 introduced a means of storing DOS attributes separately from the Unix permissions, if the Unix filesystem supports extended attributes. Currently, Samba's support for filesystem EAs is limited primarily to Linux and IRIX, but efforts are underway to support other platforms, such as FreeBSD. There are a few ways to determine whether your Linux filesystem includes support for EAs. The simplest is to check whether the filesystem was mounted with the user_xattr option:

```
$ mount
/dev/hda2 on / type ext3 (rw,acl,user_xattr)
...
```

More details about configuring Linux and the Linux kernel can be found in *Linux Kernel in a Nutshell*, by Greg Kroah-Hartman (O'Reilly).

It is also necessary to verify that Samba detected support for a sufficient EA interface at compile time, which can be done by searching for the string XATTR in the output from *smbd -b*. The following output illustrates an *smbd* daemon with support for EAs:

```
$ smbd -b | grep XATTR
    HAVE_SYS_XATTR_H
    HAVE_ATTR_XATTR_H
    HAVE_FGETXATTR
    HAVE_FLISTXATTR
    HAVE_FREMOVEXATTR
    HAVE_FSETXATTR
    HAVE_GETXATTR
    HAVE_LGETXATTR
    HAVE_LISTXATTR
    HAVE_LLISTXATTR
    HAVE_LREMOVEXATTR
    HAVE_LSETXATTR
    HAVE_REMOVEXATTR
    HAVE_SETXATTR
```

If you find that Samba did not detect the appropriate EA support libraries at compile time, make sure that the ACL and EA development packages (normally named *libacl-devel* and *libattr-devel*) are installed correctly. If they are not, it is necessary to fix the problem and recompile Samba. Unlike Samba's ACL support, which must be manually enabled using the --with-acl-support option, the *configure* script detects EA support automatically. There is no need to pass additional options in most cases.

Once support for extended attributes has been verified, you can make use of the store dos attributes share parameter to store attribute sets for both files and directories. To illustrate how this parameter works, let's begin with a share named [documents]:

```
[documents]
    path = /data/documents
    read only = no
    store dos attributes = yes
```

Next create a directory named *logs* (assume that the share's UNC path is *RAIN*\ *documents*) from the *cmd.exe* shell on a Windows XP client:

```
C:\> mkdir \\RAIN\documents\logs
C:\> attrib +h \\RAIN\documents\logs
```

You can then verify that the hidden attribute is set using the directory's properties dialog box from the Windows Explorer (shown in Figure 6-2). Make sure that you also enable viewing of hidden files through the Tools → Options... menu in the Explorer windows.

When enabled, the store dos attributes option takes precedence over the attribute mapping parameters shown earlier. However, the DOS attribute policy can be set on a per-share basis, in case you are exporting multiple filesystem types with and without EA support.

Table 6-7 includes a list of the options related to DOS attributes.

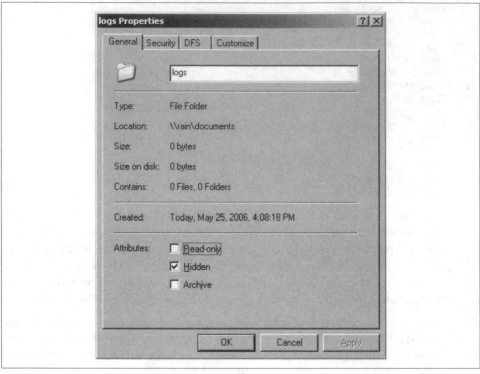

Figure 6-2. Viewing the hidden attribute on a directory

Table 6-7. DOS attribute options

Parameter	Value	Description	Default	Scope
delete readonly	boolean	Should Samba allow a user to delete a file marked as ReadOnly if allowed by the filesystem's permission?	no	Share
map archive	boolean	Maps the DOS Archive bit to the Unix owner execute permission.	yes	Share
map hidden	boolean	Maps the DOS Archive bit to the Unix world execute permission.	no	Share
map readonly	yes, no, or permissions	Maps the DOS Archive bit to the inverse of the Unix owner write permission or to evaluation of the file's ACL.	yes	Share
map system	boolean	Maps the DOS Archive bit to the Unix group execute permission.	no	Share
store dos attributes	boolean	If enabled, Samba stores the DOS attributes in the file or directory's extended attributes. This option is mutually exclusive with and takes precedence over the attribute mapping options.	no	Share

Permissions

There are two large-scale issues surrounding Unix permissions and Samba. The first, covered in this section, explores how Samba and its configuration file can take advantage of the Unix permission model. For example, how can Samba configure a group-accessible share or determine the initial permissions assigned to newly created files and directories? The second issue, covered in the upcoming section "Access Control Lists," concerns how Unix permissions and ACLs can be displayed in a format familiar to Windows users.

Let's begin with a common requirement: define a file share that can be used by members of a group in common for distributing files. In this example, users must be members of the Unix group named *staff*. Any new file or directory created within the share must be available to members of this group, so we need to ensure that new files and directories get created with the appropriate permissions.

Let's start with a basic share named [staff-docs]. We'll define a path and mark the folder writable:

```
[staff-docs]
    path = /data/staff-docs
    read only = no
```

Next we'll restrict access to the share to the *staff* group. The best security model involves multiple layers that reinforce the same policy. For example, if we choose to restrict access using the valid users option presented in the previous chapter, we should also make sure that the policy is effective if someone accesses the */data/staff-docs* directory through a means other than Samba. This means that the filesystem permissions should be set to allow group access for staff but deny access for others outside of that group. The following series of commands (executed as *root*) grant ownership of the directory to *root* and allow access only to the group *staff*. Setting the setgid bit ensures that all files and subdirectories created in the share have the correct group ownership.

```
$ chown root /data/staff-docs
$ chgrp staff /data/staff-docs
$ chmod g+rwxs,o-rwx /data/staff-docs
```

The permissions should now appear as:

```
$ ls -ld staff-docs
drwxrws--- 2 root staff 4096 2006-05-24 16:38 /data/staff-docs/
```

Now we can update the [staff-docs] share definition to restrict access via Samba as well:

```
[staff-docs]
    path = /data/staff-docs
    read only = no
    valid users = +staff
```

Adding the valid users option is not entirely necessary, because access to the share is ultimately determined by the filesystem permissions, but it does two things:

- It documents the intent of the share, in case there is ever any question as to what the permissions should be.
- It protects the share somewhat if the file permissions on */data/staff-docs* are accidentally changed to something less restrictive.

The next requirement to address is that all files and directories created within the share must be modifiable by members of the Unix *staff* group. When you create a file or directory from a Unix shell, the umask setting frequently determines the default permission set. Samba ignores the environment umask setting and instead provides its own equivalent parameters. The create mask and create directory mask options consist of octal permission sets for files and folders, respectively, that combine with the permissions requested by the user using a logical AND. Any bit not set in the mask will be removed from the final permission set. The force create mode and force directory mode options also specify octal permission sets, but are combined with the permission set using a logical OR (after applying any creation masks). Therefore, any permission bit that is set in the force mode is included in the final permissions.

The complete list of permission filters used to derive the final set is given here in the order used by Samba:

1. Apply any DOS attribute mapping options.
2. Apply the create mask settings.
3. Apply the force create mode settings.

The implication here is that the map hidden option, which acts through the world execute bit (see the earlier section "DOS Attributes"), does not work for new files if the create mask does not include this bit in its permission set.

For the sake of simplicity, assume use of the store dos attribute parameter in order to avoid any confusion with the user or group permissions. All permissions must be removed from the world set, the read and write bits must be set for files, and the read, write, and execute bits must be set for directories. The modified share definition appears as:

```
[staff-docs]
    path = /data/staff-docs
    read only = no
    valid users = +staff
    store dos attributes = yes

    # permissions masks and modes
    create mask = 0770
    force create mode = 0060
    create directory mask = 0770
    force directory mode = 0070
```

Notice that we are not concerned with the owner permissions. This example lets the user do anything with their own files. All we care about is ensuring group access. This is a clean-cut example where all relevant users belong to the same group. How can this share be extended to include users that do not share a common group?

When a user connects to a share on a Samba host, the uid, primary gid, and list of supplementary gids comprises the user's *token*. This token is then examined by Samba or the operating system kernel to determine whether the user is authorized to access a resource such as a share or file. You can instruct *smbd* to add an additional group to the user's existing list of memberships. Thus, the force user and force group options may be used to set the uid or primary gid for a user's token when working within the content of a specific share.

 Some operating systems limit the total number of groups to which a user may belong to 16 or 32. Check your operating system's documentation to determine the exact limit.

Thus, in order to allow members of the Unix *helpdesk* group to the [staff-docs] share, we must add that group to the valid users setting and then force a change to the primary group for every connected user to *staff*:

```
[staff-docs]
    path = /data/staff-docs
    read only = no
    valid users = +staff +helpdesk
    store dos attributes = yes
    force group = staff

    # permissions masks and modes
    create mask = 0770
    force create mode = 0060
    create directory mask = 0770
    force directory mode = 0070
```

Now members of both *staff* and *helpdesk* can successfully share files with each other.

This group share has one major drawback. Because the force group, create mask, and force create mode parameters define behavior for all files and within a share, we have to create a new share for every individual group. This can easily become an administrative nightmare, not to mention confusing for users who have to remember which share belongs to which group and at which drive letter the share is mounted. What is needed is a way to delegate access rights to portions of the share's directory tree.

The inherit owner and inherit permissions parameters provide the flexibility to propagate properties based on the parent of the new file or subdirectory. Using this new permission option, we can create a single file share that includes a subdirectory immediately below it for every group required. Let's look at an example using three groups: *staff*, *helpdesk*, and *devel*.

First, create the top-level directory of the share and one subdirectory for each of the three groups:

```
$ mkdir /data/groups
$ cd /data/groups
$ mkdir staff helpdesk devel
```

Next, restrict access (drwxrws---) in each of the three subfolders to the associated Unix group:

```
$ chgrp staff staff
$ chgrp helpdesk helpdesk
$ chgrp devel devel
$ chmod 2770 staff helpdesk devel
```

The final permissions appear as follows:

```
$ ls -l
total 12
drwxrws---  2 root devel    4096 2006-05-24 21:26 devel/
drwxrws---  2 root helpdesk 4096 2006-05-24 21:26 helpdesk/
drwxrws---  2 root staff    4096 2006-05-24 21:26 staff/
```

Finally, define the [groups] share in *smb.conf* like so:

```
[groups]
    path = /data/groups
    read only = no
    store dos attributes = yes
    inherit permissions = yes
```

The result is a single share that a user may mount at *G:* to access all folders for groups to which he belongs. This configuration is easier for both users and administrators.

However, very few things in life are free. If this new share solved all possible needs, it is unlikely that the force group and mask and mode family of options would still exist. In fact, the new [groups] share does not allow the sharing of files between users that have no groups in common. So you will be forced to choose between the two configurations shown in this section, should such conflicting requirements arise. One possible workaround is to make use of the [groups] share but also create [staff] using the */data/groups/staff* directory in combination with the force group parameter:

```
[staff-docs]
    path = /data/groups/staff
    read only = no
    valid users = +staff +helpdesk
    force group = staff
    store dos attributes = yes
    inherit permissions = yes
```

Table 6-8 lists short descriptions of the inheritance parameters covered here, as well as the mask and mode parameters discussed earlier in the section.

Table 6-8. File permissions and inherit options

Parameter	Value	Description	Default	Scope
create mask	octal permission set	Bits permitted in permissions when files are created in this share.	0744	Share
create directory mask	octal permission set	Bits permitted in permissions when directories are created in this share.	0755	Share
force create mode	octal permission set	Bits always set when a file is created in this share.	0000	Share
force directory mode	octal permission set	Bits always set when a directory is created in this share.	0000	Share
force group	Unix group	Primary group for a user connecting to the share.	None	Share
force user	Unix username	Primary user account for a user connecting to the share.	None	Share
inherit owner	boolean	Instructs Samba to set the owner of new files and directories based on the ownership of the immediate parent.	no	Share
inherit permissions	boolean	Instructs Samba to set the permissions of new files and directories based on the ownership of the immediate parent. Files do not inherit execute bits and the setuid bit is never inherited by files or directories.	no	Share

Access Control Lists

Windows filesystems' ACLs, sometimes referred to generically as *security descriptors*, support a wide variety of permissions masks. The Windows access masks are in fact much richer than the standard read/write/execute permissions provide by Unix systems. Therefore, Samba 3.0 supports a lossy mapping between Unix filesystem permissions and Windows ACLs. For example, when a Windows file specifying that the user *rose* has Full Control is copied to a Samba server, the Full Control access mask is mapped onto the permissions set rwx. All of the other bits in the Windows access mask, representing things such as delete and take ownership permissions, are simply thrown away. To ensure this behavior is symmetric, when translating an ACL in the reverse direction, from Unix to Windows, the rwx permissions on the Unix host are reported as Full Control to the Windows client.

 You can prevent *smbd* from reporting rwx as Full Control by disabling the map acl full control Boolean parameter in the share's definition.

The belief among Samba developers is that by supporting Read, Write, and Full Control permissions, the majority of Samba and Windows users are satisfied. The remainder of this section is dedicated to how Windows access masks are converted to Unix permission sets and vice versa, which applies whether the Samba host supports ACLs or only the standard Unix permission model. Let's begin our discussion with ACLs.

Samba supports various Unix filesystem ACL implementations. To enable Samba's compile checks for ACL support, pass the --with-acl-support option to the *configure* script. Currently Samba can support only one ACL implementation at a time. For example, if filesystem type A had one ACL interface and filesystem type B utilized a different one, Samba could interact with the ACLs on only one of those filesystems at a time. So far, this limitation has not been an issue, because most filesystems on a given operating system support a common API.

 More information about a server's ACL implementation can often be found by running man acl.

You can determine whether your Samba installation has been built to include ACL support by examining the output from *smbd -b*. A Linux host should report HAVE_POSIX_ACLS, and another operating system such as Solaris should define HAVE_SOLARIS_ACLS. The following example shows that the Samba installation on our Linux server does in fact include ACL support:

```
$ smbd -b | grep HAVE.*ACL
HAVE_POSIX_ACLS
```

If this check fails, make sure that the ACL libraries and development files are installed. On Linux hosts, these can generally be found in a package named *libacl-devel*. You should also verify that the server's filesystem included the acl option when it was mounted:

```
$ mount
/dev/hda2 on / type ext3 (rw,acl,user_xattr)
...
```

If you experience any problems with the filesystem, please refer to your operating system's documentation for possible remedies.

Before we discuss the configuration of support for Windows ACLs in *smb.conf*, we will briefly explain the POSIX ACL model. Figure 6-3 illustrates how Samba uses a POSIX ACL as the intermediate form between the Windows security descriptor and the real filesystem ACL representation.

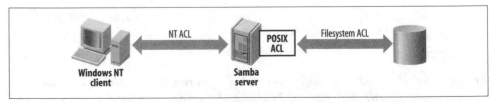

Figure 6-3. Mapping from Windows security descriptors to Unix filesystem ACLs

What's in a POSIX ACL?

The POSIX ACL standard was never finished. However, many operating systems, including Linux 2.6, implement the 1003.1e draft of the specification. A POSIX access control list is basically a Unix permission set plus four things:

- Additional named users
- Additional named groups
- A group mask
- Default ACLs for directories

Named users and groups are simply additional user and group permission sets. A POSIX ACL still has the concept of an owner (user::) and a group owner (group::). A named user or group is specified by a single character (a u for a user or a g for a group) followed by a colon and the account name, followed by another colon and the permission set. The following directory (*logs*) as shown below has an owner names *lizard*, a group owner of *webdev,* and a named user of *rose*:

```
$ getfacl logs
# file: logs
# owner: lizard
# group: webdev
user::rwx
group::rwx
mask::rwx
u:rose:r--
other::r-x
```

When evaluating the permissions granted to a particular user, the process is as follows:

1. Search for a user: entry matching the account name. This step includes comparing against the owner of the object. If a match is found, use the associated permissions set.

2. Create a permissions set by combining the access masks from all the listed groups to which the user belongs and perform a logical AND with the ACL group mask. Continue to the next check only if the user did not belong to any of the listed groups.

3. Use the world permission set.

The final addition by POSIX ACLs are the default access control entries (ACE) that may be associated with directories. These default ACLs apply to any newly created files or folders contained by the directory. This feature is similar to Samba's inherit permissions parameter. A default ACE follows the same rules as normal access entries. It may have user and group owner entries, named users and groups, a mask, and world permissions. Here is a short example of what the remainder of the *logs* directory ACL looks like:

```
default:user::rwx
default:group::rwx
```

```
default:u:rose:r-x
default:mask::rwx
default:other::r-x
```

We discuss default access control entries in more detail when we examine POSIX ACLs from the Windows Explorer security tab.

The nt acl support Parameter

Now that we have verified Samba compile support for Unix ACLs and have a solid understanding of POSIX ACLs, it is time to create an ACL-aware share in *smb.conf*. When creating a file share supporting either ACLs or the simpler Unix permission bit model, the nt acl support parameter must be enabled. Here is a share named [public] that we will use for discussion:

```
[public]
    path = /data/public
    read only = no
    nt acl support = yes
```

Windows 2000 and later Microsoft operating systems support a semidynamic model of ACL inheritance. The filesystem maintains a history of where an ACL assigned to a file or folder came from. For example, was it manually set for just this object? Or has it been inherited from its parent? The reason we refer to this as "semidynamic" is that when changing an ACE on a parent folder, the client host walks the directory tree and applies the new changes to any files or subdirectories that have inherited the setting. Samba is able to support this same semidynamic model by storing ACL inheritance information in an object's extended attributes. Refer to the previous section on DOS attributes if you need to verify support for extended attributes on your server.

In order to enable Windows ACL inheritance, you must add the map acl inherit Boolean parameter to [public]:

```
[public]
    path = /data/public
    read only = no
    store dos attributes = yes
    nt acl support = yes
    map acl inherit = yes
```

Finally, to ensure that the default ACLs on directories are propagated correctly, add the inherit acls Boolean option:

```
inherit acls = yes
```

 It is still possible to use inherit permissions in combination with ACLs, but the option will be honored only if the parent directory has no default access entries.

Before we continue on to a discussion of how these permission sets and access lists are viewed by users, Table 6-9 summarizes the ACL parameters we have covered so far.

Table 6-9. ACL options

Parameter	Value	Description	Default	Scope
acl map full control	boolean	Should Samba report the Unix permission set rwx as Full Control to Windows clients?	yes	Share
inherit acls	boolean	If enabled, ensures that default ACLs on directories are propagated to new files and folders. The default behavior is to use the mode requested by the client.	no	Share
nt acl support	boolean	Determines whether *smbd* reports support for ACLs when queried for information about the share.	yes	Share
map acl inherit	boolean	Should Samba remember an ACL's inherited properties and whether the ACL should be propagated to subfolders and files?	no	Share

Understanding the Explorer Security Tab

Understanding how the security tab displayed on a Windows client relates to the underlying filesystem permissions is the final key to making effective use of Samba's ACL support. If the file *memo.doc* has the Unix permission shown here, Figure 6-4 displays how a Windows user would view the same access rights.

```
$ ls -l memo.doc
-rw-r---- 1 lizard staff 32455 2006-05-25 09:40 memo.doc
```

Adding named users and groups to the file access list does not change the permissions display model. The end user sees more account entries, but the mapping between a Unix permissions set and Windows access mask works the same.

The display model becomes slightly more complicated once we introduce folders. Consider the ACL for the *archives* directory given here:

```
$ getfacl archives
# file: archives
# owner: lizard
# group: staff
user::rwx
group::rwx
group:helpdesk:r-x
mask::rwx
other::r-x
default:user::rwx
default:user:lizard:rwx
default:group::---
default:group:staff:rwx
default:group:helpdesk:r-x
default:mask::rwx
default:other::---
```

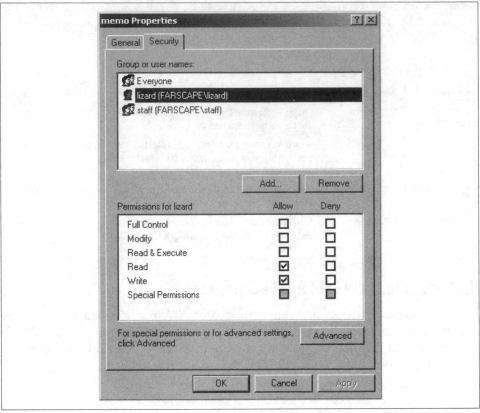

Figure 6-4. Displaying Unix permission for memo.doc using the Security dialog box

The basic permissions in this ACL are displayed by Windows as shown in Figure 6-5, and the advanced options are displayed as shown in Figure 6-6.

Several complexities involved in viewing ACLs from Windows can render them confusing. A permission is displayed in the general security tab (Figure 6-5) only if the permission applies to "This folder, subfolder, and files" (Figure 6-6). Samba interprets the access entries (e.g., group:helpdesk:r-x) to apply to "This folder." The default access entries (e.g., default:group:helpdesk:r-x) apply to "Subfolders and files." Therefore, to display the permissions in the initial security dialog box, a user or group must have both an access entry and a default entry. Users and groups do not have to have default access entries in order to function properly, but it is important to understand why an account's permissions may not be displayed on the initial security tab view. The complete security permissions are always available by navigating to the Permissions tab of the Advanced Security dialog box shown in Figure 6-6.

Next is the question of the CREATOR OWNER and CREATOR GROUP entries. Samba maps these Windows accounts to the default owner and group ACEs. In order for the owner's permissions to apply to "This folder, subfolder, and files," she must also

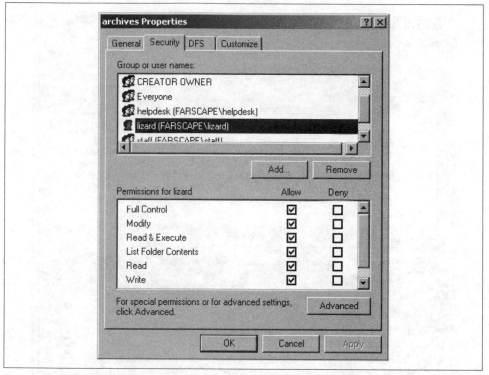

Figure 6-5. Displaying the Unix ACL for the archives folder using the Windows Security dialog box

have a named default entry. Here's an abbreviated version of the original POSIX ACL that highlights the entries needed to list both a `CREATOR OWNER` entry and to display *lizard*'s permissions in the initial security dialog box:

```
# owner: lizard
user::rwx
default:user::rwx
default:user:lizard:rwx
```

Viewing ACLs from Windows is of minimal use if you are unable to modify them. Samba converts ACL modifications sent by the client to its own filesystem representation using the inverse of the display rules just discussed. There are a few differences between Windows and Unix that you must remember:

- Unix allows only *root* or the owner to change the permissions on a file or directory.
- Only *root* or a user possessing the SeTakeOwnership privilege can assume ownership of a file or directory.
- Only *root* or a user possessing the SeRestorePrivilege privilege can set ownership to an arbitrary user.

If you wish to enforce semantics similar to those on Windows, where any user with write permissions can modify the ACL or take ownership, set dos filemode = yes in

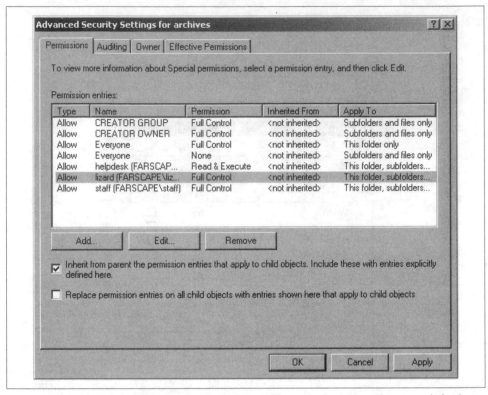

Figure 6-6. Displaying the Unix ACL for the archives folder using the Advanced Security dialog box

the share definition. This control option and a related one are summarized in Table 6-10.

Table 6-10. DOS compatibility options

Parameter	Value	Description	Default	Scope
dos filemode	boolean	Should users with write access be able to assume ownership and modify the object's ACL?	no	Share
dos filetimes	boolean	Should users with write access be able to modify the file's timestamp?	no	Share

Microsoft Distributed File Systems

Microsoft's Distributed File System (MS-DFS), not to be confused with the Distributed Computing Environment's DFS, is the Windows equivalent of the Unix automounter. All modern Microsoft clients (Windows 98, NT 4.0, and later) natively support MS-DFS. An add-on component for Windows 95 is available from Microsoft. Figure 6-7 illustrates how MS-DFS is implemented. MS-DFS links appear as folders when viewed by the client. When the user attempts to access the directory, he receives a referral to a UNC path (*CARROT\data*), which is automatically followed on his behalf by the Windows client. The user is never aware that the contents of the directory reside on another server. Because MS-DFS assumes that the credentials used to connect to the first server are also valid for connecting to the target of the referral, it is useful only within the context of an authentication domain.

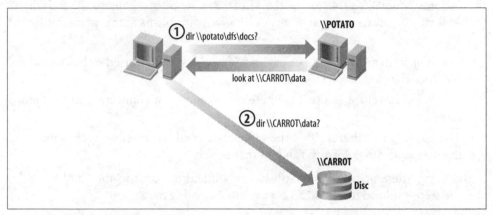

Figure 6-7. Redirection by MS-DFS

Configuring Samba to support MS-DFS root shares involves one global parameter, host msdfs, and one per share parameter, msdfs root. The following configuration defines a share named [common] that acts as a MS-DFS root share. It combines group shares managed by various departments within the network and provides an alternative to the [groups] share covered earlier in this chapter. Because we use the share to store only MS-DFS links, there is no need to provide write access to the share.

```
[global]
    host msdfs = yes

[common]
    path = /data/dfs
    read only = yes
    msdfs root = yes
```

The MS-DFS referrals are stored on the server's filesystem as symbolic links. The link name is the name of the directory displayed by clients. The target of the link represents the destination UNC path for the MS-DFS referral. The link target name follows this format:

```
msdfs:server\share[,server\share,...]
```

The msdfs keyword is used by Samba to identify the link as a MS-DFS referral. The *server\share* component is the path to the server and share returned to the client. Multiple paths can be defined; all will be returned the client, which then selects one based on internal heuristics.

The following *ln* command creates a referral from *staff* to *\\sleet\staff*:

```
$ ln -s 'msdfs:sleet\staff' staff
$ ls -l staff
lrwxrwxrwx  1 root root 17 2006-05-25 11:36 staff -> msdfs:sleet\staff
```

After reconfiguring a server or share to support MS-DFS, you will likely have to reboot the Windows client in order for it to recognize the new functionality. Once this is done, you will be able to test the MS-DFS share by browsing to the staff directory and viewing its contents. If you experience any problems at this point, verify the following:

- *smb.conf* contains no syntax errors and Samba as been restarted or has reread the file since the changes were made.
- The Windows client has been fully rebooted since last connecting to the Samba server.
- The target (e.g., *\\sleet\staff*) of the MS-DFS referral is accessible by the client and the user credentials are also valid on that server.

If you verify these items and are still having difficulties, turn to the Samba logfiles and the steps outlined in Chapter 12 for troubleshooting help.

In addition to supporting MS-DFS referrals for directories, it is possible to define a share that solely refers to another share by specifying a path in the `msdfs proxy` parameter, which can be helpful when migrating services from one server to another. For example, suppose that we have moved *\\RAIN\templates* to *\\SNOW\templates* but some clients are still trying to access it in the original location. The following share redirects users to the correct share without any client modifications:

```
[global]
    netbios name = RAIN

[templates]
    msdfs proxy = \\snow\templates
```

Table 6-11 lists the various MS-DFS related options that can be defined in *smb.conf*.

Table 6-11. MS-DFS options

Parameter	Value	Description	Default	Scope
host msdfs	boolean	If enabled, Samba reports support for MS-DFS in its global set of capabilities.	no	Global
msdfs proxy	\server\share	Defines the MS-DFS referral path returned when a client attempts sends a connection request.	None	Share
msdfs root	boolean	If enabled, Samba informs clients that a particular share supports MS-DFS referrals.	no	Share

Virtual File Systems

The *smbd* daemon interacts with files and directories on disk through a Virtual File System (VFS) module. The default VFS plug-in implements the Samba's standard file serving functionality. Other plug-ins distributed with the official Samba distribution and stored in */usr/local/samba/lib/vfs* for default installations include:

- A trash bin for saving deleted files.
- A logging module for recoding a user's access to files.
- A module to improve integration when sharing files via the Netatalk protocol.

There are also some third-party plug-ins available, such as the *samba-vscan* virus scanning plug-in (*http://www.openantivirus.org/projects.php*).

Each plug-in supports its own set of configuration settings that can be integrated into *smb.conf* using parametric options of the form *module_name:option*. In this section, we use the *recycle.so* VFS module as an example of the basic configuration steps. The complete set of VFS modules and associated documentation is included in the Samba distribution.

The purpose of the *recycle.so* library is to intercept any delete requests and move the target to a trash bin rather than removing it from disk. This is a nice safety net for users and prevents administrators from having to restore files from backup media when a user accidentally deletes an important document. Our example extends the [homes] share to provide users with a personal recycle directory.

The first step in configuring any VFS module is to define the vfs object value for the share. This parameter requires only the name of the VFS module (or modules). The *smbd* process automatically adds the necessary extension and attempts to load the plug-in from the *vfs* folder in Samba's library directory, which can be determined by running *smbd -b | grep LIBDIR*. Here is how the share definition should appear:

```
[homes]
    read only = no
    vfs object = recycle
```

The recycle module supports a variety of options for customizing how deleted files and directories should be backed up. The most common options are the directory where the deleted files are stored (repository), whether to maintain the file's original directory structure (keeptree), and which files should deleted rather than backed up (exclude). The modified share with the new VFS option syntax is:

```
[homes]
    read only = no
    vfs object = recycle
    recycle:repository = .trash
    recycle:keeptree = yes
    recycle:exclude = *.tmp, *~, *.bak
```

New VFS modules added to a share picked up in the same fashion as new configuration parameters. There is no need to restart Samba. Each new client connection is able to take advantage of the new settings. With the recycle plug-in in place, a user can safely delete files from her home directory and immediately retrieve them from the top-level *.trash* directory.

Table 6-12 lists the complete set of recycle plug-in parameters and a brief description of each. For information on other VFS modules, check the Samba documentation.

 As of the 3.0.22 release, developers still have not provided individual manpages for the various VFS plug-ins, a deficiency they have promised to correct "real soon now."

Table 6-12. VFS recycle parameters

Parameter	Value	Description	Default	Scope
directory_mode	octal permission set	The Unix permissions assigned to directories created due to the keeptree option.	0700	Share
exclude	filename pattern	List of filename patterns that should be excluded from the recycle repository. The pattern follows the Microsoft globbing syntax.	""	Share
exclude_dir	filename pattern	List of directory name patterns that should be excluded from the recycle repository. The pattern follows the Microsoft globbing syntax.	""	Share
keeptree	boolean	Should the original directory hierarchy be maintained when moving files to the repository?	no	Share
maxsize	integer	The maximum file size in bytes that should be backed up. Files larger than this size are deleted.	-1 (back up files of any size)	Share
repository	string	The absolute or relative path to the directory used to store deleted files.	*.recycle*	Share
touch	boolean	Should the access time be updated when the file is moved to the repository?	no	Share
touch_mtime	boolean	Should the modification time be updated when the file is moved to the repository?	no	Share

Executing Server Scripts

This chapter concludes with a discussion of a small but widely useful set of parameters. The preexec and postexec options allow you to define a command to be executed on the server whenever a user connects or disconnects from a share. The preexec and postexec commands are executed in the user's own context, and the root preexec and root postexec variants are executed under the context of the root account.

Scripts can be specified with arguments to pass, which are the standard Samba % variables. You are limited only by your own imagination. Some clients might connect and disconnect to shares more often that you think, so it is best not to assume that a user will connect to a share only once per session.

For an example, we'll create a share for the server's anonymous FTP directory. This step allows a user to publish files via FTP without having to resort to using an FTP client. The root preexec command creates an individual folder for the user to upload files. The share definition appears as:

```
[ftp]
    path = /var/ftp/pub
    read only = no
    force create mode = 0004
    force directory mode = 0005
    root preexec = /etc/samba/scripts/mkftpdir.sh %u
```

The contents of the *mkftpdir.sh* script are:

```
#!/bin/bash
if [ "x$1" == "x" ]; then
    exit 1
fi
if [ ! -d /var/ftp/pub/$1 ]; then
    mkdir /var/ftp/pub/$1
    chmod 755 /var/ftp/pub/$1
    chown $1 /var/ftp/pub/$1
fi
```

If desired, Samba can choose to honor or reject connections based on the return code from the preexec and root preexec commands. The preexec close (and root preexec close) can instruct *smbd* to evaluate the return code from the respective preexec command and reject the connection if the result is non-zero.

The pair of postexec commands are invoked when a user disconnects from a share. For example, when a user disconnects from a share containing removable media (such as a CD-ROM), the filesystem should be unmounted so that it can be removed. postexec commands are prime candidates for solving this category of problems.

Execution options are summarized in Table 6-13.

Table 6-13. Execution options

Parameter	Value	Description	Default	Scope
preexec	string	Specifies a command to be run under the context of the current user when connecting to the share.	""	Share
preexec close	boolean	Should *smbd* reject the share connection if the preexec command exits with a nonzero return code?	no	Share
postexec	string	Specifies a command to be run under the context of the current user when disconnecting from the share.	""	Share

Table 6-13. Execution options (continued)

Parameter	Value	Description	Default	Scope
root preexec	string	Specifies a command to be run under the context of the root user when connecting to the share.	""	Share
root preexec close	boolean	Should *smbd* reject the share connection if the root preexec command exits with a non-zero return code?	no	Share
root postexec	string	Specifies a command to be run under the context of the root user when disconnecting from the share.	""	Share

## CHAPTER 7

Printing

File serving is considered by most to be Samba's bread and butter. However, pulling up a close second in justifications for deploying Samba is its capability to centrally manage printers and to make them available across a network to Windows clients. The chapter focuses on the steps necessary to add print services to Samba's configuration as well as the details for sending print jobs from Unix and Linux clients to remote SMB/CIFS printers via *smbclient*.

Because Samba relies on a functioning, underlying print system, we will concentrate on sharing printers that have previously been configured on the server. If you need to refresh yourself on Unix printing details, three good references are *Network Printing*, by Matthew Gast and Todd Radermacher, *Essential System Administration*, by Æleen Frisch, and *Running Linux*, by Matt Welsh et al., all published by O'Reilly.

Print Shares

Samba at heart is not a printing system, but rather a spooling system. Its mantra is, "If Unix can print to it, so can I." To implement this philosophy, it must define a mechanism—an external commands or software library—to use when performing operations such as printing spooled jobs, retrieving a list of jobs in a queue, or pausing a printer.

Figure 7-1 illustrates the process of sending a print job to a Samba printer. The client opens the spool file on the server, writes the file in its entirety, and then closes the file, indicating that the job is ready to be printed.

This series of events has some important implications:

- The *smbd* daemon can hand the spooled job over to the server's printing system only after the entire file has been transmitted.
- The spooled job must be in a format that can be sent directly to the Unix print queue. Generally, this means no special Windows meta formats.

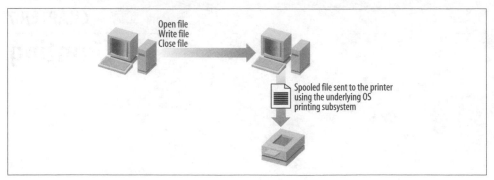

Figure 7-1. Sending a job to a Samba printer

Now it is time to define a share for a printer in the configuration file. A printer in *smb.conf* is a service section in which the mandatory print ok option has been enabled. The following is a perfectly valid, although largely useless, printer share:

```
[print-q]
    print ok = yes
```

The resulting share appears with a printer icon when viewed from a Windows client, as shown in Figure 7-2.

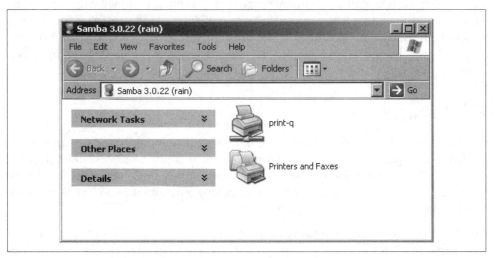

Figure 7-2. Viewing the print-q printer share from a Windows client

At this point, clients can connect to *server**print-q* and transmit print jobs. However, Samba reverts to default settings for all print-related functions. These defaults may or may not work for you. You can remove this uncertainty by explicitly defining the parameters necessary to handle print jobs.

Recall from Figure 7-1 that the client writes the entire document to the server before Samba can print it. So where is the spooled job written? The path parameter, when used in a print share, defines the directory on disk that will be used to store print jobs while they are being updated. A user must have write access to this directory in order to transmit a job to the Samba printer. Otherwise, the user will receive an error message such as "Disk is Full" or "Access denied."

Your configuration must inform *smbd* how it is to interact with the server's printing system in order to control what Samba does with a spooled job once the client has finished writing it. There are two means of defining this relationship. The first is to specify a value for the printing parameter in the printer's share definition, thus specifying a set of default commands that will be used to handle various printing operations and control how *smbd* parses the output from the printing system's *lpq* (or equivalent command). The printing option accepts a single string from the following list: SYSV, AIX, HPUX, BSD, QNX, PLP, LPRNG, CUPS.

Each one of these case-insensitve values matches a type of printing. For example, SYSV should be selected on systems such as Solaris and IRIX that use System V printing (i.e., *lpadmin* and *lpstat*). The AIX, HPUX, and QNX values represent their respective operating systems. The remaining options are matched with the printing system by the same name.

 There are two other possible printing values: NT and OS2. These are useful only when the printer in question is located on a remote Windows NT variant or an OS/2 server running a BSD printing service. Because this setup is fairly uncommon, it is possible that support for these *lpd* variants will be removed in a future Samba release.

When building Samba, the configure script attempts to determine which printing system is currently installed and set the appropriate defaults. The easiest method of determining which printing interface is being used by default is to define at least one printer, such as the [print-q] share, in *smb.conf* and parse this file using testparm:

```
$ testparm  -v -s smb.conf 2>&1 | grep 'printing.*='
    printing = bsd
```

It is also possible to see the default printing commands used to communicate with the operating system by explicitly setting the printing value in a print service and reviewing that share with testparm. Let's assume an *smb.conf* with the printing option set to BSD:

```
[print-q]
        print ok = yes
        printing = bsd
```

Running testparm on this share reveals the defaults used for BSD Samba print servers:

```
$ testparm -s smb.conf
<....output deleted....>
[print-q]
        path = /tmp
```

```
printable = Yes
printing = bsd
print command = lpr -r -P'%p' %s
lpq command = lpq -P'%p'
lprm command = lprm -P'%p' %j
```

The print command is invoked when the client has successfully written the print job to the server. Generally, this hook is used to print the file, but its flexibility allows you to do just about anything you like. For example, you could send a document to a fax machine or convert the job to a new format, such as PDF. In all cases, the print command should remove the original spooled job (%s) after it has been processed. Otherwise, the spool directory (path) eventually runs out of space as jobs continue to pile up. The lpq command and lprm command strings are used respectively to list entries in the print queue and to remove individual jobs.

 Many implementations of *lpr* or other print utilities create a copy of the original job in its own spool directory (e.g., */var/spool/lpd*). In these cases, the server requires twice the amount space as the size of the original print job. If this becomes a problem, consider placing the Samba spool directory on a different disk partition from the print system's spool directory. You can also define the min print space option in the Samba print share to require a specific amount of free space (in kilobytes) before Samba will accept a document for a given printer. If less than this amount is available, the client receives a "disk full" error message.

The %p variable shown in the three printing commands expands to the value of the printer name directive and is available only within a print service. Frequently, this parameter is omitted because its default value is the name of share itself. So in the previous output from testparm, the %p variable would be replaced at runtime with the string print-q. The complete list of variables available in print shares is listed in Table 7-1.

Table 7-1. Printing variables

Variable	Definition
%c	The page count of the print job (available only when printing from clients running Windows NT and later operating systems).
%f, %s	The full pathname of the spool file on the Samba server.
%J	The name of the print job as sent by the client.
%j	The number of the print job (for use with *lprm*, *lppause*, and *lpresume*).
%p	The name of the Unix printer.
%z	The size in bytes of the spool file.

There are more print-related commands than the three shown in the `testparm` output for the `[print-q]` service. Table 7-2 gives the list of all the printing hooks and Table 7-3 describes the default values for each printing type.

Table 7-2. Printing commands

Parameter	Value	Description	Scope
`lppause command`	string	Command to pause an individual print job in the queue.	Share
`lpq command`	string	Command to retrieve a listing of jobs in the queue.	Share
`lpresume command`	string	Command to resume a pause print job.	Share
`lprm command`	string	Command to remove an individual print job from the queue.	Share
`print command`	string	Command to send a spooled job to the printer.	Share
`queue pause command`	string	Command to pause an entire queue.	Share
`queue resume command`	string	Command to resume a paused queue.	Share

Table 7-3. Default printing command values based on printing types

Printing type	Defaults
BSD, AIX	print command = lpr -r -P'%p' %s lpq command = lpq -P'%p' lprm command = lprm -P'%p' %j
LPNRG, PLP	print command = lpr -r -P'%p' %s lpq command = lpq -P'%p' lprm command = lprm -P'%p' %j queue pause command = lpc stop '%p' queue resume command = lpc start '%p' lppause command = lpc hold '%p' %j lpresume command = lpc release '%p' %j
CUPS (when there is no library support)	print command = lpr -P'%p' %s; rm %s lpq command = lpq -P'%p' lprm command = lprm -P'%p' %j queue pause command = disable '%p' queue resume command = enable '%p' lppause command = lp -i '%p-%j' -H hold lpresume command = lp -i '%p-%j' -H resume
SYSV	print command = lp -c -d%p %s; rm %s lpq command = lpstat -o%p lprm command = cancel %p-%j queue pause command = disable %p queue resume command = enable %p
HPUX	**(same as SYSV with the following two additions)** lppause command = lp -i '%p-%j' -H hold lpresume command = lp -i '%p-%j' -H resume
QNX	print command = lp -r -P%p %s lpq command = lpq -P%p lprm command = lprm -P%p %j

This is probably a good time to mention how Samba interacts with the *Common Unix Printing System (http://www.cups.org)*.* CUPS is currently the only printing library supported by Samba. When the CUPS library has been successfully detected at compile time and the printing option has been set to the string CUPS, the printing commands are bypassed entirely. There is no need to call out to an external program to process print requests; *smbd* can call the CUPS library functions directly. The default printing values specified in Table 7-3 for printing = cups are used only when Samba has not been compiled to include CUPS library support. We provide more information on Samba and CUPS later in this chapter.

A Usable Print Share

When planning a new print share, you must know a few pieces of information. The values in parantheses are what we will use for this information in our example print share:

- The name of the printer (hp2100)
- The name of the print share (postscript)
- The type of printing supported by the OS for this queue (BSD)
- The directory that will be used to store jobs sent from clients (*/var/spool/samba*)

Using this information, we can create the following initial print share:

```
[postscript]
    print ok = yes
    printing = bsd
    path = /var/spool/samba
    print command = /usr/bin/lpr -Php2100 %s; /bin/rm %s
    lpq command    = /usr/bin/lpq -Php2100
    lprm command   = /usr/bin/lprm -Php2100 %j
    queue pause command  = /usr/sbin/lpc stop hp2100
    queue resume command = /usr/sbin/lpc start hp2100
```

To ensure that all users can send jobs to the printer, the */var/spool/samba* directory has been assign world-writable permissions (*chmod 1777 /var/spool/samba*).

We could have defined printer name = hp2100 and replaced the string hp2100 with the %p variable. In the absence of the printer name option, the %p variable defaults to the name of the share itself. So if we rename the share to [hp2100], we can simplify the service definition to the following:

```
[hp2100]
    print ok = yes
    printing = bsd
```

---

* Michael Sweet, the author of CUPS, has also written a book entitled *CUPS: Common Unix Printing System* (SAMS Publishing).

```
path = /var/spool/samba
print command = /usr/bin/lpr -P%p %s; /bin/rm %s
lpq command   = /usr/bin/lpq -P%p
lprm command  = /usr/bin/lprm -P%p %j
queue pause command  = /usr/sbin/lpc stop %p
queue resume command = /usr/sbin/lpc start %p
```

It would be nice if there were a way to define aliased names for shares. The closest possibility is the copy parameter discussed in Chapter 4. However, creating a new share named [postscript] and setting it as a copy of the [hp2100] service would break the %p variable, because the printer name option would default to postscript rather than hp2100. A satisfactory solution entails creating a postscript alias for the hp2100 in */etc/printcap*, which would appear as:

```
hp2100|postscript:\
    <remaining printcap options:....>
```

One common problem that arises using any external commands in *smb.conf* occurs when Samba is unable to locate the program or script in the current PATH setting. This is why absolute paths to the BSD printing tools are used in these examples (and why we did not simply accept the default printing values).

If all the printers on your server use the same printing hooks, you can move most of these parameters to the [global] section. The path directive is still defined in the individual printer section, however, since you would not want */var/spool/samba* to become to the default path for all file shares as well:

```
[global]
    ## set printing defaults for all queues
    printing = bsd
    print command = /usr/bin/lpr -P%p %s; /bin/rm %s
    lpq command   = /usr/bin/lpq -P%p
    lprm command  = /usr/bin/lprm -P%p %j
    queue pause command  = /usr/sbin/lpc stop %p
    queue resume command = /usr/sbin/lpc start %p

[hp2100]
    print ok = yes
    path = /var/spool/samba
```

File shares and print shares are very similar in both *smb.conf* and the CIFS protocol, so you can often reuse parameters discussed in the context of file shares for new printers. In our example, we can assign a comment to the print share by adding the following line to the [hp2100] share. Users will then be able to view the printer's description when browsing the share details:

```
comment = Classroom laser printer in RM 114
```

Some of the parameters, such as store dos attributes, are specific to file shares and make no sense for a printer, just as the print command is irrelevant for a file share. Such parameters are ignored when they are inapplicable to a given *smb.conf* service.

We can use *smbclient* to test our new example [hp2100] print share. In order to do so, we must have at least one valid user account on the Samba host. This example reuses the account named *lizard* defined in Chapter 2 and assumes an associated password of *test*. For the test, we use *smbclient* to print the local */etc/hosts* file.

```
$ smbclient //localhost/hp2100 -U lizard%test
Domain=[VALE] OS=[Unix] Server=[Samba 3.0.22]
smb: \> lcd /etc
smb: \> print hosts
putting file hosts as hosts (8.9 kb/s) (average 8.9 kb/s)
smb: \> queue
1       1083           Remote Downlevel Document hosts
```

If this command does not succeed, there are several places to start looking. First check the Samba logfiles for error messages returned by the print command option. Also ensure that the spool directory specified by the path parameter is writable by the connected user. If Samba appears to be functioning correctly but no paper appears at the printer, it is time to review Unix print system debugging techniques.

Samba and CUPS

CUPS servers are becoming more and more common in today's networks. As previously mentioned, Samba does not require external commands to be able to communicate with the CUPS printer daemon (*cupsd*). Support for this feature must be detected at compile time, however. By default, the *configure* script attempts to locate the CUPS header files and development libraries. If you wish to force Samba to build with CUPS support and fail if it cannot, use the --enable-cups option when running *configure*:

```
$ ./configure --enable-cups
....
checking for cups-config... /usr/bin/cups-config
....
```

Once support is detected, you can verify that the resulting *smbd* does in fact have support for CUPS printers by looking for HAVE_CUPS in the build options output from *smbd*:

```
$ smbd -b | grep CUPS
    HAVE_CUPS
```

Configuring Samba to work with *cupsd* is by far the easiest of all the printing types. All of the printing commands from Table 7-2 can be omitted and our example [hp2100] share can be reduced to:

```
[hp2100]
    printing = cups
    print ok = yes
    comment = Classroom laser printer in RM 114
    path = /var/spool/samba
```

This configuration assumes that Samba and the CUPS server are running on the same host. Samba can use a *cupsd* process running on a different machine by defining the cups server parameter in the [global] section of *smb.conf*. The default behavior is to use the server specified in the CUPS *client.conf* configuration file or defined by the CUPS_SERVER environment variable. The value should be either the DNS name or IP address of the remote server:

```
cups server = cups.plainjoe.org
```

CUPS allows something that is hard to do on other printing systems: you can choose when a document should be processed by the printer's filter and when the document should bypass the filter. Thus, a single CUPS print queue can be used to process raw print jobs from Windows clients and PostScript files from Unix clients. In order to do this, add the cups options parameter to the print share definition. Any number of generic CUPS arguments can be set in this parameter using a list of comma-separated options. In the following example, we just tell Samba to inform CUPS that this job is ready to be sent directly to the printer:

```
[hp2100]
    printing = cups
    print ok = yes
    comment = Classroom laser printer in RM 114
    path = /var/spool/samba
    cups options = "raw"
```

An alternative way to let a printer serve a dual purpose is to create two queues per printer, one to be used by Samba and the other to process jobs from Unix clients.

All of this ease of use is not without a price. The easier something is to configure, the more difficult it is to troubleshoot when things do not function correctly. When debugging Samba/CUPS printers, make sure to consult the *cupsd* logfiles as well as Samba's logs.

The [printers] Service

Defining individual print shares for each queue on a large print server can be tedious. To alleviate this problem, Samba provides a mechanism to dynamically create printer shares for every queue known by the host operating system. This special share named [printers] is very similar to the [homes] share. Here's how it works.

When Samba receives a request to connect to a share, it performs the following series of checks to locate the share definition.

- Check for an explicitly defined share in *smb.conf*. If a match is found, authorize this request against this share.
- Check for the [homes] service. If this share exists, look up the requested share name in the local system's list of accounts (e.g., */etc/passwd* or users in an LDAP directory). If the search succeeds, create a copy of the [homes] share named for the user found and use this new share for the connection request.

- If the [printers] share is defined, look up the requested share name in the printcap name. If a match is found, create a copy of the [printers] share named for the printer found and use this as the service in response to the client's request.

- Fall back to the default service if one is defined.

As we mentioned earlier, you can't define a user and a printer with the same name; Samba will never find the printer if both [homes] and [printers] exist in *smb.conf*. If you accidentally send print jobs to a file share, you will see spooled jobs accumulate in the top-level directory of the share.

Configuring the [printers] share involves three steps:

1. Inform *smbd* as to where it can find the list of system printers by defining the printcap name global parameter. This value varies depending on the default printing value.

2. Define the [printers] service in *smb.conf*.

3. Specify whether *smbd* should create all of the dynamic print shares at startup (allowing them to be browsed) or create them upon demand.

The printcap name parameter is indirectly linked to the printing option. In its generic form, printcap name refers to the text file that contains the list of system printers, such as */etc/printcap*. When used with certain printing systems, however, *smbd* can query the print service directly. Samba provides defaults that work most of the time; see Table 7-4 for various printing systems and the associated printcap name value assigned by default.

Table 7-4. Special printcap name values

Value of printing option	Default printcap name
CUPS	cups
SYSV, HPUX	lpstat
QNX	/qconfig

If the list of systems printers changes, you can make Samba reload all its configuration options (and thereby discover the changes in printers) through the usual mechanism of sending the *smbd* process a hangup signal (SIGHUP). But to save you the trouble of restarting *smbd*, the server can instead be instructed to periodically reparses the contents of the printcap name based on the printcap cache time global option. This parameter accepts an integer value specifying the number of seconds for which the cached list of printer names should be considered valid. In Samba 3.0.20 or greater, the printcap cache time default is 750 seconds.

In some cases, it is preferable to export a subset of system printers when using a printing type other than CUPS. This can be done by pointing Samba to a custom printcap file that contains the list of printer you wish to share (e.g., `printcap name = /etc/samba/printcap`).

The [printers] share is defined just like a normal printer. The only real requirement is to use the variables rather than hard-coded values for changeable values such as printer names.

Finally, if [global] contains `load printers = yes` (the default value), all of the printers defined in the `printcap name` file are parsed and made available for browsing when Samba is launched. Otherwise, clients may request a printer using its UNC path but may not browse for the printer.

Our resulting *smb.conf* now looks like:

```
[global]
    printing = bsd
    printcap name = /etc/printcap
    printcap cache time = 1800

    print command = /usr/bin/lpr -P%p %s; /bin/rm %s
    lpq command   = /usr/bin/lpq -P%p
    lprm command  = /usr/bin/lprm -P%p %j
    queue pause command = /usr/sbin/lpc stop %p
    queue resume command = /usr/sbin/lpc start %p

[printers]
    print ok = yes
    path = /var/spool/samba
```

Before we can test the [printers] share, we need a working */etc/printcap* file. Here are our example printer configurations. If you need a refresher on the various fields in each printer entry, refer to the `printcap` manpage.

```
hp2100:rm=rain:rp=hp2100:
slate:rm=rain:rp=slate:
quest:rm=rain:rp=quest:
```

Once Samba is started, we can browse the server and see all three printers:

```
$ bin/smbclient -L localhost -N
Anonymous login successful
Domain=[VALE] OS=[Unix] Server=[Samba 3.0.22]

    Sharename       Type    Comment
    ---------       ----    -------
    IPC$            IPC     IPC Service (Samba 3.0.22)
    hp2100          Printer hp2100
    slate           Printer slate
    quest           Printer quest
...
```

Clients will be able to connect to any one of these printers just as if it had been explicitly defined it in *smb.conf*.

Enabling SMB Printer Sharing in OS X

Because Samba comes preinstalled with Mac OS X, sharing access to a printer among Windows clients is easy. First, of course, you should set up local access using the Print Center application (located in Finder's Applications → Utilities folder). Under the Printers menu, select Add Printer..., and make the appropriate selection from the pop-up menu. For example, if the printer is directly attached, select USB; if the printer is powered on, it should appear in the list. Choose the printer, and press the Add button.

Edit */etc/smb.conf*, uncommenting the [printers] share and making any additional configuration changes you feel are necessary. Finally, enable the Samba startup item as described in Chapter 2, either by checking Windows File Sharing in Sharing Preferences or by manually editing */etc/hostconfig*. Now your printer can be used by remote Windows clients.

On Mac OS X and some other BSD-based systems, you can test your configuration using *smbutil*. The following command sends the file named *print_test_file* to the printer named printshare on the server violet:

```
$ smbutil print //violet/printshare print_test_file
```

More information on *smbutil* is in Chapter 11.

Creating a PDF Printer

The flexibility of Samba's printing hooks has inspired administrators to configure printer shares that do more than just print. One of the more common examples is a printer that converts a document to PDF and then mails the resulting file back to the user. This process is actually easier than it might sound at first. It does, however, require an external tool, such as Ghostscript's *ps2pdf* command, to convert the spooled job to PDF.

The first step in creating a PDF printer is to create the share in *smb.conf*. The caveat is that a printing type other than CUPS must be specified. Remember that the printing commands are ignored when Samba has CUPS printing support enabled. So for our example, we will use BSD printing, even though our server may not be running an *lpd* daemon:

```
[pdfgen]
    print ok = yes
    printing = bsd
    comment  = PDF Generator (requires postscript input)
    path     = /var/spool/samba
```

Next we need a script that will handle the work of converting the PostScript file to PDF and mailing it back to the user. Error checking and general paranoia has been removed from the script in order to keep it short for example purposes:

```
#!/bin/sh
## /etc/samba/pdfgen.sh <ps_file> <user> <document_name>

PSFILE=$1
USERNAME=$2
JOBNAME=$3
PDFFILE=`echo $PSFILE | cut -d. -f1`.pdf

/usr/bin/ps2pdf $PSFILE $PDFFILE

/usr/bin/mail -s "$JOBNAME PDF conversion" \
    -a $PDFFILE $USERNAME < /dev/null
```

The next step is to set the print command to execute this script. Because we are not dealing with a real printer, we set the lpq command to return an empty list, so as to prevent jobs from being displayed on the client's queue listing window:

```
print command = /etc/samba/pdfgen.sh %s %u '%J'
lpq command = /bin/true
```

Assuming that the client sends a valid PostScript file, the user should receive a copy of the document in PDF format. That is of course a large assumption, which brings us to a discussion of centrally managing Windows print drivers.

Managing Windows Print Drivers

Current versions of Samba support the downloading of print drivers on demand when clients connect to print shares. This feature is commonly referred to as *point and print* (p-n-p). The advantages of this configuration are that you are guaranteed that clients are using the print driver that you expect them to use and that you can deploy updated drivers and printer settings without touching the clients. Before you begin to think that this is too good to be true, there are a few catches.

First, the drivers must be installed on the Samba server just as one would install them on a Windows print server. However, unlike with a Windows host, you must initialize the printer registry settings on the server. (More on this later.)

Second, not all print drivers are created equal. You will find that most drivers work correctly when served from a Samba machine, but a few will be unusable due to bugs in the driver itself or a decision by the driver developers to utilize features that can be supported only by a Windows server. Luckily, for the majority of environments, Samba's level of support for p-n-p is more than adequate.

Point and Print Prerequisites

For now, assume that we have already created all of the print shares (possibly with a single [printers] share) in *smb.conf*. It is possible to create new printers at runtime via the Windows Add Printer Wizard (APW), but to keep things simple, let's just deal with the driver installation issues for now. Later we discuss how to remotely add and delete printers on a Samba host.

Samba maintains print driver metadata and files in two locations. The Windows driver files themselves are stored in a standard file share named [print$]. The service definition for this share is nothing out of the ordinary. It is important to note that all users who will be downloading drivers from the server must have read access to the data stored withing the share. However, only trusted accounts should be given the ability to add new files or modify existing ones. Because these files are downloaded automatically to clients, imagine what damage could be done if a malicious user were able to copy a virus infected DLL as part of a print driver.

Don't confuse the Windows print drivers with any driver files (e.g., PPD files or filters) specific to the underlying Unix print system.

The [print$] share defined here permits write access to members of the *ntadmin* Unix group only. All other accounts can connect but cannot modify the share contents. We also enforce world accessible permissions on files and directories.

```
[print$]
    comment              = Windows print driver files
    # Make sure the permissions on the top level directory
    # are 2775 with group ownership belonging to ntadmin
    path                 = /export/smb/printers
    read only            = yes
    write list           = +ntadmin
    inherit permissions  = yes
```

We must create two directories within the top level directory of this share. The *WIN40* directory will hold drivers for print drivers for Windows 95/98 and Millenium. The *W32X86* directory is needed for 32-bit Windows NT variants running on Intel platforms.

```
$ cd /export/smb/printers
$ mkdir WIN40 W32X86
$ chgrp ntadmin W*
$ chmod 2775 W*
```

These two directories cover the majority of clients. However, there are different directory names if you must also support Windows NT R4000 (*W32MIPS*), Windows NT Alpha_AXP (*W32ALPHA*), and Windows NT PowerPC (*W32PPC*). There are also two additional directories if you find yourself supporting newer 64-bit releases of Windows for the Itanium (*IA64*) and the AMD Opteron (*x64*).

In addition to the driver files, a print server must maintain metadata about how the driver files are grouped together (*ntdrivers.tdb*); what paper sizes are supported by the server (*ntforms.tdb*); and printer attributes such as duplex settings, page orientation, and the currently assigned driver (*ntprinters.tdb*).* All three *tdb* files are stored in a Samba lock directory (*/var/lib/samba* or */usr/local/samba/var/locks*). The authorization to update driver files is strictly controlled by the filesystem permissions and any access parameters associated with the file share. Updating information stored in these printing *tdb*s requires possession of the SePrintOperatorPrivilege. Refer to Chapter 5 if you need a refresher course on managing user rights in Samba.

Prior to 3.0.11, Samba relied on the printer admin option for authorizing users to update information in the printing *tdb*s. This parameter has since been deprecated and will be removed in a future release.

Now that we have moved past the prerequisite file shares and permissions, we can focus on installing a print driver and binding it to a printer.

Installing Print Drivers

Windows 2000 and later clients provide an interface to upload print drivers without associating the driver with any specific printer. The print driver management screen is integrated into the server properties dialog box. You can reach the Server Properties for a Samba host by browsing to the server's *Printers* folder from a client running Windows 2000 or later. Windows XP and Windows Server 2003 have renamed this folder to *Printers and Faxes*. Once you have arrived at the folder, select the File → Server Properties for the dialog box shown in Figure 7-3.

If you have connected using an account that posseses the SePrintOperatorPrivilege privilege, the Add, Remove, and Replace buttons are available. If they are disabled, make sure that your user account has the necessary privilege or that you are a member of a group that does. Also remember that updates to privilege assignments are applied only for a new CIFS session. So if the right privilege was assigned while the account was connected, you have to disconnect and relogin to the server. The most effective means of ensuring that the session is torn down and reestablished is to log out and back in again on the Windows client.

A new driver upload is begun by clicking Add. The Add Printer Driver Wizard (APDW) dialog box shown in Figure 7-4 will appear.

Click Next to get to the Driver Selection dialog box. At this point, you can either select the print drivers distributed with Windows or select an alternative location in case you have downloaded newer or additional drivers from the printer's manufacturer.

Once you have selected a driver to upload to the server, Windows prompts you to select the architectures to support with the driver to install. For example, if you wish to install a driver with support for Windows 2000 and NT clients as well as Windows 9x, it is possible to do so here. You can always upload other architectures for a

---

* Although paper sizes (i.e., forms) are installed with a specific printer, the data is stored globally across all printers. Hence the statement regarding paper sizes on the server (and not per printer).

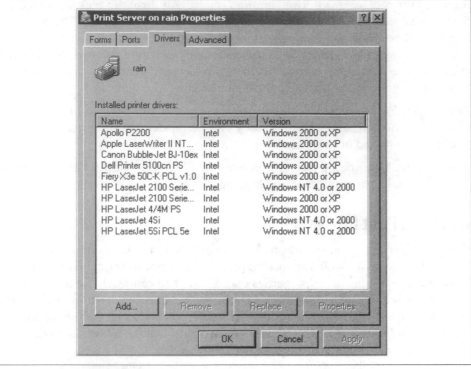

Figure 7-3. Driver tab in the Server Properties dialog box

Figure 7-4. Add Printer Driver Wizard dialog box

given driver by running the APDW again. Windows asks you for driver files for any alternative architectures that have been selected once it begins copying the files to the server.

Windows NT-only drivers are often referred to as *version 2* drivers, because the driver files are stored under *server**print$*\W32X86\2 directory. Windows 2000 and later drivers are referred to as version 3 and hence stored in \\*server**print$*\W32X86\3. The real difference between these two types of drivers is how they interact with the Windows kernel. Version 2 drivers are kernel-mode drivers, and version 3 drivers are executed in user-space.

The final dialog box allows you to begin the copying process and issue the commands to create the printer driver object on the destination machine. If the process completes successfully, you will see the newly installed driver listed in the Server Properties window. If the driver files fail to copy with an "Access Denied" error message, verify that the account used to upload the drivers has write permission to the [print$] share and its immediate subdirectories.

Assigning Print Drivers and Initializing DeviceModes

Once the driver has been installed on the server, it is time to associate it with a specific printer. A printer created on a Windows server uses the driver libraries to fill in a data structure referred to as a *DeviceMode* for options such as duplex printing features and landscape or portrait page orientation. This DeviceMode and associated registry data (PrinterDriverData) define the printer's settings. A Windows print server executes the driver when it is assigned to a printer in order to generate the required printer data. Samba is not able to natively execute Win32 code nor is it restricted to Intel hardware. Therefore, a little bit of assistance is needed to generate and store the required settings for a printer.

To bind a driver to a specific printer, first launch the printer properties dialog for that device by right-clicking the printer's icon and selecting the Properties option. You will be immediately informed that the server does not have an appropriate driver installed for the printer (because you have not assigned one yet) and asked if you would like to install a local copy of the driver. Your first inclination may be to reply Yes, because you are trying to assign a driver to the printer. However, doing so installs a new print driver on the client machine only and creates a local print object that points back to the server. You want to assign a driver to the printer object on the server, not the client. Selecting No here causes the Properties dialog box to be launched instead, as shown in Figure 7-5.

The driver selection list can be found under the Advanced tab. Selecting this dropdown list displays the names of the Windows NT and 2000/XP drivers installed on the server. Drivers that have only a Windows 9x version installed are not displayed. You can select any one of the drivers listed and then click the OK button. If all of the

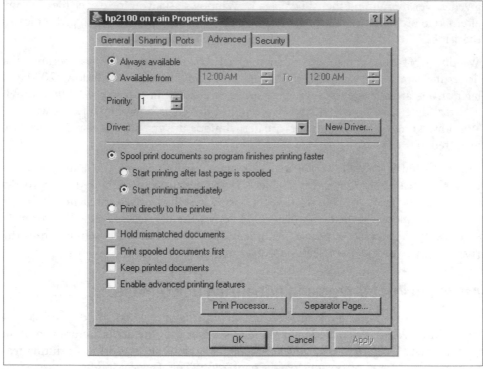

Figure 7-5. Printer Properties dialog box for \\rain\hp2100

options are disabled, this means that you have not connected to the server as a user possessing the SePrintOperatorPrivilege. (In the next section, we show how you can grant administrative rights for a single printer to a user or group.) If all goes well, the client will make the change to the printer and the dialog box will silently go away.

Upon returning to the *Printers and Faxes* folder on the Samba server, you will likely notice that the printer has been renamed to match the driver name just assigned. On a Windows print server, the printer name and the share name are stored as two different attributes of the printer. To be fully compatible and allow migrations from Windows print servers, Samba has to support renaming requests from clients such as this one. Some people like it; others find it annoying. If you would prefer to prevent clients from renaming the printer displayed in the "Printers and Faxes" window, enable the force printername parameter in the print service definition.

This time, when the printer properties dialog box is launched, you should no longer be prompted to install a driver on the client. In fact, if all has gone well, the client has already silently downloaded and installed the driver in order to display all of the associated settings. There are two things that can occur when the client attempts to launch the properties dialog box. The desired result is that window displays without any errors. However, some drivers will crash the Windows Explorer. or perhaps even the client's spooler service itself.

Print Management Extreme

When you begin print driver management in Samba, it is much easier to grasp the details by creating the print shares in *smb.conf* beforehand and focusing on the driver installation process. However, if you would like to take this one step further and create, modify, and delete printers at runtime from a remote Windows client, read on.

Samba provides two hooks that administrators can use to plug into their own scripts for adding and removing printers from the underlying printing system. These are referred to as the add printer command and the delete printer command respectively.

The add printer command is called when the client asks to create a new printer or sends a *SetPrinter()* request to change basic attributes. The script is highly site-dependent and varies from one print server to another. An example script designed for CUPS servers, named *smbaddprinter.pl*, can be found in the *examples/scripts/perl* directory of the Samba source distribution

Samba feeds seven arguments to the script:

- The printer name
- The share name
- The port name
- The driver name
- The location field
- The comment field
- The NetBIOS name of the remote client issuing the request

The script should parse these parameters and create or update the printer information for the OS.

The delete printer command, whose role is to remove the printer from the server's printing system, is given the share name as its sole argument. This tends to be a much simpler operation than adding a new printer. An example script named *smbdelprinter.pl* is in the same directory as the add printer example script.

Client crashes at this stage are caused by the lack of a printer DeviceMode. Some drivers appear to be more sensitive (or more assuming) than others. One workaround is to have *smbd* create a generic DeviceMode for the printer, by setting default devmode = yes in the print share's section of *smb.conf*. Frequently, this step is enough to at least display the printer's Properties window.

Once the properties are displayed, navigate to the Advanced tab and select the Printing Defaults... button. Windows 2000 introduced the concept of Printing Preferences, which are stored on a per-user basis, and Printing Defaults, which are stored with the printer on the server. Note that Windows NT 4.0 supports only global printer settings for all users and Windows 9x supports only printer preferences, and only on the local system. In fact, Windows 9x ignores attributes assigned to a printer on the server and initializes the local printer object to the driver defaults.

When you set a value in the Printing Defaults window, the client executes the driver on your behalf and stores the required printer data on the server. Setting any attribute stored in the DeviceMode appears to have the same effect, but the attribute that has been most tested is the page orientation. A change from portrait to landscape and back, clicking Apply between the changes, initializes the printer on the server. Figure 7-6 displays the page orientation settings for an HP LaserJet printer.

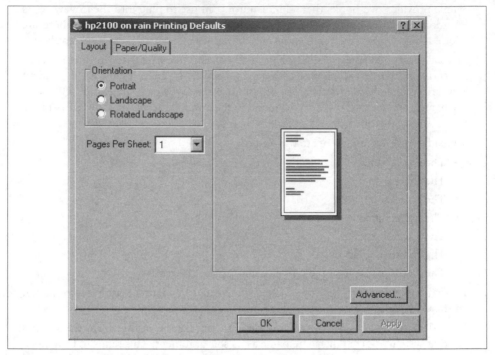

Figure 7-6. Initializing printer data using the page orientation field

Finally, exit from the property dialog boxes by clicking OK until you are back to the *Printer and Faxes* folder. The printer is now ready for use by Windows clients.

Testing Point and Print

If everything has been sucessfully completed up to this point, testing p-n-p from a client should go smoothly. Select a Windows client that matches the driver architectures installed on the server for your printer. There are many ways to establish a printer connection in Windows, and it can also vary from one OS release to another. One method that is common to all Windows clients is to browse to the server's *Printers and Faxes* folder and right-click on the printer. When you select Connect from the menu, the client downloads the driver and creates a printer connection that can be seen from the client's own *Printers* folder (Start → Settings → Printers and

Faxes). Figure 7-7 shows a connection to the printer hp2100 (HP LaserJet Series 2100 PS) served by the Samba host named rain.

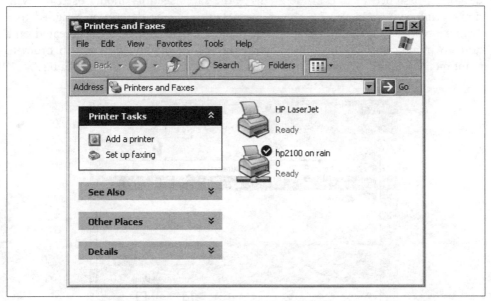

Figure 7-7. Printer connection to \\rain\hp2100 on a Windows XP client

Because they use an older printing protocol, Windows 95/98/Me never see the *Printers and Faxes* folder on the Samba server. However, it is still possible to browse to the server, right-click a print share, and select Install from the context menu. The client will download the driver and create a local printer pointing back to the server. It will not, however, associate any of the printer settings on the server, such as duplex or page size, with the local printer object. The user on these systems must manually define these settings for each printer he connects to.

Failures when connecting to a printer can often be traced to authorization failures. In the next section, we examine how to enforce security checks on on Samba print shares.

Printers and Security

The idea of controlling access to printers is a recent addition to Unix world. In order to provide a consistent and Windows-compatible view of security, Samba internally performs access checks to validate actions such as printing a document, removing a job, or changing a printer attribute. There are two levels of authorization controls related to printer operations, both of which mirror security checks done on file shares. However, a user possessing the SePrintOperatorPrivilege is granted access regardless of the access control settings.

The first access check done when connecting to a printer, assuming that the client has authorization to access the Samba server at all, is the Windows NT security descriptor assigned to that printer. This is the same security model used by Windows print servers. Figure 7-8 shows the default security descriptor assigned to a printer on standalone Samba server. The default access control entries created on a domain member server or domain controller will be slightly different in order to grant members of the *Domain Admins* group full control over printer attributes.

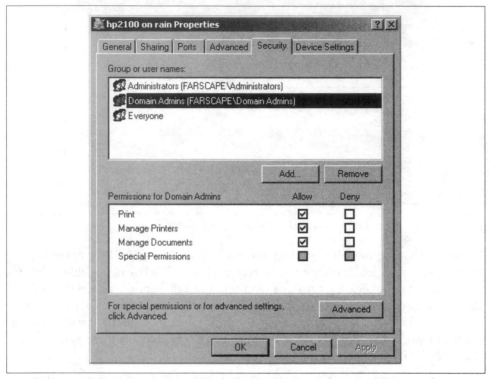

Figure 7-8. The Security tab in the printer properties dialog box of a Samba print share

The second layer of authorization controls is the standard set of *smb.conf* parameters, such as valid users and host allow. Note, however, that certain options such as force group are not currently enforced when printing from a Windows NT client variant, due to the way printer operations are carried out. For many sites, restricting access to printers via *smb.conf* setting is much easier. However, other sites require pure Windows semantics and choose to rely on the printer ACLs stored in *ntprinters.tdb*.

One final comment about Samba and print authorization: Samba currently provides no built-in means of performing page accounting for printers. This has traditionally been considered a job for the underlying printing system.

Disabling Point and Print

Under some circumstances, an administrator may wish to disable support for driver downloads and instead require that Windows clients install a driver locally when connecting to the Samba print share. This type of setup is not recommended, because it forces Samba to act in ways not normally supported by a Windows print server and hence not normally tested by Windows clients.

The p-n-p architecture rests on two supporting layers. Windows NT-based clients require that the print server support printing calls based on Microsoft Remote Procedure Call, or MS-RPC (often referred to by the named pipe over which they are implemented, *spoolss*). To disable Samba's support for the printing RPC operations without affecting the other RPC based features in Samba, such as domain membership or domain controlling, set `disable spoolss = yes` in the `[global]` section of *smb.conf*. This removes the Printers and Faxes icon from the clients' folders when they browse the server. The default value for this parameter is *no*, which means that *smbd* should support RPC-based printing.

Disabling *spoolss* support in Samba bas been known to cause Windows NT-based clients to continually poll the server for printer status updates, which results in high CPU usage by the associated *smbd* processes. Disabling *spoolss* support should be done only for very specific needs and only if you are willing to deal with the consequences.

Windows 95/98/Me clients use an older printing protocol referred to as LanMan printing. Therefore, disabling RPC-based printing has no affect on these clients.

Support for the *spoolss* set of RPC's is a global configuration option. Sometimes it is desirable to support p-n-p for the majority of printers on a Samba host, but allow clients to install a driver locally for a few specific print queues. This is a common need when the driver just doesn't work with a Samba print server.

This is one of those cases where forcing a Windows client into an untested use pattern can cause strange results. When a user connects to the driverless print queue, the client asks her to install a driver locally, as we have already seen. After doing so, the client creates a local printer object rather than a printer connection. Windows then frequently attempts to open the print queue on the server with administrative access that matches what it would expect for access to the local printer object. Of course, just because someone is a local administrator of their machine does not necessarily equate to *root* on a Unix print server. Samba (correctly) denies the request for excessive rights to the printer and the client will then display an error to the user that states, "Access denied; Unable to connect."

This is a very confusing error for the user, because she is still able to send documents to the printer without difficulty. The service option `use client driver` is designed to work around this cosmetic defect on the client. Enabling this parameter for a print share instructs Samba to map all requests for administrative access to standard print access. The result is that the client's original request succeeds. It never encounters the "Access denied" error from the server and hence never displays the confusing error message to the user.

It is important to remember that neither of these options should be enabled if the print queue is configured to support p-n-p for clients.

Printing, Queue Lists, and tdb Files

Samba has always played the role of masquerading Unix hosts as Windows servers. This role requires that certain Unix attributes be extended to present the information expected by Windows clients. Printing is no exception. Samba places a thin layer over Unix print jobs to store the additional information, such as the CIFS print job's numeric ID, the name of the print job (rather than the spool file name of *smbprnXXXX*), and the Windows security descriptor associated with the document in the queue. This information is maintained in each printer's queue cache database, located in the *printing* subdirectory of Samba's lock directory. These cache *tdb*s are used to enumerate job listings to clients such as the print queue monitor shown in Figure 7-9.

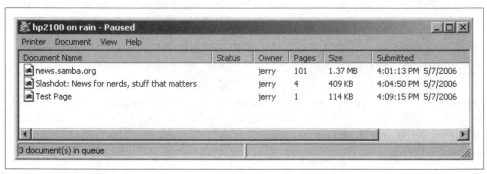

Figure 7-9. Listing of jobs in a Samba print queue from a Windows client

It can be expensive to reparse the output from the lpq command every time a client asks for an update on the status of a specific printer. The solution to this is to respond to the client request out of cache. This means that there is a lag between the real state of the Unix print queue and what is displayed to the Windows client. This lag is controlled by the integer value of the lpq cache time parameter. This value represent the expiration time in seconds of the cache file tdb contents. Current Samba releases default to a 30-second TTL.

Be very careful when tweaking this parameter. A smaller value may provide more accurate data to clients, but on a busy server with a large number of printer, the cost in CPU time is significant.

Sometimes it is desirable to restrict the maximum number of jobs accepted for a given queue. This can be done by defining the `max print jobs` option in the *smb.conf* print service. Setting the parameter to 0 (the default value) indicates that there should be no limit on the number of print jobs in the queue at any given time.

It is also possible to allow an unlimited number of jobs in the printer but restrict the number of jobs reported to a client by setting the `max reported print jobs` option. This is another performance tweaking option. It saves Samba from spending all its time composing a list of jobs to send back the client, only to find that by the time it finishes the list, its cache has already become outdated. Again, a value of 0 indicates that Samba should simply report the complete set of jobs without any restrictions on the list size.

You can thank the test engineers who believed Samba should scale to support more than 10,000 jobs in any given print queue at a time for these parameters. Of course, if you have that many jobs in a print queue, you probably have other problems with the printer. But at least Samba will happily report the situation and continue to do normal work.

Printing to Windows Printers

If you have printers connected to Windows systems, Samba can help you connect to these from Unix clients. First, it is necessary to create a printer share on the Windows system. Then, set up the printer on the Unix side by configuring a new printer and using a Samba printing program as the printer's filter.

Sharing Windows Printers

Sharing printers on Windows is not unlike sharing files. In fact, it is a little simpler. Open the Control Panel, then double-click the Printers icon to open the Printers window. Right-click the icon for the printer you want to share, and select Sharing… to open the dialog box shown in Figure 7-10 for a Windows Me system, or Figure 7-11 on a Windows Server 2003 system. (The dialog box appears slightly different on other Windows versions, but functions almost identically.)

Click the "Shared as" radio button, then click the OK button. The printer is now accessible by other systems on the network.

Adding a Unix Printer

The Samba distribution comes with three programs that assist with printing on shared printers. The *smbprint* program works with systems that use the BSD printing system, *smbprint.sysv* works with systems that use System V printing, and *smbspool* works with systems that use CUPS. In the following sections, we show you how to install printers for each system.

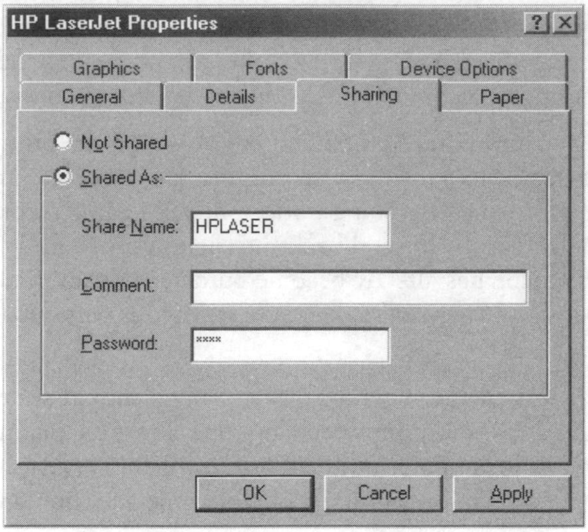

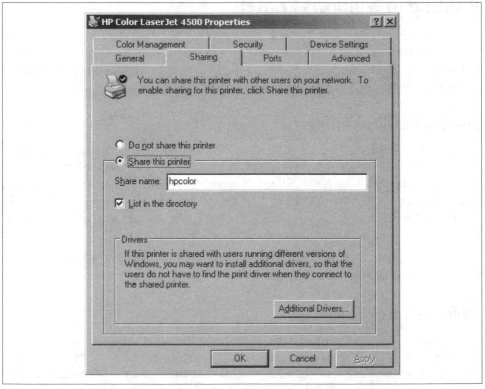

Figure 7-10. Sharing printers on Windows Me

Figure 7-11. Sharing printers on Windows 2003

BSD printers

The BSD printing system is used by many Unix variants. Here is the entry we added to our */etc/printcap* file to support our HP DeskJet 932C printer, which is shared by maya, a Windows 2003 system:

```
lp|maya-hp932c:\
    :cm=HP 932C on maya:\
    :sd=/var/spool/lpd/maya:\
    :af=/var/spool/lpd/maya/acct:\
    :if=/usr/local/samba/bin/smbprint:\
    :mx=0:\
    :lp=/dev/null:
```

The first line creates names for the printer. We are calling it maya-hp932c, to describe its location on the network and the type of printer, and lp, so that programs will use it as the default printer. The rest of the lines specify keywords and values. The cm keyword allows us to assign a comment string to the printer. The sd and af keywords assign the printer's spool directory and accounting files, respectively. The if keyword assigns the print filter. We are using the *smbprint* command to send the output to the shared SMB printer. The mx keyword is set to 0 to allow a file of any size to be printed, and lp is set to */dev/null* to discard error messages.

You can follow our model to create an entry for your own printer. If you want to go beyond the capabilities we used, refer to your system's *printcap(5)* manpage for a complete listing of keywords.

Go to your Samba source distribution's root directory and install the *smbprint* program like this:

```
$ cp examples/printing/smbprint /usr/local/samba/bin
```

Next create the printer's spool directory (as the root user):

```
$ cd /var/spool/lpd
$ mkdir maya
$ chown lp:lp maya
$ chmod 700 maya
```

The *smbprint* program looks for a file named *.config* in the printer's spool directory, which contains information on how to connect to the printer share. Therefore, create this file and fill in the required information:

```
$ cd maya
$ touch .config
$ chown lp:lp .config
$ chmod 600 .config
```

Use your preferred text editor to edit the *.config* file, and add the following:

```
server=maya
service=hpcolor
username=unix-print
password=Pr1n@ter
```

This example is for our shared printer, which has a UNC of *maya\hpcolor*. Notice that we are using a username of *unix-print* and a password of *Pr1n@ter*. It is important that these credentials do not grant access to any network resources except this printer, in case someone can read the file's contents. If possible, *unix-print* should be a special account on the Windows server used just for allowing Unix clients to access this printer.

Finally, restart the printer daemon using the normal procedure on your server. The following command works on a Linux system runing BSD printing.

```
$ /etc/init.d/lpd restart
```

You can now try printing something. Run the following command:

```
$ lpr textfile
```

If you have everything set up correctly, the file prints on the shared printer. If you get "stair stepping" of text, caused by the printer not returning to the left margin at the beginning of every line, modify the if keyword in your printcap entry to run *smb-print* with the -t option.

System V printers

Sending print jobs from a System V Unix system is a little easier than with the BSD system. Here, you need to edit the *smbprint.sysv* script in the *examples/printing* directory of the Samba distribution and do the following:

1. Change the server, service, and password parameters in the script to match the NetBIOS computer name, its shared printer service, and its password, respectively. For example, the following entries would be correct for the service in the previous example:

   ```
   server   = maya
   service  = hp
   username = unix-print
   password = Pr1n@ter
   ```

2. Run the following commands, which create a reference for the new printer (which we are naming hp_printer) in the printer capabilities file:

   ```
   $ lpadmin -p hp_printer -v /dev/null -i ./smbprint.sysv
   $ enable hp_printer
   $ accept hp_printer
   ```

After you've done that, restart the Samba daemons and try printing to hp_printer using any standard Unix program.

CUPS printers

CUPS uses a set of modules, called *backends*, to send print jobs to various destinations, such as local printers attached to parallel, serial, or USB ports, or over the network using Unix line printer daemon (LPD) protocol, Internet Printing Protocol

(IPP), AppleTalk Printer Access Protocol (PAP), and so on. The software package does not come with a backend for SMB; the Samba suite includes the *smbspool* utility for this purpose.

To enable printing to remote SMB printers using CUPS, create a symbolic link named *smb* in the CUPS backend directory pointing to *smbspool*. Depending on installation options, these could be in a number of places in the directory hierarchy, so be sure to check your system. Using a common default installation, the command would look like this:

```
$ ln -s /usr/local/samba/bin/smbspool /usr/lib/cups/backend/smb
```

Issue a HUP signal to the CUPS daemon, *cupsd*, and check for the existence of SMB support with the *lpinfo -v* command. Its output should now include a line that says network smb.

To add a printer, use the CUPS web interface, accessible on the local system at *http://localhost:631/*, or use the *lpadmin* command:

```
$ lpadmin -p hp932c -E -v smb://maya/hp932c -D "HP 932C on maya"
```

This command creates and enables a new print spool called hp932c. The -v argument specifies the printer device, which in this case is accessed over the network using an SMB URI. If the printer is not guest-accessible, you'll need to provide a username and password in the URI. The full format is as follows:

```
smb://[username[:password]@][workgroup/]server/printshare
```

The *lpadmin* command makes changes to */etc/cups/printers.conf* and sends a HUP signal to the *cupsd* daemon, resulting in the creation of a local raw printer spool. In this example, print data is passed in raw format to the Windows system, which has the necessary printer drivers and printer description files to format the data appropriately. The -D gives the printer a comment string.

Once you have the printer set up, it's time to test it out. CUPS understands both BSD-style and System V-style printing commands, so you can use whichever is more comfortable. Using the BSD *lpr* command, try something like:

```
$ lpr -P hp932c textfile
```

You should now be set up to use the printer from any application on the Unix system.

Printing Parameters

Some people would claim that printing should take a back seat to file serving or authentication services, but Samba proves that its support for the Windows printing model is not second-rate. We have shown that Samba is able to export Unix printers to Windows clients and help enable Unix clients to print to Windows print servers. And once Samba is configured for central driver management and p-n-p, only a trained eye can detect the differences between a Samba print server and a Windows one from a client's perspective.

Table 7-5 concludes this chapter with a reference of all the printing-related *smb.conf* parameters that we have discussed.

Table 7-5. smb.conf printing-related options

Parameter	Value	Description	Default	Scope
add printer command	string	External script called by Samba upon receiving an *AddPrinter( )* or *SetPrinter( )* request from a client.	None	Global
cups options	string	List of comma-separated options to be passed onto the CUPS library when printing a document.	None	Global
cups server	string	Name or IP address of the host running the cupsd daemon.	See CUPS *client.conf*	Global
default devmode	boolean	Instructs *smbd* to generate a generic DeviceMode for the print share.	no	Share
delete printer command	string	External script called by Samba upon receiving a request to remove a printer from the server.	None	Global
disable spoolss	boolean	Determines whether Samba should support the RPC printing protocol used by Windows NT-based client.	no	Global
force printername	boolean	Determines whether Samba should disallow storing the printer name as a separate attributer separate from the share name.	no	Share
load printers	boolean	Determines whether *smbd* should create print services for all entries in the printcap name file when starting, assuming that a valid [printers] share has been defined.	yes	Global
lpq cache time	integer	Integer value representing the time in seconds that a queue cache *tdb* should be considered valid.	30	Share
max print jobs	integer	Places an upper limit on the number of jobs that are allowed in a the print queue at any given time.	0	Share
max reported print jobs	integer	Places an upper limit on the number of jobs in a queue that are reported to clients at any given time.	0	Share
min print space	integer	An integer value defining the amount of free space in kilobytes that must be present in order for Samba to accept a new print job for this queue.	0	Share

Table 7-5. smb.conf printing-related options (continued)

Parameter	Value	Description	Default	Scope
path	string	When used in the context of a print share, this parameter defines the directory used to store jobs as they are being spooled from clients.	*/tmp*	Share
print ok	boolean	Defines the service as being a print share.	no	Share
printcap cache time	integer	Integer value specifying the interval in seconds used to poll the printcap name file for new or deleted printer entries.	750	Global
printcap name	string	Defines the file or service used to obtain a list of valid printers on the system.	Determined at compile time	Global
printer name	string	The name used to derive the value for the %p printing variable.	%S	Share
printing	enum	Defines the type of printing used for a specific file share. The available printing types are SYSV, AIX, HPUX, BSD, QNX, PLP, LPRNG, CUPS.	Determined at compile time	Share
use client driver	boolean	Determines whether Samba should map requests for administrative access to a printer to a lesser privilege value.	no	Share

## CHAPTER 8

Name Resolution and Network Browsing

Name resolution is critical to Samba's operation, because names are used to find the servers that share files or printers. *Network browsing* takes the task of finding servers to a new level of sophistication by allowing a user to delve down into a hierarchy of networks, domains, hosts, and services offered by each server. Although there are many ways to locate services on a network—such as the Service Location Protocol (SLP), Universal Plug-and-Play (UPnP), or even use of LDAP queries to search Active Directory—our focus is solely on Samba's role in browsing NetBIOS-based services.

Name resolution and browsing are not difficult to configure. However, some complexity is introduced by the variety of available name-resolution systems. Historically, Unix and other TCP/IP users have moved from a flat *hosts* file to the DNS, with the NIS or LDAP directory services as other popular choices. Meanwhile, Microsoft moved from a broadcasting system to a simple, LAN-only name server called WINS, and then to DNS.

All of these historical name resolution systems are still in use today. Finding a host is so crucial to networking that sites want robust name-resolution systems with fallback mechanisms in case the main system fails. Browsing is also complicated by the frequent need to show hosts in other subnets. This chapter shows you how to configure your network to handle name resolution and browsing any way you want.

Some of the differences between Unix and Microsoft networking implementations are the result of fundamental design goals. Unix networking was originally designed largely to implement a relatively formal group of systems that were assumed to be small in number, well-maintained, and highly available; that have static IP addresses; and that wouldn't physically move from place to place. Bringing a new server online was a labor-intensive task, but it did not have to be performed frequently. In contrast, Windows networking was originally developed as a peer-to-peer collection of small personal computers on a single subnet, having no centrally or hierarchically organized structure.

SMB networking is dynamic. Computers are allowed to leave the network at any time, sometimes without warning, and to join or rejoin the network at any time. Furthermore, any user in a Windows network can theoretically add a new shared resource to the network or remove a resource that was previously added. The change in the network's configuration is handled automatically by the rest of the network, without requiring any action by a system administrator.

Name Resolution

TCP/IP networks identify systems by IP addresses, and use a name resolution scheme to associate these addresses with more human-readable text names. In Microsoft's earliest networking implementations (for MS-DOS and Windows for Workgroups), the translation of names to network addresses was carried out in a manner similar to the Address Resolution Protocol (ARP) used on Ethernet networks today. When a system on the network needed an IP address corresponding to a name, it broadcasted the name to every other system on the network and waited for the system that owned the name to respond with its IP address.

The main problem with performing name resolution using broadcast packets is poor performance of the network as a whole, including CPU time consumed by each host on the network, which has to accept every broadcast packet and decide whether to respond to it. Also, broadcast packets usually aren't forwarded by routers, limiting name resolution to the local subnet. Microsoft's solution was to add Windows Internet Name Service (WINS) support to Windows NT, so that the computers on the network could perform a direct query of the WINS server instead of using broadcast packets.

Modern Windows clients use a variety of methods for translating hostnames into IP addresses. The exact method varies depending on the version of Windows the client is running and how the client is configured (i.e., whether a DNS server and/or WINS server is provided). In general, Windows uses some combination of the following methods:

- Looking up the name in its cache of recently resolved names
- Querying DNS servers
- Using a local *hosts* file
- Querying WINS servers
- Using a local *LMHOSTS* file
- Performing broadcast name resolution

The first method is self-explanatory. A hostname is checked against a cache of hostnames that have been recently resolved to IP addresses. This check helps to save time and network bandwidth for resolving names that are used frequently.

It is possible, although uncommon, for a Windows system to consult a local hosts file, as described in Chapter 3. DNS servers are very common in modern networks. When a Windows system is configured with the IP address of at least one DNS server, it can use DNS to resolve fully qualified domain names, such as those for sites on the Internet. The DNS servers can be either Windows or Unix systems. You can learn more about DNS and DNS server configuration in the book *DNS and BIND*, by Paul Albitz and Cricket Liu (O'Reilly).

WINS Clients and Server Interaction

There are two types of interaction between a WINS client and a server: the client keeps its own NetBIOS name (or names) registered with the server and queries the server to get the IP address corresponding to the NetBIOS name of another system.

When a WINS client joins the network, it registers its NetBIOS name with the WINS server, which stores it along with the client's IP address in the WINS database. This entry is marked *active*. The client is then expected to *refresh* the registration of its name periodically (typically, every four days) to inform the server that it is still using the name. This period is called the *time to live*, or TTL. When the client leaves the network by being shut down gracefully, it informs the server, and the server marks the client's entry in its database as *released*.

When a client leaves the network without telling the WINS server to release its name, the server waits until after it fails to receive the expected registration renewal from the client and then marks the entry as released.

In either case, the released name is available for use by other clients joining the network. It might persist in the released state in the WINS database, and if it is not reregistered, the entry is eventually deleted.

More information on WINS can be found in the Microsoft white paper "Windows Internet Naming Service (WINS) Architecture and Capacity Planning," which can be downloaded from the Microsoft web site (*http://www.microsoft.com*).

Setting Up Samba As a WINS Server

You can set up Samba as a WINS server by enabling the `wins support` parameter in the `[global]` section of the configuration file, like this:

```
[global]
    wins support = yes
```

The *wins.dat* file was mentioned in Chapter 2 while discussing Samba's database files. It is important to remember that the file does not reflect the current state of *nmbd*'s WINS database, but rather a snapshot of the registered names at a previous point in time. The file is read when *nmbd* starts and is synchronized with the in-memory tables periodically.

Samba 3.0 cannot currently replicate its database with any other WINS servers. If you are using Samba as your WINS server, you must make sure not to allow any Windows systems or other Samba servers on your network to be configured as WINS servers. If you do, their WINS databases will not synchronize, resulting in potentially inconsistent name resolution.

 Development code in Samba 4 supports the Windows WINS replication protocol and communicates with other WINS servers. Although this code is not part of the current Samba production releases, it can be installed as a separate service to handle your WINS infrastructure.

Proxying name resolution requests to DNS

Because Windows tries all possible mechanisms for translating a name to an IP address, a client might ask a WINS server to resolve the name of a server that has no relation to a NetBIOS service. For example, when a web browser tries to access an unqualified hostname, the name could be checked against Samba's WINS service. Therefore, unless configured otherwise, a Samba WINS server checks with the system's DNS server if a requested hostname (of type <00> or <20>) cannot be found in its WINS database. The *nmbd* daemon spawns a child process to handle the DNS lookups, so that the main process can continue to handle other incoming name requests. This method is similar to Microsoft's WINS and DNS implementation, which can share records in a common database.

Typical Unix systems maintain the IP address of the DNS server in */etc/resolv.conf*. The following configuration file indicates that the host should append a domain of *plainjoe.org* to unqualified hostnames when sending queries to the DNS server located at 192.168.1.56:

```
domain plainjoe.org
search plainjoe.org
nameserver 192.168.1.56
```

If you would prefer to restrict *nmbd* to search only its WINS database when answering name resolution requests, disable the dns proxy option in *smb.conf*:

```
[global]
    wins support = yes
    dns proxy = no
```

This option has no effect if Samba's WINS server functionality has not been enabled.

Catching WINS database modifications

The wins hook global option allows you to run a script or other program whenever the WINS database is modified. The script is passed four parameters that describe the modification:

- The command that was executed: add, delete, or refresh
- The name being modified

- The resource byte in hex of the name being modified
- The TTL of the request

When you define the WINS hook parameter in *smb.conf*, provide the absolute path to the external utility, as shown here:

```
[global]
    wins support = yes
    wins hook = /usr/local/bin/dns_update
```

The original design goal of this parameter was to provide a mechanism by which *nmbd* could synchronize a dynamic DNS server with a its WINS database. The *dns_update* script referred to in the previous *smb.conf* example is included in the *examples/scripts/wins_hook* directory of the Samba distribution.

Setting Up Samba to Use Another WINS Server

You can configure Samba to use one or more WINS servers somewhere else on the network by providing it with their IP addresses as values to the wins server directive:

```
[global]
    wins server = 192.168.1.2 192.168.1.3
```

The two servers in this example implicitly belong to a single, logical WINS group. It is assumed that the all servers within a group share a synchronized databases of registered names. Samba directs WINS registration and resolution requests to the first server in the group, failing over to the next host only when the first is unavailable.

The wins support and the wins server parameters are mutually exclusive; you cannot simultaneously offer Samba as the WINS server and use another system as the server. Typically, one Samba server is set up as the WINS server using wins support, and all other Samba servers are configured with the wins server parameter pointing to the Samba WINS server.

Configuring a WINS proxy

If you have a Samba server on a subnet that contains clients but has no WINS server, and the Samba server has been configured to use a WINS server on another subnet, you can tell the *nmbd* server to forward any name-resolution requests with the wins proxy option:

```
[global]
    wins server = 192.168.1.2 192.168.1.3
    wins proxy = yes
```

Use this only in situations where the WINS server resides on another subnet. Otherwise, the broadcast will reach the WINS server regardless of any proxying.

The lmhosts File

Chapter 3 explained how Windows systems can make use of an *LMHOSTS* file as an alternative to the WINS server for name resolution. Although its use is discouraged, Samba also can use an *lmhosts* file (default */usr/local/samba/lib/lmhosts*). Samba's *lmhosts* follows a limited form of the syntax provided by the Windows equivalent. A simple Samba *lmhosts* file might look like this:

```
192.168.1.1      TUMNUS
192.168.1.10     TURKISH
```

The names on the right side of the entries are NetBIOS names, so you can assign resource types to them and add additional entries for computers:

```
192.168.1.1      NARNIA#1B
```

Here, we've made TUMNUS the primary domain controller of the NARNIA domain. This line starts with TUMNUS's IP address, followed by the name NARNIA and the resource type <1B>.

If you wish to place an *lmhosts* file somewhere other than the default location, notify the *nmbd* process upon startup by using the -H option, followed by the name of your *lmhosts* file. However, because there is curently no way to instruct *smbd* to read an *lmhosts* from a location other than the one defined when the binaries were compiled, it is best to simply use the path returned from smbd -b | grep LMHOSTSFILE (or to avoid its use entirely).

 A bug existed in all versions of Samba 3.0 up until 3.0.21b that resulted in a failure to read any *lmhosts* filename specified using the -H option to *nmbd*. This is perhaps a testimony to how little *lmhosts* files are used on Samba servers.

Configuring Name Resolution for the Samba Suite

Daemons and tools in the Samba suite need to perform name resolution for internal use. For example, when *smbd* is required to contact a remote domain controller or *smbclient* connects to a host, Samba must act as a name resolution client. You can define the order in which the programs try each name-resolution method through the name resolve order parameter, like this:

```
[global]
    name resolve order = wins lmhosts hosts bcast
```

The parameter value list may be made up of up to four strings:

lmhosts
: Uses the Samba server's local *lmhosts* file.

hosts
: Uses the standard Unix name-resolution methods provided by the *gethostbyname()* C library call. Depending on how the server's operating system is configured, this call may result in a local *hosts* file lookup or a query to some name service such as DNS.

`wins`
> Use the WINS server, which may be the local Samba system itself, defined in *smb.conf.*

`bcast`
> Use a broadcast name resolve query.

The order in which the values are specified is the order in which name resolution is attempted. In our example, Samba attempts to use its WINS server first for name resolution (if one has been specified), followed by the *lmhosts* file on the local system (if it exists). Next, the `hosts` value tells it to ask the operating system to resolve the name. This is possible only if the name is for a server (a resource byte of <00> or <20>) or a domain controller.* Finally, if those three attempts fail, the server performs a broadcast name resolution.

Name-Resolution Configuration Options

A summary of Samba's name-resolution options discussed in this chapter is shown in Table 8-1.

Table 8-1. Name-resolution options

Parameter	Value	Description	Default	Scope
`wins support`	boolean	Controls whether *nmbd* will function as a WINS server.	no	Global
`wins server`	string (IP address or DNS name)	Identifies one or more WINS servers to use for name registration and resolution.	None	Global
`wins proxy`	boolean	Allows Samba to act as a proxy to a WINS server on another subnet.	no	Global
`wins hook`	string	External command to run when the WINS database changes.	None	Global
`dns proxy`	boolean	If set to yes, allows a Samba WINS server to search DNS if it cannot find a server name in WINS.	yes	Global
`name resolve order`	string	The order of methods used to resolve NetBIOS names.	`lmhosts wins host bcast`	Global

Network Browsing

Browsing was developed by Microsoft to help users find shared resources on the network. In a networked computing environment where users can add or remove shares

---

* Chapter 10 explains how Samba is able to use DNS when locating domain controllers for Active Directory domains.

at any time, it is important to have some automatic means of keeping track of the shared resources and allowing users to "browse" through them to find the ones they wish to use.

Before browsing was added to SMB networking, when anyone added a new share, the people with whom they wished to share the data or printer would have to be informed of the share's UNC, using some relatively low-tech method such as speaking to them in person or over the phone. Already this was very inconvenient in large organizations. To further complicate matters, the users working on client computers had to type in the share's UNC to connect to it. The only way to get around typing in the share's UNC every time it was used was to map a network drive to it, and with a large number of shares on the network, this could easily get out of hand.

Browsing in a Windows Network

To keep things simple, we first describe network browsing in a network that contains only Windows systems, and then show you how to add a Samba server.

The basic way browsing works is that one computer in the network takes on the role of the local master browser (LMB) and keeps a list of all the computers on the local subnet that are acting as CIFS servers. You might also see the LMB referred to as the *browse master*, the *browse server*, or simply the *master browser*. The list of computers is called the *browse list* and includes Samba servers, Windows NT-based systems, and any Windows 9x systems that have the File and Printer Sharing for Microsoft Networks networking component installed. The browse list also contains the names of all workgroups and domains. At this level, browsing is limited to the local subnet, because the browsing protocol depends on broadcast packets, which are typically not forwarded to other subnets by routers.

A user at any Windows system can view the browse list by opening up the My Network Places, as you saw in Chapter 1. Alternatively, the net view command can be used from a Windows command prompt to display the servers in our workgroup:

```
C:\> net view
Server Name            Remark
-------------------------------------------------------------
\\RAIN                 Samba 3.0.22
\\LETTUCE              Lee Zard's WinXP development box
\\XPOP                 Office Print Server
\\TRINITY              Office File Server
The command completed successfully.
```

Then, net view can be used with a computer name as an argument to contact a server directly and list the resources it is sharing:

```
C:\> net view \\RAIN
Shared resources at \\RAIN

Samba 3.0.22
```

```
Share name  Type   Used as  Comment
-------------------------------------------------------------
data        Disk            Test share for ACLs
hp2100      Print           HP LaserJet 2100 Series PCL 6
lizard      Disk   H:       Home directory of lizard
netlogon    Disk            Net Logon service
pdfgen      Print
public      Disk   P:       Public Access
The command completed successfully.
```

The computers on the network involved in browsing are more than just the master browser and its clients. There are also backup browsers, which maintain copies of the browse list and respond to client requests for it. Backup browsers are therefore able to take over the role of master browser seamlessly in case it fails. The master browser usually doesn't serve the browse list directly to clients. Instead, its job is mainly to keep the master copy of the browse list up-to-date, and also periodically update the backup browsers. Clients are expected to get their copies of the browse list from backup browsers, selecting among them randomly to help to distribute the load on the backup browsers more evenly. Ideally, the interaction between any client and the master browser is limited to the client announcing when it joins or leaves the network (if it is a server) and requesting a list of backup browsers.

There can be more than one backup browser. A workgroup will have a backup browser if two or more computers on the subnet are running a Windows desktop operating system with file and print sharing enabled. For every 32 additional computers, another backup browser is added.

In addition to acting as the local master browser, the Primary Domain Controller (PDC) acts as the domain master browser (DMB), which ties subnets together and allows browse lists to be shared between master and backup browsers on separate subnets. This is how browsing is extended to function beyond the local subnet. Each subnet functions as a separate browsing entity, and the domain master browser synchronizes the master browsers of each subnet. In a Windows-only network, browsing cannot function across subnets unless a PDC exists on the network.[*]

By default, each computer that participates in a browse election is considered a *potential browser*. It can be ordered by the browse master to become a backup browser or can identify itself as a backup browser and accept the role on its own.

Browser Elections

When no master browser is running on the subnet, potential browsers choose a new master browser among themselves in a process called an *election*. An election is

---

[*] Because all domain controllers in an AD domain are technically considered to be equals, one must be designated as the PDC emulator.

Browsing, Anonymous Sessions, and Security

Whether networks have become more hostile in recent years, or whether the hostility was always there and we have just recently become less trusting, the end result is that operating system vendors, Microsoft included, are reducing the amount of information that can be anonymously obtained about a host system. Network browsing originally relied upon being able to enumerate shares on a server without any user credentials, because many networks lacked any type of central authentication service at all.

Today the landscape is much different. Vendors attempt to protect their software from disclosing unnecessary information to unknown users. The simplicity of browsing on SMB/CIFS networks has become a casualty in the war against computer crime. No longer can you enumerate shares anonymously on modern Windows servers; however, if you are joined to a Windows domain where authentication is handled centrally, you probably haven't noticed.

However, if you are trying to follow the browsing examples in the chapter but receive "Access Denied" messages, or are prompted to log on every time you connect to a server, chances are that you need to either manually synchronize your password on the target servers or work within the context of an authentication domain.

If you don't have an existing domain, feel free to jump ahead to Chapter 9 and implement your own Samba-based domain.

started by a computer in the subnet when it discovers that no master browser is currently running. If a master browser is shut down gracefully, it broadcasts an election request datagram, initiating an election by the remaining computers. If the master browser fails, the election can be started by a client computer that requests a list of backup browsers from the master browser or by a backup browser that requests to have its browse list updated from the master browser. In each case, the system fails to receive a reply from the master browser and initiates the election.

Browser elections are decided in multiple rounds of self-elimination. During each round, potential browsers broadcast election request datagrams containing their qualifications to notify other potential browsers that an election is happening and that if the recipient is more qualified, it should also broadcast a bid. When a potential browser receives an election request datagram from a more qualified opponent, it drops out, disqualifying itself from becoming the master browser. Otherwise, it responds with its own election request datagram. After a few rounds, only one potential browser is left in the election. After an additional four rounds of sending out an election request datagram and receiving no response, it becomes the master browser and sends a broadcast datagram announcing itself as the local master browser for the subnet. It then assigns runners-up in the election as backup browsers, as needed.

A potential browser's qualifications include the following:

- Whether it has recently lost an election
- The version of the election protocol it is running
- Its election criteria
- The amount of time the system has been up
- The computer's NetBIOS name

If the potential browser has lost an election recently, it immediately disqualifies itself. The version of the election protocol it is running is checked, but so far, all Windows systems (and Samba) use the same election protocol, so the check is not very meaningful. The election criteria usually determine which computer becomes the LMB. There are two parts to the election criteria, shown in Tables 8-2 and 8-3.

Table 8-2. Operating system values in an election

Operating system	Value
Windows NT/2000/2003 domain controllers	32
Windows NT/2000/XP/2003 (domain member and standalone servers)	16
Windows 95/98/Me	1
Windows for Workgroups	1

Table 8-3. Computer role settings in an election

Role	Value
Domain master browser	128
WINS client	32
Preferred master	8
Running master	4
Recent backup browser	2
Backup browser	1

The operating system type is compared first, and the system with the highest value wins. The values have been chosen to cause the PDC, if there is one, to become the local master browser. Otherwise, a Windows NT/2000/XP/2003 system wins over a Windows for Workgroups or Windows 95/98/Me system.

When an operating system type comparison results in a tie, the role of the computer is compared. A computer can have more than one of the values in Table 8-3, in which case the values are added together.

A domain master browser has a role value of 128 to weigh the election so heavily in its favor that it also becomes the local master browser on its own subnet. Although the PDC (which is always the domain master browser) will win the election based solely on its operating system value, sometimes there is no primary domain controller on the network, and the domain master browser would not otherwise be distinguished from other potential browsers.

Systems that are using a WINS server for name resolution are weighted heavily over ones that use broadcast name resolution with a role value of 32.

A *preferred master* is a computer that has been selected and configured manually by a system administrator to be favored as the choice master browser. When a preferred master starts up, it forces a browser election, even if an existing master browser is still active. A preferred master has a role value of 8, and the existing master browser gets a value of 4.

A backup browser that has recently been a master browser and still has an up-to-date browse list is given a role value of 2, and a potential browser that has been running as a backup browser gets a value of 1.

If comparing the operating system type and role results in a tie, the computer that has been running the longest wins. In the unlikely event that the two have been up for the same amount of time, the computer that wins is the one with the NetBIOS name that sorts first alphabetically.

You can tell if a machine is a local master browser by using the Windows *nbtstat* command. Place the NetBIOS name of the machine you wish to check after the *-a* option:

```
C:\> nbtstat -a rain

Local Area Connection:
Node IpAddress: [192.168.1.88] Scope Id: []

        NetBIOS Remote Machine Name Table

    Name                Type       Status
    ---------------------------------------------
    RAIN           <00>  UNIQUE     Registered
    RAIN           <03>  UNIQUE     Registered
    RAIN           <20>  UNIQUE     Registered
    .._ _MSBROWSE_ _.<01> GROUP     Registered
    GARDEN         <00>  GROUP      Registered
    GARDEN         <1B>  UNIQUE     Registered
    GARDEN         <1C>  GROUP      Registered
    GARDEN         <1D>  UNIQUE     Registered
    GARDEN         <1E>  GROUP      Registered
```

The resource entry that you're looking for is .._ _MSBROWSE_ _.<01>. This entry indicates that the server is currently acting as the local master browser for the current subnet. The group entry with the workgroup name and a resource byte of <1D> is also indicative of a host operating as the LMB. All hosts that participate in browsing elections register the <1E> group name. The <1B> group name is registered only by the domain master browser. As mentioned before, Windows clients do not differentiate between the DMB and the primary domain controller function, so we also know that RAIN is the PDC for the GARDEN domain. As you will see in Chapter 9, all domain controllers register the <1C> group name.

Each instance of a workgroup on a given subnet has its own LMB, so the <1D> group name is never registered with WINS. You must use a broadcast query to resolve the name and should receive only one reply. The -M option to the *nmblookup* command can be used to locate the local master browser for a workgroup. The following example locates the LMB for the GARDEN workgroup at address 192.168.1.88:

```
$ nmblookup -M garden
querying garden on 192.168.1.255
192.168.1.88 garden<1d>
```

If the machine is a Samba server, you can also check the Samba *nmbd* logfile for an entry such as this:

```
nmbd/nmbd_become_lmb.c:become_local_master_stage2(406)
*****
Samba name server RAIN is now a local master browser for
workgroup GARDEN on subnet 192.168.1.0
```

 When *nmbd* receives a HUP signal, it dumps its current brows list of servers and workgroups to its logfile.

It is possible to find all machines that are potential browse servers on a subnet by performing a broadcast querying the <1E> group name:

```
$ nmblookup 'garden#1e'
querying garden on 192.168.1.255
192.168.1.88 garden<1e>
192.168.1.10 garden<1e>
192.168.1.132 garden<1e>
```

The domain master browser name is registered with the WINS server, because all LMB servers must be able to locate it. You can query the WINS server for the DMB's address by sending a directed name query to the WINS server at 192.168.1.74 (-U option) and setting the recursion bit in the request packet (-R option):

```
$ nmblookup -U 192.168.1.74 -R 'garden#1b'
querying garden on 192.168.56.1
192.168.1.88 far scape<1b>
```

Server Announcements

Each server on the network announces itself to the network to allow the master and backup browsers to build their browse lists. When first joining the network, a host sends server announcements every minute, but the interval is gradually stretched out to every 12 minutes. When a server is shut down gracefully, it sends an announcement that it is going offline to allow the master and backup browsers to remove it from the browse list. However, when a server goes offline by crashing or by some other failure, the master browser notices its disappearance only because it stops receiving server announcements. The master browser waits for three of the server's announcement periods before deciding that it is offline, which can take up to 36 minutes. Because backup browsers have their browse lists updated from the master browser once every 15 minutes, it can take up to 51 minutes for clients to be informed of a failed server.

For more detailed information on Microsoft's browsing protocols, consult the Microsoft documents "Browsing and Windows 95 Networking" and "CIFS/E Browser Protocol." You can find these by searching for the titles on the Microsoft web site: *http://www.microsoft.com*.

Configuring Samba for Browsing

Samba has full support for network browsing and can participate as a master browser, a backup browser, a domain master browser, a potential browser, or just a server that doesn't participate in browsing elections. By default, *nmbd* participates in elections. If you want to prevent this, simply disable the local master parameter in *smb.conf*:

```
[global]
    local master = no
```

Usually, Samba should be available as a local master or at least a backup browser. In the simplest case, you don't need to do anything, because Samba's default is to participate in browsing elections with its operating system value set to 20, which beats any Windows system less than a domain controller (see Table 8-2). The operating system value Samba reports for itself in browser elections can be set using the os level parameter:

```
[global]
    os level = 33
```

The preceding value allows Samba to beat even a Windows server acting as a primary domain controller. As we show in the following section, though, forcing Samba to win this way is not recommended.

If you want to allow a Windows XP system to be the master browser, you need to set Samba lower:

```
[global]
    os level = 8
```

The maximum value for os level is 255. Supposing we wanted to make absolutely sure that our Samba server is the local master browser at all times, we might say:

```
[global]
    local master = yes
    os level = 255
    preferred master = yes
```

The addition of the preferred master parameter instructs *nmbd* to initiate a browser election as soon as it starts up, and the os level of 255 allows it to beat any other system on the network. This includes other Samba servers, assuming they are configured properly. If another server is using a similar configuration file (with os level = 255 and preferred master = yes), the two will fight each other for the master browser role, winning elections based on minor criteria, such as uptime or their current role. To avoid this, other Samba servers should be set with a lower os level and not configured to be the preferred master.

Samba As the Domain Master Browser

Previously, we mentioned that for a Windows workgroup or domain to extend into multiple subnets, one system has to take the role of the domain master browser. The DMB propagates browse lists across each subnet in the workgroup. This works because each local master browser periodically synchronizes its browse list with the domain master browser. During this synchronization, the local master browser passes on the name of any server that the domain master browser does not have in its browse list, and vice versa. Each local master browser eventually holds the browse list for the entire domain.

There is no election to determine which machine assumes the role of the domain master browser. Instead, it has to be manually configured by an administrator. By Microsoft's design, however, the domain master browser and the PDC both register a resource type of <1B>, so the roles—and the machines—are inseparable. If you have a Windows server on the network acting as a PDC, do not configure Samba to become the domain master browser. More about Samba's domain controlling functions is covered in Chapter 9.

If there is no existing PDC, Samba can assume the role of a domain master browser for all subnets in the workgroup with the following options:

```
[global]
    domain master = yes
    preferred master = yes
    local master = yes
    os level = 33
```

The final three parameters ensure that the server is also the local master browser, which is vital for it to work properly as the domain master browser. You can verify that a Samba machine is in fact the domain master browser by checking the *nmbd* logfile:

```
nmbd/nmbd_become_dmb.c:become_domain_master_stage2(118)
*****
Samba name server RAIN is now a domain master browser for
workgroup GARDEN on subnet 192.168.1.0
```

You previously saw how to query a WINS server for the <1B> group name, but you can also use a broadcast name query, as shown here:

```
$ nmblookup 'GARDEN#1b'
Sending queries to 192.168.1.255
192.168.1.88 GARDEN<1b>
```

Samba Browsing Enhancements

You must remember three rules when creating a workgroup/domain that spans more than one subnet:

- You must have either a Windows NT-based host or a Samba server acting as a local master browser on each subnet in the workgroup/domain.
- You must have a Windows PDC or a Samba server acting as a domain master browser somewhere in the workgroup/domain.
- A WINS server should be on the network, with each system on the network configured to use it for name resolution.

If your entire browsing infrastructure is run by Samba, some additional features are available to work around deviations from the standard LMB/DMB/WINS browsing architecture. Consider the subnets shown in Figure 8-1.

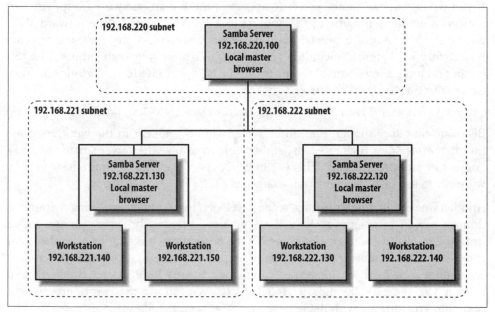

Figure 8-1. Multiple subnets with Samba servers

Under normal circumstances, hosts on one subnet would learn of servers on another subnet by browse list propagation through the workgroup's DMB. Samba, however, is not tied to the DMB requirement and can use the `remote announce` configuration option to make sure that computers in different subnets are sent broadcast announcements about itself, which has the effect of ensuring that the Samba server appears in the browse lists of foreign subnets. To achieve this effect, the directed broadcasts must reach the local master browser on the other subnet. Be aware that many routers do not allow directed broadcasts by default; you might have to change this setting on the router for the directed broadcasts to get through to its subnet.

With the `remote announce` option, list the broadcast or IP addresses that should receive the announcement. For example, to ensure that machines in the 192.168.220 and 192.168.222 subnets get broadcast information from your Samba server, specify the following:

```
[global]
    remote announce = 192.168.220.255 192.168.222.255
```

Instead of supplying the broadcast address of the remote subnet, you can specify the exact address where broadcasts should be sent if the local master browser on the foreign subnet is guaranteed to always have the same IP address, such as when a Samba host has been configured to always win the browse election.

If you would like the Samba server to appear in more than one workgroup, you can append a workgroup name to the address to each address using the forward slash character (/). The `remote announce` setting allows you to send server announcements for arbitary workgroups, including additional groups on your own subnet. The following example allows Samba to be seen in the PARK and PICNIC workgroups in addition to our own on the 192.168.221 subnet:

```
    remote announce = 192.168.221.255/PARK 192.168.221.255/PICNIC
```

Be aware that even though the Samba server will now appear in the workgroup list on the remote subnet, clients must still be able to resolve the server's name to an IP address in order to access it. This is why WINS is considered a requirement for any widespread use of browsing within a large network.

Another means of implementing some level of cross subnet browsing without a domain master browser is to have the Samba local master browser synchronize its browse list directly with one or more Samba servers, each acting as a local master browser on a different subnet. For example, let's assume that our Samba server is configured as a local master browser, and that Samba local master browsers also exist at 192.168.220.100 and 192.168.222.120. We can use the `remote browse sync` option to sync directly with the remote Samba servers, as follows:

```
[global]
    remote browse sync = 192.168.220.100  192.168.222.120
```

You can also use directed broadcasts with this option if you do not know specific IP addresses of local master browsers. However, the `remote browse sync` functionality works only with other Samba servers.

Browsing Options

Table 8-4 shows options that specify how Samba should handle browsing tasks.

Table 8-4. Browsing configuration options

Parameter	Value	Desscription	Default	Scope
`local master`	boolean	If yes, allows Samba to participate in browsing elections.	yes	Global
`preferred master`	boolean	If yes, allows Samba to use the preferred master browser bit to attempt to become the local master browser.	yes (if both local master and domain master options are enabled)	Global
`domain master`	boolean	If yes, allows Samba to become the domain browser master for the workgroup or domain.	no	Global
`os level`	numeric (0–255)	Operating system level of Samba in an election for local master browser.	20	Global
`remote browse sync`	string (list of IP addresses)	Samba servers with which to synchronize browse lists.	None	Global
`remote announce`	string (IP address / workgroup pairs)	Subnets and workgroups to send directed broadcast packets to, allowing Samba to appear in their browse lists.	None	Global

## CHAPTER 9

Domain Controllers

Our discussion of Samba up to this point has focused on file and print servers that authenticate users against a local set of accounts; these accounts had to previously be added to the system hosting Samba using either *pdbedit* or *smbpasswd*. Standalone servers (also called workgroup servers) have the advantages of being easy to set up and possessing no dependencies on external services. However, managing user accounts on more than two or three of these servers quickly becomes onerous.

Our systems administration mantra is, "Reduce redundancy through consolidation." Creating a Samba domain removes duplicate users and groups from each standalone server by consolidating these accounts onto a small set of domain controllers that can process authentication requests on behalf of domain member servers. Coupled with Microsoft's networking facility that allows a user to log in to her local workstation via a domain account, a Samba domain provides a means to centrally manage all authentication, not just access to file and print services.

In this chapter, we show you how to configure Samba as a Primary Domain Controller (PDC) with one or more Samba Backup Domain Controllers (BDC), and how to join Windows clients to this domain. Domains by themselves have little relevance without users and groups, so we also explore the mechanisms to manage and store user and group accounts. After you have a solid understanding of how to configure Samba's domain controller functionality, we explain how to migrate a Windows NT 4.0 domain to a Samba domain and retain the complete list of accounts and user settings. We conclude with a discussion of remotely monitoring and managing Samba hosts using tools such as the Windows Event Viewer, the Service Control Manager, and the Performance Monitor.

Samba Domains: NT 4.0 or Active Directory?

Before we dive into the technical details of Samba's domain controller functionality, it is important that you understand what a Samba domain offers, what it currently lacks, and where the project is headed. As stated in Chapter 1, Samba 3.0 can act as a Windows NT 4.0 domain controller, with one major exception. It does not implement the Windows System Account Manager (SAM) replication protocol. This means that it cannot participate as a domain controller with Windows DCs in either an NT 4.0 or mixed-mode Active Directory domain. However, this limitation is not usually a deterrent to deploying a Samba domain. As you will see later in this chapter, it is possible to configure a domain composed solely of Samba DCs. Samba 3.0 cannot at this time act as a domain controller for an Active Directory domain.

Configuring a Samba PDC

To build a Samba Primary Domain Controller, it is best to begin with a working standalone file server. We assume the following configuration:

```
[global]
    netbios name = STORK
    workgroup = ORA
    security = user
    encrypt passwords = yes

[public]
    path = /data/public
    read only = no
```

There are five minimum requirements that must be met by a Samba PDC:

1. User mode security (security = user)
2. Support for encrypted passwords (encrypt passwords = yes)
3. A properly configured [netlogon] file share
4. Configuration as a Domain Master Browser (domain master = yes)
5. Configuration as a logon server (domain logons = yes)

Our initial *smb.conf* meets the first two requisites. The next step is to add a [netlogon] file share that emulates the NETLOGON service on Windows domain controllers. The share itself must be readable by all domain users, so that they can access items such as policy files and login scripts (covered later in this chapter), but should restrict write access solely to administrators. This example specifies the share as read only, but includes the *ntadmin* group in the write list; *ntadmin* is our primary group for systems administrators:

```
[netlogon]
    comment = Net Logon service
    path = /data/netlogon
    read only = yes
    write list = +ntadmin
```

Enabling the domain master parameter in the global section of *smb.conf* causes *nmbd* to register the *DOMAIN<0x1b>* name (ORA<0x1b> in our example). This name is used by Windows clients to locate the PDC for a domain. When searching for any domain controller, not necessarily just the PDC, a Windows client attempts to resolve the *DOMAIN*<0x1c> name. You can instruct *nmbd* to register this name (e.g., ORA<0x1c>) by setting the domain logons option in *smb.conf*. Our PDC's new global configuration looks like this:

```
[global]
    netbios name = STORK
    workgroup = ORA
    security = user
    encrypt passwords = yes

    ## enable PDC functionality
    domain master = yes
    domain logons = yes
```

It is not required that the PDC act as the local master browser, but most are configured to operate in this role as well. To achieve this, add the following browsing-related parameters to the global section. Review the previous chapter if you need a reminder regarding any of these three parameters.

```
os level = 33
preferred master = yes
local master = yes
```

After making these changes, it is best to restart both *smbd* and *nmbd*. Wait approximately one minute for *nmbd* to complete its name registration process. Then use *nmblookup* to verify that both the 0x1c and 0x1b names have been claimed. It is normal to see more than one IP address when querying for the 0x1c name if you have one or more backup domain controllers configured on your network. In our case, we have only the PDC so far:

```
$ nmblookup 'ORA#1b' 'ORA#1c'
querying ORA on 192.168.1.255
192.168.1.88 ORA<1b>
querying ORA on 192.168.1.255
192.168.1.88 ORA<1c>
```

You can also verify the name registration in *nmbd*'s logfile. A successful logon server (0x1c) registration generates a log entry like the following.

```
become_logon_server_success: Samba is now a logon server
    for workgroup ORA on subnet 192.168.1.88
```

When configured as the DMB, *nmbd* logs this message:

```
Samba server STORK is now a domain master browser for
    workgroup ORA on subnet 192.168.1.88
```

Setting Up Domain Joins

Now that you have a working Samba DC, the next step is to add Windows clients to the domain. Before moving to that topic, however, let's go over some background on computer accounts.

When joining a domain, the client establishes a password known only to itself and the domain controller. This password is called the machine trust account password and is used to prove the identity of the computer each time it contacts the DC (normally upon booting). For security purposes, hosts running Windows 2000 and later require that you provide credentials for an administrative account that can potentially create the new machine account and assign it a random password.

Originally, Windows NT 4.0 allowed an administrator to create the client's machine trust account in advance using the Server Manager application. This new account was then assigned a predefined password based on the machine name. Therefore any user who knew the name could then join a computer to the domain.

The goal, then, is to complete the following tasks:

- Create the Domain Admins group for the purpose of managing user rights.
- Provide a set of users with administrative rights to join hosts to the domain.
- Implement the infrastructure necessary to manage these machine accounts.

Domain Admins

Domain Admins is a special group in Windows domains. The group's RID is always 512. When a Windows client joins a domain, it adds this domain group to its local Administrators group. The result is that members of Domain Admins automatically gain administrative privileges on all domain members. Samba honors membership in the Domain Admins group as well, by granting all Domain Admins the ability to manage the user rights assignments necessary to authorize users to join hosts to the domain.*

 Samba 3.0 does not currently support localized versions of the Domain Admins group name, such as the German name Domänen-Administratoren.

In order to create a group mapping entry for this special domain RID, you must first look up the SID of the ORA domain. You must be *root* for all the command examples in this section. Get the SID as follows:

```
# net getlocalsid ORA
SID for domain ORA is: S-1-5-21-3489264249-1556752242-1837584028
```

Now append the Domain Admins RID to the domain SID and create a group mapping entry for it:

```
# net groupmap add sid=S-1-5-21-3489264249-1556752242-1837584028-512 \
    ntgroup="Domain Admins" unixgroup=ntadmin
Successfully added group Domain Admins to the mapping db
```

---

* Remember to set enable privileges = yes in *smb.conf*.

Now all members of the *ntadmin* Unix group will be seen as domain administrators by both Samba and Windows clients.

 Depending on your version of Samba and which passdb has been configured, it may be necessary to use *net groupmap*'s modify command instead of add. Try add first, and then try modify if add fails.

Required privileges

Samba uses the SeMachineAccountPrivilege right to authorize a user or group to join a computer to the domain. Now is a good time to review the "User Privilege Management" section in Chapter 5 if you need a refresher on the *net rpc rights* command. Remember that new privilege assignments, like membership in a new group, are not applied to the user's token until the next session.

The best way to manage user rights is to assign a privilege to a group and then add the appropriate users to that group. In order to grant and revoke privileges, you must connect either as *root* or a member of the Domain Admins group. Our examples connect using the account *cindy*, who is a member of Domain Admins.

When a client joins a Samba domain, it performs the network equivalent of running *pdbedit -a machinename*. Normally, this type of request must be executed as *root*. But you can create a group mapping entry and assign it the SeMachineAccountPrivilege privilege to make *smbd* perform the account creation for members of this group as *root*.

Create the Server Admins Windows group based on the Unix group *srvadmin* and grant then the powers to manage users. The following commands create the group mapping entry and then (using the *cindy* account) assign the "Add machines to domain" right to the group:

```
# net groupmap add unixgroup=srvadmin ntgroup="Server Admins"
Successfully added group Server Admins to the mapping db

# net rpc rights grant 'ORA\Server Admins' SeMachineAccountPrivilege \
  -S stork -U cindy
Password: <enter cindy's password>
Successfully granted rights.
```

All Samba users must possess a matching Unix account. Therefore, Samba lets administrators create a matching Unix account at the time a host is joined to the domain. The add machine script option refers to an external utility that *smbd* invokes to generate the Unix account when it receives the network request to create a machine account. If the matching Unix account already exists, the script is ignored.

Because the process of creating users varies widely from one Unix platform to another, Samba does not include a default setting for this option. Usually it is possible to use some variant of a tool provided by the operating system.

The following example of a setting for add machine script comes from a Samba PDC running on Linux. The script invokes the *useradd* command to create the account referenced by the %u variable, assign its primary group membership to the *hosts* Unix group (which already exists), and set its login shell to */bin/false*. Thanks to the login shell setting, the user cannot log in and cause any mischief on the Linux host; all she can do is access Samba files.

```
add machine script = /usr/sbin/useradd -g hosts -s /bin/false '%u'
```

The *ldapsam passdb* supports a distinct search suffix for machine accounts. The ldap machine suffix works just like the ldap user suffix, but is intended for storing machine accounts. There is no harm in omitting this parameter. If no machine search suffix is defined, *smbd* falls back to the user search base. However, if you plan to use a separate subtree for storing machine accounts and are integrating the Samba attributes with the posixAccount object class, make sure that the server's LDAP NSS library can find both users and machines. This is commonly achieved by specifying multiple *passwd* search bases in the library's configuration file.

Table 9-1 gives a summary of the new *smb.conf* option presented in this section. In the next section we'll test the new configuration.

Table 9-1. The add machine script option

Parameter	Value	Description	Default	Scope
add machine script	string	Defines the external command to invoke when *smbd* must create a Unix user for a machine trust account.	" "	Global

Joining a Windows client

The best way to understand how domain joins and the add machine script work together is to actually join a client to our domain. We'll use a Windows XP Professional client in the following examples. Remember from Chapter 3 that Windows XP Home Edition has been crippled to remove its domain join capabilities.

Begin by navigating to the System Properties dialog box. You can access this in several ways, but the one that works most consistently is to run *control.exe sysdm.cpl* from a command prompt or from the Run... option in the Start Menu. In the properties window, navigate to the Computer Name tab (called Network Identification in Windows 2000) and select Change (Properties in Windows 2000). The dialog boxes should appear similar to Figure 9-1. Here you can change the client's machine name or domain membership.

After entering the domain name ORA and clicking OK, you will be presented with a dialog box requesting credentials to join the domain (Figure 9-2). Continue to use the account details for cindy, because she is also a member of the srvadmin Unix group, which was granted the rights necessary to join hosts to the domain.

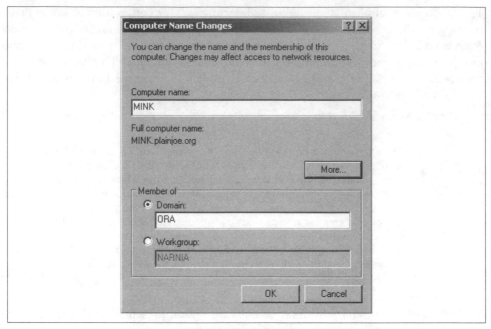

Figure 9-1. Computer Name Changes dialog on Windows XP

Figure 9-2. Entering credentials to join the domain

The Windows client then contacts the Samba PDC and uses these credentials to send the request to create the machine account and sets its password. If all of this succeeds, you will be greeted with the success message shown in Figure 9-3: "Welcome to the ORA domain."

Figure 9-3. Welcome message upon successful registration

There are a couple of places where this process can fail. The most common errors are:

Access Denied
> The user account does not possess the sufficient privilege to join clients to the domain. Verify the account's assigned rights using *net rpc rights*.

Logon Failure
> Ensure that you entered the user's password correctly.

The username could not be found
> The add machine script failed to create the Unix account. Make sure that the script is functioning as expected. Clues to the root cause of the failure can be found in Samba's logfiles. For example, a typo in the primary group name when calling *useradd* might result in a message such as useradd: Unknown group hoss.

If you find an error not listed here, try increasing the Samba debug log levels to search for more clues and consider some of the techniques described in Chapter 12.

After a successful join and client reboot, you are able to select the domain when logging into the Windows console. Figure 9-4 displays the drop-down list of domains shown on our XP client. The local machine name MINK is present in the list, as is the ORA domain. The BOOKS domain is an Active Directory domain that is trusted by ORA. We examine domain trusts later in this chapter.

Managing Users and Groups

The main purpose of a domain is to centralize authentication services. With this in mind, we turn our attention to users and groups. Traditionally, Windows administrators have used the User Manager for Domains application (sometimes referred to simply as *usrmgr.exe*) to create, modify, and remove accounts within NT 4.0 domains. Windows NT 4.0 server administration tools such as *usrmgr.exe* can be found in the latest Windows NT 4.0 service pack from *http://www.microsoft.com*.

> Neither the Windows 2000/XP local user tools such as *lusrmgr.msc* or the Active Directory domain tools support managing users and groups in Windows NT 4.0 equivalent domains.

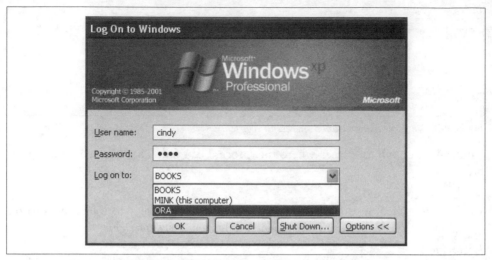

Figure 9-4. The Ctrl+Alt+Del logon dialog box showing a drop-down list of domains

Enabling remote account management support in Samba requires a few additional configuration pieces. Samba divides responsibilities between the list of accounts in its own *passdb* and those underlying Unix users and groups to which the *passdb* entries correspond. Samba continues to manage its own account attributes, but *smbd* requires help to manage these Unix identities just as it did for machine accounts. This is achieved through a collection of scripts defined in the global section of *smb.conf* that allow Samba to perform the following actions:

- Create a new user (add user script)
- Remove an existing user (delete user script)
- Change the login name associated with a user (rename user script)
- Create a new group (add group script)
- Remove an existing group (delete group script)
- Set a user's primary group (set primary group script)
- Assign a secondary group to a user (add user to group script)
- Remove a group from a user's list of supplementary groups (delete user from group script)

You'll notice that there is no parameter for renaming groups. The name stored in the group mapping table is handled by Samba independently of the Unix group name. When renaming a group, only the group map entry is updated.

Similar to our earlier discussion regarding machine accounts, creating a user or group is very platform-specific. Therefore, you must find a solution that works for your server. Following is one example of how to set up these scripts on a Linux server. The following list of configuration parameters makes use of the tools in the *pwdutils* package included with Novell's SuSe Linux. However, such values should be portable across most Linux distributions. The %u and %g variables are expanded to the user and group names sent in the client's request.

```
[global]
    add user script = /usr/sbin/useradd -m '%u'
    delete user script = /usr/sbin/userdel '%u'
    rename user script = /usr/sbin/usermod -l '%unew' '%uold'
    add group script = /usr/sbin/groupadd '%g'
    delete group script = /usr/sbin/groupdel '%g'
    add user to group script = /usr/sbin/groupmod -A '%u' '%g'
    delete user from group script = /usr/sbin/groupmod -D '%u' '%g'
    set primary group script = /usr/sbin/usermod -g '%g' '%u'
```

These commands are fairly intuitive and do what you would expect. For example, *useradd* creates the Unix user, and *usermod* can be used to rename an account. More information on the specifics of *useradd* and other account management tools can be found in the server operating system's manpages.

> The *smbldap-tools* package included in the */examples/LDAP* subdirectory of the Samba source distribution is a set of user management scripts for hosts configured to use the *ldapsam passdb* backend. They assume a certain namespace and layout within the LDAP DIT. More information can be found at *http://samba.idealx.org*.

Once this infrastructure is in place, any user possessing the SeAddUsersPrivilege on the server can create and modify accounts directly from a Windows desktop. Don't be confused by the name. This privilege that purports to "Add users and groups to the domain" can also modify existing accounts. The following command allows members of Server Admins to manage users and groups:

```
# net rpc rights grant 'ORA\Server Admins' SeAddUsersPrivilege \
  -S stork -U cindy
Password: <enter cindy's password>
Successfully granted rights.
```

> When run on a Windows 2000/XP/2003 host, a bug in User Manager for Domains prevents it from being able to manipulate user rights on a Samba (or Windows NT 4.0) DC. For this reason, it is recommended that you always use *net rpc rights* to manage privilege assignments on Samba hosts.

Commands that grant privileges are cumulative. You can review the list of privileges assigned to a user or group using the *net rpc rights list* command. The following command anonymously (through the -U% option) enumerates the rights possessed by the Server Admins group:

```
# net rpc rights list accounts 'ORA\Server Admins' -U% -S stork
SeMachineAccountPrivilege
SeAddUsersPrivilege
```

Now launch User Manager for Domains. You will be greeted with a list of users and groups and should be able to match the output from *pdbedit -L -w* to the list of users and the output from *net groupmap list* to the list of groups. Figure 9-5 shows the users and groups in the ORA domain. The following commands confirm that the list of accounts matches what is reported from Samba's own tools. The output has been trimmed to list solely the user and group names for easier reading. Also notice that the machine accounts (ones ending with a dollar sign) are not listed by User Manager, which filters them from the display.

```
# pdbedit -L -w | cut -d: -f 1
KNOT$
DORN$
POLE$
MINK$
jerry
BOOKS$
lizard
STORK$
cindy

# net groupmap list | cut -d \( -f 1
Printer Admins
staff
Domain Users
Server Admins
helpdesk
Administrators
Linux Users
Domain Admins
Users
```

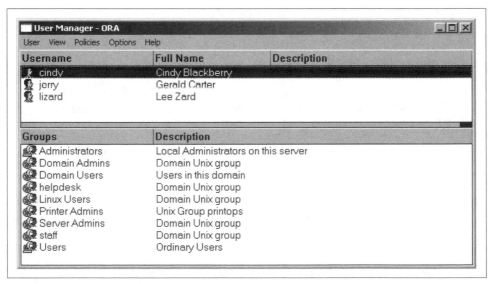

Figure 9-5. Users and groups in the ORA domain

You can launch the New User dialog from the the User menu. Figure 9-6 shows the creation of a new account named mark; Figure 9-7 illustrates how to manage *mark*'s group membership.

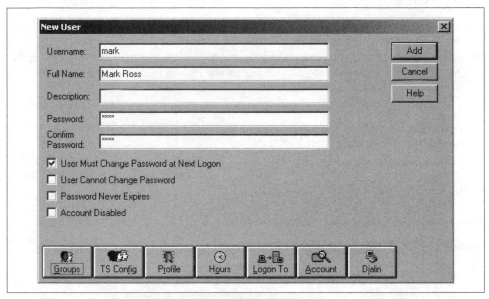

Figure 9-6. Creating a new user named mark

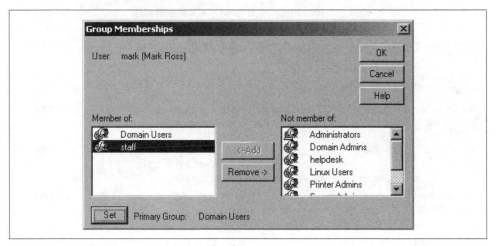

Figure 9-7. Managing a user's group membership

After adding the new account, verify that it was created by examining */etc/passwd* and Samba's passdb. The new Unix account should be present in the system *passwd* file:

```
$ grep mark: /etc/passwd
mark:x:10026:1008::/home/mark:/bin/bash
```

The output from *pdbedit* also confirms the new Samba account:

```
# pdbedit -L -w mark
mark:10026:01FC5A6BE7BC6929AAD3B435B51404EE:0CB6948805F797BF2A82807973B89537:
[U]:LCT-44D8C4C1:
```

If you observe any failures in *usrmgr.exe*, the troubleshooting tips for resolving domain join failures, described in Chapter 10, apply to managing users. Verify that the connected user has been granted the appropriate level of privileges and scan the Samba logfiles for more information regarding the reason for the failure.

 After remote account management has been enabled, you can also use the *net rpc user* and *net rpc group* commands covered in Chapter 11 to manage your Samba DC.

Table 9-2 provides a brief listing of the account management parameters introduced in this section.

Table 9-2. User and group management options

Parameter	Value	Description	Default	Scope
add group script	string	External command to invoke when *smbd* must create a Unix group.	" "	Global
add user script	string	External command to invoke when *smbd* must create a Unix user.	" "	Global
add user to group script	string	External command to invoke when *smbd* must add a group to a user's list of secondary groups.	" "	Global
delete group script	string	External command to invoke when *smbd* must remove a Unix group.	" "	Global
delete user script	string	External command to invoke when *smbd* must delete a Unix user.	" "	Global
delete user from group script	string	External command to invoke when *smbd* must remove a group from a user's list of secondary groups.	" "	Global
rename user script	string	External command to invoke when *smbd* must rename a Unix user. The old name is expanded from %uold and the new name is expanded from %unew.	" "	Global
set primary group script	string	External command to invoke when *smbd* must change a Unix user's primary group membership.	" "	Global

User Profiles

User roaming profiles, sometimes called roving profiles, provide a way for a domain user to customize elements of his environment such as the desktop wallpaper, application defaults, and desktop shortcuts. Such profiles give users a more "at home" feeling when they move from machine to machine. Figure 9-8 displays the User Environment Profile setting dialog box provided by *usrmgr.exe*. With the exception of the Terminal Server settings, we'll discuss each one of these fields shortly.

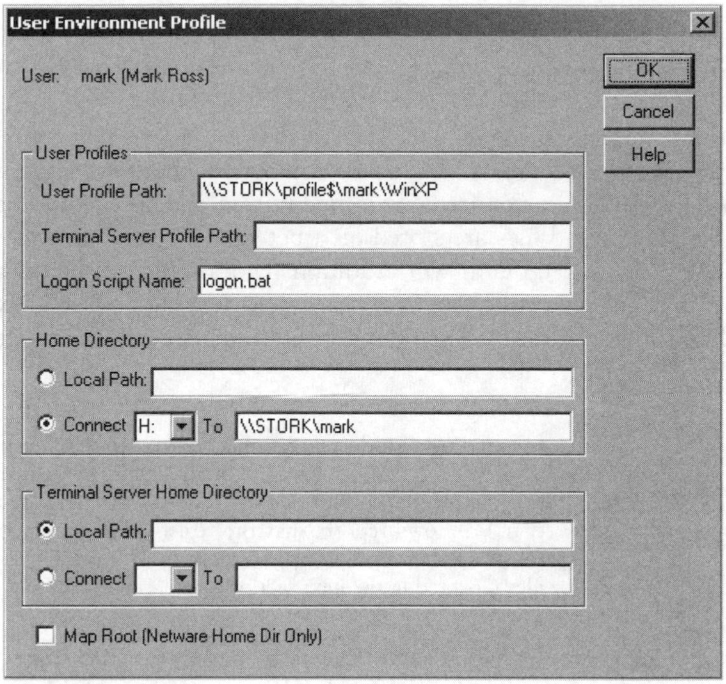

Figure 9-8. The User Environment Profile dialog box in User Manager for Domains

Our focus is on making a Samba DC support Windows user profiles, not on Windows-specific tasks such as editing the registry or updating shortcuts. More information on these topics can be found in the plethora of currently available Windows administration books and online articles. A definitive guide to user profiles can be found in the white paper titled "Implementing Policies and Profiles for Windows NT 4.0," available through a search at *http://www.microsoft.com*.

First it is important to understand exactly what composes a user profile. Roughly speaking, a profile is a collection of application settings. Some of these settings may be stored in the user's registry hive (*NTUSER.DAT*), and others may be stored as files on disk. The following is a list of the top-level files and directories composing a Windows XP user profile:

```
$ ls -l
total 880
drwx-----T+ 5 cindy helpdesk   4096 Aug  8 13:33 Application Data
drwx-----T+ 2 cindy helpdesk   4096 May 21 20:52 Cookies
drwx-----T+ 2 cindy helpdesk   4096 May 21 15:26 Desktop
drwx-----T+ 3 cindy helpdesk   4096 Aug  6 16:32 Favorites
drwx-----T+ 4 cindy helpdesk   4096 Aug  6 16:32 My Documents
-rwx------  1 cindy helpdesk 786432 Aug  8 14:20 NTUSER.DAT
drwx-----T+ 2 cindy helpdesk   4096 May 21 15:26 NetHood
drwx-----T+ 2 cindy helpdesk   4096 May 21 15:26 PrintHood
drwx-----T+ 2 cindy helpdesk   4096 Aug  8 12:07 Recent
```

```
drwx-----T+ 2 cindy helpdesk   4096 Aug  6 16:31 SendTo
drwx-----T+ 3 cindy helpdesk   4096 May 21 15:26 Start Menu
drwx-----T+ 2 cindy helpdesk   4096 May 21 20:42 Templates
-rwx------  1 cindy helpdesk   1024 Aug  8 14:20 ntuser.dat.LOG
-rwx------  1 cindy helpdesk    328 Aug  8 14:22 ntuser.ini
```

Storing per-user settings on a central file server can provide several benefits to administrators. For example, new machines can be deployed without worrying about having to transfer the user's customized environment from one host to another. If all of the user's documents and files are stored on a network file share as well, machines can practically be swapped out at will. Additionally, a profile can be updated while the user is offline and have the changes appear at the next logon. Useful examples of this are adding shortcuts to the Start Menu or editing application settings found in the *NTUSER.DAT* registry hive.

 One oddity surrounding Windows and the registry is that clients refuse to load a binary registry file, for example *NTUSER.DAT*, if the DOS ReadOnly bit is set on the file. The only clue as to the cause of the failure is that Windows reports that the registry file is corrupt, when in fact it is perfectly fine. This applies both to user profiles and system policy files (covered in the next section).

To support roaming profiles, your server needs to dedicate a file share to storing these per user settings, and you must inform the Windows clients of this share so that the user profile can be download at logon time. The following excerpt from *smb.conf* uses the logon path parameter to specify the location of the user's roaming profile.

The %U variable is used to separate profiles based on username. The %a variable is used to separate the profiles based on client OS. This is important, because a profile created by Windows 2000 may not be 100% compatible with one created by Windows XP. The [profile$] share is a normal file share. The trailing $ is included to prevent the share from being displayed by Windows client when browsing the server. You could have disabled the browseable parameter to achieve the same effect.

```
[global]
    logon path = \\STORK\profile$\%U\%a

[profile$]
    comment = User roaming profiles
    path = /data/profiles
    read only = no
    inherit permissions = yes
```

Each user must be able to write to a subdirectory matching his login name in */data/ profiles* (i.e., */data/profiles/mark*). One way to meet this requirement is to create the top-level directory before the user first logs on. It is also a good idea to prevent other users from accessing a profile other than their own. Run the following commands as root to create the necessary profile directory for the user mark:

```
# mkdir -p /data/profiles/mark
# chown mark  /data/profiles/mark
# chmod 700 /data/profiles/mark
```

Windows itself will handle creating the directory based on the %a value. Here is the profile directory for a user who has logged on to clients running various operating systems:

```
$ ls -l
total 16
drwx------  14 cindy helpdesk 4096 Aug  6 21:18 Win2K
drwx------  13 cindy helpdesk 4096 Jul 22 10:23 Win2K3
drwx------  15 cindy helpdesk 4096 Aug  6 17:29 WinNT
drwx------  13 cindy helpdesk 4096 Aug  8 12:02 WinXP
```

> Roaming profiles can be disabled by setting the logon path to an empty string.
>
> ```
> logon path = ""
> ```

In addition to a roaming environment, it is beneficial to provide users with a private network file share in which to store data. Personal files, along with application settings, can then follow a user from machine to machine. Windows connects to the user's home directory automatically if you define the logon home parameter in *smb.conf*. The driver letter used by in the connection is controlled by the logon drive option. The following example connects the home directory (*STORK**username*) to the *H:* drive:

```
[global]
    logon home = \\STORK\%U
    logon drive = H:

[homes]
    comment = Home directory for %U
    read only = no
    valid users = %S
```

> In spite of the default values, it is recommended that you never store users' profiles in their home directories. It is too easy to lose data when the profile is copied from the Windows client back to the network file share.

You may wish to do more when a user logs on than just connect her to a home directory. The logon script parameter points to a Windows batch file that is run on the client when a user logs on. The script value is the DOS path to the batch file relative to the root of the [netlogon] share. For example, to run a script based on the user's primary group, set the following in *smb.conf*:

```
[global]
    logon script = %G.bat
```

For a user whose primary group is *ntadmin*, *smbd* will expand the %G before sending the UNC path *stork**netlogon**ntadmin.bat* to the client. Frequently, the logon script is configured to point to a master batch file that performs certain actions based on the user's group membership. The *ifmember.exe* tool included in the Windows Server 2003 resource kit allows you to test for membership in a group and perform a specific action if the test succeeds. Other more power-scripting languages such as Perl or Python may be used as well, but these must be invoked from the original batch file.

 Batch files should be in DOS text. There are many methods and tools to do this. The simplest is to find an editor that supports DOS text. Other methods of converting Unix text files to a DOS format are covered in Chapter 11.

Table 9-3 summarizes the user profile parameters discussed in this section.

Table 9-3. User profile options

Parameter	Value	Description	Default	Scope
logon drive	string	The drive letter that a Windows client should use when connecting to the user's home directory.	" "	Global
login home	string	The UNC path to the user's home directory.	\\%N\%U	Global
login path	string	The UNC path to the user's roaming profile.	\\%N\%U\profile	Global
login script	string	The DOS path (relative to the root of the [netlogon] share) to a batch file that will be executed on the client when a user logs on.	" "	Global

System Policies

A Windows NT 4.0 system policy file, usually named *ntconfig.pol* and stored in the [netlogon] share, is a collection of registry settings used to enforce specific settings on client machines and users or groups. NT 4.0 system policies are very different from AD Group Policy Objects. The latter is a feature of Active Directory and not supported by Samba's current domain controlling capabilities.

Figure 9-9 displays the Windows NT 4.0 Policy Editor (included in the latest Windows NT 4.0 Service Pack). The dialog box shows specific policy objects for the Server Admins group, the user *mark*, and the computer *mink*. If a user or host does not match any of the specific policies, the default user or default computer policy will be applied.

System policies are retrieved by the client as part of the user logon process. By default, the client searches the [netlogon] share for a file named *ntconfig.pol* and then attempts to merge this file with either the HKEY_LOCAL_MACHINE or the HKEY_CURRENT_USER registry hive, depending on the type of policy object.

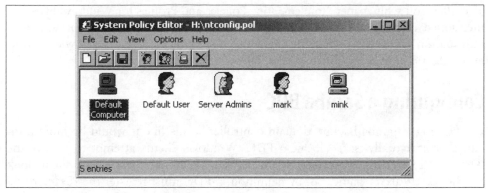

Figure 9-9. The User Environment Profile dialog box in User Manager for Domains

You can accomplish a lot with system policies. Figure 9-10 illustrates a few user settings that can be managed via policy settings. This example highlights settings such as restricting screen locks and excluding certain directories from being synchronized as part of the user's roaming profile.

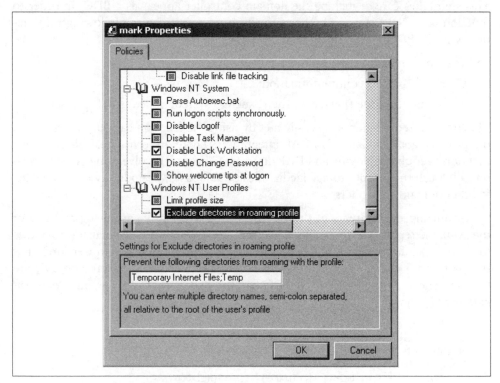

Figure 9-10. User system policy settings

The Microsoft white paper "Implementing Policies and Profiles for Windows NT 4.0," mentioned in the context of roaming user profiles, is also an excellent source of information for system policies. It might also be helpful to read MS Knowledge Base article 225087, "Writing Custom ADM Files for System Policy Editor."

Configuring a Samba BDC

Configuring a Samba backup domain controller seems like it would be more difficult than it actually is. To locate a PDC, Windows clients attempt to resolve the *DOMAIN*<0x1b> NetBIOS name. To locate all available domain controllers, clients look for the *DOMAIN*<0x1c> name. So, by definition, a BDC must register the <0x1c> name but not <0x1b>. This requirement translates into the following *smb.conf* settings:

```
[global]
    domain master = no
    domain logons = yes
```

Everything else about the BDC's configuration is identical to that of the PDC.

This step takes care of making the domain controller appear as a BDC. In order to function as a BDC, the Samba hosts must also synchronize the following information with the PDC:

- The domain SID
- User and group account information
- The contents of the [netlogon] share, such as system polices and logon scripts

The first two requirements are easily met by using the *ldapsam* passdb. In fact, this is the primary goal for Samba's LDAP integration. There are other possible solutions that don't require deploying an LDAP directory. These all involve using *rsync* to periodically push the passdb storage media (files or databases) periodically from the PDC to other domain controllers.

Synchronizing the contents of the [netlogon] share is fairly easy using any one of the available replication tools. Our preferred method is to run *rsync*, using SSH keys for authentication, periodically from a *cron* job. The following script ensures that the [netlogon] shares (i.e., */data/netlogon*) on the two BDCs, turtle and owl, are kept in sync with the PDC. Each BDC has the PDC's root SSH key in *~root/.ssh/authorized_keys*.

```
#!/bin/sh
HOSTS="turtle.example.com owl.example.com"
NETLOGON=/data/netlogon
for h in ${HOSTS}; do
    rsync -a -e ssh –delete ${NETLOGON}/ ${h}:${NETLOGON}/
done
```

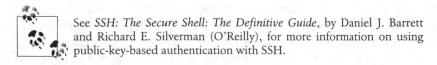 See *SSH: The Secure Shell: The Definitive Guide*, by Daniel J. Barrett and Richard E. Silverman (O'Reilly), for more information on using public-key-based authentication with SSH.

Not all information is synchronized between the PDC and BDCs. For example, because the UNC path to home directories and roaming user profiles can be stored in the user's passdb entry, these file shares must be maintained on a central server. There are several ways to prevent these shares from being a single point of failure, such as maintaining two servers that run high availability software such as Heartbeat (*http://www.linux-ha.org*) and a shared storage backend. This and other HA solutions are beyond the scope of our discussion.

passdb Recommendations

Chapter 5 covered the technical details of the three passdb plug-ins distributed with Samba: *smbpasswd*, *tdbsam*, and *ldapsam*. Our focus here is to address which one to use on a Samba domain controller. This discussion is less technical and more philosophical. We will reiterate some of the points made in earlier chapters that should also be considered in the context of Samba domains. Each passdb has its pros and cons. The ultimate choice is up to you.

Samba's *smbpasswd* file has the advantage of being very simple. It's a text file with one record per line and a small number of fields per record. Its main intended use is on standalone file and print servers. Because such servers merely have to authenticate users, all they need to store in the *smbpasswd* file are a username, a password, and possibly password expiration calculations. The user's SID is generated at runtime based on an internal algorithm and the user's Unix account. This means that if the uid ever changes, so will the user's SID: this situation can break roaming profiles. The lack of persistent SID storage is the main reason why we recommend against using the *smbpasswd* passdb on a domain controller.

The *tdbsam* passdb is targeted at both standalone servers and Samba domains with a single PDC. It can store a more complete set of user attributes than *smbpasswd*. For example, the logon options such as logon script can be set on a per-user basis rather than relying on a single default value from *smb.conf*. The *tdbsam* passdb also stores the user's SID, a feature that is required to migrate a Windows NT 4.0 domain to a Samba domain controller. However, the lack of replication makes *tdbsam* unsuitable for domains with multiple Samba domain controllers.

The *ldapsam* backend has the completeness of *tdbsam* with the added overhead of an LDAP directory. Very LDAP-savvy administrators may find it appealing (although it is not recommended) to edit user or group attributes directly, something impossible to do with *tdbsam*.

The attraction of directory services is to consolidate information that was previously duplicated across network services. Therefore, the *ldapsam* `passdb` module is intended as a means of sharing information between multiple Samba domain controllers. Because *ldapsam*, like *tdbsam*, stores the full SID in user and group entries, it is not a way to share this information between multiple standalone servers. Each host would have a different machine SID and hence would recognize only accounts matching its own SID. A user created by one workgroup server would be ignored by another.

Table 9-4 provides some basic rules to consider when choosing an account storage plug-in for your new Samba server. Remember that these are recommendations and not rules. You are the final judge concerning which `passdb` to deploy. For example, *ldapsam* may be completely acceptable on a standalone server if you have only one Samba host on the network and already have an LDAP directory available for use. If you need advice or someone to bounce ideas off of, the Samba mailing lists mentioned in Chapter 12 are good places to get peer review of your configurations.

Table 9-4. passdb recommendations

passdb	Standalone server	Samba domain with a single DC	Samba domain with a multiple DCs
smbpasswd	Yes	No	No
tdbsam	Yes	Yes	No
ldapsam	No	No	Yes

Migrating an NT 4.0 Domain to Samba

Earlier, we stated that Samba 3.0 does not support the Windows NT 4.0 SAM replication protocol. This is true in the sense that you cannot configure Samba to receive incremental change sets from a Windows PDC (or vice versa). However, developers have implemented enough of the protocol to allow what is referred to as *SAM synchronization*. Windows servers do this when a BDC is first brought online. It synchronizes its local SAM with the domain SAM by requesting the complete set of users and groups from the PDC. By requesting this initial synchronization operation with a Windows NT 4.0 PDC, Samba can obtain a complete list of users and groups along with passwords and account details, thus providing a means of migrating from the Windows domain controller to a Samba-based domain.

The basic steps for migrating an NT 4.0 domain from Windows to Samba are:

1. Ensure that all Samba daemons are stopped.
2. Configure the Samba host's *smb.conf* as a BDC for the domain, including the user management family of scripts.
3. Synchronize the Samba's machine SID stored in *secrets.tdb* with the domain SID.
4. Create a BDC account on the Windows PDC for the Samba server.

---

5. Join the domain.

6. Issue the SAM synchronization request.

7. Reconfigure Samba as a PDC.

8. Shut down the Windows PDC.

9. Start *smbd* and *nmbd* on the Samba server.

Most of effort necessary for migrating a domain is in generating a working set of user management scripts. These are required so that Samba can generate the new Unix users and groups before creating the user accounts or group mapping entries in its passdb. However, one major hurdle is that many Unix account utilities restrict the format of a new user or group name. For example, the Linux *groupadd* command fails if the group name contains whitespace:

```
# groupadd "Domain Admins"
groupadd: Invalid group name `Domain Admins'.
```

One workaround is to bypass the OS tools and manually create the Unix groups. On Linux at least, the rejection of white space in group names is a tool issue, not a limitation of */etc/group* or the *libnss_files.so.2* library. The following excerpt from */etc/group* illustrates these group names:

```
Domain Admins:!:1000:
Domain Users:!:1001:
Domain Guests:!:1002:
Account Operators:!:1003:
Server Operators:!:1004:
Backup Operators:!:1005:
Print Operators:!:1006:
```

If you have a large number of groups, however, such manual creation may be too tedious. In this case, customize the user management scripts called by Samba to accept valid Windows user and group names.

The next question is which passdb backend to use. Our recommendation is to begin with *tdbsam*. The reasons are simple. *tdbsam* is easier to configure than an LDAP backend and more robust than an *smbpasswd* file. Additionally, it is easier to remove *tdb* files than to rebuild an LDAP DIT when performing migration experiments. You can always convert Samba's users and groups from a *tdb* backend to an LDAP directory service later using the following command:

```
# pdbedit -i tdbsam -e ldapsam:ldap://ldap.example.com/
```

With these recommendations in mind, let's begin the example by defining the following *smb.conf* for our soon-to-be Samba PDC. All the parameters should be familiar at this point. The Windows NT domain that we are migrating is named DOA. Remember to disable the domain master option when configuring a backup domain controller. The [netlogon] share is not required for the migration process, but will be necessary once we swap the Samba server to a PDC. Finally, we have omitted any support for roaming user profiles, because this feature is independent of transferring accounts. We will, however, revisit some specific issues surrounding the user environment profile after completing the migration.

```
[global]
    netbios name = CAT
    workgroup = DOA
    security = user
    encrypt passwords = yes
    passdb backend = tdbsam

    domain logons = yes
    domain master = no

    add user script = /usr/sbin/useradd -m '%u'
    delete user script = /usr/sbin/userdel '%u'
    rename user script = /usr/sbin/usermod -l '%unew' '%uold'
    add group script = /usr/sbin/groupadd '%g'
    delete group script = /usr/sbin/groupdel '%g'
    add user to group script = /usr/sbin/groupmod -A '%u' '%g'
    delete user from group script = /usr/sbin/groupmod -D '%u' '%g'
    set primary group script = /usr/sbin/usermod -g '%g' '%u'

[netlogon]
    path = /data/netlogon
    read only = yes
    write list = +"Domain Admins"
```

After the initial *smb.conf* has been created, the next step is to synchronize Samba's machine SID with the domain SID. This is done by running the *net rpc getsid* command against the Windows PDC. Because you are writing directly to *secrets.tdb*, these commands must be run as *root*. In the example, *medic* is the name of the PDC for the DOA domain.

```
# net rpc getsid -S medic
Storing SID S-1-5-21-406022937-1377575209-526660263 for Domain DOA in secrets.tdb
```

Samba's machine SID must be manually set to match this domain SID using *net setlocalsid*. If the command succeeds, you are immediately returned to a shell prompt with no additional output.

```
# net setlocalsid S-1-5-21-406022937-1377575209-526660263
```

The next two steps, creating the BDC account and joining the domain, should be executed in immediate succession in order to prevent an attacker from hijacking the machine account. Ideally, this should be done on a separate, secure network, but that is not always possible when migrating a production domain. When experimenting, consider moving a Windows BDC to an isolated network and promoting it to a PDC.

Figure 9-11 shows the Server Manager (*srvmgr.exe*) application and the Add Computer to Domain dialog boxes. Use these to create a BDC account for the Samba host.

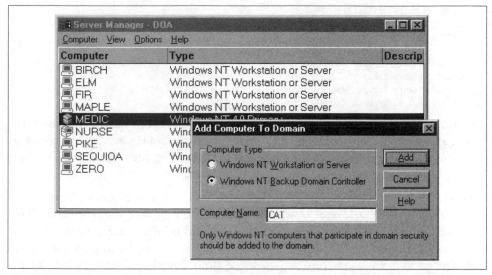

Figure 9-11. Using Server Manager to create a BDC account for the Samba host CAT

Next, join the domain using *net rpc join*. We'll provide much more detail about joining Windows (and Samba) domains in the next chapter. For now, this one command is enough to get the job done:

```
# net rpc join
Joined domain DOA.
```

You are finally ready to migrate the users and groups from the DOA domain into Samba's passdb. Assume that all group names containing whitespace have been previously created in */etc/group* by hand. Begin the migration process by running *net rpc vampire*. The -S option is used to define the name of the Windows NT 4.0 PDC to contact. After the migration completes, it is a good idea to verify the new users and groups both in the server's Unix accounts and in Samba's passdb.

```
# net rpc vampire -S medic
Fetching DOMAIN database
Creating unix group: 'testgroup'
Creating unix group: 'testgroup2'
Creating account: Administrator
Creating account: Guest
Creating account: foo
Creating account: foo2
Creating account: foo3
Creating account: user1
Creating account: NURSE$
Creating account: CAT$
Group members of Domain Admins: Administrator,
Group members of Domain Users: Administrator(primary),foo2(primary),
   user1(primary),foo3(primary),NURSE$(primary),CAT$(primary),
Group members of Domain Guests: nobody,
Group members of testgroup: foo(primary),
```

```
Group members of testgroup2: foo,
Creating unix group: 'LocalTestGrp'
Fetching BUILTIN database
skipping SAM_DOMAIN_INFO delta for 'Builtin' (is not my domain)
Creating unix group: 'Administrators'
Creating unix group: 'Guests'
Creating unix group: 'Replicator'
Creating unix group: 'Users'
```

The final steps are to shut down the Windows PDC and launch the new Samba PDC. Before starting *smbd* and *nmbd*, make sure to enable the domain master parameter so that Samba registers the DOA<0x1b> name and the Windows client recognizes the new PDC.

Here are a few pieces of advice. Migrating a domain is tricky business. You should expect to run through several test migrations before disabling the Windows PDC. Also consider any additional services such as file and printer shares, web servers, or other applications offered by the Windows PDC. These must be migrated individually. The good news is that you have to successfully complete the migration process only once.

Domain Trusts

Samba 3.0 was the first version to support Windows NT 4.0 style one-way trusts, which can be used to connect Samba domains to both NT and Active Directory domains. Initiating a trust relationship is very similar to the process of joining a domain described earlier in this chapter. The trusted domain creates a domain trust account that has a purpose analogous to a machine trust account. The trusting domain then establishes the relationship by joining the trust. We'll next walk you through an example of configuring a Samba domain to trust an AD domain.

First, you must have a fully configured Samba domain. Samba restricts the right to create domain trusts to members of the Domain Admins group, so it is necessary to configure an appropriate group mapping entry for this if you have not already done so. You also must either create the necessary Unix user account for the domain trust using the name of the trusting domain followed by a $ character (e.g., *books$*), or configure a working add machine script in *smb.conf*.

Use the *net rpc trustdom* command to create the domain trust account on the Samba PDC. The add subcommand accepts the name of the domain (BOOKS) followed by the new trust account password (sambapw):

```
$ net rpc trustdom add BOOKS sambapw -S stork -U cindy
Password: <enter cindy's password>
```

If all goes well, you are returned immediately to a shell prompt. You can verify that the account was created using *pdbedit*. The I account flag is used to mark this as a domain trust account. (Note that the following output has been wrapped for better readability.)

```
# pdbedit -L -w books$
BOOKS$:10018:A01531C54AE6F75CAAD3B435B51404EE:
    45F9E3989DD87751210C054A9B3A134E:[I         ]:LCT-44DA55A9:
```

Now establish the trust account from the Windows domain controller. Figure 9-12 shows the *books.plainjoe.org* domain properties, as displayed by the Windows 2000 Active Directory Domains and Trusts MMC plug-in. The top section of this dialog is used to connect to a trusted domain. There are no existing domain trust relationships in the screenshot.

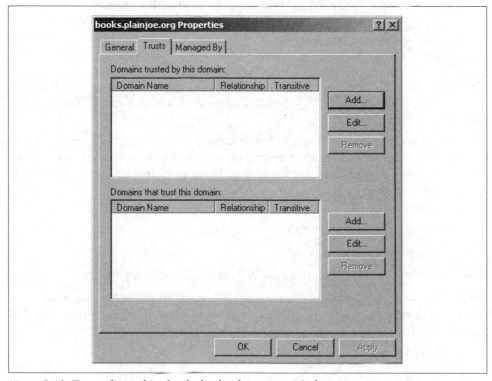

Figure 9-12. Trust relationships for the books.plainjoe.org AD domain

Now select Add from the top section and enter the name of the Samba domain (ORA) along with the password specified in the *net rpc trustdom add* command. You should be greeted with a dialog box similar to the one in Figure 9-13, indicating that the trust has been established and verified.

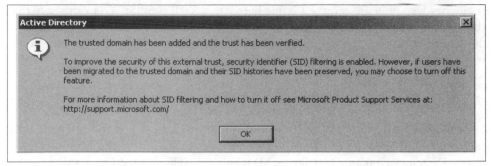

Figure 9-13. Confirming a successfully established trust between Samba and AD

You can use *smbclient* to test the trust relationship by connecting to a share on any member server in the BOOKS domain as a user from the ORA domain:

```
$ smbclient //windc/public -U cindy -W ORA
Password: <enter cindy's password>
Domain=[BOOKS] OS=[Windows 5.0] Server=[Windows 2000 LAN Manager]
smb: \>
```

Next, it is time to create the trust relationship in the other direction. This time, create the trust account on the Windows DC using the lower half of the Trusts dialog box shown in Figure 9-12.

You will initially receive a message that Windows cannot verify the trust. This is because you have not established the trust on the Samba DC yet. To do so, run the *net rpc trustdom establish* command, giving the trusted domain name as the sole parameter. This must be done as *root* so that the net tool can write the new password to *secrets.tdb*.

```
# net rpc trustdom establish BOOKS
Password: <enter trust password here>
Trust to domain BOOKS established
```

You should now be able to return to the Windows DC and verify the trust.

You can view the list of current trusts using the *net rpc trustdom list* command. This command does not display any information about the status of the trust, only that Samba has a trust account entry or password for the listed domain.

```
# net rpc trustdom list -U cindy
Password: <enter cindy's password>
Trusted domains list:
BOOKS              S-1-5-21-4200961138-2496335650-1239021823

Trusting domains list:
BOOKS              S-1-5-21-4200961138-2496335650-1239021823
```

In order to connect to the Samba server using an account from the BOOKS domain, the server requires some method to deal with users and groups from the trusted domain. The best way to do this is with Winbind. Conceptually, these trusted users and groups on a Samba PDC are no different from domain users and groups on a Samba member server. To set up Winbind on a Samba DC, follow the same steps you would for a Samba member server (described in Chapter 10) with the exception of maintaining the security = user setting instead of one of the domain mode security settings. On a DC, Winbind allocates uids and gids only for accounts outside of its own domain.

Table 9-5 completes our discussion of domain trusts with an overview of the *net rpc trustdom* commands.

Table 9-5. net rpc trustdom commands

Command	Options	Description
add	DOMAIN password	Create a domain trust account for a trusting domain using the specified password.
del	DOMAIN	Remove a domain trust account.
establish	DOMAIN	Establish a trust relationship with a trusted domain.
revoke	DOMAIN	Disconnect a trust relationship with a trusted domain.
list	none	List the currently configured domain trust relationships.

Remote Server Management

Windows provides a large number of remote management applications. You've already seen two examples of these: Server Manager and User Manager for Domains. Other tools provide the capability to manage file shares, stop and start services, search logfiles, and monitor system resources. Supporting tools familiar to Windows administrators can help to distribute the burden of server administration without requiring you to retrain your staff. In the following sections, we show you to configure Samba to support these types of remote management applications.

File Shares

Figure 9-14 shows a listing of shares on our server using the Microsoft Management Console. Our goal is to be able to manipulate new and existing shares using this application. To do so, we need to meet two requirements:

- Authorize a user or group to manage file shares.
- Configure *smbd* so that it is able to modify its own *smb.conf* dynamically.

Granting the SeDiskOperatorPrivilege right allows a user or group to manage Samba's file shares, including changing a share's security ACL. The *net rpc rights* command should be very familiar by now. We'll continue to use Server Admins as our primary administrative group and grant it the necessary privilege with the following command:

```
$ net rpc rights grant 'ORA\Server Admins' SeDiskOperatorPrivilege \
  -S stork -U cindy
Password: <enter cindy's password>
Successfully granted rights.
```

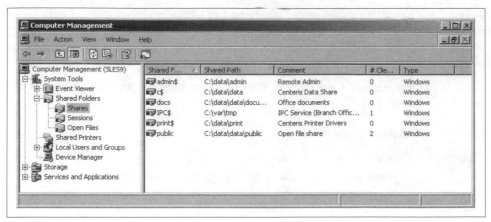

Figure 9-14. Using the Computer Management MMC plug-in to view available Samba shares

Samba provides three parameters referring to external commands that modify *smb.conf* whenever a file share is added, modified, or removed. The add share command is used to create a new file share to *smb.conf*. When called by *smbd*, it is passed the following five parameters:

- The absolute path to *smb.conf*
- The name of the new share
- The directory path to be shared
- A comment string
- The maximum number of simultaneous connections allowed

The change share command updates basic share properties and is invoked with the same set of parameters as the add share command.

The delete share command removes a file share from *smb.conf*. The parameter list consists solely of:

- The path to *smb.conf*
- The name of the share to be removed

An example share management program is distributed with Samba in *examples/scripts/shares/perl*. The *modify_share_command.pl* script is intended to be an example of how the various *smb.conf* share commands work, but it can be used in production. However, because it strips comments and reorders the configuration file (similar to SWAT), it may not be suitable for all servers.

The following excerpt from *smb.conf* shows how to integrate these new options into an existing configuration. The script uses the number of defined parameters to determine whether it should add/update a share or remove one, which allows us to use one program for all three commands.

```
[global]
    add share command = /etc/samba/scripts/modify_share_command.pl
    change share command = /etc/samba/scripts/modify_share_command.pl
    delete share command = /etc/samba/scripts/modify_share_command.pl
```

We can now use the MMC Shared Folders plug-in to create a new share named [graphics]. Figure 9-15 shows the Create A Shared Folder Wizard, which can be launched from the Action → New File Share... menu option. The shared directory path must be entered as a DOS path, but is converted to a Unix path by *smbd* before passing it off to the add or change share parameters.

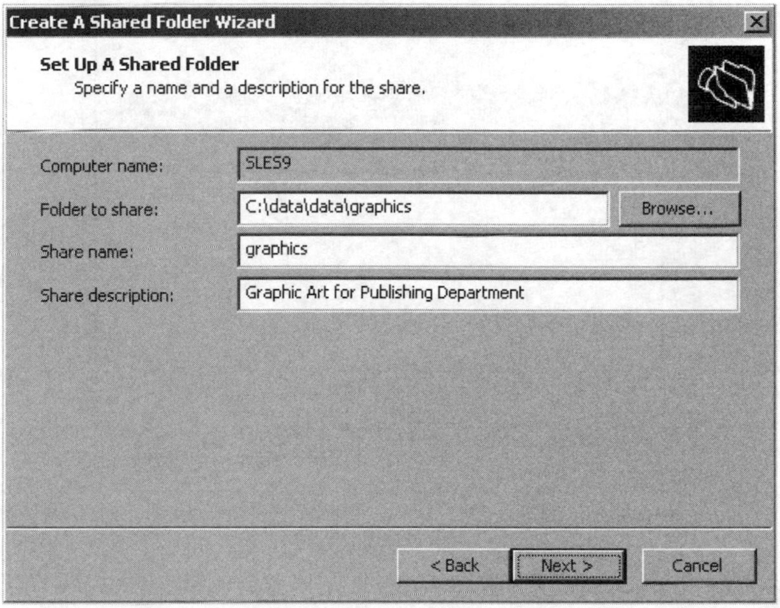

Figure 9-15. Creating a new Samba share from Windows

The resulting share created by the add share command is shown here:

```
[graphics]
    max connections = 0
    comment = Graphic Art for Publishing Department
    path = /data/data/graphics
```

Creating shares using MMC or other RPC-based management tool does not give you access to the full range of *smb.conf* parameters. The parameter most notably absent is valid users. However, you can customize the share's security descriptor to achieve the same effect. Share permissions, stored in *share_info.tdb*, are independent of the filesystem ACLs discussed in Chapter 6 and are thus available even on systems without that feature. Figure 9-16 shows the share permissions for [graphics]. Here the

ORA\artists group has been given full access, while all other users are granted only read access to the share.

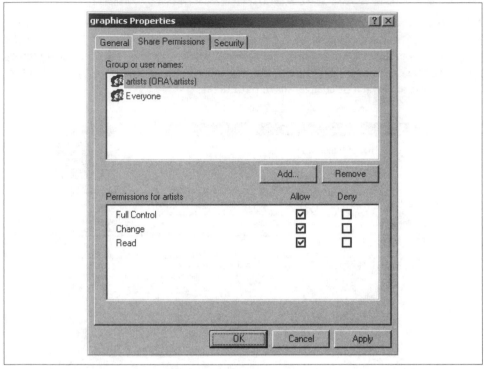

Figure 9-16. Share permissions for graphics

Services

The Windows Service Control API can be used to manage Unix daemons via the System V init script interface. Figure 9-17 lists configured services on a Samba host.

The registry service is not linked to any configuration setting and therefore is always present. But a few of these services are handled internally by *smbd* or *nmbd* because they are linked to specific *smb.conf* parameters:

- The Print Spooler (disable spoolss)
- Net Logon (the [netlogon] file share)
- WINS (wins support)
- Remote Registry Service

Of these four internal services, only the Print Spooler will accept start or stop commands. Its main purpose is to support the Microsoft Print Migrator tool (*http://www. microsoft.com/printserver*).

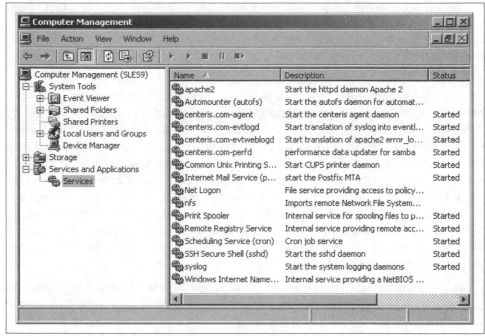

Figure 9-17. Listing services on the Samba host \\SLES9

You can include additional services using the svcctl list parameter. The *smb.conf* setting corresponding to the listing in Figure 9-17 is:

```
[global]
    svcctl list = syslog nfs sshd postfix cron autofs \
    centeris.com-agent apache2 cups centeris.com-evtlogd \
    centeris.com-perfd centeris.com-evtweblogd
```

The svcctl list directive specifies the services that should be listed by the Windows Service Control Manager. To actually stop and start a service, you must add a SysV init script using the name listed in *smb.conf* to the *svcctl* folder of Samba's *lib* directory (e.g., */usr/local/samba/lib/svcctl*). In most cases, adding a symbolic link to the operating system's init script in */etc/init.d* is sufficient. This file listing shows symlinks for *apache2*, *autofs*, *cron*, *nfs*, *postfix*, *sshd*, and *syslog*:

```
$ ls -l
total 8
drwxr-xr-x  2 root root 4096 Aug 10 23:35 .
drwxr-xr-x  9 root root 4096 Aug 10 23:35 ..
lrwxrwxrwx  1 root root   19 Jul 14 15:49 apache2 -> /etc/init.d/apache2
lrwxrwxrwx  1 root root   18 Jul 14 15:49 autofs -> /etc/init.d/autofs
lrwxrwxrwx  1 root root   16 Jul 14 15:49 cron -> /etc/init.d/cron
lrwxrwxrwx  1 root root   15 Jul 14 15:49 nfs -> /etc/init.d/nfs
lrwxrwxrwx  1 root root   19 Jul 14 15:49 postfix -> /etc/init.d/postfix
lrwxrwxrwx  1 root root   16 Jul 14 15:49 sshd -> /etc/init.d/sshd
lrwxrwxrwx  1 root root   18 Jul 14 15:49 syslog -> /etc/init.d/syslog
<...remaining output deleted...>
```

Samba expects the init script to support three command line options: start, stop, and status. For all three commands, *smbd* assumes that a nonzero return code indicates an error and that the service is not running. If your OS does not provide initialization scripts for service startup and shutdown, or does not obey Samba's assumptions, it will be necessary to write your own.

Each service has an assigned security descriptor, just like files or printers, which can be set to allow a specific user or group the right to stop and restart a service. By default, only members of the local Administrators group (S-1-5-32-544) are authorized to manage services. At least initially, it is necessary to create a group mapping entry for this SID. You could, however, change a service's ACL to allow members of the *Web Admins* group to restart Apache and restrict the *Mail Admins* group to managing Postfix. Sadly, Microsoft does not provide a graphical interface to manage service access lists. However, it is possible to use *sc.exe* utility shipped with Windows XP to set the ACL using its Security Descriptor Definition Language (SDDL). For more information on *sc.exe*, access the tool's help screen using the */?* switch or search *http://technet.microsoft.com*.

Figure 9-18 shows service management in action as the Postfix Mail Server is launched by selecting Start from the context menu provided by a right click on the service name.

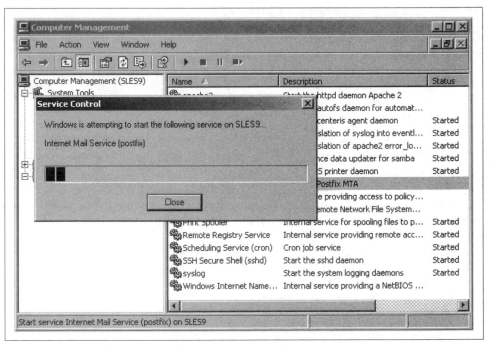

Figure 9-18. Starting Postfix from MMC

Table 9-6 summarizes the `svcctl list` option present in this section.

Table 9-6. Listing services in smb.conf

Parameter	Value	Description	Default	Scope
svcctl list	string	Define a list of service names to enumerate when queried using the Windows Service Control API.	" "	Global

Eventlogs

The Windows Event Viewer is limited, compared to many logging tools. It is, however, familiar to Windows admins and is distributed as part of the operating system. For this reason alone, it is worth investigating, as it allows existing EventLog API-based monitoring tools to audit both Unix hosts and their Windows counterparts.

The first step when enabling this feature is to configure the list of EventLogs that should be reported to Windows clients by defining the `eventlog list` global parameter in *smb.conf*. The following setting enumerates five logfiles: *Application*, *System*, *Security*, *SyslogLinux*, and *WebServer*:

```
eventlog list = Application, System, Security, SyslogLinux, Webserver
```

Samba does not parse system logfiles directly. Instead, it reads log records from an associated *tdb* stored in the *eventlog* folder of its `lock directory` (e.g., */var/lib/samba/eventlog*). These *tdb* files are created by using an external tool to parse the system logfiles and then writing entries to the database using the *eventlogadm* tool. An example Perl script which is able to parse syslog-generated logfiles is included in the *examples/scripts/eventlog* directory of the Samba source distribution. To generate the Security EventLog *tdb*, pipe */var/log/secure* through the *parselog.pl* script and then feed the output to the *eventlogadm* tool, giving the EventLog name as the single command-line argument:

```
# tail -f /var/log/secure | parselog.pl | eventlogadm Security
```

This command continuously feeds log messages into *security.tdb*, which is accessed by *smbd* to generate the log entries shown in Figure 9-19. Here you can see the successful SSH login by *root* from host 192.168.56.1.

 To fully decode logfiles in Event Viewer, Windows requires a message file DLL that can be downloaded from the server's [C$] share. More information on Message Files and EventLogs can be found at *http://msdn.microsoft.com*.

Table 9-7 provides a short description of the `eventlog list` setting.

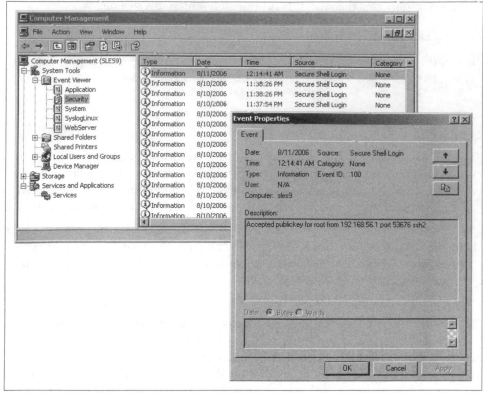

Figure 9-19. Viewing a Unix host's /var/log/secure file in the Windows Event Viewer

Table 9-7. Listing event logs in smb.conf

Parameter	Value	Description	Default	Scope
eventlog list	string	Define a list of logfile names to enumerate when queried using the Windows EventLog API.	" "	Global

Performance Monitor

Our final management application falls more into the remote monitoring category. The Performance Monitor (*perfmon.exe*) utilizes the Windows registry interface to periodically poll a server for performance data such as CPU usage, disk utilization, and available memory. Similar to its relationship with EventLogs, Samba acts as a interface to performance data that has been collected by an external tool or daemon.

There are many ways to collect performance data. On Linux hosts, a great deal of information can be collected by reading files stored in */proc*. An implementation based on this method is distributed in the *examples/perfcounter* directory of the Samba source tree. Build instructions and a simple *Makefile* are included as well. Once the daemon has been compiled, it can be launched to generate an example set of performance counters stored in the *perfmon* folder of Samba's lock directory (*/var/lib/samba/perfmon*). To launch the program as a daemon, run the following command as *root*:

```
# ./perfcount -d
```

This command creates two *tdb* files: *names.tdb* and *data.tdb*. Samba uses these files to service any requests to read from the HKEY_PERFORMANCE_DATA registry hive. Figure 9-20 displays a *perfmon.exe* session that is monitoring the System and User CPU usage on a Unix host during a software compile. It is interesting to compare the Performance Monitor data with the output from *vmstat* during the same period. You will find that the graph closely matches *vmstat*'s CPU usage report:

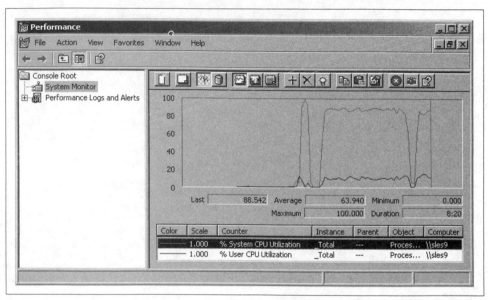

Figure 9-20. Viewing System versus User CPU usage in the Windows perfmon.exe tool

```
$ vmstat 5
procs        ----cpu----
 r  b <...> us sy id wa
 1  0 <...>  2  4 93  2
 1  0 <...> 11 89  0  0
 1  0 <...> 10 89  0  0
 1  0 <...> 10 90  0  0
 1  0 <...> 11 89  0  0
 1  0 <...> 11 88  1  1
 0  1 <...> 12 87  0  1
 1  0 <...> 11 58 21 10
 0  1 <...>  3 16 80  1
 1  0 <...> 13 80  0  6
 1  0 <...> 14 86  0  0
```

Samba developers continue to support new remote management interfaces and improve existing ones. For the latest information on features related these and other tools, review the *WHATSNEW.txt* file included with the latest Samba release.

## CHAPTER 10

Domain Member Servers

Windows domains are based on centralized authentication services provided by domain controllers. A moderately sized domain has a limited number of DCs, but can possibly host hundreds of file and print servers. The number of servers in a large domain can exceed this amount by a factor of 10 or more.

In many networks, Samba is leveraging these domain authentication services and standing side by side with Windows. First introduced in 1998, Samba's support for participating in Windows domains as a member server has helped administrators integrate Unix servers with Windows clients. In 2003, Samba 3.0 advanced this feature by adding support for Kerberos authentication and LDAP directory services, yielding improved integration with Microsoft Active Directory domains.

Chapter 5 began by discussing the concepts of authentication and authorization. These tasks apply not only to local users but also to domain member servers. For all but the smallest domain, manual synchronization of user and group account information between Unix hosts and Windows domains can consume a large portion of your time. Our focus in this chapter is on decreasing the amount of effort necessary to deploy Samba member servers by leveraging both the authentication and authorization data maintained by Windows domain controllers. We address the steps necessary for Samba to join and participate in both Windows NT 4.0 and Active Directory domains, including how to configure any required external software dependencies such as the Kerberos client libraries, time synchronization, and the DNS client resolver. We also examine Winbind's account management features and its benefits to member servers.

Joining a Domain

Adding a new machine to a domain is much like adding a new user. In the case of a human user, the new account is first created on the domain controller. Then the user is informed of his login name and credentials. The user remembers this password in order to access available network services such as email or printing. When a computer joins a domain, it also establishes a random password that is known only by the domain controllers and itself. The client stores this password locally, in the registry or some other local database.

We described the process used to authenticate a connection request to a share on a standalone server in Chapter 1. If necessary, now might be a good time to review the section "Connecting to a CIFS File Share" as a refresher on session setup requests. Standalone servers provide an excellent starting point for examining domain authentication, because the basics of the connection process are identical for both standalone and member servers. The primary difference is how the server ultimately validates the credentials sent by the client.

Samba 3.0 and Windows NT 4.0 domain controllers use a *Remote Procedure Call* (RPC) mechanism, by which a member server can establish a secure means of communication and then request that the DC authenticate a user session. This concept is illustrated in simplified diagram shown in Figure 10-1. The client, named \\FOX, connects to the file server \\HOUND, who in turn asks the domain controller \\RABBIT to authenticate a session request for the user *rose*. The *NetRequestChallenge()* and *NetAuth2()* RPCs used the password stored as part of the domain join process to establish the identity of \\HOUND. The third RPC, *NetSamLogon()*, is the authentication request on behalf of the user. After receiving the *NetSamLogon()* reply from the domain controller, the file server either responds successfully or returns the error code, such as Logon Failure or Password Expired, specified by the DC.

When participating in an AD domain, Windows 2000 and later clients are capable of using *Kerberos 5* (Krb5) authentication services.* We say "capable," because Active Directory domains still support NTLM authentication and the RPC mechanisms just described. A full discussion of Kerberos is beyond the scope of this book. Two excellent sources of information on the subject are *Kerberos: The Definitive Guide*, by Jason Garman (O'Reilly), and *Network Security: Private Communication in a Public World*, by Charlie Kaufman et al. (Prentice Hall). The former discusses implementation issues for Kerberos administrators and the latter is an in-depth examination of Kerberos and other security protocols.

Figure 10-2 illustrates what occurs when a user connects to a file server using Kerberos authentication. Again, the client machine \\FOX connects to the server \\HOUND, except this time a domain controller is not needed to authenticate the session request. The file server decrypts the Kerberos ticket locally, therefore verifying that the user has been previously authenticated by the DC.

* Active Directory domains do not support Kerberos v4.

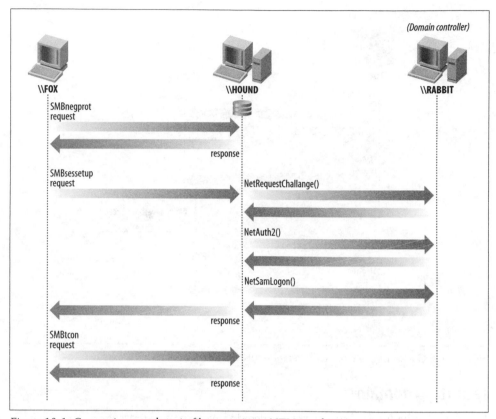

Figure 10-1. Connecting to a domain file server using NTLM and RPC

Domain and ADS Security Modes

Samba provides two modes of operating within a domain, security = domain and security = ads. Both allow Samba to leverage the central authentication service provided by domain controllers. Both modes support the NTLM and NTLMv2 authentication protocols. The ads mode, however, also provides support for Kerberos authentication, but domain does not. A good rule of thumb is to select the ads method if you are joined to an AD domain, regardless of whether the domain runs in mixed or native mode.

If you plan to configure Samba for security = ads, remember to follow the instructions given in Chapter 2 to verify that your Samba installation does in fact possess support for Kerberos, LDAP, and Active Directory. There are no such external software dependencies for enabling domain security; this mode is always provided.

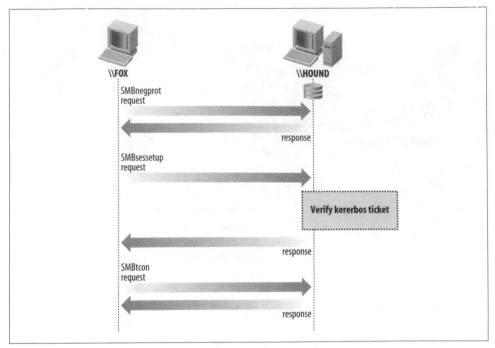

Figure 10-2. Connecting to a file server in an Active Directory domain

security = domain

Joining a Samba host using security = domain involves two steps:

1. Define the domain and member server settings for your environment in *smb.conf*.
2. Establish the machine account credentials by joining the domain.

The first parameter to set is the security option. Start by defining domain mode security in the [global] section of *smb.conf*:

```
[global]
    security = domain
```

Supporting password encryption is a requirement for member servers, so you should set it explicitly, even though it is enabled by default:

```
    encrypt password = yes
```

Finally, specify the name of the domain to which your server will belong. Samba, like Windows, reuses the workgroup parameter for this setting. Here, we are joining the GLASS Windows NT 4.0 domain:

```
    workgroup = GLASS
```

Once *smb.conf* has been configured, use the *net* command to establish the server's credentials in the domain. You need a user account that is properly authorized to join your server to the domain.* When in doubt, an account that is a member of the Domain Admins group will always work. Next, run the net join command from a root shell to join the domain, using the -U option to define the connecting user name:

```
$ net join -U Administrator
Administrator's password: <enter password for Administrator>
<...intermediate output deleted...>
Joined domain GLASS.
```

If you are greeted by the "Joined domain ..." message, *net* was able to successfully establish the machine account credentials and your server is now a part of the domain. If not, there are three common reasons why this process may fail, described next.

First, if you receive the following message, make sure that you entered the correct user name and password:

```
Could not connect to server XXX
The username or password was not correct.
```

Second, if you entered the correct credentials but the account does not possess the sufficient rights to join the server to domain, you will receive this error message:

```
error setting trust account password: NT_STATUS_ACCESS_DENIED
Unable to join domain XXX.
```

The third common error is the inability to locate a DC for the domain specified in *smb.conf*. This error is signaled by the following message:

```
Unable to find a suitable server
```

This situation is frequently caused by a mistyped name, so verify your *smb.conf* settings before proceeding. If your configuration is correct, it could be that this error is caused by a name service failure. We cover how Samba attempts to locate domain controllers shortly.

If you are joining a Samba domain, you may encounter the additional following error:

```
Creation of workstation account failed
```

This error is normally caused by some failure in the add machine script. Or possibly the script succeeded, but *smbd* is unable to locate the Unix account it created, a situation frequently caused by running the Name Service Cache Daemon (*nscd*) on the Samba DC. To resolve this problem, ensure that the DC's */etc/nsswitch.conf* file is set up correctly, that the add machine script did in fact create the trust account, and that *nscd* is using up-to-date information.

You can verify your server's trust account at any time by running this command:

```
$ net rpc testjoin
Join to 'GLASS' is OK
```

---

* Domain Administrators can grant rights or privileges to users to join a specific host or a collection of hosts to the domain.

security = ads

From the perspective of an end user, a server configured to use ads security behaves identical to one using domain security. From our perspective as administrators, the additional Kerberos support provided by the ads method is made apparent by the extra configuration steps necessary to join a domain. Instead of the two steps described for security = domain, this time there are four to complete:

1. Define the domain and member server settings for your environment in *smb.conf*.
2. Synchronize the server's clock with the domain controller.
3. Configure the Kerberos client library and DNS resolver settings.
4. Establish the machine account credentials by joining the domain.

Basic Samba settings

Once again, we start with configuring the server's *smb.conf* file. Our initial file defines ads security and includes the required encrypted password support:

```
[global]
    security = ads
    encrypt passwords = yes
```

Next, include the realm of the AD domain. In Active Directory domains, the Kerberos realm is the same as the uppercase version of the domain's DNS name.* So the AD domain *blue.plainjoe.org* is defined as:

```
realm = BLUE.PLAINJOE.ORG
```

The workgroup parameter specifies the short name of the domain, which is commonly the same as the first portion of the realm name. However, this setup is not guaranteed. If you define the wrong value, the *net* tool complains when it joins the domain and reminds you to set the correct value. In our example, the short domain name is the first component of the realm name, so we specify the workgroup as follows:

```
workgroup = BLUE
```

Time synchronization

Time synchronization is a prerequisite for Kerberos authentication. Therefore, Microsoft chooses to make all AD domain controllers act as time servers. Non-Microsoft clients can synchronize their system clocks with an AD DCs by using version 4 of the Simple Network Time Protocol (SNTP). The *ntpdate* tool, included in the NTP distribution from *http://www.ntp.org*, can synchronize the server's local

---

* In pure Kerberos 5 implementations, the realm and DNS domain are not required to match. However, Active Directory consolidates the two into a single name when running *dcpromo.exe*.

clock with an AD DC. Most systems already have some form of the NTP tools included.

Kerberos Terminology 101

For the purposes of our discussion, understanding some basic terminology can be helpful to map Kerberos concepts onto Active Directory functionality:

Principal
> A user or computer in a Kerberos authentication database (e.g., a user or computer object in AD).

Realm
> A collection of Kerberos principals. In AD, this is the same as the DNS domain.

Ticket Granting Ticket (TGT)
> An encrypted blob of data issued to a principal, which can be used to requests tickets to other principals.

Service Ticket
> An encrypted blob of data that can be used to access application services such as a mail, web, or file server.

Key Distribution Center (KDC)
> The Kerberos database server.

Authentication Server (AS)
> The service responsible for issuing TGTs.

Ticket Granting Service (TGS)
> The service responsible for issuing service tickets.

Secret Key
> The hashed version of a principal's passphrase. This is also referred to as the long-term key, because it does not expire or change based on an individual session.

Session Key
> A short-term key valid only for the life of a specific application session or Kerberos ticket. Windows 2000 and later systems use this key to encrypt certain communications between clients and servers.

In most implementations, Microsoft and Unix alike, the KDC, AS, and TGS are all implemented in the same service, although each has a logically separate function. An AD domain controller fulfills all three of these roles. Frequently, the term KDC is used to refer to the KDC+AS+TGS server.

To set your server's clock to match the time on the domain controller named *bluedc1.blue.plainjoe.org*, run the following command as *root*:

```
$ ntpdate bludc1.blue.plainjoe.org
17 Jun 12:46:46 ntpdate[16773]: step time server 192.168.1.148 offset 8.734885 sec
```

If you receive the error message, "no server suitable for synchronization found," confirm that the hostname used is valid and reachable. If the name is correct, an administrator of the DC (possibly you) must verify the *w32time.exe* service. More information about Active Directory and time synchronization can be found by searching *http://support.microsoft.com* for the keyword "w32time.exe."

The *ntpdate* command can be run periodically as a cron job to prevent the Samba server's clock from drifting. Another option is to run the *ntpd* daemon and have it synchronize the local clock on a continuing basis. To use this method, specify the domain controllers using a server line in */etc/ntp.conf* and then have the daemon started as part of the system boot process. More on configuring NTP clients can be found in the book *Essential System Administration*, by Æleen Frisch (O'Reilly).

Encryption types

The next item on the list is to configure the server's Kerberos client libraries, which Samba will use to validate user connections. Although this process can vary slightly depending the Krb5 distribution you are using, either Heimdal or MIT, thankfully the configuration files used by the two implementations are extremely compatible with each other. By default, both distributions use the file */etc/krb5.conf* to define client-side settings. The options of interest are what encryption types the client supports and how it locates a KDC for a given realm.

Active Directory realms implement three Krb5 encryption types:

- RC4-HMAC
- DES-CBC-MD5
- DES-CBC-CRC

AD domain controllers always prefer the strongest encryption algorithm for which a principal has assigned keys. The most secure encryption type in our list is RC4-HMAC. Remember from Chapter 2 that this new encryption type is supported in open source Kerberos distributions beginning only with MIT krb5 1.3 and with Heimdal 0.6.1. Krb5 authentication still works on systems with older Kerberos libraries such as RedHat Enterprise Linux 3, but only DES keys will be available.

We limit the client libraries to use the same list of encryption types supported by Microsoft. This is important, because by default, Unix Kerberos implementations prefer the Advanced Encryption Standard (AES) or triple-DES (3DES) methods, which are not currently supported by Windows domain controllers. There are several points during Krb5 communications where an encryption type mismatch can cause failure. If the Samba server cannot decrypt a user's ticket, that user cannot be authenticated. To be safe, we use a single list for obtaining TGTs, service tickets, and any session-key-based encryption that may be performed by adding three options (default_tgs_enctypes, default_tkt_enctypes, and preferred_enctypes) to the [libdefaults] section of *krb5.conf*.

```
[libdefaults]
    default_tgs_enctypes = RC4-HMAC DES-CBC-MD5 DES-CBC-CRC
    default_tkt_enctypes = RC4-HMAC DES-CBC-MD5 DES-CBC-CRC
    preferred_enctypes   = RC4-HMAC DES-CBC-MD5 DES-CBC-CRC
```

Realm/domain and KDC lookups

Next, we define the client library's default realm, just as we did in *smb.conf*. This realm is used whenever the Krb5 libraries are given an unqualified principal name. For example, if asked to retrieve a TGT for the user *Administrator*, Krb5 uses the principal *Administrator@BLUE.PLAINJOE.ORG*. The default realm also goes in *krb5.conf*'s [libdefaults] section:

```
default_realm = BLUE.PLAINJOE.ORG
```

Finally, we have to make a choice concerning how the Krb5 libraries will locate a KDC for a realm. The simplest means is to use the same DNS service as the AD domain. The reasoning behind this recommendation is that there is no need to duplicate information that Active Directory already maintains. If you find that KDC DNS lookups are not available on your platform or if you do not wish to use them, you must manually configure the KDC addresses in *krb5.conf*. We'll show both methods in the following sections.

Using DNS for KDCs lookups. The goal of this configuration is to enable the Kerberos client libraries to find a KDC by generating a query to the DNS server. If you configure the use of DNS, a request to contact a KDC for a realm results in DNS SRV lookups for *_kerberos._udp.<domain>* or *_kerberos._tcp.<domain>*. For example, locating a KDC in the realm BLUE.PLAINJOE.ORG results in a DNS query for the SRV record *_kerberos._udp.blue.plainjoe.org*. Lookups for the corresponding TCP record result when the Krb5 replies are too large for UDP and must be retried over TCP.

The Heimdal Kerberos client implementation has always supported locating KDC via DNS SRV lookups. The MIT distribution has also possessed support for several releases, but did not enable the feature by default until the 1.4 release. DNS queries for KDCs can be enabled in older version of MIT Kerberos by defining the KRB5_DNS_LOOKUP and KRB5_DNS_LOOKUP_KDC preprocessor macros at compile time.

To configure the Kerberos libraries for DNS lookups, first configure */etc/resolv.conf* to point to the DNS servers used by the AD clients and servers. Also be sure to set the DNS search suffix to the name of the AD domain. For our example, the DNS servers for the *blue.plainjoe.org* domain are at 192.168.1.101 and 192.168.2.101, which gives us the following *resolv.conf* file:

```
search blue.plainjoe.org
nameserver 192.168.1.101
nameserver 192.168.2.101
```

The only other step is to instruct the Krb5 libs to query DNS for the name and address of KDCs by enabling the dns_lookup_kdc option in the [libdefaults] section:

```
dns_lookup_kdc = true
```

Manually configuring KDCs lookups. Although we recommend the use of AD for lookups whenever possible, as shown in the previous section, you can instead configure KDC addresses manually in *krb5.conf*. To do so, add a section for each realm that may be contacted in the [realms] section. Assuming that we have no trusted domains, a single entry for BLUE.PLAINJOE.ORG will suffice.

In this example, we have one KDC named *bluedc1.blue.plainjoe.org*. Multiple KDCs may be specified by including additional kdc lines in the realm's configuration.

```
[realms]
    BLUE.PLAINJOE.ORG = {
        kdc = bluedc1.blue.plainjoe.org
    }
```

Final steps

Before moving a client to the final stage of joining the AD domain, it is a good idea to verify that the Kerberos client configuration is functioning properly. The easiest way to do this is to use *kinit* to obtain a TGT for an existing domain user. Our example uses the built-in Administrator account:

```
$ kinit Administrator
Password for Administrator@BLUE.PLAINJOE.ORG: <password for Administrator>
```

The MIT variant of *kinit* does not provide any feedback unless the TGT request is unsuccessful. Heimdal's *kinit* indicates success by providing the maximum lifetime of the obtained TGT. Regardless of the Krb5 distribution used, it is possible to view the current ticket cache using the *klist* command:

```
$ klist
Default principal: Administrator@BLUE.PLAINJOE.ORG

Valid starting     Expires            Service principal
06/18/06 20:49:03  06/19/06 06:49:05  krbtgt/BLUE.PLAINJOE.ORG@BLUE.PLAINJOE.ORG
        renew until 06/19/06 20:49:03
```

The command output proves that we have obtained a TGT for Administrator by listing the ticket for the principal *krbtgt/BLUE.PLAINJOE.ORG@BLUE.PLAINJOE.ORG*, the standard principal name given to the Kerberos authentication server for our realm.

There are a few errors that can commonly occur at this stage. The most common errors and potential solutions are:

Unable to locate a KDC for the requested realm
> The client was unable to determine a KDC for the principal's realm. Verify that the default_realm value in *krb5.conf* is spelled correctly. If so, verify that either the kdc parameter is specified for the realm in the [realms] section or dns_lookup_dns is enabled in [libdefaults]. When using DNS SRV queries to locate a KDC, use either *nslookup* or the *host* utility to confirm that the SRV record for the *_kerberos._udp* hostname is resolvable in the domain.

KDC has no support for encryption type while getting initial credentials

Verify that the list of supported encryption types in */etc/krb5.conf* includes RC4-HMAC. If you are using an older version of Kerberos libraries that do no support this encryption type, it is recommended that you upgrade your Kerberos libraries if possible. However, you may be able to work around the error by changing the Administrator's password once to generate the user's necessary DES Krb5 keys.

Preauthentication failed

Confirm that you are entering the correct password for the user's account.

Clock skew too great

By default, all AD domain controllers require that the clocks on both clients and servers are within five minutes of each other. Go back and resync the system's time to match that of the DC.

Once you have confirmed a working Krb5 client installation, the existing ticket cache should be cleared using the *kdestroy* command. This command prevents the *net* command from ignoring the user credentials that are entered on the command line. Both the Heimdal and MIT implementation of this tool return directly to a command prompt upon success with no additional messages.

With all the preliminary steps completed, it is now time to perform the net join. The command-line arguments are identical to the ones used to join using security = domain; once again, this command must be run as *root*:

```
$ net join -U Administrator
Administrator's password: <enter password for Administrator>
Using short domain name - BLUE
Joined 'OAK' to realm 'BLUE.PLAINJOE.ORG'
```

Any failures during the join process can usually be traced to Kerberos errors or *net* failures, both of which have been previously discussed. If you have misspelled or omitted the workgroup in *smb.conf*, the join process may succeed, but will inform you of an error. Make sure to correct this mistake in *smb.conf*:

```
The workgroup in smb.conf does not match the short
domain name obtained from the server.
Using the name [BLUE] from the server.
You should set "workgroup = BLUE" in smb.conf.
Using short domain name - BLUE
```

We can verify our machine account at any time in AD by running the following command:

```
$ net ads testjoin
Join is OK
```

Integrating Kerberized Unix services

Even before its adoption by Microsoft, Kerberos always supported machine principals. For example, an SSH server may use the principal name *host/machine.example.com*, and an LDAP directory server may use *ldap/machine.example.com*. These are different principals even though they are hosted by the same machine. The secret keys for these service principals are stored in a keytab file (usually */etc/krb5.keytab*). In AD domains, these secret keys are derived from the machine trust account password.

Samba will manage a server's keytab file if the use kerberos keytab option is enabled in *smb.conf*:

```
[global]
    use kerberos keytab = yes
```

If this parameter is enabled when joining the domain, the *net join* command creates the keytab file automatically. If you decide to make use of a keytab file after the member server has been configured, you can create a keytab file by using the *net ads keytab* command. The create subcommand generates initial entries for the *host/machine* principal. This command must be run as *root*, because it requires access to Samba's *secrets.tdb* file and must be able to write the keytab records to */etc/krb5.keytab*:

```
$ net ads keytab create -P
```

 It is possible to define a custom location for the keytab file by defining the KRB5_KTNAME environment variable.

New service principals can be added to the machine's account in AD and to the keytab file using *net ads keytab add*. All that is needed is the principal (service) name, not the full *principal/instance* syntax. The -P option uses the machine account and prevents you from having to enter user credentials. For example, to add a keytab entry for the *HTTP/machine.example.com* service principal used by Apache kerberos modules, we would execute:

```
$ net ads keytab add HTTP -P
Processing principals to add...
```

This command adds a new servicePrincipalName to the server's account in AD and stores the new key in the local keytab file. Tables 10-1 and 10-2 summarize the keytab-related parameters and tools covered in this section.

Table 10-1. Keytab-related parameters

Parameter	Value	Description	Default	Scope
use kerberos keytab	boolean	Enables Samba's keytab management functionality.	no	Global

Table 10-2. *net ads keytab management options*

Command	Description
add	Adds a new service principal value for the server's machine account.
create	Generates a keytab file based on the existing service principal values associated with the server in AD.
flush	Removes all entries from the keytab file.

Locating a Domain Controller

In default configurations, Samba attempts to automatically find domain controllers for any domain that it must contact. These auto lookups rely heavily on network name services. Remember that the order in which these services are queried is controlled by the name resolve order global option.

When configured for security = domain, NetBIOS name services are used to resolve the *DOMAIN<0x1b>* name when searching for the PDC and the *DOMAIN<0x1c>* name when any DC will do. Thus, unless the server will communicate only with domain controllers on its own subnet, Samba must be configured to use the WINS server (or servers) for the domain.

In an Active Directory domain, Samba is able to use DNS, just as Windows 2000 and later clients do. If the DNS lookup fails to return one or more domain controller names, Samba may fall back to NetBIOS name queries, much as it did when using domain mode security, assuming that the disable netbios parameter has not been enabled.

> Prior to the 3.0.23 release, Samba queried for the SRV record *_ldap._tcp.<domain>* when searching for an AD domain controller. Beginning with 3.0.23, Samba searches for the *_ldap._tcp.dc._msdcs.<domain>* record, just as Windows clients do.

You can exert a little more control over which domain controller is used by Samba for its own domain by setting the global password server option. This parameter accepts a list of one or more domain controllers using the standard *smb.conf* delimiters (whitespace or commas). Names of these preferred DCs can be NetBIOS names, hostnames, or fully qualified DNS names, but they must be resolvable to an address. For instance, to restrict Samba to using the domain controllers named *dc1* and *dc2*, add the following line to the server's *smb.conf* file:

```
password server = dc1 dc2
```

Samba attempts to contact the host at *dc1* first and continues to contact *dc2* only if the first server cannot be contacted. As long as *dc1* is available, *dc2* is not used. Adding the wildcard character (*) to the list instructs Samba to include any domain controllers found using its internal auto lookup support. This means you can use a local DC, but still fall back to any DC, should the preferred DC become unavailable.

> ## NetBIOS: Rest in Peace
>
> It is feasible to remove NetBIOS from your network, but only when operating in an AD
> environment. Even then, many administrators find it very difficult to remove all appli-
> cations that have a dependency on some piece of this legacy protocol. However, if you
> are feeling adventurous, Microsoft operating systems, starting with Windows 2000,
> can be configured to drop all support for NetBIOS by relying on DNS for name services
> and using TCP and UDP for the transport protocols. In order to configure Samba to
> behave the same way, define the following group of parameters:
>
> ```
>     [global]
>         smb ports = 445
>         disable netbios = yes
>         name resolve order = hosts
> ```
>
> At this point, there is no reason to support network browsing, either, because it does
> not function properly without the presence of NetBIOS name services. So there is no
> reason to run the *nmbd* daemon at all, as it is responsible only for NetBIOS name reg-
> istrations, acting as a WINS server, and participating in browsing elections.

A word of caution before moving on. It is frequently better to allow Samba to find a
domain controller on its own. As with most parameter values, developers work
extremely hard to make Samba robust and efficient. In some cases, it is necessary to
manually specify the DC that your server will use, but it is recommended that you do
this only as a last resort.

Table 10-3 concludes this section by giving a brief listing of the parameters recently
covered.

Table 10-3. Domain controller location parameters

Parameter	Value	Description	Default	Scope
disable netbios	boolean	Controls Samba use of NetBIOS name services.	no	Global
password server	list	List of domain controllers Samba should prefer when operating as a member server.	*	Global

Matching Domain Users to Local Accounts

Remember from Chapter 5 that every user accessing the Samba server must be associated with a Unix uid. *smbd* goes through several steps in its attempt to find a
matching Unix account. This is true for users who are authenticated locally as well as
those validated by a remote domain controller.

The first step is to process the username map option, which may translate the current
account name to another string. For standalone servers, this is done before the
authentication request is processed, but for domain members, this transformation

occurs after authentication. As a result, any domain names in map entries must be fully qualified.*

Qualified domain names take two forms. When the server is using security = ads and not running Winbind, it is necessary to add an entry that qualifies the user by prefixing the complete realm in order to deal with Kerberos logins. Without *winbindd* (the Winbind daemon), Samba has no way to convert realm names to short names. NTLM login requests provide the short name of the domain, so we must also include an entry of the form *DOMAIN\user*. The complete entry for the user *leezard* in the AD domain *eden.plainjoe.org* (with a short name of EDEN) would appear as:

```
lizard = EDEN.PLAINJOE.ORG\leezard EDEN\leezard
```

 Beginning with Samba 3.0.21, *smbd* can obtain the short name of the domain from the Kerberos ticket, thus removing the need for the REALM\user username map entries.

When *winbindd* is available to convert realm names into short names, or when only NTLM authentication is supported (i.e., security = domain), the previous entry should be simplified to:

```
lizard = EDEN\leezard
```

But as you will soon see, when using *winbindd*, a username map may be entirely unnecessary.

Once any relevant mapping records have been processed, *smbd* queries the operating system for a uid matching the login name. If the user name is still in the fully qualified format, Samba searches for the qualified name first and falls back to look for the user name minus the domain if the qualified search fails to yield a match. Once a uid is located, Samba creates a token for the user containing the uid and all group memberships.

This search process implies that there is an implicit match between a local Unix user and a domain user possessing the same name. This implication may cause confusion when a user from a trusted domain accesses the server. Both *EDEN\adam* and *FRUIT\adam* map to the same Unix user, *adam*. In order to prevent a user from a trusted domain gaining access to files owned by a user of the same name in our domain, it is recommended that you disable domain trusts on the Samba host by setting:

```
[global]
    allow trusted domains = no
```

Returning to our search, if no matching uid can be found, *smbd* has two options: reject the login or map the user to the guest account. The map to guest parameter,

---

* This requirement was introduced in the 3.0.8 release.

first presented in Chapter 5, has a special setting that is valid only on domain member servers. When set to the value bad uid, Samba silently maps a domain user to the guest account if no corresponding Unix account can be found. This behavior allows you to require domain users to be authenticated without being concerned with creating any local accounts. The original 3.0 releases removed this functionality, which was the default behavior in Samba 2.2. But it was later included again as part of the map to guest option in version 3.0.20.

Winbind

So far, we have assumed that each domain account would be mapped to a preexisting Unix user or group. You may wish to deploy a Samba server with no preexisting Unix account infrastructure. In this cases, Winbind, the name given to the *winbindd* daemon and set of libraries that act as an intermediary between Unix services and Windows domain controllers, offers a means to manage domain users and groups without the overhead of local accounts.

In its most common configuration, Winbind maintains a database of domain accounts matched to Unix uids and gids. These Unix identifiers are allocated to domain users and groups from a range specified in *smb.conf*. Winbind then makes these SID-to-uid/gid mappings available to Unix applications via the Name Service Switch (NSS) interface so that lookups for a user such as *EDEN\leezard* returns an entry resembling a line from */etc/passwd*:

```
EDEN\leezard:*:10000:10002:Lee Zard:/home/EDEN/leezard:/bin/false
```

Winbind is currently supported on the following platforms: AIX, FreeBSD 5.x, HP-UX 11.x, IRIX, Linux, and Solaris. If you are using vendor-provided Samba packages for any of these platforms, chances are good that *winbindd* and its associated pieces are already installed. If you compile Samba yourself on a supported platform, the following files will be created:

winbindd

> The long-running daemon that communicates with domain controllers on behalf of other Unix processes, including *smbd*.

libnss_winbind.so

> This library provides the support functions for the passwd and group NSS databases listed in */etc/nsswitch.conf*. The library extension, *.so*, may vary depending on the convention used by your server's operating system.

pam_winbind.so

> A PAM module utilizing *winbindd* to provide NTLM authentication and password change support. This library is built only if you have enabled the --with-pam option when compiling Samba. Its extension, *.so*, may vary depending on the convention used by your server's operating system.

---

ntlm_auth
> A command-line interface providing features similar to the *pam_winbind.so* library. The tool is commonly used to provide challenge/response authentication to Unix services such as dial-in and web proxy servers.

wbinfo
> A command line utility for interacting with *winbindd*. Although it can be used in shell scripts, its main purpose is as an administrative testing tool to ensure that *winbindd* is functioning properly.

 You can force Winbind to be compiled by specifying the --with-winbind option when running the *configure* script. This option can be useful when porting Winbind to a new platform.

By default, Samba's *make install* process places *winbindd* in */usr/local/samba/sbin* and the *ntlm_auth* and *wbinfo* tools to */usr/local/samba/bin*. However, due to paranoia about copying files to operating system directories and the subtle differences between systems, neither the PAM nor NSS libraries are installed by default. These must be manually copied.

The target directory for the *pam_winbind* library varies, depending on your platform. The most common location is */lib/security/*. However, 64-bit Linux servers use */lib64/security*. Make sure to check your operating system's documentation for specifics. The following set of commands, executed as *root* on a 32-bit Linux host, installs the PAM module to the correct location and sets the appropriate ownership and permissions. It is assumed that you have already navigated to the top level of the Samba source tree.

```
$ cp source/bin/pam_winbind.so /lib/security/
$ chown root /lib/security/pam_winbind.so
$ chgrp root /lib/security/pam_winbind.so
$ chmod 755 /lib/security/pam_winbind.so
```

Next, install the NSS library. Once again, the target directory varies, depending on your server's operating system. In most cases, it is the */lib* directory. The library name is a bit less standard. On modern Linux systems, the library is called *libnss_winbind.so.2*, and on Solaris hosts it should be *nss_winbind.so.1*. Usually, you can just follow the convention of other NSS libraries on your system. As an example, these commands install the library on a 32-bit Linux host. Executing *ldconfig* at the end creates the symbolic link from *libnss_winbind.so.2* to *libnss_winbind.so*:

```
$ cp source/nsswitch/libnss_winbind.so /lib/libnss_winbind.so
$ chown root /lib/libnss_winbind.so
$ chgrp root /lib/libnss_winbind.so
$ chmod 755 /lib/libnss_winbind.so
$ ldconfig
```

Early versions of Samba 3.0 did not correctly set the internal version for the *libnss_winbind.so* library, and therefore require that you create the symbolic link manually.

After installing the NSS library, add the `winbind` service to the `passwd` and `group` databases in */etc/nsswitch.conf*. This step enables the operating system to query *winbindd* when searching for users and groups. Winbind will happily coexist in *nsswitch.conf* with other services such as NIS or LDAP. This example instructs the operating system to query local files, an LDAP directory service, and finally *winbindd* when searching for users and groups:

```
passwd: files ldap winbind
group:  files ldap winbind
```

The last step before starting *winbindd* is to specify a range of uid and gid values in *smb.conf* that can be allocated for domain users and groups. These allocations are then stored in the *winbindd_idmap.tdb* file, where they can be found after the system reboots. Each range, one for users and one for groups, must be continuous and must not overlap any existing accounts. On older Unix implementations that supported only 16-bit uid/gid values, this could be a problem. On newer platforms, the possibility of 4 billion uid values provided by 32-bit identifiers lessens the contention a bit. Here's an example that allots uids from 200,000 to 300,000 for *winbindd*'s use:

```
[global]
    idmap uid = 200000 - 300000
```

There is no absolute requirement that the `idmap gid` parameter use the same range as the uids, but this is a common convention:

```
    idmap gid = 200000 - 300000
```

It may seem that 100,000 users or groups would be plenty. It frequently is. There is, however, a potential mathematical problem. Each domain can potentially possess a total sum of users and groups just under 2^{32}. Although this limit is rarely reached in a single domain, mapping accounts from multiple trusted domains might reach the limit of the idmap ranges in *smb.conf*. We have never actually seen this occur in practice, because uids are allocated only when a domain user accessed the Samba server. It is rare for every user in a domain to access the same file server.

Once *smb.conf* has been modified, it is time to start *winbindd*. The daemon supports most of the command-line options common to *smbd* and *nmbd*. It does not, however, support being started from *inetd*. Normally *winbindd* is launched as part of the system boot process. To initially test your setup, start the server from the command line:

```
$ /usr/local/samba/sbin/winbindd
```

The internals of *winbindd* have been rewritten several times; most recently, in the 3.0.20 Samba release. In all of the 3.0 releases, you will see at least two *winbindd* processes. In Samba 3.0.20 and later, you may see more, depending on the number of trusts supported by your domain.

winbindd does not respond to network requests as *smbd* and *nmbd* do. It listens on two Unix domain sockets in */tmp/.winbindd* and the directory specified in the lock directory configuration option (normally */usr/local/samba/var/locks/winbindd_ privileged*). The former is accessible by any user for queries such as enumerating users or groups and resolving names to and from SIDs. In contrast, the *winbindd_ privileged* pipe is available only for *root*. Certain operations, such as NTLM challenge/response authentication and allocating a uid or gid, must be restricted from nonadministrative users for security reasons.

You can test that *winbindd* is responding correctly by using *wbinfo* to send it a ping request:

```
$ wbinfo -p
Ping to winbindd succeeded on fd 4
```

If you receive the message "could not ping winbindd!", make sure that *winbindd* is in fact running. If the server immediately exited, it may be helpful to start it interactively with a high debug level. The following examples show *winbindd* failing to start because it does not believe that it has been correctly joined to the domain:

```
$ winbindd -d 10 -i
<...intermediate output deleted...>
Could not fetch our SID - did we join?
unable to initialize domain list
```

Once you know that *winbindd* is responding to requests, verify that it can properly communicate with a domain controller. Running *wbinfo -t* validates Samba's machine trust account much in the same way as when we ran *net ... testjoin*. The difference in this case is that you are asking *winbindd* to validate the credentials rather than doing it yourself using the *net* command.

```
$ wbinfo -t
checking the trust secret via RPC calls succeeded
```

If you observe any failures at this point, recheck the trust account using *net ... testjoin* and follow the troubleshooting steps presented earlier in the chapter.

Next, verify *winbindd*'s ability to authenticate users. Using the -a option to *wbinfo*, ask *winbindd* to send a *NetSamLogon()* authentication request to the appropriate DC using a set of credentials passed in on the command line. The backslash is the default separator between the domain and login name and must be either quoted or escaped when specified in a shell environment. This delimiter can be changed to an alternate character by specifying the winbind separator option in *smb.conf*. The % character is used to separate the password from the username:

```
$ wbinfo -a "EDEN\leezard%test"
plaintext password authentication succeeded
challenge/response password authentication succeeded
```

If the previous tests have succeeded, this one should succeed as well. The plaintext authentication is similar to what is provided by *pam_winbind*. However, the challenge/ response authentication requires access to *winbindd*'s privileged pipe operations and therefore can succeed only if *wbinfo -a* is run as well. If both of these fail, ensure that you have entered the correct credentials.

There are quite a few more options to *wbinfo*. In fact, every query supported by *winbindd* has an analogous *wbinfo* command-line switch. Table 10-4 summarizes the remaining arguments supported by the tool. Note that some options possessing a long description string have no single-character equivalent.

Table 10-4. wbinfo options

Short option	Long option	Argument	Description
-a	--authenticate	*username%password*	Attempt to authenticate a user using NTLM.
-D	--domain-info	domain	List information regarding the domain.
	--getdcname	domain	Find a domain controller for a specific domain.
-g	--domain-groups		Enumerate domain groups.
-G	--gid-to-sid	gid	Convert a gid to a SID.
-?	--help		Display the help listing.
-m	--trusted-domains		Display the list of trusted domains.
-n	--name-to-sid	name	Convert a name into a SID.
-p	--ping		Ping the *winbindd* daemon.
-r	--user-groups	username	List the gids for groups to which the user belongs.
	--separator		Print the winbind separator character.
	--sequence		Display the current sequence number for all trusted domains, including our own.
-s	--sid-to-name	SID	Convert a SID to a user or group name.
-S	--sid-to-uid	SID	Convert a SID to a uid.
-t	--check-secret		Verify the machine account credentials.
	--user-domgroups	SID	Print the SIDs for the domain groups to which the user belongs.
	--user-sids	SID	Print the SIDs for the all groups to which the user belongs.
-u	--domain-users		Enumerate domain users.
-U	--uid-to-sid	uid	Convert a uid to a SID.
-Y	--sid-to-gid	SID	Convert a SID to a gid.

Next, verify that the NSS library is properly installed by issuing a call to retrieve a user from *libnss_winbind*. The resulting output also confirms *winbindd*'s ability to allocate uids and gids for users and groups. Many operating systems provide the *getent* tool for querying NSS databases. You can issue a query for a specific user by executing the following command. Remember to either quote the username or escape the backslash so that *getent* doesn't misinterpret the following l as a control character. If the *libnss_winbind* library is not installed in the correct location or has improper permissions, the test fails to locate the user.

```
$ getent passwd "EDEN\leezard"
EDEN\leezard:*:10000:10002:Lee Zard:/home/EDEN/leezard:/bin/false
```

If your operating system doesn't include a *getent* or equivalent command, the same test can be performed using Perl's *getpwnam( )* function:

```
$ perl -e '@pw = getpwnam("EDEN\\leezard"); print "@pw\n";'
EDEN\leezard * 10000 10002 Lee Zard /home/EDEN/leezard /bin/false
```

The home directory path and login shell values are filled in by the *smb.conf* parameters template homedir and template shell. The home directory location defaults to the path /home/%D/%U. %D and %U are *smb.conf* variables, documented in Chapter 4, for the user's domain and login name. The shell defaults to /bin/false, although you will see later how to change this to a valid shell in order to allow domain users access to non-Samba services using *pam_winbind*.

It is a good idea to rerun the *getent* test, but this time, search for a domain group:

```
$ getent group "EDEN\Domain Admins"
EDEN\domain admins:x:10003:EDEN\gcarter,EDEN\administrator
```

You are now ready to start both *smbd* and *nmbd* and connect as a domain user. The easiest way to view *winbindd* in action is to connect to a share using *smbclient* and examine the output from *smbstatus*. For the example here, assume that the server named ZERO is providing a file share named [public]:

```
$ smbclient //zero/public -U leezard -W EDEN
Password: test
Domain=[EDEN] OS=[Unix] Server=[Samba 3.0.22]
smb: \>
```

Running *smbstatus* on the server while still connected with *smbclient* shows that the the user *EDEN\leezard* has attached to the share public. The important bit of data is the username, which has been provided Winbind's NSS library:

```
$ smbstatus

Samba version 3.0.22
PID     Username      Group            Machine
-------------------------------------------------------------
13854   EDEN\leezard  EDEN\domain users  zero (127.0.0.1)

Service     pid     machine     Connected at
-------------------------------------------------------
public      13854   zero        Tue Jul  4 21:12:29 2006

No locked files
```

When *winbindd* performs actions such as authenticating a user or querying the membership of a group, it remembers certain information in an attempt to minimize network communication. In AD domains, it is almost guaranteed that cached user and group information will be flushed from the *winbindd_cache.tdb* file regularly at an interval specified in seconds by the `winbind cache time` option. This parameter defines the number of seconds before *winbindd* queries a DC to determine whether its local cache is still current. At most sites, the default of 5 minutes is sufficient, although you may wish to experiment with longer periods, depending on the replication period between your DCs. Rest assured that uids and gids allocated to users and groups are not part of this cache and persist across restarts and server reboots.

One very expensive operation in both in time and bandwidth, regardless of any amount of caching, is enumerating users and groups. This problem, coupled with the fact that current Windows service packs and hot fixes make it increasingly difficult to retrieve this information with only the machine account credentials, have led Samba developers to recommend that both the `winbind enum users` and `winbind enum groups` parameters be disabled. These two parameters are used to enable or disable Winbind NSS support for the *getpwent( )* and *getgrent( )* set of functions, which have historically been used to iterate over available user accounts. Developers agree that these functions are highly inefficient and that an application should use the *getpwnam( )* or *getgrnam( )* function when looking for a specific user or group. Nevertheless, there are a still a few older applications that may fail if you disable user and group enumeration. Our advice is to get a newer version of the application. If you ever need to enumerate accounts, *wbinfo*'s -u and -g options will continue to work, as these are independent of the NSS library.

Table 10-5 concludes our initial setup of Winbind by summarizing the *smb.conf* parameters presented in this section.

Table 10-5. Basic Winbind options

Parameter	Value	Description	Default	Scope
idmap uid idmap gid	integer range	Range of uid and gid values from which *winbindd* can allocate for domain users and groups.	None	Global
template homedir	string	Home directory path used to fill in *passwd* entries for domains users.	/home/%D/%U	Global
template shell	string	The shell used to fill in *passwd* entries for domain users.	/bin/false	Global
winbind cache time	integer	The number of seconds for which *winbindd* assumes that cached information is valid.	300	Global
winbind enum users winbind enum groups	boolean	If enabled, *winbindd* supports enumerating users and groups via the *getpwent( )* and *getgrent( )* NSS calls.	yes[a]	Global
winbind separator	character	The character used to separate the domain name from the user or group name when displaying domain accounts.	\	Global

[a] These two parameters are disabled by default starting with release 3.0.23.

idmap Backends

In some scenarios, you may wish to have more control over how *winbindd* allocates uids and gids for domain accounts, or want to share mappings between Winbind installations on multiple servers. The idmap backend parameter allows you to specify an alternative SID-to-uid/gid database, which may also provide alternative uid and gid allocation semantics. We have already mentioned one backend: tdb. The default tdb idmap implementation stores uid and gid allocations in the local database file *winbindd_idmap.tdb*.

Samba 3.0.22 currently ships with four supported idmap backend modules:

tdb

> The default backend used for local uid and gid allocation. Its main advantage is that it requires very little setup or maintenance. Its main disadvantage is that a user is allocated a different uid on each Winbind server installation, thus making it incompatible with NFS.

ldap

> Support for storing SID-to-uid/gid mappings in an LDAP directory service was added to address the problems with NFS and the tdb backend. If your network already has an available LDAP directory, this backend provides a simple means of ensuring consistent mapping tables among multiple Winbind installations.

rid

> The RID backend shared library provides a central mapping solution for single domain installations. It is built only when the --with-shared-modules=idmap_rid option is passed to the *configure* script. The RID backend guarantees consistent one-to-one mappings between domain SIDs and Unix accounts by generating the Unix ID value based on the Windows Relative Identifier. Because a user's or group's RID does not change for the lifetime of the account, you are ensured that the uid or gid will be the same in every Winbind install. However, because Windows domain allocates RIDs in a monotonic fashion beginning with 1,000, it does not support trusted domains, as accounts in multiple domains may be mapped to the same local Unix uid/gid.

ad

The AD backend utilizes POSIX information stored in Active Directory rather than allocating any uid or gid local values, and currently supports only a domain with the Services for Unix (SFU) schema extensions. To create this plug-in, you must specify the --with-shared-modules=idmap_ad option when building Samba. Note that although this option gains you the most flexibility for managing specific uid and gid values, it also requires that you manually manage additional attributes for accounts in AD.

With the exception of tdb, let's look at the specific configuration details of each backend. The default tdb configuration was covered in the previous section as part of our initial Winbind installation.

idmap backed = ldap

Winbind's LDAP backend shares much of its configuration settings with the ldapsam passdb backend discussed in Chapter 5. If Samba has been compiled to include LDAP support, the ldap idmap feature is included in *winbindd*. Based on the parameters presented in conjunction with the ldapsam module, our initial *smb.conf* contains the following parameters:

```
[global]
    ldap admin dn = cn=smbadmin,ou=people,dc=example,dc=com
    ldap suffix = dc=example,dc=com
```

We also assume that *smbpasswd -w* has been run to store the admin DN's password in *secrets.tdb* and that the LDAP directory service has already loaded Samba's distributed schema file.

The next step is to specify where the SID-to-uid/gid mappings will be stored in the directory using the ldap idmap suffix parameter. All that is required is that this DN exists and may be modified by the account specified in the ldap admin dn option. *winbindd* will handle the rest. The server in our example uses an organizational unit directly below the directory root for storing idmap entries:

```
    ldap idmap suffix = ou=idmap
```

idmap modules use a syntax similar to their passdb counterparts for defining configuration settings. Parameters are appended to the module name using a colon followed by the option's value. The only parameter that this module supports is the LDAP server's URI. The following setting in *smb.conf*'s [global] section informs *winbindd* to contact the LDAP server named *ldap.example.com*:

```
    idmap backend = ldap:ldap://ldap.example.com
```

As with the user and group information in Chapter 5, the best solution is to allow *winbindd* to manage its LDAP entries without any interference. It will keep track of the next available uid and gid values and ensure that each is allocated atomically and store in the directory. Other instances of *winbindd* then query the LDAP directory prior to allocating a new uid or gid. The use of the SID as the RDN value prevents two servers from creating multiple records for a given user or group.

The LDIF entry shows the the next available uid (207250) and gid (204932) values maintained by *winbindd* in the ldap idmap suffix:

```
    dn: ou=idmap,dc=example,dc=com
    objectClass: organizationalUnit
    objectClass: sambaUnixIdPool
    ou: idmap
    uidNumber: 207250
    gidNumber: 204932
```

When *winbindd* needs to allocate a new Unix user, it increments the `uidNumber` attribute by one and store the SID and allocated uid in the directory. The following LDIF represents a mapping between the SID S-1-5-21-406022937-1377575209-526660263-8188 and the uid 205342:

```
dn: sambaSID=S-1-5-21-406022937-1377575209-526660263-8188,
  ou=idmap,dc=example,dc=com
objectClass: sambaIdmapEntry
objectClass: sambaSidEntry
uidNumber: 205342
sambaSID: S-1-5-21-406022937-1377575209-526660263-8188
```

If you observe any failures in the *winbindd* logfiles when attempting to access the LDAP directory, check whether you have specified the correct `ldap suffix` and `ldap idmap suffix` values and that the directory service's access controls allow modification to those locations by the `ldap admin dn` account.

idmap backed = rid

The *idmap_rid* plug-in, like the ldap idmap module, provides consistent uid and gid allocation across servers. It is much easier to configure, mainly because it is able to make use of existing domain account information rather than requiring an extra directory service other than the Windows domain itself. However, it is less flexible in terms of support for trusted domains and administrative control over uid and gid assignments. Still, its ease of use and compatibility with both Windows NT 4.0 and Active Directory domains make it very attractive for many administrators.

To build the *idmap_rid* (or *rid*) shared library, you must specify `--with-shared-modules=idmap_rid` when running the Samba's configure script.[*] Even if you are relying on Samba packages provided by a vendor, you may find it necessary to compile the library yourself, as it is not always included. Once built, the *idmap_rid* library should be installed in */usr/local/samba/lib/idmap* as part of the *make install* process.

Next, configure the idmap parameters in *smb.conf*. In this example, we'll set the `idmap uid` and `idmap gid` options exactly as we did before, except that this module does require that both parameters specify the same range. The `idmap backend` option need only refer to the *rid* plug-in by name:

```
[global]
    idmap uid = 200000 - 300000
    idmap gid = 200000 - 300000
    idmap backend = rid
```

Because the rid plug-in officially supports only a single domain, you must also disable support for trusted domains in *smb.conf*:

```
allow trusted domains = no
```

---

[*] Operating system support for shared libraries is also a requirement.

To calculate the uid or gid assigned to a domain user or group, add the RID to the lower end of the idmap range and verify that the resulting value is less than the upper boundary of the range. So a user with the SID S-1-5-21-3493585492-4029240144-3226775320-1168 would be assigned the uid of 201168 (1168 + 200000).

Although the rid idmap module does not officially support trusted domains, it can be built with unofficial support by defining the `IDMAP_RID_SUPPORT_TRUSTED_DOMAINS` macro when running *make*.

```
$ make -DIDMAP_RID_SUPPORT_TRUSTED_DOMAINS bin/rid.so
```

The resulting library allows you to split up the idmap range between domains by defining the subrange as an option to the `idmap backed = rid` directive. The following setting splits the range (200000–300000) between the domains EDEN and PERSIA. Always use the short name of the domains here, even when joined to an AD domain. The ranges cannot overlap, or exceed the original idmap uid and gid ranges.

```
idmap backend = rid:EDEN=200000-26000,PERSIA=260001-300000
```

The main disadvantage in this configuration, and mostly likely why it is not officially supported by Samba developers, is that if the first domain ever outgrows the allotted ids, there is no way to expand the available range without changing all of the uids and gids allocated to the second domain.

idmap backed = ad

The final idmap module examined here is the *idmap_ad* library, which uses the Microsoft's SFU schema extensions for managing Unix users and group attributes in AD. Like the *rid* plug-in, it also requires that you include it in the list of shared modules (`--with-shared-modules=idmap_ad`) when compiling Samba. The resulting library (named *ad.so* or *idmap_ad.so*, depending on your Samba version and platform) is installed in */usr/local/samba/lib/idmap/* by default.

 The *ad* library included in Samba 3.0.23 also works with the RFC2307 schema support in Windows 2003 R2.

The setup is remarkably easy. All that is required is to enable the module using the `idmap backend` parameter:

```
idmap backend = ad
```

Because the uid and gid information is maintained in Active Directory, there is no need to specify an available range in *smb.conf*. This approach does, however, require some coordination between Unix and AD administrators because *winbindd* does not check whether a uid from AD overlaps with any local Unix users.

Normally the home directory path and login shell values for users in Winbind's NSS output would be filled in from the `template homedir` and `template shell` options.

However, the SFU schema also supports storing these attributes in AD. The `winbind nss info` option allows us to specify whether we want to retrieve the real attributes from AD (`sfu`) or to fill them in with template values (`template`). To make use of the SFU attributes, add the following line to the global section of *smb.conf*:

```
winbind nss info = sfu
```

Figure 10-3 shows the SFU attributes for a user in a Windows 2003 domain named *ocean.plainjoe.org*. And here is corresponding passwd record returned from *libnss_winbind*:

```
$ getent passwd "OCEAN\phish"
OCEAN\phish:*:10007:10027:Peter Trout:/home/phish:/bin/bash
```

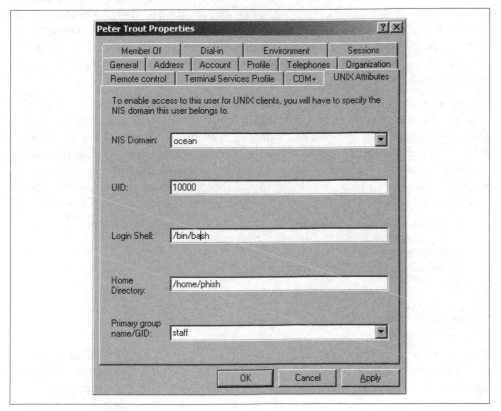

Figure 10-3. SFU attributes for a user in AD

Table 10-6 provides a brief summary of the parameter introduced in this section.

Table 10-6. Winbind NSS sources

Parameter	Value	Description	Default	Scope
winbind nss info	template, sfu[a]	The data source used to fill in Unix attributes other than the numeric uid or gid.	template	Global

[a] Samba 3.0.23 will also support the additional value rfc2307 for Windows 2003 R2 domains.

Additional Winbind Features

Winbind is most known for its ability to create Unix accounts for Windows domain users and groups. However, it possesses some lesser-known but equally useful functionality. These features can further help you consolidate authentication, unify authorization controls, and provide accounts in Samba domains for trusted domain users and groups.

PAM and Domains

Winbind's PAM interface provides Unix services other than Samba a means to authenticate domain users. Consider the case of providing domain users access to an IMAP or POP mail server without requiring a second password. Any Unix service using PAM authentication may be configured to support domain credentials in this manner. We'll use an OpenSSH server as an example, due to its pervasiveness in Unix networks.

It may seem obvious, but we must remind you to verify that the Unix service in question has been compiled to include PAM support. Few things are more frustrating than spending a hour in attempt to deduce why the server is not recognizing the PAM changes and finally realizing that the configuration file is being completely ignored. Vendors usually provide documentation regarding the features that were enabled when the software was built. In the absence of this, a quick check with *ldd* or the *strings* utility will indicate whether a binary has been linked with *libpam.so*:

```
$ ldd /usr/sbin/sshd | grep pam
      libpam.so.0 => /lib/libpam.so.0 (0x4008f000)
$ strings /usr/sbin/sshd | grep pam
pam_get_item
pam_getenvlist
pam_end
pam_chauthtok
pam_authenticate
<...remaining output deleted...>
```

If both of these checks fail to return any output, there's a high probability that the server does not include PAM support. If that is the case, you may be able to find an updated package from your OS vendor or, if all else fails, to recompile the server software yourself.

It is also a good idea to verify that any runtime PAM configuration settings are turned on as well. For example, OpenSSH requires that the UsePAM option be enabled in its configuration file (usually */etc/ssh/sshd_config*):

```
UsePAM yes
```

If you make any changes to the *sshd_config* file, make sure to send a HUP signal to *sshd* so that it will reload its configuration.

Once you know that the server is honoring its PAM configuration file, you can add the *pam_winbind* library to the stack. For OpenSSH, this means editing either */etc/pam.conf* or */etc/pam.d/ssh* (depending on your server's operating system) and adding a line to the list of auth modules. The following snippet from */etc/pam.d/ssh* on a SUSE Linux host specifies that *sshd* will attempt to authenticate the user against local files first and fall back to Winbind if this fails:

```
auth    sufficient    pam_unix2.so
auth    required      pam_winbind.so  use_first_pass
```

pam_winbind also supports the PAM account module type. This configuration from */etc/pam.d/ssh* at least verifies that your *libnss_winbind* is functioning properly:

```
account sufficient      pam_unix2.so
account required        pam_winbind.so
```

Now let's take another look at the *getpwnam()* reply returned by *winbindd* that was presented earlier:

```
EDEN\leezard:*:10000:10002:Lee Zard:/home/EDEN/leezard:/bin/false
```

Winbind fills in the home directory location (here, */home/EDEN/leezard*) from the template homedir parameter (assuming that you use an idmap backend other than the ad plug-in). But Winbind does not verify that the directory path exists or attempt to create it. These jobs are commonly handled by another PAM module or some means outside of PAM. For ease of use, our example configuration loads the *pam_mkhomedir* module as part of the session configuration to create the user's home directory and populate it with basic shell initialization files:

```
session required    pam_unix2.so
session required    pam_mkhomedir.so  skel=/etc/skel/ umask=0022
```

The *pam_unix2* library performs auditing, such as writing session information to the system's utmp logs.

The *pam_winbind* library is omitted from this section of */etc/pam.d/ssh*, because it does not implement PAM session support.

Before anyone attempts to log in, you must give users a valid shell. Set the template shell parameter to whatever shell you prefer:

```
template shell = /bin/bash
```

After restarting *winbindd*, verify that the parameter has taken effect:

```
$ getent passwd "EDEN\leezard"
EDEN\leezard:*:10000:10002:Lee Zard:/home/EDEN/leezard:/bin/bash
```

Now we can finally log in to the server zero using an SSH client:

```
$ ssh -l "eden\leezard" zero
Password: <password for leezard>
Creating directory '/home/EDEN/leezard'.
Creating directory '/home/EDEN/leezard/Documents'.
Creating directory '/home/EDEN/leezard/public_html'.
```

```
Have a lot of fun...

EDEN\leezard@zero:~> whoami
EDEN\lizard

EDEN\leezard@zero:~> id
uid=10004(EDEN\leezard) gid=10002(EDEN\domain users)
groups=10002(EDEN\domain users),10015(EDEN\linux admins)
```

If the login fails, enable additional debugging in *sshd* and examine its logfiles. You can also make *pam_winbind* generate additional debugging information by passing it the debug parameter as part of the PAM configuration. The discussion of tracing processes presented Chapter 12 may also be of use in this case.

Some users find typing the fully qualified *DOMAIN\username* login string to be annoying or just confusing. Although there is no cure for this for users in trusted domains, it is possible to instruct Winbind to assume its own domain if one is not specified when authenticating non-Samba services. This is done by enabling the winbind use default domain global option, shown in Table 10-7, in *smb.conf*:

```
winbind use default domain = yes
```

The user *EDEN\leezard* can now log on to the server by simply executing *ssh leezard@zero*. Table 10-7 summarizes this configuration option.

Table 10-7. Winbind PAM option

Parameter	Value	Description	Default	Scope
winbind use default domain	boolean	If enabled, Winbind assumes that unqualified user and group names are to be looked up in the domain to which it has been joined.	no	Global

Of course, you may not wish to allow all domain users to log in to your Unix server. The require_membership_of option allows you to specify the SID of a group to which the user must belong in order for the authentication to succeed. Remember that you can use *wbinfo -n* to resolve a domain account name to a SID. For example, here we obtain the SID for the *EDEN\Linux Admins* group:

```
$ wbinfo -n "EDEN\linux admins"
S-1-5-21-4200961138-2496335650-1239021823-1209 Domain Group (2)
```

We can then add this SID to the auth line for *pam_winbind* to prevent anyone who is not a member of EDEN's *Linux Admins* domain group from logging on via SSH. The *pam_winbind* configuration line has been wrapped for readability:

```
auth  sufficient  pam_unix2.so
auth  required    pam_winbind.so  use_first_pass
    require_membership_of=S-1-5-21-4200961138-2496335650-1239021823-1209
```

pam_winbind also supports changing of a user's domain password. We can let the */etc/pam.d/passwd* file set the credentials for either a local account or a domain account by specifying the follow two lines:

```
password   sufficient   pam_unix2.so
password   required      pam_winbind.so
```

We'll conclude this section with Table 10-8, which gives a complete list of *pam_winbind*'s configuration parameters.

Table 10-8. pam_winbind options

Parameter	Description
debug	Enable additional log messages from *pam_winbind*.
require_membership_of=SID require-membership-of=SID	Restrict authentication to users belonging to a specific domain group.
try_first_pass	Attempt to use the initial password entered by the user before prompting for new credentials.
unknown_ok	Ignore any failures for users who cannot be found via *getpwnam( )* calls. This option is relevant only in the account module configuration.
use_authtok	Use PAM's authentication token when changing passwords.
use_first_pass	Use only the initial password entered by the user. Do not prompt for new credentials if the initial one cannot be validated.

Local Nested Groups

Windows offers several types of groups. We won't attempt to explain all of them, but it is important to understand how local groups function in order to understand Samba's implementation of them.

Under Windows NT 4.0, a local group (sometimes referred to as an *alias*) was local to a machine or group of domain controllers. The local group existed under the domain of the local machine's SID. Microsoft extended this model in AD and made local groups defined on the domain controllers available to all domain members. Samba implements the Windows NT 4.0 model of local groups.

The important feature that makes local groups attractive is that they can contain local users, domain users, or domain groups. This is how all Domain Admins gain administrative access to machines joined to a domain. The Windows client adds the *Domain Admins* group to the local *Administrators* group upon joining the domain. Figure 10-4 shows the *EDEN\Domain Admins* group as a member of the *Administrators* group on a Windows XP member server.

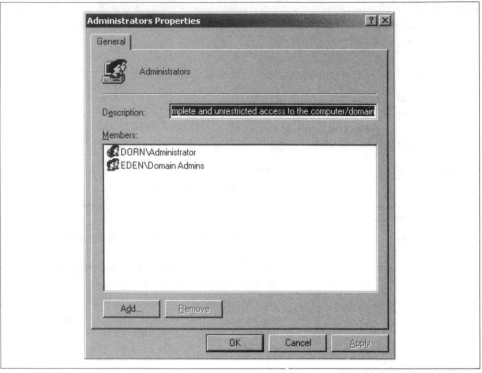

Figure 10-4. Local Administrators group on a Windows XP client containing Domain Admins group

Winbind provides Samba's support for local group nesting by creating Unix groups in its idmap table and unrolling the group membership before returning a list of users via NSS. In other words, Samba returns a single flat list of users, even if some of those users were buried in various nested group memberships.

You must begin with a working Winbind installation using the tdb or ldap idmap backend. This means that the idmap uid and gid ranges have been defined in *smb. conf*, the *libnss_winbind* library has been installed, */etc/nsswitch.conf* has been updated for the Winbind services, and *winbindd* is successfully answering requests.

Next, add the following line to Samba's configuration to turn on the local group feature and restart *winbindd*:

```
[global]
     winbind nested groups = yes
```

Use the *lusrmgr.msc* tool from a Windows client to create a new group, as shown in Figure 10-5. You can add domain groups as members, as well as users. In the figure, we have added the *EDEN\Linux Admins* domain group and a local user named *slug* to the local *ZERO\sysadmin* groups.

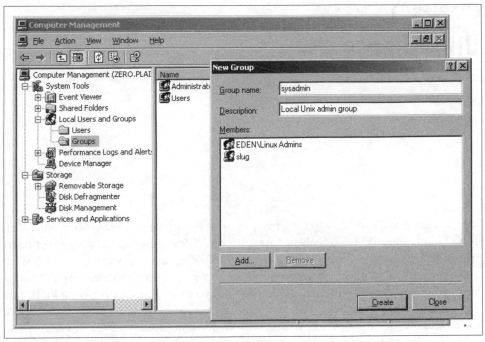

Figure 10-5. Creating a local group on a Samba server with the Windows XP MMC

When we expand the group using the *getent* tool, the *Linux Admins* group has been expanded to its individual members: *EDEN\leezard* and *EDEN\adam*.

```
$ getent group 'zero\sysadmin'
ZERO\sysadmin:x:10011:slug,EDEN\lizard,EDEN\adam
```

The real advantage of doing this, from a Unix administrator's perspective, is that you can now use the gid 10011 in filesystem ACLs or other Unix authorization policies and it will apply to members of the Linux Admins domain group. With a little imagination, you can find many ways to take advantage of group nesting on your servers. Table 10-9 finishes up our discussion regarding local groups with a brief summary of the new parameter presented.

Table 10-9. Winbind group nesting options

Parameter	Value	Description	Default	Scope
winbind nested groups	boolean	Enables Winbind's support for providing and expanding local group membership via NSS.	no	Global

CHAPTER 11
Unix Clients

Samba's fame and popularity come from its ability to serve pervasive Microsoft Windows clients, but SMB/CIFS clients are also available on a wide variety of platforms and operating systems from desktops to handhelds, running your choice of Windows, Linux, Mac OS X, or any number of other operating systems. By providing SMB/CIFS support on heterogeneous systems, you can standardize your local area network, allowing everybody to use, for instance, the cross-platform OpenOffice.org suite (*http://www.openoffice.org*). Users on Windows, Linux, and OS X systems will be able to access both local and remote documents in the same fashion. Files can be shared by saving them to the SMB/CIFS share just as if it were a local hard disk. This method can also be part of a migration strategy for moving users from one operating system to another.

The most transparent means of accessing SMB/CIFS file shares is to provide a filesystem that understands the protocol. In this chapter, we explore the native SMB/CIFS filesystem support available on Linux, OS X, and FreeBSD systems.

In the absence of an SMB/CIFS filesystem, you can turn to tools provided by Samba, such as *smbclient*. Although command-line utilities do not provide the seamless integration of a filesystem, they are extremely portable. This portability means that you can develop your own administration scripts utilizing *smbclient* and be assured that they will run on Linux, Solaris, HP-UX, or any other Unix server on which Samba is available.

Finally, we examine some of Samba's tools that can help you to perform remote administration tasks from Unix clients. One example is the *net* tool, which can perform common tasks such as managing users and groups, restarting services, and rebooting servers.

The Linux CIFS Filesystem

We'll begin by exploring the new CIFS filesystem included in the Linux 2.6 kernel. A patch for 2.4 kernels is available from the project's web site at *http://linux-cifs.samba. org*. Here you will also find the latest released source code, which may not have been integrated into the mainline kernel tree yet. We won't go into the details of compiling a Linux kernel. If you require details about how to do this, *Running Linux*, by Matt Welsh et al., or *Linux Kernel in a Nutshell*, by Greg Kroah-Hartman (O'Reilly) are good places to find out more.

Linux's original SMB/CIFS filesystem client, named *smbfs*, was written by Volker Lendecke, an active Samba developer. The *cifs* kernel VFS module has since superseded *smbfs*. However, there is still some confusion among Linux users and admins alike which one should be used. The *smbfs* kernel module and user space tools (*smbmount*, *smbumount*, and *smbmnt*) will likely continue to be included in Linux and Samba for some time, but none of these pieces has an active maintainer. Therefore any reported bugs will very likely not be fixed. If you have Linux systems that are currently set up to use *smbfs*, now is a good time to begin thinking about migrating them to use the *cifs* module instead.

The primary difference between the *cifs* and *smbfs* kernel modules is that *cifs* was originally written to work only against servers running Windows NT 4.0 or later (as well as Samba servers). In the 2.6.15 Linux kernel, however, *cifs* picked up support for connecting to shares on Windows 9x/Me hosts, which makes it only a matter of time before the *smbfs* code is removed entirely.

Installation

The Linux CIFS filesystem is composed of two parts: the kernel code (referred to by the name of the kernel module, *cifs*) and the user-space mount tools. The *cifs* kernel filesystem support is generally built as a module and loaded when a user attempts to connect to an SMB/CIFS file server using the *mount* command. The easiest way to tell whether your Linux host possesses *cifs* support is to examine the contents of */proc/filesystems*. Check this file and look for the term *cifs* listed in the output:

```
$ cat /proc/filesystems | grep cifs
nodev   cifs
```

If *grep* fails to match anything in the file, try manually loading the *cifs* kernel module with the help of the *modprobe* command. You must run the following command as *root*:

```
$ modprobe cifs
```

If you are returned immediately to a shell prompt, the module loaded correctly. Examine */proc/filesystems* again; *cifs* should be listed this time. However, if the kernel was built without the *cifs* feature enabled, you will see the following error:

```
FATAL: Module cifs not found.
```

Either rebuild the system's kernel and enable the *cifs* filesystem, or (if you obtained your system through a license with a vendor) contact your vendor to receive a new kernel.

Next verify that the *cifs* mount and unmount utilities have been installed as */sbin/mount.cifs* and */sbin/umount.cifs*, respectively. If the files do not exist, check that you have the appropriate packages installed. Novell provides a separate *cifs-mount* RPM, and Red Hat includes the two binaries in their *samba-client* package. Debian, ironically enough, includes the *cifs* mount tools in the *smbfs* package.

Because the source files for *mount.cifs* and *umount.cifs* are included in the Samba source tree, you can manually build both tools by running these commands:

```
$ gcc -o mount.cifs client/mount.cifs.c
$ gcc -o umount.cifs client/umount.cifs.c
```

 Newer releases allow you to build these tools automatically by specifying the --with-cifsmount option when running *source/configure* to build Samba.

You should then copy these files to the */sbin* directory. Running the following commands as *root* ensures that the utilities are installed with the correct ownership and permissions:

```
# cp -p mount.cifs umount.cifs /sbin
# chown root.root /sbin/mount.cifs /sbin/umount.cifs
# chmod 755 /sbin/mount.cifs /sbin/umount.cifs
```

Manpages for both *mount.cifs* and *umount.cifs* are included with the Samba distribution files, and additional information is available in the *fs/cifs/README* file included in the Linux kernel source tree.

Mounting a SMB/CIFS File Share

You now have the pieces in place to mount a SMB/CIFS share as part of your local filesystem. Mounting filesystems is normally restricted to the *root* account. We'll show you how to allow users to mount and unmount SMB/CIFS shares shortly. For the moment, make sure to run the *mount* and *umount* commands as *root*. The general syntax for accessing a SMB/CIFS file share is:

```
$ mount -t cifs //server/share mount_point [-o options]
```

The -t option specifies the filesystem type (cifs) and enables *mount* to know what external helper in the */sbin* directory should be invoked (i.e., *mount.cifs*) to access the remote filesystem. The *//server/share* format is identical to what we've shown when using *smbclient* in prior chapters. The *mount_point* is the path to a local directory where the share will be mounted. Numerous options can be specified with the -o flag. One common value is the login name of the account used to connect to the remote server: user=*name*. If you do not specify this option, *mount.cifs* uses the value found in the USER environment variable.

Here is an example of connecting the share public provided by the Windows XP host *fox* to the local directory */cifs/public*. Because *mount.cifs* does not use NetBIOS name services, it is assumed that the hostname *fox* can be resolved to an IP address using a simple lookup in */etc/hosts* or a DNS query. If this is not the case, you may specify the remote server's IP address using the ip=*aaa.bbb.ccc.ddd* option. The user *zoe* is a local account on the Windows system.

```
$ mount -t cifs //fox/public /cifs/public -o user=zoe
Password: <enter password for zoe>
```

The underlying *mount.cifs* helper prompts for a password if one is not provided in some other form. There are three methods for handling noninteractive mount requests. The first is to specify the password on the command line using the pass=*password* option. Using this option, our original mount request would appear as follows:

```
$ mount -t cifs //fox/public /cifs/public -o user=zoe,pass=FY23d^g
```

 At the time of writing, *cifs* does not support Kerberos authentication.

The second possibility is to store the password string in the environment variable PASSWD or to store it in a file specified by either the PASSWD_FD or PASSWD_FILE variable. If you use this option, make sure to export the variable to the environment so that it will be available to *mount.cifs*. This method can be useful when issuing mount requests from a script, but be careful to not leave passwords lying around in the environment where they can be read by other users.

The final possibility is to store the username and password in a file referenced by the cred parameter and read by *mount.cifs* at startup. Each line in the credentials file consists of a parameter=*value* pair. The three supported parameter values are:

- username
- password
- domain

In order to convert the original mount request to use the cred option, first create a file named *.cifsrc* in *root*'s home directory containing the following lines:

```
username=zoe
password=FY23d^g
```

Notice that the domain was omitted in this listing. Any of the three parameters not specified in the credentials file may be defined as a command-line argument if desired.

Protect the *.cifsrc* file with permissions that prevent others from reading the file, such as the octal permissions 600. Now the *mount* command listing no longer includes the username or password on the command line for other users to see:

```
$ mount -t cifs //fox/public /cifs/public -o cred=$HOME/.cifsrc
```

Running *mount* with no arguments lists all mounted filesystems, included the *cifs* share that was just connected:

```
$ mount
<...output deleted...>
//fox/public on /cifs/public type cifs (rw,mand)
```

Once the share has been mounted you can access files using normal tools:

```
$ cd /cifs/public
$ ls -l
total 4392
drwxrwxrwx  1 root root       0 Jul 23  2006 .
drwxr-xr-x  4 root root    4096 Jul 23 13:43 ..
-rwxrwSrwt  1 root root 2986038 Sep  1  2005 lastgold.bmp
-rwxrwSrwt  1 root root  239023 Jul 22 04:30 lookupsid.pcap
<...remaining output deleted...>
$ echo "hello" > foo.txt
$ cat foo.txt
hello
```

When you mount shares from Windows servers, all files and directories will be reported as being owned by the user that mounted the share, and the group ownership will reflect the user's primary group. In our example, the user and group were *root*. When the *cifs* client connects to servers that support the CIFS Extensions for Unix, such as Samba, it reports the correct ownership and file permissions. (More on this in the next section.) Barring such support, you can control the reported ownership using the uid and gid parameters when mounting the share. Each accepts either the name or numeric id of a respective user or group on the local Linux host. To see how this works, first unmount the share from */cifs/public*:

```
$ umount /cifs/public
```

Next, mount the share again, but this time add the options uid=zoe and gid=users to report files as being owned by *zoe* and the group *users*:

```
$ mount -t cifs //fox/public /cifs/public -o user=zoe,uid=zoe,gid=users
Password: <enter password for zoe>
```

Now, when listing the files, the ownership and group ownership is displayed as requested by the uid and gid mount options:

```
$ ls -l /cifs/public
total 4392
```

```
drwxrwxrwx  1 zoe users        0 Jul 23  2006 .
drwxr-xr-x  4 root root     4096 Jul 23 13:43 ..
-rwxrwSrwt  1 zoe users  2986038 Sep  1  2005 lastgold.bmp
-rwxrwSrwt  1 zoe users   239023 Jul 22 04:30 lookupsid.pcap
```
<...remaining output deleted...>

You probably also noticed the file permissions in the previous listing. Without help, *cifs* has no way of mapping Windows file ACLs to POSIX permissions. The file_ mode and dir_mode options allow you to specify the permissions reported by the kernel for files and directories. By defining file_mode=0640 and dir_mode=0755 when mounting *fox\public*, you can restrict files from being accessed by accounts outside of *root*, *zoe*, and the *users* group, while still allowing everyone to scan the filesystem:

```
$ ls -l /cifs/public
drwxr-xr-x  2 zoe users        0 Jul 23  2006 docs
-rw-r-----  1 zoe users  2986038 Sep  1  2005 lastgold.bmp
-rw-r-----  1 zoe users   239023 Jul 22 04:30 lookupsid.pcap
<...remaining output deleted...>
```

The uid, gid, file_mode, and dir_mode options control the file attributes used by the Linux kernel when performing authorization checks. In reality, there are two access checks for every file. The server uses the file's security descriptor to verify that the connected user has the appropriate access rights, and the Linux kernel determines whether the local user should be granted access based on the calculated Unix permission set. So if the user who connected to the share is not authorized by the server's permissions to access a file, no amount of tweaking permissions on the client will give him access to it.

> The *cifs* client has experimental support for multiuser mounts, which is disabled by default. This feature is controlled by the value stored in */proc/fs/cifs/MultiuserMount*.

Table 11-1 completes this section by listing the common parameters to *mount.cifs* we've covered. Be sure to consult the utilities' manpage for a current list of options.

Table 11-1. mount.cifs -o options

Key	Value	Function
user	string	Provides the username for authentication.
dom	string	Defines the user's authentication domain.
pass	string	Provides the share or domain password, if it hasn't been supplied by another means.
cred	filename	Name of file containing the username, domain, and password values.
ip	IP address	Specifies the IP address of the remote SMB/CIFS server.
uid	name or numeric	User ID to apply to all files and directories of the mounted share.
gid	name or numeric	Group ID to apply to all files and directories of the mounted share.
file_mode	octal	Permissions to apply to files.
dir_mode	octal	Permissions to apply to directories.

Allowing Normal User CIFS Mounts

Windows clients allow normal users to map a UNC path to a drive letter such as *H:*. Linux users frequently expect this same capability. In order to allow non-*root* users to mount SMB/CIFS file shares using *mount.cifs*, you have two options. The most flexible solution for users is to add the setuid bit for both *mount.cifs* and *umount.cifs* so the users are able to call *mount.cifs* directly instead of *mount -t cifs*. The remaining command-line arguments needed to mount a SMB/CIFS share are the same. To enable the setuid permission bit, run the following commands while logged in as *root*:

```
$ chmod u+s /sbin/mount.cifs /sbin/umount.cifs
```

Some administrators are uncomfortable with setuid binaries. To be fair, this is an extremely powerful privilege to grant to a program. Any potential flaws in the utility could be leveraged by an attacker to gain superuser privileges on the system.

The alternative method of allowing user mounts is to add a line to */etc/fstab* referencing the remote filesystem and target mount point, and specifying the user mount option. The user option in this context is not the same as the *mount.cifs* user parameter. For example, the following line allows normal users to mount */cifs/cdrom* from the UNC path *media.example.com**cd*. The noauto directive is used to prevent the filesystem from being mounted at boot time. Rather than placing it in */etc/fstab*, the username sent in the SMB/CIFS connection request is pulled from the USER environment variable.

```
//media.example.com/cd     /cifs/cdrom     noauto,user  0 0
```

A non-*root* user can now simply invoke *mount /cifs/cdrom* to access the CD-ROM shared by the host *media.example.com*. More details regarding defining user mounts in */etc/fstab* can be found in the *mount* and *fstab* manpages.

CIFS Extensions for Unix Clients

It is easy to view SMB/CIFS as a Windows protocol. Its history, however, extends before and beyond Microsoft. Although CIFS is not an open standard, extensions to the protocol have been developed and documented. These include the Mac extensions and the Unix extensions, both of which are described in the *CIFS Technical Reference* from the Storage Network Industry Association (*http://www.snia.org*).

The Unix extensions, as they are commonly called, were first developed in 1996 by Hewlett-Packard. Since then, they have received attention and updates from various companies and individuals, including Linux kernel engineers and Samba developers. The most notable features provided by these extensions are filename case sensitivity, symbolic links, POSIX locking semantics, and proper reporting of Unix ownership and permissions.

Both the *cifs* filesystem and Samba support the Unix extensions by default. Samba controls this behavior using the unix extensions Boolean parameter in *smb.conf*. You can manipulate Linux *cifs* client's support of the Unix extensions by flipping the value in */proc/fs/cifs/LinuxExtensionsEnabled* between 0 and 1. The following command enables Unix extension support in the Linux client:

```
$ echo 1 > /proc/fs/cifs/LinuxExtensionsEnabled
```

The most visible enhancement to *cifs* provided by these extensions is the ability to report the correct ownership of files and directories. For example, the following *cifs* mount from a Samba host shows the real uid and gid ownership of files within the share:

```
drwxr-xr-x   4 rose    users      0 Jun  3 10:09 iTunes
drwxr-xr-x  11 lizard  guest      0 May 22 16:27 Documents
drwx------   2 1217    hosts      0 Jun 15 11:05 vc6_sp5
```

The requirement for reporting correct ownership on *cifs* filesystems is the same as the one needed by NFS mounts: namely, that the uid and gid are assigned to the same user and group on both the client and server. In our example, both *rose* and *lizard* are the same on the client and server. However, the client has not assigned the uid 1217 to a user. The easiest way to handle common assignments for uids and gids is to make use of a directory service such as LDAP for distributing user and group information.

 If the users and groups on both the client and server are not synchronized, you may wish to disable the local permission check and just rely on the server's security by setting the noperm option when mounting the filesystem.

Table 11-2 provides a brief summary of the new *smb.conf* parameter.

Table 11-2. Samba's Unix extensions option

Parameter	Value	Description	Default	Scope
unix extensions	boolean	Enables support for the CIFS Extensions for Unix clients.	yes	Global

FreeBSD's smbfs

FreeBSD, Darwin, and Mac OS X all provide the *smbutil* and *mount_smbfs* programs for connecting to SMB/CIFS shares. Neither of the programs is part of Samba; however, we include them to give you a little additional support in case you have BSD-related Unix systems on your network.*

---

* The examples in this section are based on FreeBSD 6.1.

smbutil

The *smbutil* program provides functionality similar to some of the Samba suite's command-line utilities. It can be used to list the shares available on an SMB server or perform NetBIOS name lookups.

The first argument given to *smbutil* is one of a number of subcommands and is usually followed by arguments specific to the subcommand. For example, to list the resources offered by a server, use the *view* subcommand and enter your server password when prompted:

```
$ smbutil view //elm
Password: <enter password>
Share       Type        Comment
----------------------------------------------------------------
public      disk
SS2500      printer     Stylus Scan 2500
IPC$        pipe        IPC Service (Samba 3.0.22)
lizard      disk        User Home Directories

4 shares listed from 4 available
```

 If the *smbfs.ko* kernel module is not loaded, you will see this error message:

```
smbutil: smb_lib_init: can't find kernel module
```

You can load the module manually by running the following command as *root*:

```
$ kldload smbfs.ko
netsmb_dev: loaded
```

If you wish to connect to the server with a username that differs from the one you are currently logged in as, you can specify it on the command line by preceding the name of the server with the username and using an at-sign (@) as a separator:

```
$ smbutil view //lizard@elm
```

You can also include the password after the username, using a colon (:) as a separator, to avoid being prompted for it:

```
$ smbutil view //lizard:secret@elm
```

Typing your password in the open like this is strongly discouraged. An alternative is to use *smbutil* to generate a password hash using the *crypt* subcommand:

```
$ smbutil crypt secret
$$1625a5723293f0710e5faffcfc6
```

This hash can then be used in place of a clear-text password. However, the encryption is not particularly strong and will foil only the most casual inspection. The only reasonably secure method of providing a password is to be prompted for it.

While starting up, *smbutil* reads the file *.nsmbrc* in the user's home directory. A list of common configuration parameters is summarized at the end of this section in Table 11-3.

For example, to keep your password in your *~/.nsmbrc* file, you can create an entry in the file such as the following:

```
[ELM:LIZARD]
    password=$$1625a5723293f0710e5faffcfc6
```

The section heading in brackets specifies the SMB server's NetBIOS name and the username to which the subsequent parameter settings apply. (The hostname and username must be supplied in uppercase characters.) Section headings can also consist of just a hostname or can contain a share name as a third element for specifying parameters applicable to a single share. Finally, if a [default] section is present, the settings in it apply to all connections.

The following example *.nsmbrc* shows some of the other parameters you might use:

```
[default]
    # NetBIOS name server
    nbns=192.168.1.74

[ELM]
    # server IP address
    addr=192.168.1.46
    workgroup=TEST

[ELM:LIZARD]
    password=$$1625a5723293f0710e5faffcfc6
```

Directives in per-user configurations can be overridden on a systemwide basis by storing directives in the file */etc/nsmb.conf*. This method provides you with a means to apply mandatory settings to all users. Directives can be placed in this file using the section and parameter format similar to that of the Samba configuration file.

smbutil is somewhat of a hybrid of Samba's *smbclient* and *nmblookup* tools. The *lookup* subcommand returns the IP address associated with a given NetBIOS hostname. A NetBIOS name server can be optionally specified with the -w argument:

```
$ smbutil lookup -w 192.168.1.74 ELM
Got response from 192.168.1.74
IP address of ELM: 192.168.1.46
```

mount_smbfs

The *mount_smbfs* program performs essentially the same function as *mount.cifs* on Linux. It mounts an SMB/CIFS share on a directory in the local filesystem. The share can then be accessed just like any other directory. The command synopsis for *mount_smbfs* is:

```
mount_smbfs [options] Share-UNC mount-point
```

where *Share-UNC* is of the form:

```
//[workgroup;][username[:password]@]server[/share]
```

For example:

```
$ mount_smbfs //TEST;lizard:$$1625a5723293f0710e5faffcfc6@elm/lizard\
  /smb/lizard
```

A list of common configuration parameters and command-line options is provided in Table 11-3.

Table 11-3. Common smbutil and mount_smbfs options

Command-line option	Configuration file parameter	Description
-I *hostname*	addr	Avoid NetBIOS name resolution and connect to the server using the specified DNS hostname or IP address.
-N	None	Do not prompt for a password.
-R *count*	retry_count	Number of times to retry connection before giving up.
-T *seconds*	timeout	Timeout, in seconds, per connection request.
-U *username*	username	Username to use for authentication. Defaults to Unix username.
-W *workgroup*	workgroup	Name of workgroup of remote server.
-d *mode*	None	Permissions to apply to directories in the mounted share. Defaults to the same as the file permissions, plus an execute (search) bit whenever the read bit is set.
-f *mode*	None	Permissions to apply to files in the mounted share. Defaults to the same as the permissions set on the directory used as the mount point.
-g *group*	None	Name or numeric gid to apply to all files and directories in the mounted share. Defaults to the group of the directory used as the mount point.
-u *username*	None	Username or numeric UID to apply as the owner of all files and directories in the mounted share. Defaults to the owner of the directory used as the mount point.

The ownership and permissions of the mount point determine the default ownership and permissions for files and directories in the mounted share. These can be modified with command-line arguments, like this:

```
$ mount_smbfs -u lizard -g admin -f 0750 -d 0755 \
  //lizard@elm/lizard /smb/lizard
```

In this example, the files and directories in the mounted share are owned by the user *lizard* and the group *admin*, with files and directories having permissions 750 and 755, respectively. As usual, the permissions are specified in the octal format used by the Unix *chmod* command.

The *mount_smbfs* command also makes use of settings in */etc/nsmb.conf* and *~/.nsmbrc*, as described earlier.

Mac OS X

In addition to *smbutil* and *mount_smbfs*, OS X includes a graphical interface to the functionality they provide.* If you know the path to the share you desire, it is possible to map it directly using the Connect to Server... option from the Go menu. Instead of using a UNC, specify the share in the form of a Uniform Resource Identifier (URI) with a prefix of smb:// entered in the Address field. Figure 11-1 shows how a connection to \\elm.plainjoe.org\public would appear. You can specify a server, share, workgroup, username, and password (optionally encrypted with *smbutil crypt*) in the URI, in the same format as the UNC argument to *mount_smbfs*. As usual for Mac OS X, shares are mounted under */Volumes*, but show up in the root of the Finder hierarchy.

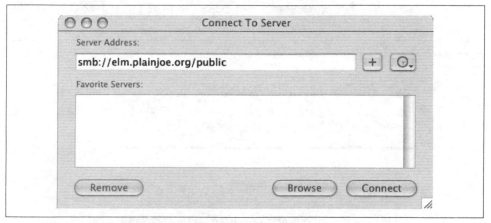

Figure 11-1. OS X Connect To Server dialog box

If you don't specify a share name in the URI, pressing Connect will present you with a window that lets you choose from a list of shares available to mount. Figure 11-2 displays the shares provided by the server *smb://elm.plainjoe.org*.

Only guest-accessible shares show up in the list until you've authenticated. After pressing the Authenticate button, you'll be prompted for a workgroup, username, and password, as shown in Figure 11-3. You'll also see this dialog box if you provide a share name in the URI, but not a username and password.†

If you don't know the name of a server to which you wish to connect, you can browse for it in the network section of the Finder window. If you have a WINS server on your network, you can provide the server's IP address using the SMB service in

---

* The examples in this section are based on OS X 10.3.

† If you've previously stored your authentication information in a keychain, you will instead be prompted for your keychain password.

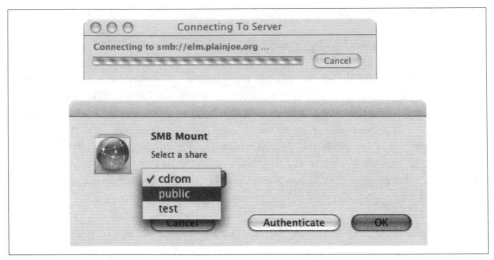

Figure 11-2. Selecting a share to mount

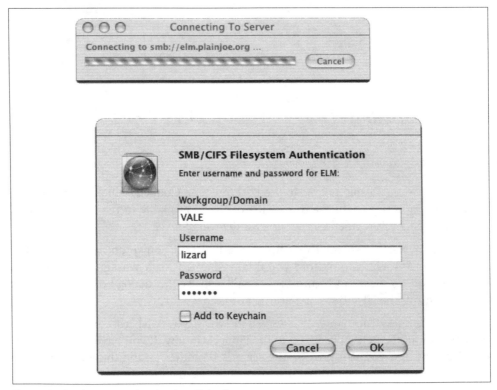

Figure 11-3. The user authentication dialog box

Apple's Directory Access application, or by using the wins server parameter in /etc/smb.conf. Figure 11-4 displays the Finder Network browser, which appears very similar to My Network Places on Windows clients.

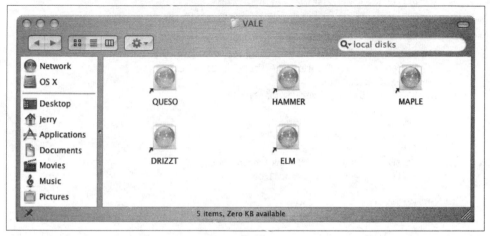

Figure 11-4. Browsing servers in Finder's Network

smbclient

smbclient is a basic part of the Samba suite and a very versatile tool. It can be used for browsing shares on servers, testing configurations, debugging, accessing shared printers, backing up shared data, and automating administrative tasks in shell scripts. And unlike the native filesystem support we have previously discussed, *smbclient* is portable to all Unix variants that support Samba.

In Chapter 2, we showed you how to use *smbclient* to test your Samba installations, and we've already covered *smbclient*'s printing functionality in Chapter 7. In this section, we focus mostly on running *smbclient* as an interactive shell, using its *ftp*-like commands to access shared directories on the network. A complete reference to the tool can be found in Appendix A.

Listing Shares and Workgroups

The -L option can be used with *smbclient* to list the resources on a single computer. Assuming that the Samba server is configured to take the role of the master browser, we can also obtain a list of the computers in the domain or workgroup. The following command attempts to anonymously (-N option) enumerate the shares and browse list from the server *maple.plainjoe.org*:

```
$ smbclient -L maple.plainjoe.org -N
Anonymous login successful
Domain=[VALE] OS=[Unix] Server=[Samba 3.0.22]
```

```
        Sharename      Type      Comment
        ---------      ----      -------
        netlogon       Disk      NETLOGON Service
        profile$       Disk      User roaming profiles
        print$         Disk      Print Drivers
        public         Disk      Public access file share
        software       Disk      Software Repository
        C$             Disk      Administrative share
        IPC$           IPC       IPC Service (Samba 3.0.22)
        hp2100         Printer   HP LaserJet 2100 Series PCL 6
Anonymous login successful
Domain=[VALE] OS=[Unix] Server=[Samba 3.0.22]

        Server              Comment
        ---------           -------
        ELM                 Samba 3.0.22
        HAMMER              XP Development box
        MAPLE               Samba 3.0.22

        Workgroup           Master
        ---------           -------
        AD                  SPUD
        GLASS               CRYSTAL
        VALE                MAPLE
```

The first section of output contains the enumerated file and printer shares on *maple*. This list includes only shares with a name that does not exceed 12 characters in length.* The three hosts listed in the Server column of section 2 are the ones in *maple*'s browse list. Remember from Chapter 8 that each browse master maintains a list of servers in its workgroup. The workgroups and master browsers known by *maple* are listed in the final section.

Running the same command against the Windows XP host *hammer* generates an ACCESS_DENIED error when enumerating the shares:

```
$ smbclient -L hammer -N
Anonymous login successful
Domain=[VALE] OS=[Windows 5.1] Server=[Windows 2000 LAN Manager]

        Sharename      Type      Comment
        ---------      ----      -------
Error returning browse list: NT_STATUS_ACCESS_DENIED
```

Chapter 8 described anonymous browsing as a casualty of the security war. The solution is to provide credentials when connecting to the server. The -U option allows you to specify a username other than your Unix account name when connecting. Without the parameter (and unless you explicitly ask for an anonymous login using

---

* This length limitation was removed in Samba 3.0.23.

---

the -N option), *smbclient* obtains the username from either the USER or LOGNAME environment variables:

```
$ smbclient -L hammer -U lizard
Password: <enter password for lizard>
Domain=[VALE] OS=[Windows 5.1] Server=[Windows 2000 LAN Manager]

        Sharename      Type      Comment
        ---------      ----      -------
        public         Disk
        IPC$           IPC       Remote IPC
        Users          Disk
        ADMIN$         Disk      Remote Admin
        C$             Disk      Default share
```

smbclient makes use of the same mechanisms for retrieving passwords as the Linux *mount.cifs* tool. For noninteractive sessions, you can specify a password using the PASSWD environment variable or point to a file containing the password using the PASSWD_FD or PASSWD_FILE environment settings. You can also specify a credentials file using the -A (or --authentication-file) command-line option. Finally, you can also specify the password on the command line by appending it to the username with the % character.

An Interactive smbclient Session

A common use for *smbclient* is to create an *ftp*-like shell to access SMB resources on the network. To begin a session, *smbclient* must be provided with the UNC of a resource (which you can find using the -L option) on the command line. Forward slashes are accepted by *smbclient* for the share's UNC, which makes entering the UNC on the command line easier. Backslashes can also be used, but they must be quoted or escaped, and it is somewhat more difficult to type '\\elm\public' or \\\\elm\\public. You can optionally follow the UNC path with a password to avoid being prompted.

```
$ smbclient //elm/public
Domain=[VALE] OS=[Unix] Server=[Samba 3.0.22]
Password: <enter password>
smb: \>
```

After connecting to the share, *smbclient* displays the smb: \> prompt and waits for a command to be entered. Commands are similar to those with which you might be familiar in *ftp* and are also somewhat similar to Unix shell commands. To retreive a list of *smbclient* commands, use the help command:

```
smb: \> help
?                altname   archive   blocksize   cancel
case_sensitive   cd        chmod     chown       del
dir              du        exit      get         getfacl
hardlink         help      history   lcd         link
lowercase        ls        mask      md          mget
mkdir            more      mput      newer       open
print            prompt    put       pwd         q
```

```
queue        quit      rd      recurse       reget
rename       reput     rm      rmdir         setmode
stat         symlink   tar     tarmode       translate
volume       vuid      logon   listconnect   showconnect
!
```

Some commands in the previous list are synonyms for other commands. For example, the ? command is a synonym for help. You can give this command the name of another command as an argument to get a concise reminder of what the command does and how to use it:

```
smb: \> help ls
HELP ls:
        <mask> list the contents of the current directory
```

The term <mask> refers to a file-matching pattern as commonly found in Unix shells and utilities. For example, the following command lists all files ending in *doc* in the current directory on the remote system. The columns show the filename followed by the file's MS-DOS attributes, size, and time of last modification.

```
smb: \> ls *doc
  ms-ProfPol-wp.doc         A      131  Tue Jun 18 09:12:34 2006
  smbclient.doc             A    33969  Mon Jun 10 20:22:24 2006
  smbmount.doc              A     7759  Mon Jun 10 20:20:00 2006

        48590 blocks of size 524288. 40443 blocks available
```

As with any other Unix utility, *smbclient* maintains a working directory on the local host, which can be modified with the lcd command, and a working directory on the remote SMB share, which can be changed using cd. For example, to change to the *trans* directory in the SMB/CIFS share, execute the following command. The smb: \> prompt changes to reflect the remote working directory.

```
smb: \> cd trans
smb: \trans\>
```

To change your current directory on the local system, use the *lcd* command:

```
smb: \trans\> lcd /data/snd
the local directory is now /data/snd
```

Most of *smbclient*'s commands perform operations on remote files and directories. There is no command for listing the contents of the local directory. However, *smbclient* does allows a shell escape. Any command preceded by an exclamation point (!) is interpreted as a shell command and is run in a subshell on the local system. Therefore, to display the contents of the current local working directory, invoke the *! ls* command.

```
smb: \trans\> !pwd && ls -l
/data/snd
total 16
drwxrwxr-x   2 lizard  users   4096 Jan 10 14:46 data
-rw-rw-r--   1 lizard  users    131 Jan 10 02:22 releasenotes.html
```

The put and get commands transfer files to and from the remote server. For example, the following command uploads the file *releasenotes.html* to *\\elm\public\trans*:

```
smb: \trans\> put releasenotes.html
putting file releasenotes.html as \trans\releasenotes.html
   (127.9 kb/s) (average 10.7 kb/s)
```

Unlike *ftp*, *smbclient* does not have *ascii* and *binary* commands to set the type of the file that is being transferred. All files are transferred byte for byte with no modification of the original file. The only place where this is an issue is when dealing with ASCII text files. Unix systems used the carriage return (CR) character to delimit lines of text. while DOS and Windows systems use a combination of carriage return and line feed (LF) for the same purpose.

> Before transferring a text file from a Unix system to a Windows system, you might want to use the GNU *unix2dos* command to reformat newlines in the file to match the carriage return/line feed (CRLF) standard:
>
> ```
> $ unix2dos text_file > text_file.txt
> ```
>
> A complementary *dos2unix* command can handle the reverse conversion. In the long run, it is probably easier to provide users with a text editor that is capable of handling both file formats.

The mget and mput commands transfer a list of files or a set of files matching a DOS-style wildcard pattern. Thus, to copy all files from the remote subdirectory *plain*, using the wildcard pattern plain/*, enter:

```
smb: \trans\> mget plain/*
```

By default, *smbclient* issues prompts to confirm the transfer of each file:

```
smb: \trans\> mget plain/*
Get file tomm.wav? y
Get file toml.wav? y
Get file tomh.wav? y
Get file snare.wav? n
Get file rim.wav? n
Get file handclap.wav? y
Get file bassdrum.wav? n
```

You can toggle this prompting behavior on and off by issuing the prompt command:

```
smb: \> prompt
prompting is now off
```

If you specify the name of a directory to the mget command, *smbclient* does not copy its contents by default. To transfer the entire directory tree, set the recurse option:

```
smb: \> recurse
directory recursion is now on
```

After disabling prompting and enabling recursive gets, we can copy a directory tree with the mget command. The original folder hierarchy will still be intact on the new system:

```
smb: \> mget winadmin
getting file \winadmin\bin\putty.exe of size 380928 as putty.exe (6200.0 kb/s)
(average 6200.0 kb/s)
getting file \winadmin\bin\dhcpadmn.cnt of size 1849 as dhcpadmn.cnt (180.6 kb/s)
(average 5340.1 kb/s)
getting file \winadmin\bin\dhcpadmn.exe of size 238352 as dhcpadmn.exe (8313.0 kb/s)
(average 6189.5 kb/s)
getting file \winadmin\bin\dhcpadmn.hlp of size 56486 as dhcpadmn.hlp (6895.2 kb/s)
(average 6242.8 kb/s)
<...remaining output deleted...>
```

Directory recursion applies to all commands, so if an ls command is used while directory recursion is on, all files in the directory tree are listed. To turn directory recursion off again, reenter the recurse command. At the same time, you might also wish to toggle prompting back to its initial state:

```
smb: \trans\> recurse
directory recursion is now off
```

Samba 3.0.12 gave *smbclient* support for MS-DFS (covered in Chapter 6). This means that you can follow MS-DFS referrals by changing directories. This next example connects to an MS-DFS root share named dfs on the server *primary*:

```
$ smbclient //primary/dfs -U Administrator
Password:
Domain=[COLOR] OS=[Windows 5.0] Server=[Windows 2000 LAN Manager]
smb: \> dir
  .                        D        0  Mon May  9 15:06:14 2005
  ..                       D        0  Mon May  9 15:06:14 2005
  printmig.exe             A   215632  Fri Feb 18 09:13:08 2005
  spud                     D        0  Fri Apr  1 10:00:00 2005

        63881 blocks of size 32768. 4851 blocks available

smb: \> cd spud
smb: \spud\> ls
  .                        D        0  Tue Feb 28 11:35:51 2006
  ..                       D        0  Tue Feb 28 11:35:51 2006
  ad.plainjoe.org.txt      A      458  Tue Feb 28 11:35:51 2006
  dns.log                  A      116  Tue Feb 28 11:34:45 2006

        63881 blocks of size 32768. 4851 blocks available
```

The showconnect command displays the UNC path of the current working directory. For non-DFS shares, this will always be the original path to which you connected. But for MS-DFS root shares, the path displayed can vary depending on your working directory. In the following output you can see that the directory *spud* is a referral to the UNC path *spud\public:*

```
smb: \spud\> showconnect
//spud/public
```

You can view the list of servers *smbclient* has connected to during its current session using the listconnect command. In the following example, entry 0 is the DFS referral already discussed, line 1 refers to the original UNC path specified when launching *smbclient*, and line 2 is a connection initiated by *smbclient* itself when checking for MS-DFS support.

```
smb: \spud\> listconnect
0:      server=spud, share=public
1:      server=primary, share=dfs
2:      server=primary, share=IPC$
```

There are other *smbclient* commands that you might find useful. The mkdir command can be used to create a directory, rmdir removes a directory, rm deletes a file, and rename changes a file's name. These behave very similarly to their Unix shell counterparts.

To exit *smbclient*, use the exit or quit command:

```
smb: \trans\> quit
```

Backups with smbclient

Another popular use of *smbclient* is to create and restore backups of SMB/CIFS file shares. *smbclient* supports the creation of backups using the standard *tar* format, making them easy to work with and portable among different versions of Unix. Using *smbclient* on a Unix server to run network backups can result in a more centralized and easily managed solution for providing data integrity, because both SMB shares and NFS filesystems can be backed up on the same system.

You can perform backups in two ways. To back up an entire share, the simplest method is to use the -Tc option on the command line. In this scenario, we are backing up *hammer\public*. The resulting *tar* filename encodes the date in the form YYYY-MM-DD (e.g., *hammer-2006-07-25.tar.gz*).

```
$ smbclient //hammer/public -A ~/.smbpw -Tc  |\
  gzip -9 > hammer-`date +%Y-%m-%d`.tar.gz
```

By using the -D option, it is possible to back up an individual directory in the share, rather than the whole share. The following command causes *smbclient* to change its working directory to the *documents* directory of the *hammer\public* share before starting the backup:

```
$ smbclient //hammer/public -A ~/.smbpw -D documents -Tc  |\
  gzip -9 > hammer-`date +%Y-%m-%d`.tar.gz
```

It is also possible to use *smbclient*'s tar command in interactive mode, which can be useful when developing noninteractive scripts, to ensure that they are doing the right thing. The tarmode command is used to control the behavior of the tar command when copying files. The following example instructs *smbclient* to tar all files, including those with the System and Hidden DOS attributes set:

```
$ smbclient //hammer/public
Password: <enter password>
smb: \> cd documents
smb: \documents\> tarmode full hidden system quiet
smb: \documents\> tar c hammer-2006-07-25.tar
```

The previous command backs up only the *hammer\public\documents* subdirectory, using the settings specified in the tarmode command. To have this type of backup run automatically from a script, embed the commands in a -c option:

```
$ smbclient //hammer/public -A ~/.smbpw \
  -c "cd trans; tarmode full hidden system quiet; \
  tar c hammer-`date +%Y-%m-%d`.tar"
```

When runing the tar command (or the -T option), it is necessary to specify either the c option to create a backup archive or the x option to extract (restore) one. Other options can be appended to the option string and are explained in the section on *smbclient* in Appendix A. They allow you to create incremental backups, specify which files to include or exclude from the backup, and specify a few other miscellaneous settings.

 An alternative to extracting the tar archive directly to the SMB share is to use the Unix system's *tar* command to extract it to a directory on the Unix server, and then copy the desired files to a shared directory. This allows a greater amount of control over the restoration process, as when correcting for an accidental file deletion or reverting a set of files to a previous condition.

For example, suppose that we wish to create an incremental backup of a share and reset the archive bit on the files to set things up for the next incremental backup. There are two ways to achieve this. We could run the following interactive commands:

```
smb: \> tarmode inc reset quiet
smb: \> tar c backup.tar
```

Or we could specify the -Tcgaq option on the *smbclient* command line.

The best strategy for using *smbclient* for network backups depends on your local configuration. If you have only a few Windows systems sharing a small amount of data, you might create a script containing *smbclient -Tc* commands to back up each share to a separate tar file, placing the files in a directory that is included with regular backups of the Unix system. If you have huge SMB/CIFS shares on your network, you might prefer to write the backup directly to a tape drive. This can be done with *smbclient* just as you would with a Unix *tar* command:

```
$ smbclient //homeserver/users -A ~/.smbpw -Tc > /dev/tape
```

Programming with smbclient

We'll finish our coverage of *smbclient* with some general comments about including the tool in your own shell scripts. You've seen that *smbclient* allows a list of commands to be passed on the command line using the -c option. For instance, we can noninteractively copy the file *\\elm\public\files\memo.txt* to */data/files* using the following single command:

```
$ smbclient //elm/public -A ~/. smbpw -c \
    "lcd /data/files; cd files; get memo.txt"
```

Everything that *smbclient* needs to know to perform the operation has been specified in the command. There is no password prompting, so a command such as this can easily be placed inside a shell script.

 Readers interested in more details on shell scripts should refer to *Classic Shell Scripting*, by Arnold Robbins and Nelson H. F. Beebe (O'Reilly).

By using *smbclient* in this manner, it is possible to create customized commands using shell functions, scripts, or aliases. For example, suppose that we wanted a command to print a short listing of files in a shared directory, showing just the names of the files. Using a *bash* function, we could define a function *smbls* as follows:

```
## ~/.profile
function smbls
{
    share=`echo $1 | cut -d '/' -f '1-4'`
    dir=`echo $1 | cut -d '/' -f '5-'`
    smbclient $share -c "cd $dir; ls" -A ~/.smbpw | \
        grep "^  " | cut -d ' ' -f 3 - | sort
}
```

After defining this function and importing it into our shell, we can use *smbls* like this:

```
$ smbls //elm.plainjoe.org/public
CD-images
lectures
ms-ProfPol-wp.doc
profile-map
trans
$ smbls //elm.plainjoe.org/public/trans
.

..
lecture1.mp3
lecture2.mp3
lecture3.mp3
lecture4.mp3
```

smbclient subscribes to the Unix philosphy of chaining tools together to achieve one task. This is just one simple example. If you develop a very clever or elaborate solution to a common administrative problem, consider making it available to others in the Samba community using one of the mailing lists covered in Chapter 12!

Remote Administration with net

The *net* command was mentioned in Chapter 5, when we discussed Samba's group mapping and user privileges features and again in Chapter 10 as the tool used to join Samba servers to a domain. Its original design mimicked the *net.exe* command found on Windows hosts. Since the tool's introduction in Samba 3.0.0, it has become the kitchen sink of Samba administration tools and a stable alternative to the more developer oriented *rpcclient* utility.

There are two roles for *net*. One is the protocol administration tool used for such things as managing users or groups to remote servers. The other is the local database administration role for manipulating such things as group mapping entries. Our primary concern this section is the first side, the protocol interface to remote administration functions.

net supports three administration protocols identified by the following case-insensitive keywords:

RAP

> The CIFS *Remote Administration Protocol* (RAP), used primarily by Windows 9x/Me clients and OS/2 hosts. RAP should be considered to be historical at this point in time and of interest only to CIFS developers.[*]

RPC

> Microsoft's Remote Protocol Call (RPC) implementation, loosely based on the Distributed Computing Environment/Remote Procedure Call (DCE/RPC) specification. This is the primary interface for managing Windows clients and servers.

ADS

> Active Directory specific functions based upon Lightweight Directory Access Protocol (LDAP) requests, with a small dash of RPC when necessary. This protocol can be used only when communicating with AD domain controllers.

There is a great deal of overlap in subcommands between these three administration methods. For example, all three interfaces return identical results, only differing in order, when enumerating users:

```
$ net rap user -S windc -U Administrator
Password: <enter Administrator's password>
Administrator
```

---

[*] OS/2 administrators might disagree on this point.

```
Guest
krbtgt
IWAM_WIN2K-KDC
IUSR_WIN2K-KDC
gcarter
TsInternetUser
lizard

$ net rpc user -S windc -U Administrator
Password: <enter Administrator's password>
Administrator
gcarter
Guest
IUSR_WIN2K-KDC
IWAM_WIN2K-KDC
krbtgt
lizard
TsInternetUser

$ net ads user -S windc -U Administrator
Password: <enter Administrator's password>
Administrator
Guest
IWAM_WIN2K-KDC
IUSR_WIN2K-KDC
krbtgt
gcarter
TsInternetUser
lizard
```

If we were to examine the traffic on the network, however, we would see very different search queries.

This brings up the next question: which method is preferable? As a general rule, we recommend using either RPC or ADS, depending on which provides the functionality you desire. As you will soon see, some features are available only in one or the other.

net rpc

The first task discussed here is managing users and groups. *net rpc* provides two subcommands, user and group, for viewing and manipulating accounts. You can find out more about each subcommand using the help option. The following command demonstrates the available features of the user subcommand. This help listing shows that the user subcommand is available for all three interfaces: RAP, RPC, and ADS:

```
$ net rpc help user
net [<method>] user [misc. options] [targets]
        List users
<...output deleted...>
Valid methods: (auto-detected if not specified)
        ads             Active Directory (LDAP/Kerberos)
        rpc             DCE-RPC
        rap             RAP (older systems)
```

The miscellaneous options for user are composed of information such as the user credentials used in the connection request (-U option) or the log level (--debuglevel option). A valid target is generally a specific server (-S option), workgroup (-w option), or IP address (-I option). The order of command-line arguments prefaced by an option flag does not matter. You can string these options and parameters together to enumerate users on a CIFS server by running this command:

```
$ net rpc user -S windc -U lizard
Password: <enter password for lizard>
Administrator
gcarter
Guest
IUSR_WIN2K-KDC
IWAM_WIN2K-KDC
krbtgt
lizard
TsInternetUser
```

If you wish to find out the groups to which a particular user belongs, add the info argument to the user subcommand.

```
$ net rpc user info lizard -S windc -U lizard
Password: <enter password for lizard>
Linux Users
Domain Admins
Printer Admins
Domain Users
```

You may add, delete, and rename users as well. For example, you can create a new user account for *jsmith* and then rename the account to *smitty*. Although you do not have to run the *net* command as *root*, you do have to specify an account with sufficient rights, such as *Administrator*, on the target server to change user or group settings.

```
$ net rpc user add jsmith -S windc -U Administrator
Password: <enter password for Administrator>
Added user jsmith
```

```
$ net rpc user rename jsmith smitty -S windc -U Administrator
Password: <enter password for Administrator>
Renamed user from jsmith to smitty
```

One of the most tedious jobs that system administrators often have to perform is resetting forgotten passwords for users. The *net rpc password* command allows you to do this for accounts on any Windows or Samba server from your Unix desktop. As an example, the following command sets the password for the account just created to be LeAv3:. If all goes well, you will be returned immediately to a shell prompt.

```
$ net rpc password smitty LeAv3: -S windc -U Administrator
Password: <enter password for Administrator>
```

You can always check the return code from *net* to determine success or failure. A simple *echo $?* at a shell prompt or *test $? -eq 0* in a script will inform you whether the command succeeded.

After creating a new user, you can add the account to specific groups using the group subcommand. The following example adds the user *smitty* to the *Domain Admins* group on the host windc, which is a domain controller in the BOOKS domain. Note that *net rpc group addmem* provides feedback only when the operation fails, not when it is completed successfully.

```
$ net rpc group addmem "Domain Admins" smitty -S windc -U Administrator
Password: <enter password for Administrator>

$ net rpc group members "Domain Admins" -S windc -U Administrator
Password: <enter password for Administrator>
BOOKS\Administrator
BOOKS\gcarter
BOOKS\smitty
```

Table 11-4 gives a summary of the subcommands available to *net rpc user* and *net rpc group*.

Table 11-4. Parameters for the net rpc subcommands user and group

Command	Subcommand	Options	Description
user			Enumerate user accounts.
	add	*username* [*password*]	Create a user account with an optional password.
	delete	*username*	Remove a user account.
	info	*username*	List the group membership for a user account.
	rename	*oldname newname*	Rename a user account from oldname to newname.
group			Enumerate groups.
	list	[global|local|builtin]	Enumerate groups of a specific type.
	add	*name*	Create a new group.
	delete	*name*	Remove a group.
	members	*name*	List the members of a group.
	addmem	*group user*	Add *user* to *group*.
	delmem	*group user*	Remove *user* from *group*.

Shares

In addition, with *net* you can manage shared resources on a server just as you manage user and group accounts. The share option to *net rpc* allows you to view existing shares, migrate data, and add or remove resources.

We'll start by enumerating the shares on a particular server. *net rpc share* doesn't list as many details as *smbclient -L*, but it does include shares with long names:

```
$ net rpc share -S windc -U Administrator
Password: <enter password for Administrator>
public
IPC$
print$
NETLOGON
CertEnroll
ADMIN$
SYSVOL
C$
files
```

You can create new SMB/CIFS shares for existing directories. Assume that the path *C:\users* has been previously created on the host windc. You can create a file share named UserHome that points to this directory by running this command. No response is displayed unless the command fails.

```
$ net rpc share add "UserHome=c:\\users" -S windc -U Administrator
Password: <enter password for Administrator>
```

If you enumerate the shares again, you will see the new UserHome share in the output. There is also a complementary delete option to *net rpc share*. This command only stops the server from sharing the directory. It does not remove any files on the server.

Table 11-5 describes the various *net rpc share* options.

Table 11-5. net rpc share commands

Parameter	Options	Description
None		Enumerate shares on the server.
add	*sharename=path*	Create a new file share for the path on the server.
allowusers	*sharename*	Display or set a list of SIDs which are allowed to access this share.
delete	*sharename*	Stop sharing the directory path on the server.
migrate	<all|files|security|share> [*share*]	Migrate share settings from the remote server to the local server.

Services

Like Unix, Windows hosts possess numerous long-running processes that operate in the background to perform specific tasks. You can enumerate the services using the *net rpc service list* command. The lefthand column presents the service name and the righthand column gives its more friendly display name:

```
$ net rpc service list -S windc -U Administrator
Password: <enter password for Administrator>
<...output deleted...>
UPS            "Uninterruptible Power Supply"
UtilMan        "Utility Manager"
```

```
VMTools        "VMware Tools Service"
W32Time        "Windows Time"
WinMgmt        "Windows Management Instrumentation"
WINS           "Windows Internet Name Service (WINS)"
Wmi            "Windows Management Instrumentation Driver Extensions"
wuauserv       "Automatic Updates"
WZCSVC         "Wireless Configuration"
```

The status subcommand provides more detail about the current state of a service:

```
$ net rpc service status w32time -S windc -U Administrator
Password: <enter password for Administrator>
w32time service is running.
Configuration details:
        Controls Accepted    = 0x1
        Service Type         = 0x20
        Start Type           = 0x2
        Error Control        = 0x1
        Tag ID               = 0x0
        Executable Path      = C:\WINNT\System32\services.exe
        Load Order Group     =
        Dependencies         = /
        Start Name           = LocalSystem
        Display Name         = Windows Time
```

If the need arises, you can stop and start a specific service using its shorter service name. The following commands stop and then restart the *w32time* service on a Windows host:

```
$ net rpc service stop w32time -S windc -U Administrator
Password: <enter password for Administrator>
.............................
w32time service is stop pending.

$ net rpc service start w32time -S windc -U Administrator
Password: <enter password for Administrator>
.
Successfully started service: w32time
```

Sometimes, however, restarting a single service is not enough to restore a host to a working state. In these cases, a reboot is necessary. You can use the shutdown command to reboot a host. The -r flag instructs the host to reboot after the shutdown and the -t option defines the number of seconds to delay the reboot process. You may also specify an informational message using the -C option. Following is an example that reboots a server in 120 seconds and informs any logged-on user of the server maintenance. The client sees the reboot dialog box shown in Figure 11-5.

```
$ net rpc shutdown -r -t 120 \
  -C "Maintenance reboot required.  Please log off"
  -S dorn -U Administrator
Password: <enter password for Administrator>
Shutdown of remote machine succeeded
```

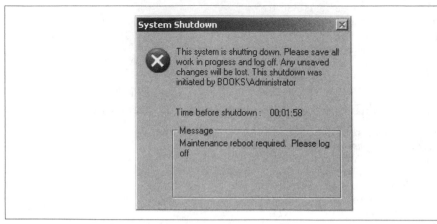

Figure 11-5. Reboot dialog box issued by net rpc shutdown

If you change your mind, there is an abortshutdown command that can cancel your previous reboot request.

Table 11-6 finishes this section with a short summary of the commands to manage services using *net rpc service*.

Table 11-6. net rpc service commands

Parameter	Options	Description
list		Enumerate installed services on the server.
pause	*servicename*	Pause the service. Not all services support this control, which is the equivalent of using ^Z to stop a job in a Unix shell.
start	*servicename*	Start the service.
status	*servicename*	Display the service configuration and current status.
stop	*servicename*	Stop the service.
resume	*servicename*	Resume a paused service.

net ads

The ADS method of the *net* command shares some of the same functions as the RPC method. For example, you can reset passwords and manage users and groups. The main advantage of *net ads* over *net rpc* is the ability in ADS to use Kerberos tickets for authentication and to communicate with Active Directory using LDAP. Using Kerberos removes the need to enter a password every time you run the *net* command. To observe how this works, first initialize your Krb5 ticket cache using the *kinit* command:

```
$ kinit Administrator
Password for Administrator@BOOKS.PLAINJOE.ORG: <enter password>
```

You can now list users in the AD domain by running *net ads user*:

```
$ net ads user
Administrator
Guest
IWAM_WIN2K-KDC
IUSR_WIN2K-KDC
krbtgt
gcarter
TsInternetUser
lizard
smitty
```

Upon examining your ticket cache, you will see that you now possess a service ticket for a DC in your domain. In our example, the machine account *windc$* is one of the domain controllers in the *books.plainjoe.org* AD domain:

```
$ klist
Ticket cache: FILE:/tmp/krb5cc_0
Default principal: Administrator@BOOKS.PLAINJOE.ORG

Valid starting     Expires            Service principal
07/26/06 17:46:58  07/27/06 03:46:35  krbtgt/BOOKS.PLAINJOE.ORG@BOOKS.PLAINJOE.ORG
        renew until 07/27/06 17:46:58
07/26/06 17:47:21  07/27/06 03:46:35  windc$@BOOKS.PLAINJOE.ORG
        renew until 07/27/06 17:46:58
```

Because Active Directory can be searched using LDAP queries, the *net ads* command provides a simple search interface as an alternative to tools such as *ldapsearch*. The search command accepts an LDAP search filter, followed by an optional list of attribute names to return. The following example looks up the SID assigned to the user *smitty*. The sAMAccountName attribute stores the value for user and machine account names, so the LDAP filter matches against it.

```
$ net ads search "(sAMAccountName=smitty)" objectSID
Got 1 replies
objectSid: S-1-5-21-4200961138-2496335650-1239021823-1273
```

This next search returns a list of all machines in the domain, including their operating systems if available, by matching the computer object class value:

```
# net ads search "(objectclass=computer)" sAMAccountName
Got 6 replies

operatingSystem: Windows 2000 Professional
sAMAccountName: BLITZ$

operatingSystem: Windows XP Professional
sAMAccountName: LETTUCE$

operatingSystem: Windows XP Professional
sAMAccountName: DORN$
```

```
operatingSystem: Windows 2000 Professional
sAMAccountName: POLE$

sAMAccountName: zero$

operatingSystem: Windows 2000 Server
sAMAccountName: WINDC$
```

net ads search can be a valuable auditing and debugging tool and is much faster than firing up a graphical LDAP search tool, especially if that approach involves logging onto a Windows client.

## CHAPTER 12

Troubleshooting Samba

Samba is extremely robust. Once you have everything set up the way you want it, you'll probably forget that it is running. When trouble occurs, it's typically during installation or when you're trying to reconfigure the server. Fortunately, a wide variety of resources are available to diagnose these troubles. Although we can't describe in detail the solution to every problem you might encounter, you should be able to get a good start resolving the problem by following the advice given in this chapter.

The first section of this chapter lists what's in the tool bag, a collection of utilities available for troubleshooting Samba; the second section is a detailed how-to; and the final section lists extra resources you can use to track down particularly stubborn problems.

This chapter doesn't address problems specific to domain member servers. Due to the intimate relationship of joining a new server to a domain and troubleshooting this process, the information has been consolidated into a single chapter, Chapter 10. This chapter does provide the means to verify that basic network services are in order, which is a prerequisite to joining a Samba host to a domain.

The Tool Box

Sometimes Unix seems to be made up of a grab bag of applications and tools. There are tools to troubleshoot tools. And of course, there are several ways to accomplish the same task. When trying to solve a problem related to Samba, a good plan of attack is to use the following:

- Samba logs
- Unix utilities
- Fault tree
- Documentation and FAQs
- Samba newsgroups and mailing lists

We go over each of these in the following sections.

Samba Logs

Your first line of attack should always be to check the Samba logfiles. These can help diagnose the vast majority of the problems faced by beginning- to intermediate-level Samba administrators.

Samba is quite flexible when it comes to logging. You can set up the server to log as little or as much information as you desire. Variables in the Samba configuration file allow you to isolate individual logs for each system, share, or combination thereof.

The quickest way to determine the default location of the logfiles on your Samba server is to look for the LOGFILEBASE setting in the output from *smbd -b*. The following output is from a server that was compiled using only default settings:

```
$ smbd -b | grep LOGFILEBASE
    LOGFILEBASE: /usr/local/samba/var
```

You can specify a log directory to use with the -l flag on the command line when starting the Samba daemons. For example:

```
$ smbd -l /var/log/samba
$ nmbd -l /var/log/samba
```

Alternatively, you can override the location and name using the log file configuration option in *smb.conf*. This option accepts variables, so you could easily have the server keep a separate log for each connecting client system by specifying the following absolute path:

```
[global]
    log file = /var/log/samba/log.%m
```

Another useful trick is to have the server keep a log for each service (share) that is offered, especially if you suspect a particular share is causing trouble. To do this, use the %S variable, like this:

```
[global]
    log file = /var/log/samba/log.%S
```

Log Level

The level of logging that Samba uses can be set in the *smb.conf* file using the global log level option or its synonym debug level. The logging level is an integer that can range from 0 to 10.[*] At level 0, only critical errors such as client disconnections or system-call-related failures are logged. Higher values result in more voluminous logging.

For example, let's assume that we will use a Windows client to browse a directory on a Samba server. For a small amount of log information, you can use log level = 1,

---

[*] In reality, Samba's log level exceeds 100 in some code. However, levels 0 to 10 are the ones primarily used by both administrators and developers.

which instructs Samba to show only cursory information; in this case, only the connection itself:

```
[2006/02/20 19:13:19, 1] smbd/service.c:make_connection_snum(924)
  client (192.168.236.10) connect to service public
  initially as user lizard (uid=1004, gid=100) (pid 18450)
```

Higher debug levels produce more detailed information. Usually, you won't need more than level 3, which is fully adequate for most Samba administrators. Levels above 3 are primarily used by developers. These higher levels quickly consume disk space with megabytes of excruciating detail concerning Samba's internal operations.

Here is an example of output at levels 2 and 3 for the same operation. Don't worry if you don't understand the intricacies of an SMB connection; the point is what types of information are shown at the different logging levels. Note that timestamps have been removed (debug timestamp = no) to reduce the noise in the log excerpts.

```
/* Level 2 */
check_ntlm_password: authentication for user [lizard] ->
  [lizard] -> [lizard] succeeded
client (192.168.236.10) connect to service public
  initially as user lizard (uid=1004, gid=100) (pid 18491)
Serving public as a Dfs root

/* Level 3 */
Transaction 6 of length 82
switch message SMBtconX (pid 18535) conn 0x0
setting sec ctx (0, 0) - sec_ctx_stack_ndx = 0
Connect path is '/export/u1/public' for service [public]
se_access_check: user sid is S-1-5-21-3489264249-1556752242-1837584028-2560
se_access_check: also S-1-5-21-3489264249-1556752242-1837584028-1201
se_access_check: also S-1-1-0
se_access_check: also S-1-5-2
se_access_check: also S-1-5-11
se_access_check: also S-1-22-2-16
se_access_check: also S-1-22-2-33
se_access_check: also S-1-5-21-3489264249-1556752242-1837584028-512
se_access_check: also S-1-22-2-1003
se_access_check: also S-1-22-2-1004
se_access_check: also S-1-22-2-1006
se_access_check: also S-1-5-32-544
Initialising default vfs hooks
setting sec ctx (1004, 100) - sec_ctx_stack_ndx = 0
client (192.168.236.10) connect to service public
  initially as user lizard (uid=1004, gid=100) (pid 18535)
setting sec ctx (0, 0) - sec_ctx_stack_ndx = 0
Serving public as a Dfs root
tconX service=PUBLIC

[... deleted ...]
```

We cut off the log level 3 listing after the one packet. Log level 3 is extremely useful for following exactly what the server is doing, and most of the time it is clear where an error occurs after glancing through the logfile.

Using a high log level (5 or higher) *seriously* slows down the Samba server. Remember that every log message generated causes a write to disk (an inherently slow operation) and log levels greater than 2 produce large amounts of data. Essentially, you should turn on logging level 3 or higher only when you're actively tracking a problem in the Samba server.

 You might find it necessary to generate a level 10 debug log for submitting a bug report or when working with other administrators in the Samba community to track down a problem. We recommend these *smb.conf* settings:

```
[global]
    log level = 10
    max log size = 0
    log file = /var/log/samba/log.%m
```

Then archive and compress the entire contents of */var/log/samba* before sending it to the relevant parties.

Activating and Deactivating Logging

To turn logging on and off, set the appropriate level in the [global] section of *smb.conf*. Then either restart Samba or force the current daemon to reprocess the configuration file by sending it a hangup (HUP) signal. You also can monitor and control the current log level for a particular *smbd* process using the *smbcontrol* utility. The following example, run as the *root* user, determines that the current log level for the *smbd* with process id of 18637 is 0 and then sets the overall log level to 5. The final command verifies that the log level was in fact set to 5.

```
$ smbcontrol 18637 debuglevel
PID 18637: all:0 tdb:0 printdrivers:0 lanman:0 smb:0
   rpc_parse:0 rpc_srv:0 rpc_cli:0 passdb:0 sam:0 auth:0
   winbind:0 vfs:0 idmap:0 quota:0 acls:0 locking:0 msdfs:0
$ smbcontrol 18637 debug 5
$ smbcontrol 18637 debuglevel
PID 18637: all:5 tdb:5 printdrivers:5 lanman:5 smb:5
   rpc_parse:5 rpc_srv:5 rpc_cli:5 passdb:5 sam:5 auth:5
   winbind:5 vfs:5 idmap:5 quota:5 acls:5 locking:5 msdfs:5
```

Logging by Individual Client Systems or Users

An effective way to diagnose problems without hampering other users is to assign different log levels for different systems in the [global] section of the *smb.conf* file. We can do this by building on the strategy we presented earlier:

```
[global]
    log level = 0
```

```
log file = /var/log/samba/log.%m
include = /usr/local/samba/lib/smb.conf.%m
```

These options instruct Samba to use unique configuration and logfiles for each client that connects. Now all you have to do is create an *smb.conf* file for a specific client system (e.g., */usr/local/samba/lib/smb.conf.lettuce*) with a log level = 3 entry in it (the others will pick up the default log level of 0), and then use that logfile to track down the problem.

Similarly, if only particular users are experiencing a problem—and it travels from system to system with them—you can isolate logging to a specific user by adding the following to the *smb.conf* file:

```
[global]
    log level = 0
    log file = /var/log/samba/log.%U
    include = /usr/local/samba/lib/smb.conf.%U
```

Then you can create a unique *smb.conf* file containing the configuration option log level = 3 for each user you wish to monitor (e.g., */usr/local/samba/lib/smb.conf.rose*) and only those users will get more detailed logging.

Unix Utilities

Sometimes it's helpful to use a tool outside the Samba suite to examine what's happening inside the server. Two diagnostic techniques that can be of particular help in debugging Samba troubles are to monitor the system calls made by the server daemons and to monitor the network traffic between the client and the server.

Tracing System Calls

The *trace* command masquerades under several different names, depending on the operating system. On Linux it is *strace*; on Solaris and AIX you'll use *truss*; SGI has *padc* and *par*; and HP-UX has *trace* or *tusc*. All have essentially the same function, which is to display each operating system function call as it is executed. This display allows you to follow the execution of a program, such as *smbd*, and often pinpoint the exact call that is causing the difficulty.

A sample *strace* output for the Linux operating system follows. This is a small section of a larger file created during the opening of a directory on the Samba server. Each line lists a system call and includes its parameters and the return value. If there was an error, the error value (e.g., ENOENT) and its explanation are also shown. You can look up the parameter types and the errors that can occur in the appropriate *trace* manual page for the operating system you are using.

```
chdir("/pcdisk/public")                = 0
stat("mini/desktop.ini", 0xbffff7ec)   = -1 ENOENT (No such file or directory)
stat("mini", {st_mode=S_IFDIR|0755, st_size=1024, ...}) = 0
stat("mini/desktop.ini", 0xbffff7ec)   = -1 ENOENT (No such file or directory)
```

```
open("mini", O_RDONLY)                       = 5
fcntl(5, F_SETFD, FD_CLOEXEC)                 = 0
fstat(5, {st_mode=S_IFDIR|0755, st_size=1024, ...}) = 0
lseek(5, 0, SEEK_CUR)                         = 0
SYS_141(0x5, 0xbfffdbbc, 0xedc, 0xbfffdbbc, 0x80ba708) = 196
lseek(5, 0, SEEK_CUR)                         = 1024
SYS_141(0x5, 0xbfffdbbc, 0xedc, 0xbfffdbbc, 0x80ba708) = 0
close(5)                                      = 0
stat("mini/desktop.ini", 0xbffff86c)          = -1 ENOENT (No such file or directory)
write(3, "\0\0\0#\377SMB\10\1\0\2\0\200\1\0"..., 39) = 39
SYS_142(0xff, 0xbffffc3c, 0, 0, 0xbffffc08) = 1
read(3, "\0\0\0?", 4)                         = 4
read(3, "\377SMBu\0\0\0\0\0\0\0\0\0\0\0\0"..., 63) = 63
time(NULL)                                    = 896143871
```

This example shows several *stat()* calls failing to find the files they were expecting. You don't have to be an expert to see that the file *desktop.ini* is missing from that directory. However, be warned that failures reported by the *trace* tool are not always server errors. In this example, it might be perfectly normal that the *desktop.ini* file did not exist. With a little bit of detective work and deductive reasoning, many difficult problems can be identified by looking for obvious, repeatable errors with *trace*.

Tracing is also useful when diagnosing abnormally high CPU usage in Samba. An *smbd* process that continually consumes the majority of available CPU cycles is sometimes a symptom of a corrupt tdb file or possibly a source level bug. In this case, it is helpful to identify what operation the process is spending its time executing. A continually repeated operation such as an *fcntl()* call is a good place to look for clues. Perhaps the file descriptor associated with the *fcntl()* call can give some clue to as to what the process is doing.* However, sometimes high CPU usage is caused by a very active client. So don't jump to conclusions, and don't be too quick to rule out client or application bugs.

Network Packet Captures

There are a variety of programs for capturing network traffic (a.k.a. network *sniffing*) and saving it to a file for later analysis. Almost all Unix/Linux operating systems include some type of tool for this purpose. Solaris has the *snoop* utility, HP-UX has *nettl*, AIX has *iptrace* and *ipreport*, and Linux provides *tcpdump*. Like most tools on Linux, *tcpdump* (*http://www.tcpdump.org*) is available for various platforms. There's even a Windows port named WinDump (*http://www.winpcap.org/windump*).

By far, the best freely available application for dissecting the SMB/CIFS protocol is Wireshark (*http://www.wireshark.org*), formerly Ethereal. This network analyzer allows

---

* There are various ways to determine the file on disk associated with an open file descriptor in a process. On Linux, the contents of */proc/<pid>/fd* contains a list of open files. A more operating-system-agnostic method is to use the *lsof* tool.

---

you to examine very specific protocol minutia such as request flags or server support for specific protocol features, and is able to read the file formats of most free and commercial network capture applications. Wireshark packages are available for various Unix and Linux platforms as well as Windows and include a command packet capture tool. You probably could rely on it for all of your network analysis needs.

To begin our network analysis discussion, we'll separate the process of capturing the packets and analyzing them. This way, you can use whatever sniffer tool is provided by the operating system vendor and still use Wireshark for analyzing the SMB/CIFS conversation. We use *tcpdump* in the examples, primarily because it is available on a wide variety of platforms.

When capturing packets, the important points to consider are:

- How much of each packet should you store? For the SMB/CIFS protocol and particularly MS-RPC, it is best not to truncate the data at all.
- Where should the data be stored?
- What network interface should be monitored?
- Which packets should be saved? Perhaps you are concerned only with a conversation with a specific client or packets on a specific TCP or UDP port.

Most capture programs have command-line parameters that allow you to control these aspects of sniffing. The following example shows how to capture the conversation between our server (192.168.236.86) and the client used for testing (192.168.236.10).

```
$ tcpdump -s 0 -w cifs.pcap -i eth0 \
  "host 192.168.236.86 and host 192.168.236.10 and (port 139 or port 445)"
```

The -s 0 options instructs *tcpdump* to save the full packet, the -w parameter is used to define the file used for storing the data, the -i option refers to the network interface used for the capture (*eth0* in this instance), and the remaining string enclosed in double quotes describes the capture filter.[*] This filter restricts *tcpdump* to saving packets on ports 139 or 445 between the two hosts at 192.168.236.10 and 192.168.236.86. The full filter syntax is covered in the *tcpdump* manpage. The capture session can be terminated by typing CTRL-C.

Next, we can open the file *cifs.pcap* in Wireshark for further analysis.

Using Wireshark

Wireshark is a *protocol analyzer*, meaning that it can dissect a packet and label individual bits according to a network protocol specification. This dissection can help to locate points where the communication between two hosts takes an unexpected path. Wireshark can also provide some network statistics summaries, such as I/O

---

[*] The *tcpdump* utility included with AIX 5 interprets a snap length of 0 to mean capture 0 bytes of each packet. In such cases, use the size of an Ethernet frame (1,514 bytes).

throughput and packet retransmission. More information on using Wireshark can be found at *http://www.ethereal.com* and Angela Orebaugh's book *Ethereal Packet Sniffing* (Syngress).

Figure 12-1 shows a client searching for a file that does not exist, as can be seen from the error STATUS_NO_SUCH_FILE. Just as in the case of errors reported by *trace*, this missing file could be a simple innocuous search caused by the client's PATH setting. Or it could be the reason for an application failing to launch.

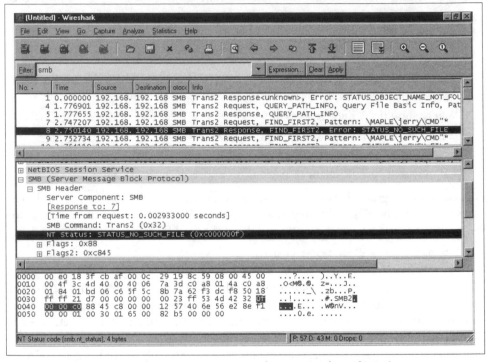

Figure 12-1. Using Wireshark to view a conversation between Samba and Windows

The Fault Tree

The fault tree presented in this section is for diagnosing and fixing problems that occur when you're installing and reconfiguring Samba. Before you set out to troubleshoot any part of the Samba suite, you should know the following information:

- Your client IP address (we use 192.168.236.10)
- Your server IP address (we use 192.168.236.86)
- The netmask for your network (typically 255.255.255.0)
- Whether the systems are all on the same subnet (our example systems are)

For clarity, we've renamed the server in the following examples to server.example.com, and the client system to client.example.com.

How to Use the Fault Tree

Start the tests here, without skipping forward; it won't take long (about five minutes) and might actually save you time backtracking. Whenever a test succeeds, you will be given a name of a section to which you can safely skip.

Troubleshooting Low-Level IP

The first series of tests is that of the low-level services that Samba needs to run. The tests in this section verify that:

- The IP software works
- The Ethernet hardware works
- Basic name service is in place

Subsequent sections add the Samba daemons *smbd* and *nmbd*, host-based access control, authentication and per-user access control, file services, and browsing. The tests are described in considerable detail to make them understandable by both technically oriented end users and experienced systems and network administrators.

 Beware of firewalls! The Windows XP SP2 firewall will disable the host from answering basic network requests such as ping. For these tests, consider disabling any firewall settings on both the client and server if possible.

Testing the networking software with ping

The first command to enter on both the server and the client is ping 127.0.0.1. This tries to send data to the loopback address and indicates whether any networking support is functioning. On both Windows and Unix, you can run ping 127.0.0.1 from a command shell and usually interrupt it after a few lines. Here is an example on a Linux server:

```
$ ping 127.0.0.1
PING localhost: 56 data bytes 64 bytes from localhost (127.0.0.1):
icmp-seq=0. time=1. ms 64 bytes from localhost (127.0.0.1):
icmp-seq=1. time=0. ms 64 bytes from localhost (127.0.0.1):
icmp-seq=2. time=1. ms ^C
----127.0.0.1 PING Statistics----
3 packets transmitted, 3 packets received, 0% packet loss round-trip (ms)
min/avg/max = 0/0/1
```

Some versions of *ping* let you set a limit on how many times it makes the round trip, so you don't have manually interrupt the command. For instance, on Linux you could enter ping -c5 to stop automatically after five transmissions.

If you get ping: no answer from _._._._ or 100% packet loss, you have no IP networking installed on the system. The address 127.0.0.1 is the internal loopback address and doesn't depend on the computer being physically connected to a network. If this test fails, you have a local problem. TCP/IP isn't installed, it's misconfigured, or a firewall might be preventing ICMP packets. See your operating system documentation if it's a Unix server. If it's a Windows client, follow the instructions in Chapter 3 to install networking support.

 If you're the network manager, some good references are *TCP/IP Network Administration*, by Craig Hunt, and *Windows Server 2003 Network Administration*, by Craig Hunt and Roberta Bragg, both published by O'Reilly. An excellent resource for understanding the TCP/IP protocol suite is Richard Stevens' *TCP/IP Illustrated*, Vol. 1 (Addison-Wesley).

Testing local name services with ping

Next, try to ping localhost from a shell on the Samba server. The name localhost is the conventional hostname for the 127.0.0.1 loopback interface, and it should resolve to that address. After typing ping localhost, you should see output similar to the following:

```
$ ping localhost
PING localhost: 56 data bytes  64 bytes from localhost (127.0.0.1):
icmp-seq=0. time=0. ms  64 bytes from localhost (127.0.0.1):
icmp-seq=1. time=0. ms  64 bytes from localhost (127.0.0.1):
icmp-seq=2. time=0. ms  ^C
```

If this succeeds, try the same test on the client. Otherwise:

- If you get unknown host: localhost, there is a problem resolving the hostname *localhost* to a valid IP address. (This might be as simple as a missing entry in a local *hosts* file.) From here, skip down to the section "Troubleshooting Name Services" later in this chapter.

- If you get "ping: no answer," or "100% packet loss," but pinging 127.0.0.1 worked, name services is resolving to an incorrect address. Check the file or database (typically */etc/hosts* on a Unix system) that the name service is using to resolve addresses to ensure that the entry is correct.

Testing the networking hardware with ping

Next, ping the server's network IP address from itself. This should get you exactly the same results as pinging 127.0.0.1:

```
$ ping 192.168.236.86
PING 192.168.236.86: 56 data bytes 64 bytes from 192.168.236.86 (192.168.236.86):
icmp-seq=0. time=1. ms 64 bytes from 192.168.236.86 (192.168.236.86):
icmp-seq=1. time=0. ms 64 bytes from 192.168.236.86 (192.168.236.86):
icmp-seq=2. time=1. ms ^C
----192.168.236.86 PING Statistics----
3 packets transmitted, 3 packets received, 0% packet loss round-trip (ms)
min/avg/max = 0/0/1
```

If this test works on the server, repeat it for the client. Otherwise:

- If *ping network_ip* fails on either the server or client, but ping 127.0.0.1 works on that system, you have a TCP/IP problem that is specific to the Ethernet network interface card on the computer. Check with the documentation for the network card or host operating system to determine how to configure it correctly. However, be aware that on some operating systems, the *ping* command appears to work even if the network is disconnected, so this test doesn't always diagnose all hardware problems.

Testing connections with ping

Now, ping the server by name (instead of its IP address)—once from the server and once from the client. This is the general test to determine whether your network is working:

```
$ ping server
PING server.example.com: 56 data bytes 64 bytes from server.example.com (192.168.236.
86):
icmp-seq=0. time=1. ms 64 bytes from server.example.com (192.168.236.86):
icmp-seq=1. time=0. ms 64 bytes from server.example.com (192.168.236.86):
icmp-seq=2. time=1. ms ^C
----server.example.com PING Statistics----
3 packets transmitted, 3 packets received, 0% packet loss round-trip (ms)
min/avg/max = 0/0/1
```

If successful, this test tells you four things:

- The hostname (e.g., server) is being found by your local name server.
- The hostname has been expanded to the full name (e.g., server.example.com).
- The host's address is being returned (192.168.236.86).
- The client and server can successfully send and receive packets to each other.

If this test isn't successful, one of several things can be wrong with the network:

- First, if you get ping: no answer, or 100% packet loss, you're not connecting to the network, the other system isn't connecting or isn't responding, or one of the addresses is incorrect. Verify that the server does not have an active firewall preventing it from receiving or replying to ICMP packets. Also check the addresses that the *ping* command reports on each system, and ensure that they match the ones you set up initially.

  If the addresses do not match, try entering the command *arp -an*, and see whether there is an entry for the other system. (The *arp* command stands for the Address Resolution Protocol. The *arp -an* command lists all the addresses known on the local system.) Here are some things to try:

  — If you receive a message like 192.168.236.86 at (incomplete), the Ethernet address of 192.168.236.86 is unknown. This message indicates a complete lack of connectivity, and you're likely having a problem at the very bottom of the TCP/IP protocol stack—the Ethernet interface layer.

— If you receive a response similar to server (192.168.236.86) at 8:0:20:12:7c:94, the server has been reached at some time, or another system is answering on its behalf. However, this means that *ping* should have worked: because it hasn't, you may have an intermittent networking or ARP problem.

— If the IP address from ARP doesn't match the address you expected, investigate and correct the addresses manually.

— If each system can ping itself but not another, something is wrong on the network between them.

• If you get `ping: network unreachable` or `ICMP Host Unreachable`, you're not receiving an answer, and more than one network is probably involved.

It is much simpler to deal with hosts on the same subnet. However, networking, like life, is not always ideal. At this point, it is time to rely on your (or a good friend's) TCP/IP administration skills. Check the default gateway settings on the host and verify that the router IP address is correct. Then try to ping the gateway. If this fails, go through the troubleshooting steps for failing to ping the server from the client or vice versa. This failure is at the network layer. If you can ping the router, but not the host on the other side of it, use the gateway's documentation to verify that packets are successfully being routed from one network to the other.

If possible though, try to test a server and client that are on the same network:

1. First, perform the tests for `ping: no answer` described earlier in this section. If these don't help you identify the problem, the remaining possibilities are that an address is wrong, your netmask is wrong, a network is down, or the packets have been stopped by a firewall.

2. Check both the address and the netmasks on source and destination systems to see whether something is obviously wrong. Assuming that both systems really are on the same network, they both should have the same netmasks, and *ping* should report the correct addresses. If the addresses are wrong, you'll need to correct them. If they are correct, the programs might be confused by an incorrect netmask. See the section "Netmasks" later in this chapter.

3. If the commands are still reporting that the network is unreachable and neither of the previous two conditions are in error, one network really might be unreachable from the other. This is a general networking issue; if you have a separate network manager at your site, he or she may have to investigate. This, too, is an issue for the network manager.

• If you get `ICMP Administratively Prohibited`, you've struck a firewall of some sort or a misconfigured router. Again, if you have a separate network manager at your site, that person may have to investigate.

• If you get `ICMP Host redirect` but *ping* reports that packets are getting through, this is generally harmless: you're simply being rerouted over the network.

- If you get a host redirect and no *ping* responses, you are being redirected, but no one is responding. Treat this situation just like the Network unreachable response, and check your addresses and netmasks.

- If you get ICMP Host Unreachable from gateway *hostname*, ping packets are being routed to another network, but the other system isn't responding and the router is reporting the problem on its behalf. Again, treat this like a Network unreachable response, and start checking addresses and netmasks.

- If you get ping: unknown host *hostname*, your system's name is not known. This tends to indicate a name service problem, which didn't affect localhost. Have a look at "Troubleshooting Name Services," later in this chapter.

- If you get partial success—with some pings failing but others succeeding—you have either an intermittent problem between the systems or an overloaded network. Ping a bit longer, and see whether more than about 3 percent of the packets fail. If so, take the necessary steps to reduce the network problem or contact a network manager if that role is fulfilled by someone other than you. However, if only a few fail, or if you happen to know some massive network program is running, don't worry. The TCP/IP suite of protocols is able to compensate for the occasional lost packets.

- If you get a response such as smtsvr.antares.net is alive when you actually pinged server.example.com, either you're using someone else's address or the system has multiple names and addresses. If the address is wrong, the name service is clearly the culprit; you'll need to change the address in the name service database to refer to the correct system. This is discussed in "Troubleshooting Name Services," later in this chapter.

  Servers are often *multihomed*—i.e., connected to more than one network, with different names on each net. If you are getting a response from an unexpected name on a multihomed server, look at the address and see whether it's on your network (see the section "Netmasks" later in this chapter). If so, you should use that address, rather than one on a different network, for both performance and reliability reasons.

  Servers can also have multiple names for a single Ethernet address, especially if they are web servers. This is harmless, albeit startling. You should probably use the official (and permanent) name, rather than an alias that might change.

- If everything works but the IP address reported is 127.0.0.1, you have a name service error. This error typically occurs when an operating system installation program generates an */etc/hosts* line similar to 127.0.0.1 localhost *hostname.domainname*. The localhost line should say something similar to 127.0.0.1 localhost or 127.0.0.1 localhost.localdomain. Correct it, lest it cause failures in the negotiations over who is the master browse list holder and who is the master browser. It can also cause hard-to-diagnose errors in later tests.

If this command works from the server, repeat it from the client.

Troubleshooting Server Daemons

Once you've confirmed that basic networking is working properly, the next step is to make sure that the daemons are running on the server. This determination takes three separate tests, because no single one of the following tests can decisively prove that everything is functioning properly.

To be sure that the daemons are running, you need to find out whether they:

1. Have started
2. Are registered or bound to a TCP/IP port by the operating system
3. Are actually listening for incoming connections

Tracking daemon startup

First, check the Samba logs. If you've started the daemons, the message smbd version *release* started should appear. If it doesn't, you need to restart the Samba daemons.

If the daemon reports that it has indeed started, look out for bind failed on port *XXX* socket_addr=0 (Address already in use). This means another daemon has been started on port 139 or 445 (*smbd*). Also, *nmbd* will report a similar failure if it cannot bind to port 137 or 138. Either you've started a daemon twice, or the *inetd* server has tried to provide a daemon for you.* If it's the latter, we'll diagnose that in a moment.

Another useful trick for locating a startup failure is to start the failing service from the command line and monitor its progress. All Samba daemons support the -i command-line option for just such a purpose. Combined with a high debug level dumping to standard output, this option should help you to locate the exact point of startup. The following example illustrates the message displayed when you try to launch *smbd* when a previous instance was still running:

```
$ smbd -d 10 -i
....
ERROR: smbd is already running. File /var/run/smbd.pid exists
    and process id 31654 is running.
talloc report on 'null_context' (total 453 bytes in 73 blocks)
        lp_talloc     contains     453 bytes in  72 blocks
```

From here, you can check the process listing to verify whether the existing process is in fact *smbd*. It is possible that a previous instance of *smbd* has exited but not cleaned up its pid file, and that another process exists with that same pid. Use the *ps* command on the server with the "long" option for your system type (commonly ps ax or ps -ef), and see whether *smbd* and *nmbd* are already running. This often looks like the following:

---

* We use the name *inetd* for the TCP/IP metadaemon or superserver that runs on many Unix and Linux servers; the actual command is usually either *inetd* or the newer *xinetd*.

```
$ ps ax | grep mbd
31654 ?        Ss     0:00 smbd -D -d3
31656 ?        Ss     0:02 nmbd -D -d3
31657 ?        S      0:00 smbd -D -d3
```

This example illustrates that *smbd* and *nmbd* have already started as standalone daemons (the -D option) at log level 3 (-d3).

Looking for daemons bound to ports

Both *smbd* and *nmbd* have to register with the operating system so that they can get
access to the necessary TCP/IP ports. The *netstat* command will tell you if this has
been done. Run the command netstat -a on the server, and look for lines mentioning netbios-ns (137/udp), netbios-dgm (138/udp), netbios-ssn (139/tcp), or
microsoft-ds (445/tcp):

```
$ netstat -an | egrep ':(137|138|139|445)'
tcp       0      0 *:139           *:*         LISTEN
tcp       0      0 *:445           *:*         LISTEN
udp       0      0 *:137           *:*
udp       0      0 *:138           *:*
```

Although you may see additional lines listed, there should be at least two UDP lines,
one for the NetBIOS name service port (137) and one for the NetBIOS datagram service (138), indicating that the *nmbd* server is registered and (we hope) is waiting to
answer requests. There should also be at least one TCP line for each of the values of
the smb ports parameter in *smb.conf*. The default value includes both ports 139 and
445, so frequently you will see a TCP line for each one. Additionally, these ports
should be in the LISTEN state. This means that *smbd* is up and waiting to accept
connections.

There might be other TCP lines indicating connections from *smbd* to clients, one for
each client. These are usually in the ESTABLISHED state. If there are *smbd* lines in
the ESTABLISHED state, *smbd* is definitely running. If there is only one line in the
LISTEN state, you can't be sure yet. If both of the lines are missing, a daemon has
not succeeded in starting, so it's time to check the logs, and then go back to
Chapter 2.

If there is a line for each client, it might be coming either from a Samba daemon or
from the meta-daemon, *inetd*. It's quite possible that your *inetd* startup file contains
lines that start Samba daemons without your realizing it; for instance, although such
behavior is becoming increasingly rare, the lines might have been placed there if you
installed Samba as part of a Linux distribution. The daemons started by *inetd* prevent ours from running. This problem typically produces log messages such as bind
failed on port XXX socket addr=0 (Address already in use).

Check your */etc/inetd.conf* file or */etc/xinetd.d/* directory; unless you're intentionally
starting the daemons from there, any servers bound to the netbios-* or microsoft-ds
ports should be disabled. Refer to Chapter 2 for details concerning Samba and *inetd*.

```
```

Checking smbd with telnet

The easiest way to test that the *smbd* server is actually working is to send it a meaningless message and see if it is rejected. Try something such as the following:

```
$ echo "hello" | telnet localhost 139
Trying
Trying 192.168.236.86 ...
Connected to server. Escape character is '^]'.
Connection closed by foreign host.
```

This command sends an erroneous but harmless message to *smbd*. If you get a Connected message followed by a Connection closed message, the test was a success. You have an *smbd* daemon listening on the port and rejecting improper connection messages. On the other hand, if you get telnet: connect: Connection refused, most likely no daemon is present. A less likely explanation is that you have attempted to connect to the wrong port. Remember that the ports used by *smbd* are controlled by the smb ports option. Make sure you use one of these ports. If all else fails, check the logs and go back to Chapter 2.

Regrettably, there isn't an easy test for *nmbd*. If the *telnet* test and the *netstat* test both say that an *smbd* is running, there is a good chance that *netstat* will also be correct about *nmbd* running. *nmbd* is tested further later in this chapter when we troubleshoot network browsing problems.

Testing daemons with testparm

Once you know there's a daemon, you should always run *testparm*, in hopes of getting something such as the following:

```
$ testparm
Load smb config files from /usr/local/samba/lib/smb.conf
Processing section "[homes]"
Processing section "[printers]" ...
Processing section "[tmp]"
Loaded services file OK. ...
```

The *testparm* program normally reports the processing of a series of sections and responds with Loaded services file OK if it succeeds. If there is something wrong with the file, *testparm* reports one or more of the following messages, which also appear in the logs as noted:

WARNING: You have some share names that are longer than 12 characters.
: This error is for anyone using Windows Me and older clients. They fail to connect to shares with long names.

WARNING: [*name*] service MUST be printable!
: A printer share lacks a print ok = yes option.

WARNING: No path in service name - making it unavailable!
: Current versions of Samba disable any service other than [homes] that does not have an explicit path set.

NOTE: *name* is flagged unavailable
: Just a reminder that you have used the available = no option in a share.

Can't find include file [*name*]
: A configuration file referred to by an include option did not exist. If you were including the file unconditionally, this is an error and probably a serious one: the share will not have the configuration you intended. If you were including it based on one of the % variables, such as %a (architecture), you must decide whether, for example, a missing Windows XP configuration file is a problem. It often isn't.

Can't copy service name, unable to copy to itself.
: You tried to copy an *smb.conf* section into itself.

Unable to copy service—source not found: [*name*]
: Indicates a missing or misspelled section in a copy = option.

Ignoring unknown parameter name.
: Typically indicates an obsolete, misspelled, or unsupported option.

Global parameter name found in service section.
: Indicates that a global-only parameter has been used in an individual share. Samba ignores the parameter.

After the first *testparm* test, repeat it with (exactly) three parameters: the name of your *smb.conf* file, the name of your client, and its IP address:

```
$ testparm /usr/local/samba/lib/smb.conf client 192.168.236.10
```

This command runs one more test that checks the hostname and address against hosts allow and hosts deny options and might produce the Allow connection from hostname to service and/or Deny connection from hostname to service messages for the client system. These messages indicate that you have hosts allow and/or hosts deny options in your *smb.conf*, and they prohibit access from the client system.

Troubleshooting SMB Connections

Now that you know the servers are up, you need to make that sure they're running properly. Start by placing a simple *smb.conf* file in the */usr/local/samba/lib* directory.

A minimal smb.conf file

In the following tests, we assume that you have a [temp] share suitable for testing, plus at least one valid user account (we'll use one named *rose*). An *smb.conf* file that includes just these is as follows:

```
[global]
    workgroup = EXAMPLE
    security = user
```

```
[homes]
    read only = no

[temp]
    path = /data/tmp
    read only = no
```

Testing locally with smbclient

The first test ensures that the server can list its own services (shares). Run the command `smbclient -L localhost -N` to anonymously connect to the server from itself. You should see the following:

```
$ smbclient -L localhost -N
Anonymous login successful
Domain=[EXAMPLE] OS=[Unix] Server=[Samba 3.0.22]]

    Sharename      Type      Comment
    ---------      -----     ----------
    temp           Disk
    homes          Disk
    IPC$           IPC       IPC Service (Samba 3.0.22)
...
```

If you received this output or something similar, move on to the next section, "Testing connections with smbclient." On the other hand, if you receive an error, check the following:

- If you get `Connection to localhost failed`, either you've spelled its name wrong or there actually is a problem (which should have been seen back in "Testing local name services with ping"). In the latter case, move on to the section "Troubleshooting Name Services," later in this chapter.

- If you get `Error connecting to xxx.xxx.xx.xx (Connection refused)`, the server was found, but it wasn't running an *smbd* daemon. Skip back to "Troubleshooting Server Daemons," earlier in this chapter, and retest the daemons.

- If you're using *inetd* (or *xinetd*) instead of standalone daemons, be sure to check your */etc/ inetd.conf* (or *xinetd* configuration files) and */etc/services* entries against their manpages for errors as well.

- If you get the message `NT_STATUS_ACCESS_DENIED`, you aren't permitted access to the server. This could mean you have a `hosts allow` option that doesn't include the server or a `hosts deny` option that does. Recheck with the command `testparm smb.conf your_hostname your_ip_address` (see the section "Testing daemons with testparm"), and correct any unintended prohibitions. The error could also be caused by a `restrict anonymous` setting in *smb.conf*.

Testing connections with smbclient

Run the command smbclient //*server*/temp to connect to the server's [temp] share and to see if you can connect to a file service. We assume that a valid account for the user named *rose* has already been created. You should get the following response:

```
$ smbclient //server/temp -U rose
Password: <enter password>
Domain=[EXAMPLE] OS=[Unix] Server=[Samba 3.0.22]
smb: \> quit
```

If you get Get_Hostbyname: Unknown host name or Connect error: Connection refused, see the previous section, "Testing locally with smbclient," for the possible diagnoses.

Now, at the Password: prompt, provide the password for the account given as the -U argument value. If you then get an smb: \> prompt, the connection works. Enter quit and continue on to the next section, "Testing connections with net use."

A response of NT_STATUS_LOGON_FAILURE indicates either that you are using an invalid account name or that the password you used didn't match the credentials for the account. It is a good idea to verify that the account exists by running pdbedit --verbose *rose*.

An error message referring to NT_STATUS_BAD_NETWORK_NAME can be caused by any one of the following:

- A wrong share name: you might have spelled it wrong, it might be too long, it might be in mixed case, or it might not be available. Check that it's what you expect with *testparm* (see the earlier section, "Testing daemons with testparm").

- An invalid users or valid users option in your *smb.conf* file that doesn't allow your account to connect. Recheck using testparm smb.conf *your_hostname your_ip_address* (see the earlier section, "Testing daemons with testparm").

- A valid hosts option that doesn't include the server, or an invalid hosts option that does. Also test this with *testparm*.

- There is one more reason for this failure that has nothing at all to do with passwords: the path parameter in your *smb.conf* file might point somewhere that doesn't exist. This will not be diagnosed by *testparm*. You will have to check it manually.

Once you have connected to [temp] successfully, repeat the test, this time logging in to your home directory (e.g., connect to the network path //*server*/*rose*). If you have to change anything to get that to work, retest [temp] again afterward.

Testing connections with net use

Run the following command on the Windows client to see whether it can connect to the server:

```
C:\> net use * \\server\temp /user:rose
```

You should be prompted for a password whether or not the password for *rose* on the Samba server is different than the one you used to logon to the Windows console. Once the correct password has been transmitted, you should see the response:

```
The command was completed successfully.
```

If that worked, congratulations! You have completed all of these tests successfully, and your server should be ready to accept connections from users. Otherwise:

- If you get `The specified shared directory cannot be found`, or `Cannot locate specified share name`, the directory name is either misspelled or not in the *smb.conf* file.

- If you get `The computer name specified in the network path cannot be located` or `Cannot locate specified computer`, the directory name has been misspelled, the name service has failed, there is a networking problem, or the `hosts deny` option includes your host.

  - If it is not a spelling mistake, you need to double back at least to the section "Testing connections with smbclient" to investigate why it doesn't connect.

  - If *smbclient* does work, there is a name service problem with the client name service, and you need to proceed to the section "Testing the server with nmblookup" and see whether you can look up both the client and server with *nmblookup*.

- If you get `The password is invalid for \\server\temp`, verify that you are using the correct credentials. If you provide your password again and it still fails, your password is not being matched on the server, or possibly the configuration file has a `valid users` or `invalid users` list denying you permission.

- You might have the NetBEUI protocol bound to the Microsoft client. This often produces long timeouts and erratic failures and is known to have caused failures to accept passwords in the past. Unless you absolutely need the NetBEUI protocol, remove it.

Troubleshooting Browsing

Finally, we come to browsing. We've left this for last, not because it is the most difficult, but because it's both optional and partially dependent on network topology. Browsing is simply a way to find the servers on your network and the resources that they provide. But problems with browsing are hard to diagnose if you don't already know that all the other NetBIOS and SMB/CIFS services are running properly.

Testing the Server with nmblookup

This section tests the "advertising" system used for Windows name services and browsing. Advertising works by broadcasting one's presence or willingness to provide services; it uses broadcasts and UDP packets.

The *nmblookup* program can broadcast name queries for the hostname you provide and returns its IP address and the name of the system, much as *nslookup* does with DNS. Here, the -B option is used to define the broadcast address to use when sending the name query. If you do not list a specific broadcast address, *nmblookup* defaults to sending a request using the broadcast address of each available network interface (or the subset defined by the interfaces option).

First, check the server locally. Run *nmblookup* with a -B option specifying your server's name (to tell it to send the query to the Samba server) and a parameter of _ _SAMBA_ _ (two underscores on each side) as the symbolic name to look up:

```
$ nmblookup -B server __SAMBA__
querying __SAMBA__ on 192.168.236.86
192.168.236.86 __SAMBA__<00>
```

You should get the IP address of the server, followed by the name _ _SAMBA_ _, which means that the server has successfully advertised that it has a service called _ _SAMBA_ _, and therefore that at least part of NetBIOS name service works.

If you get name_query failed to find *name* _ _SAMBA_ _, chances are that you either have a problem with name resolution, or *nmbd* is not running. Check to make sure you spelled the server's hostname correctly, then try again with nmblookup -B *ip_address*. If that fails too, *nmbd* isn't running. Go back briefly to the earlier section, "Troubleshooting Server Daemons."

Testing the Client with nmblookup

Next, check the IP address of the client from the server with *nmblookup* using the -B option for the client's name and a parameter of '*' meaning "anything," as shown here:

```
$ nmblookup -B client '*'
querying * on 192.168.236.10
192.168.236.10 *<00>
```

You might get the following errors:

- If you receive name_query failed to find name *, the client software on the PC isn't installed, started, or bound to TCP/IP. Refer to Chapter 3 and ensure that you have a client installed that is listening to the network. Windows XP clients (at least those with Service Pack 2) do not seem to respond to the '*' name. These hosts will respond to queries for their own names, so retest using the client machine name in place of *.

- If nmblookup -B *client_name* fails but nmblookup -B *client_IP_address* succeeds, there is a name service problem with the client's name; go to "Troubleshooting Name Services," later in this chapter.

Testing the Network with nmblookup

Run the command *nmblookup* again with a parameter of `'*'`, this time without a specific broadcast address. Here we are testing the ability of programs (such as *nmbd*) to use broadcasts. It's essentially a connectivity test, done via a broadcast to the default broadcast address.

The results lists the hosts on the network that respond. Samba might not catch all the responses in the short time it listens, so you won't always see all the SMB/CIFS hosts on the network. However, you should see most of them:

```
$ nmblookup '*'
192.168.236.191 *<00>
192.168.236.228 *<00>
192.168.236.86 *<00>
192.168.236.79 *<00>
192.168.236.206 *<00>
192.168.236.10 *<00>
192.168.236.217 *<00>
192.168.236.72 *<00>
```

In case of failure:

- If this doesn't give at least the client address you previously tested, the default broadcast address is wrong (or it is running Windows XP). Try `nmblookup -B 255.255.255.255 '*'`, which is a last-ditch variant. If this draws responses, the broadcast address you've been using before is wrong. Troubleshooting these is discussed in the "Broadcast Addresses" section, later in this chapter.

- If the address 255.255.255.255 fails too, check your notes to see whether your PC and server are on different subnets, as mentioned in the earlier section, "Testing connections with ping." You should try to diagnose this step with a server and client on the same subnet, but if you can't, you can try specifying the remote subnet's broadcast address with `-B`. Finding that address is discussed in the section "Broadcast Addresses" later in this chapter. The `-B` option will work if your router supports directed broadcasts; if it doesn't, you might be forced to test with a client on the same network.

As usual, you can check the Samba logfiles for additional clues.

Testing Browsing with smbclient

From the server, try listing its own shares using *smbclient* with a `-L` option and your server's name. We'll stick to port 139 (`-p` option) since NetBIOS sessions are a required component of network browsing.[*] A server that is not configured to receive

---

[*] Windows clients do not support separating NetBIOS name services (137/udp) from NetBIOS session services (139/tcp). The client either supports NetBIOS in its entirety or does not support any of its services. We'll take the same approach when configuring Samba.

SMB/CIFS connections on port 139 will frequently have problems with participating in browsing and elections. You should get something resembling the following:

```
$ smbclient -L server -N -p 139
Anonymous login successful
Domain=[EXAMPLE] OS=[Unix] Server=[Samba 3.0.22]

        Sharename       Type        Comment
        ---------       -----       ----------
        temp            Disk
        homes           Disk
        IPC$            IPC         IPC Service (Samba 3.0.22)


        Server          Comment
        ---------       -------
        SERVER          Samba 3.0.22
        CLIENT


        Workgroup       Master
        ---------       -------
        EXAMPLE         SERVER
```

Problems can be diagnosed as follows:

- If you didn't get a Sharename list, the server is not allowing you to browse any shares. This should not be the case if you've tested any of the shares with Windows Explorer or the *net use* command. If you haven't done the smbclient -L localhost -N test yet (see the earlier section, "Testing locally with smbclient"), do it now. Also check the *smb.conf* file to make sure that you do not have the option browsable = no anywhere in it: we suggest using a minimal *smb.conf* file (see the earlier section, "A minimal smb.conf file"). You need to have browsable enabled (which is the default) to see the share.

  Windows 2000 and later hosts do not allow you to browse for shares anonymously and return NT_STATUS_ACCESS_DENIED. You will, however, still be able to enumerate any servers or workgroups of which the host is aware.

- If you didn't get a browse list of servers or workgroups, the host might not be providing information about the systems on the network. At least one system on the net must support browse lists. Make sure that your Samba host has local master = yes and browse list = yes (both are enabled by default unless configured otherwise) in the *smb.conf* file if you want Samba to be the local master browser.

- If you didn't get a workgroup list with your workgroup name in it, it is possible that your workgroup is set incorrectly in the *smb.conf* file.

- If you get nothing, try once more with the additional options -I *ip_address* -d3. Remember that the -d3 option sets the log/debugging level to 3. Then check the Samba logs for clues.

If you're still getting nothing, you shouldn't have gotten this far; double back to at least "Troubleshooting Low-Level IP" and "Troubleshooting Server Daemons." On the other hand:

- If you get `NT_STATUS_ACCESS_DENIED`, you aren't permitted access to the server. If this is a Samba host, verify that the `hosts allow` option includes the server itself and the loopback address. If this is a Windows 2000 or later host, you must use a valid user account to connect (the `-U` option) instead of requesting an anonymous session (the `-N` option).

- If you attempt to connect with user credentials (the `-U` option) and instead get `NT_STATUS_LOGON_FAILURE`, verify that the account exists and you have the correct login name and password. Sometimes it might also be necessary to specify the domain name (the `-W` option) if you are connecting to a domain member server.

- If you get `Connection refused`, the *smbd* server is not currently running. Check that it's up, running, and listening to the network with *netstat*. See the earlier section, "Troubleshooting Server Daemons."

- If you get `Connection to hostname failed`, you've made a spelling error, there is a mismatch between the Unix and NetBIOS hostname, or there is a name service problem. Start name service debugging as discussed in the earlier section, "Testing connections with net use." If this works, suspect a name mismatch, and go to the later section, "Troubleshooting NetBIOS Names."

- If you get `Session request failed`, the server refused the connection. This message usually indicates an internal error, such as insufficient memory to fork a process or perhaps some problem with inordinate name resolution delays.

Testing Client Browsing with net view

On the client, run the command `net view \\server` in an MS-DOS (command prompt) window to see whether you can connect to the client and ask what shares it provides. You should get back a list of available shares on the server.

 As was discussed in Chapter 8, anonymous browsing of servers has been one of the casualties in the effort to tighten network security. In some environments, anonymous browsing may still work. If you receive any messages indicating "Access denied," try retesting using a valid user account. The *net.exe* command allows you to specify the account credentials with the `/user:username` command-line option.

If this test works, you have no further problems. Otherwise:

- If you get `Network name not found` for the name you just tested in the earlier section, "Testing the Client with nmblookup," there is a problem with the client software itself. Double-check this diagnosis by running *nmblookup* against the client; if it works and *net view* doesn't, the client is at fault. If *nmblookup* fails, there is a NetBIOS name service problem, as discussed in the later section, "Troubleshooting NetBIOS Names."

- If you get `You do not have the necessary access rights`, or `This server is not configured to list shared resources`, you probably have a `hosts allow` or `hosts deny` line that prohibits connections from your system. These problems should have been detected by the *smbclient* tests starting in the earlier section, "Testing browsing with smbclient."

- If you get `The specified computer is not receiving requests`, you have misspelled the name, the system is unreachable by broadcast (tested in the earlier section, "Testing the network with nmblookup"), or the system is not running *nmbd*.

Browsing the Server from the Client

From My Network Places window, try to browse the server. You will probably first have to expand the Entire Network link. Your Samba server should appear in the browse list of your local workgroup. You should be able to double-click the name of the server to get a list of shares.

- If you receive an `Unable to browse the network` error, one of the following has occurred:
  - You have looked too soon, before the broadcasts and updates have completed. Wait 30 seconds and try again.
  - There is a network problem you haven't yet diagnosed.
  - There is no browse master. Add the configuration option `local master = yes` to your *smb.conf* file.
- If you receive the message `\\server is not accessible`:
  - The system really isn't accessible.
  - The system doesn't support browsing.

If you've made it this far and the problem is not yet resolved, either the problem is one not yet covered here, or it is a problem related to a topic already covered, and further analysis is required. Name resolution is often related to difficulties with Samba, so we cover it in more detail in the next sections. If you know that your problem is not related to name resolution, skip to the "Extra Resources" section at the end of the chapter.

Troubleshooting Name Services

This section looks at simple troubleshooting techniques for all the name services that you'll encounter, but only for the common problems that affect Samba.

There are several good additional references for troubleshooting particular name services: Paul Albitz and Cricket Liu's *DNS and Bind* (O'Reilly) covers DNS, and the Windows Internet Name Service (WINS) and *LMHOSTS* files are discussed in a wide variety of documentation available from *http://www.microsoft.com*.

The problems addressed in this section are as follows:

- You don't know which name services are in use.
- A hostname can't be looked up.
- The long (FQDN) form of a hostname works, but the short form doesn't.
- The short form of the name works, but the long form doesn't.
- A long delay occurs before the expected result.

Identifying What's in Use

First, determine whether both the server and the client are using DNS, WINS, or local files to resolve names. Each operating system has a different preference:

- Windows NT tries WINS, then broadcast, then the *LMHOSTS* file, and finally *HOSTS* and DNS.
- Windows 2000 and later follow the same rules as Windows NT unless NetBIOS support has been disabled in the network settings. In that case, the client relies solely on DNS and a local *hosts* file.
- Samba daemons use *lmhosts*, WINS, the Unix system's name resolver (i.e., the *gethostbyname()* function), and then NetBIOS broadcasts (depending on the name resolve order parameter in *smb.conf*).
- Unix systems can be configured to use any combination of DNS, a local *hosts* files, or WINS and generally in any order.

A good rule of thumb is to always configure clients and servers to prefer a centralized directory service such as DNS or WINS over local files for resolving names to addresses. Local settings such as */etc/hosts* and *lmhosts* have a tendency to get out of sync over time when deployed on multiple systems. By consolidating on a central name service, you have a single database to troubleshoot when clients are unable to resolve names: you know that either the name service is broken or the client or server is misconfigured. We recommend that both the client systems use WINS and DNS, and that Samba be configured to use WINS and the host operating system's name resolver. The Unix server itself should be configured to use DNS and fall back to the */etc/hosts* file only in case of failure. You'll have to look at your notes and the actual systems to see which is in use.

On the clients, the name services are all set in the TCP/IP Properties panel of the Networking Control Panel, as discussed in Chapter 3. You might need to check there to see what you've actually turned on. On the server, see whether a */etc/resolv.conf* file exists. If it does, you're using DNS. You might be using the other name resolution options as well, though.

Check for a */etc/nsswitch.conf* file on Unix operating systems. If you have one, look for a line that begins with host: followed by files dns, or both. These are the name services to use, in order, with optional extra material in square brackets. The files keyword is for using a local *hosts* files, while dns (sometimes using the keyword bind for the Berkeley Internet Name Daemon) refers to using the Domain Name System.

Cannot Look Up Hostnames

If you have isolated a problem to a name lookup and know from the previous section which service your local system is using, try the following:

DNS

Use the *nslookup* or *host* command to resolve the machine name. If this fails, look for a */etc/resolv.conf* error, an inaccessible DNS server, or a short name/ FQDN problem (see the next section). Try the following solutions:

- Confirm that your */etc/resolv.conf* file contains one or more nameserver lines, each with an IP address. These are the addresses of your DNS servers.
- Ping each server address you find. If this fails for one system, check that connectivity and DNS service on the system. If it fails for all, check your network.
- Retry the lookup using the full domain name including the finalizing period (e.g., server.example.com.) if you tried the short name first, or the short name if you tried the FQDN first. If results differ, skip to the next section.

Broadcast

The broadcast mechanism supports only short names such as server, and not the FQDN variants, such as server.example.com. Run nmblookup -S server. This reports everything broadcast has registered for the name. In our example, it looks like this:

```
$ nmblookup -S server
querying server on 192.168.236.255
192.168.236.86 SERVER<00>
Looking up status of 192.168.236.86
        SERVER          <00> -          M <ACTIVE>
        SERVER          <20> -          M <ACTIVE>
        EXAMPLE         <00> - <GROUP> M <ACTIVE>
        EXAMPLE         <1e> - <GROUP> M <ACTIVE>
```

The required entry is SERVER <00>, which identifies server as being this system's NetBIOS name. You should also see your workgroup mentioned one or more times. If these lines are missing, NetBIOS broadcasts cannot look up names and will need attention.

WINS

WINS is similar to the NetBIOS broadcast methods, and debugging WINS issues is very similar to debugging broadcast name resolution problems. The only real difference is that *nmblookup* must send the name query directly to the WINS server itself. This is accomplished by sending a unicast packet to the WINS server IP address (the -U option) and setting the recursive flag (the -R option) in the request. If *nmblookup* can resolve the name successfully, it will proceed to issue a node status request to the target server as it did with the broadcast mechanism. Assuming that we are using a WINS server at 192.168.1.74, the command and its output would appear as:

```
$ nmblookup -U 192.168.1.74 -R -S server
querying server on 192.168.1.74
192.168.236.86 SERVER<00>
Looking up status of 192.168.236.86
        SERVER          <00> -          M <ACTIVE>
        SERVER          <20> -          M <ACTIVE>
        EXAMPLE         <00> - <GROUP> M <ACTIVE>
        EXAMPLE         <1e> - <GROUP> M <ACTIVE>
```

The server and workgroup entries should display the same information as described in the broadcast tests. If there is an error, verify that the network and SMB/CIFS software are on the target machine.

hosts

Inspect the *HOSTS* file on the client (*%SYSTEMROOT%\system32\drivers\etc\hosts*). Each line should have an IP number and one or more names, with the primary name first and then any optional aliases. An example follows:

```
127.0.0.1          localhost
192.168.236.1      dns.svc.example.com
192.168.236.10     client.example.com client
192.168.236.11     backup.example.com loghost
192.168.236.86     server.example.com server
192.168.236.254    router.svc.example.com
```

On Unix, localhost should always be 127.0.0.1. On the client, check that there are no #XXX directives at the ends of the lines; these are LAN Manager/NetBIOS directives and should appear only in *LMHOSTS* files.

LMHOSTS

This file is a local source for LAN Manager (NetBIOS) names. It has a format similar to *HOSTS* files, but it does not support long-form domain names (e.g., server.example.com) and can have a number of optional #XXX directives following the NetBIOS names. There is usually an *lmhosts.sam* (for sample) file located in *%SYSTEMROOT%\system32\drivers\etc* on Windows clients, but it's not used unless it is renamed to *lmhosts* in the same directory.

Long and Short Hostnames

Where the FQDN form of a hostname works but the short name doesn't (for example, client.example.com works but client doesn't), consider the following:

DNS

> This usually indicates that there is no default domain in which to look up the short names. Look for a default or domain line in */etc/resolv.conf* on the Samba server containing your domain, or look for a search line containing one or more domains. One or the other might need to be present to make short names usable; which one is needed depends on the vendor and version of the DNS resolver. Try adding domain *your_domain* to *resolv.conf*, and ask your network or DNS administrator what should be in the file.

Broadcast/WINS

> The broadcast and WINS NetBIOS name services do not support fully qualified domain names; it won't suffer from this problem.

hosts

> If the short name is not in */etc/hosts*, consider adding it as an alias. If you can, avoid short names as primary names (the first one on a line). Have them as aliases if your system permits.

LMHOSTS

> LAN Manager doesn't support names other than the short versions, so it won't suffer from this problem.

On the other hand, if the short form of the name works and the long form doesn't, consider the following:

DNS

> This is not a normal or expected error. Troubleshoot the DNS server configuration or contact your DNS administrator if you do not manage that service.

Broadcast/WINS

> This is normal; NetBIOS name services can't use an FQDN. Optionally, consider DNS for locating specific servers wherever possible.

hosts

> Add the long name as at least an alias, and preferably as the primary form. Also consider using DNS if it's practical.

LMHOSTS

> This is normal. LAN Manager can't use an FQDN; consider switching to DNS or *hosts*.

Unusual Delays

When there is a long delay before the expected result:

DNS
Test the same name with the *nslookup* or *host* command on the system that is slow (client or server). If *nslookup* is also slow, you have a DNS problem. If the lookup is slower on a client, you might have too many protocols bound to the Ethernet card. Eliminate NetBEUI, which is infamously slow, assuming you don't need it. You can also use Wireshark to analyze the cause of any DNS delays.

Broadcast/WINS
Test the client using *nmblookup*; if it's faster, you probably have the protocols problem mentioned in the previous item.

hosts
The *HOSTS* file, if of reasonable size, is always fast. You probably have the protocols problem mentioned previously under DNS.

LMHOSTS
This is not a name lookup problem; *LMHOSTS* files are as fast as *hosts* files.

Localhost issues

When a localhost isn't 127.0.0.1, try the following:

DNS
There is probably no record for `localhost. A 127.0.0.1`. Arrange to add one, as well as a reverse entry, `1.0.0.127.IN-ADDR.ARPA PTR 127.0.0.1`.

Broadcast/WINS
Not applicable.

hosts
Add a line that says `127.0.0.1 localhost`.

LMHOSTS
Not applicable.

Troubleshooting Network Addresses

A number of common problems are caused by incorrect routing of Internet addresses or by the incorrect assignment of addresses. This section helps you determine your addresses.

Netmasks

Using the netmask, it is possible to determine which addresses can be reached directly (i.e., which are on the local network) and which addresses require forwarding packets through a router. If the netmask is wrong, the systems will make one of two mistakes. One is to route local packets via a router, which is an expensive waste of time—it might work reasonably fast, it might run slowly, or it might fail utterly. The second mistake is to fail to send packets from a remote system to the router, which will prevent them from being forwarded to the remote system.

The netmask is a number like an IP address, with one bits for the network part of an address and zero bits for the host portion. It is used as a bitmask to mask off parts of the address inside the TCP/IP code. If the mask is 255.255.0.0, the first two bytes are the network part and the last two are the host part; this is sometimes known (somewhat anachronistically) as the netmask for a class B network. More common is the class C netmask 255.255.255.0, in which the first three bytes are the network part and the last one is the host part.

For example, let's say your IP address is 192.168.1.10 and the Samba server is 192.168.236.86. If your netmask happens to be 255.255.255.0, the network part of the address is the first 3 bytes, and the host part is the last byte. In this case, the network parts are different, and the systems are on different networks:

Network part	Host part
192 168 001	10
192 168 236	86

If your netmask happens to be 255.255.0.0, the network part is just the first 2 bytes. In this case, the network parts match, and so the two systems are on the same network:

Network part	Host part
192 168	001 10
192 168	236 86

Make sure that the netmask in use on each system matches the structure of your network. On every subnet, the netmask should be identical on each system.

Broadcast Addresses

The broadcast address is a normal address, with the hosts part all one bits. It means "all hosts on your network." You can compute it easily from your netmask and address: take the address and put one-bits in it for all the bits that are zero at the end of the netmask (the host part). The following table illustrates this:

	Network part	Host part
IP address	192 168 236	86
Netmask	255 255 255	000
Broadcast	192 168 236	255

In this example, the broadcast address on the 192.168.236 network is 192.168.236. 255. There is also an old "universal" broadcast address, 255.255.255.255. Routers are prohibited from forwarding these, but most systems on your local network will respond to broadcasts to this address.

Network Address Ranges

A number of address ranges have been reserved for testing and for nonconnected networks; we use these for the examples in this book. If you don't have an address yet, feel free to use one of these to start. They include one class A network, 10.*.*.*, a range of class B network addresses, 172.16.*.* through 172.31.*.*, and 254 class C networks, 192.168.1.* through 192.168.254.*. The domain example.com is also reserved for unconnected networks, explanatory examples, and books.

If you're actually connecting to the Internet, you'll need to get an appropriate IP address and a domain name, probably through the same company that provides your connection.

Finding Your Network Address

If you haven't recorded your IP address, you can learn it through the *ifconfig* command on Unix or the *ipconfig.exe* command on Windows. Check your manual pages for any options required by your brand of Unix. For example, ifconfig -a works on both Linux and Solaris. You should see output similar to the following:

```
$ ifconfig -a
eth0  Link encap:Ethernet  HWaddr 00:14:A4:82:36:E0
      inet addr:192.168.236.86  Bcast:192.168.236.255  Mask:255.255.255.0
      UP BROADCAST RUNNING MULTICAST  MTU:1500  Metric:1
      RX packets:54509 errors:2199 dropped:0 overruns:0 frame:2199
      TX packets:45497 errors:1 dropped:0 overruns:0 carrier:0
      collisions:0 txqueuelen:200
      RX bytes:19202254 (18.3 Mb)  TX bytes:5060379 (4.8 Mb)
      Interrupt:11 Memory:f92e0000-f92f0000

lo    Link encap:Local Loopback
      inet addr:127.0.0.1  Mask:255.0.0.0
      UP LOOPBACK RUNNING  MTU:16436  Metric:1
      RX packets:291088 errors:0 dropped:0 overruns:0 frame:0
      TX packets:291088 errors:0 dropped:0 overruns:0 carrier:0
      collisions:0 txqueuelen:0
      RX bytes:75847323 (72.3 Mb)  TX bytes:75847323 (72.3 Mb)
```

One of the interfaces will be loopback (in our examples, lo), and the other will be the regular IP interface. The flags should show that the interface is running, and Ethernet interfaces will also say they support broadcasts (PPP interfaces don't).

Troubleshooting NetBIOS Names

Historically, SMB protocols have depended on the NetBIOS name system, also called the LAN Manager name system. This was a simple scheme where each system had a unique 15-character name (plus one byte for the resource type) and broadcast it on the LAN for everyone to know. With TCP/IP, we tend to use names such as client.example.com, stored in */etc/hosts* files or DNS.

The usual mapping of DNS names such as server.example.com to NetBIOS names uses the server part as the NetBIOS name and converts it to uppercase. Alas, this approach doesn't always work, especially if you have a system with a 16-character name; not everyone uses the same NetBIOS and DNS names. In this case, it would not be unusual to have a host with a NetBIOS name of corpvm1 and a DNS name of vm1.corp.com.

A system with a different NetBIOS name and DNS name is confusing when you're troubleshooting; we recommend that you try to avoid this wherever possible. NetBIOS names are discoverable with *smbclient*:

- If you can list shares on your Samba server with smbclient -L *short_name*, the short name is the NetBIOS name.

- If you get Get_Hostbyname: Unknown host *name*, there is probably a mismatch. Check in the *smb.conf* file to see whether the NetBIOS name is explicitly set.

- Try to list shares again, specifying -I and the IP address of the Samba server (e.g., smbclient -L server -I 192.168.236.86). This command overrides the name lookup and forces the packets to go to the IP address. If this attempt works, there was a mismatch.

- Try with -I and the full domain name of the server (e.g., smbclient -L server -I server.example.com). This tests the lookup of the domain name, using whatever scheme the Samba server uses (e.g., DNS). If it fails, you have a name service problem. You should reread the earlier section "Troubleshooting Name Services" after you finish troubleshooting the NetBIOS names.

- If nothing is working so far, repeat the tests specifying -U *username* and -W *workgroup*, with the username and workgroup in uppercase, to make sure you're not being derailed by a user or workgroup mismatch.

- If still nothing works and you had evidence of a name service problem, troubleshoot the name service (see the earlier section, "Troubleshooting Name Services") and then return to the NetBIOS name service.

Extra Resources

At some point during your work with Samba, you'll want to turn go online for news, updates, and aid.

Documentation and FAQs

Samba ships with a large set of documentation files, and it is well worth the effort to at least browse through them, either in the distribution directory on your computer under *docs* or online at the Samba web site: *http://www.samba.org*. The most current FAQ list, bug information, and distribution locations are located at the web site, with links to all the Samba manual pages and HOWTOs. There is also a newly launched Wiki for the Samba community, hosted at *http://wiki.samba.org*.

Samba Mailing Lists, Newsgroups, and IRC

The following are mailing lists for support with Samba. See *https://lists.samba.org* for information on subscribing and unsubscribing to these mailing lists:

samba@samba.org
>   This is the primary mailing list for the Samba user community and for general questions and discussion regarding Samba.

samba-technical@samba.org
>   This mailing list focuses on the Samba development and is where Samba programmers coordinate discussion of the Samba code.

samba-announce@samba.org
>   This low-noise list is for receiving news regarding Samba, such as announcements of new releases.

samba-cvs@samba.org
>   By subscribing to this list, you automatically receive a message every time one of the Samba developers updates the Samba source code in the subversion repository. You might want to do this if you are waiting for a specific bug fix or feature to be applied. To avoid congesting your email inbox, we suggest using the digest feature, which consolidates messages into a smaller number of emails.

Searchable versions of the Samba mailing list archives can be found online at *http://marc.theaimsgroup.com*.

When posting messages to the Samba mailing lists, keep in mind that you are sending your message to a large audience. A well-formulated, concise question or comment with a precise and informative subject line is more likely to be answered, and a poorly considered message is *very* likely to be ignored. Once you post a request for help, keep poking at the problem yourself. Most of us have had the experience of posting a message containing hundreds of lines of intricate detail, only to solve the problem an hour later after the article has blazed its way across several continents. The rule of thumb goes something like this: the more folks who have read your request, the more likely that at least one person will be able to identify a solution.

The primary newsgroup for Samba is *comp.protocols.smb*. And although the main Samba discussion is now on the project's mailing lists, this vast pool of Usenet knowledge has developed into something that has made it into an invaluable resource: a memory. Archival and search sites such as the one at Google (*http:// groups.google.com/advanced_group_search*) have made sifting through years of valuable solutions as simple as a few mouse clicks.

When searching a newsgroup, try to be as specific as possible, but not too wordy. Searching on actual error messages is best. If you don't find an answer immediately in the newsgroup, resist the temptation to post a request for help until you've done a bit more work on the problem. You might find that the answer is in an FAQ or one of the many documentation files that ship with Samba, or a solution might become evident when you run one of Samba's diagnostic tools.

If you prefer interactive discussion, both users and developers have formed a community at *irc.freenode.net* on the *#samba* and *#samba-technical* channels. The former is for talking to other Samba users and dealing with installation or configuration issues. You will find random technical discussions between developers on the latter channel.

Filing a Bug Report

Sometimes no amount if troubleshooting can diagnose an error because you have found a legitimate bug in Samba. Samba developers use Bugzilla for tracking defects. You can search the open bug reports and file your own at *https://bugzilla.samba.org*. When filing a new bug, remember to include these important pieces of information:

- The version of Samba that exhibits the defect.
- Details of the server's operating system, including patch level and kernel revision.
- The CIFS client that exposes the problem. For Windows clients, include the operating system and installed service pack.
- The steps to be taken to reproduce the bug.
- What behavior you expected from Samba.

Be prepared to supply any additional logs or network traces that might be requested by developers. It is also a good idea to continue to try to reproduce the failure against the most current production Samba release. If the defect has been fixed, make sure that you update the bug report and let the developers know.

Summary of Samba Daemons and Commands

This appendix is a reference listing of command-line options and other information to help you use the programs that come with the Samba distribution.

SMB URI Syntax

Commands that make use of Samba's *libsmbclient* library frequently prefer (or require) the SMB URI syntax instead of the UNC path when accessing SMB/CIFS servers. The SMB URI syntax is similar to the URIs used to access resources on the Internet, such as *ftp://ftp.samba.org/pub/samba/* or *http://www.samba.org/samba/docs/index.html*.

The *smb://* syntax can be used to enumerate browse lists of workgroups or shares on servers. The following two URI examples enumerate the contents of a workgroup's browse list and a servers collection of shares:

smb://workgroup/
smb://server/

These next two examples connect to a share on a specific server.

smb://server/share
smb://workgroup/server/share

These final two examples are used to connect to the same shares as in the previous listing, but include user credentials in the URI string:

smb://username:password@server/share
smb://username:password@workgroup/server/share

More information on the SMB URI syntax can be found in the latest copy of the draft-crhertel-smb-uri Internet draft at *http://ubiqx.org/cifs*.

Samba Daemons

The following sections provide information about the command-line parameters for *smbd*, *nmbd*, *winbindd*, and *swat*. Some options are shared by all four daemons:

`-?|--help`

Print usage information for the command.

`--usage`

Print a brief command usage description.

`-d|--debuglevel debug_level`

Set the debug (sometimes called logging) level. The level normally ranges from 0 to 10. Specifying the value on the command line overrides the value specified in the *smb.conf* file. Debug level 0 logs only the most important messages; level 1 is normal; levels 3 and above are primarily for debugging and can slow the daemon considerably.

`-l|--log-basename log_directory`

Send the log messages to somewhere other than the location compiled into the executable or specified in the *smb.conf* file. If the directory does not exist, Samba's compiled-in default will be used.

`-s|--configfile configuration_file`

Specify the location of the Samba configuration file, overriding any compile time default location.

`-V|--version`

Print the daemon's version information.

The following additional options are available only to *smbd*, *nmbd*, and *winbindd*:

`-F|--foreground`

Run smbd in the foreground (i.e., do not detach from the terminal). This option is primarily of use when running Samba under the *daemontools* services (*http://cr.yp.to/daemontools.html*).

`-i|--interactive`

Run the binary interactively, rather than as a daemon. All debug messages are written to standard output, which can be very useful for quick debugging sessions. You can terminate the daemon by pressing CTRL+C.

`-S|--log-stdout`

Log all debug messages to standard output rather redirecting to a logfile. This option is frequently used in conjunction with the `--foreground` option and the daemontools service management tools.

smbd

The *smbd* program provides Samba's file, printer, and authentication services, using one daemon per TCP/IP stream, which usually equates to one *smbd* process per connected client. It is controlled by a configuration file named *smb.conf*, although certain settings can be overridden by command-line options.

The configuration file is automatically re-evaluated every three minutes. If it has changed (or if the list of included files has changed), most new options are immediately effective. You can force Samba to reload the configuration file immediately by either sending a HUP signal to a specific *smbd* process or by running *smbcontrol smbd reload-config*. Reloading the configuration file does not normally affect any clients that are already connected (unless of course the changes introduced a bad configuration).

Other signals

To shut down an *smbd* process, send it the termination signal SIGTERM (15), which allows it to die gracefully, instead of a SIGKILL (9).

Command synopsis

    smbd [options]

Additional options

-b|--build-options
> Display options and configure test results used to build *smbd*.

-D|--daemon
> Run the *smbd* program as a daemon. This is the recommended way to use *smbd*. It is also the default action when *smbd* is run from an interactive command line. In addition, *smbd* can be run from *inetd*.

-p|--port *port_number*
> Set the TCP/IP port number from which the server will accept requests. The default is to service TCP ports 139 for traffic over the NetBIOS session layer and 445 for SMB/CIFS traffic directly over TCP.

nmbd

The *nmbd* program is Samba's NetBIOS name service and browsing daemon. It replies to NetBIOS over TCP/IP (also called NetBT or NBT) name-service requests broadcast from SMB clients, and optionally to Microsoft's Windows Internet Name Service (WINS) requests. Both are versions of the name-to-address lookup required by NetBIOS clients. The broadcast version uses UDP, broadcast on the local subnet only, while WINS uses TCP, which can be routed. If running as a WINS server, *nmbd* keeps a current name and address database in the file *wins.dat* stored in Samba's lock dircetory.

An active *nmbd* daemon also responds to browsing protocol requests used by the Windows My Network Places. This protocol provides a dynamic directory of servers, as well as the disks and printers that the servers are providing. If *nmbd* is acting as a local master browser, it stores the browsing database in the file *browse.dat* also stored in in Samba's lock directory.

Signals

Like *smbd*, the *nmbd* program responds to several Unix signals. Sending *nmbd* a SIGHUP signal causes it to dump the names it knows about to the *namelist.debug* file in its lock directory. To shut down an *nmbd* process and allow it to die gracefully, send it a SIGTERM (15) signal, rather than a SIGKILL (9).

Command synopsis

    nmbd [*options*]

Additional options

-D|--daemon
: Run the *nmbd* program as a daemon. This is the recommended way to use *nmbd*. It is also the default action when *nmbd* is run from an interactive command line. In addition, *nmbd* can be run from *inetd*.

-H|--hosts *lmhosts_file*
: Specify the location of the *lmhosts* file for name resolution. This file is used only to resolve names for the local server, not to answer queries from remote systems.

-p|--port *port_number*
: Set the UDP port number from which the server accepts requests. The default is to service the name service UDP port 137 and the NetBIOS datagran UDP port on 138.

winbindd

The *winbindd* daemon is part of the Winbind service and is used to allow Unix systems to obtain user and group information from a Windows or Samba domain. Winbind maps Windows relative IDs (RIDs) to Unix uids and gids and allows domain accounts to be used for Unix authentication. Its purpose is to ease integration of Microsoft and Unix networks when a preexisting domain is set up to handle authentication and authorization responsibilities.

The daemon is accessed by users via the name service switch and PAM. Both services use Samba provided libraries to send requests to *winbindd* over Unix domain sockets. *winbindd* then communicates with domain controllers on behalf of the Unix programs.

Winbind is discussed extensively in Chapter 10.

Command synopsis

    winbindd [*options*]

Additional options

`-n|--no-caching`
    Disable caching of domain user and group information. Under normal circumstances, account data is cached according the `winbind cache time` setting in *smb.conf*.

swat

The Samba Web Administration Tool (SWAT) is used to configure a server's *smb.conf* file and to provide some basic user management features. It can be run only from *inetd*, as described in Chapter 2.

Options

`-a|--disable-authentication`
    Disable authentication checks in SWAT. This flag should be used only when debugging new installations.

`-P|--password-menu-only`
    Restrict access to all pages in SWAT except the password change dialog box. This is useful as a browser-based password change application for users rather than running the *smbpasswd* command manually.

Samba Client Programs

This section lists the command-line options and subcommands provided by each nondaemon program in the Samba distribution.

Common Options

Many Samba commands share groups of command-line parameters. The common options fall into three categories:

General options

`-?|--help`
    Print usage information for the command.

`--usage`
    Print a brief command usage description.

`-d|--debuglevel debug_level`
    Set the debug (sometimes called logging) level. The level normally ranges from 0 to 10. Specifying the value on the command line overrides the value specified in the *smb.conf* file. Debug level 0 logs only the most important messages; level 1 is normal; levels 3 and above are primarily for debugging Samba and can slow the tool considerably.

`-l`|`--log-basename` *log_directory*

> Send the log messages to somewhere other than the location compiled into the executable or specified in the *smb.conf* file. If the directory does not exist, Samba's compiled-in default will be used.

`-s`|`--configfile` `configuration_file`

> The location of the Samba configuration file, overriding any compile time default location.

`-V`|`--version`

> Print the program's version information.

Authentication options

`-A`|`--authentication-file` *filename*

> Specify a file containing the user credentials to be used for the connection request rather than passing the information as command-line parameters. Parameters in the file can be one of three keywords: `username`, `password`, or `domain`. Each keyword is followed by an equal sign (=) and the option's value. The format of the file is as follows:

```
username = value
password = value
domain   = value
```

> Parameters defined in the authentication file take precedence over their command-line counterparts. The permissions on the file should be very restrictive (0600, for example) to prevent access by unwanted users. You can find examples of authentication files in Chapter 11.

`-k`|`--kerberos`

> Enable Kerberos 5 authentication when connecting to the remote server. This requires that you have previously obtained a TGT using the *kinit* command. When you enable Kerberos authentication, the `-U` and `-A` options will be ignored. More information about Kerberos can be found in Chapter 10.

`-N`|`--no-pass`

> Request an anonymous connection.

`-P`|`--machine-pass`

> Use the machine's trust account when connecting to remote servers.

`-S`|`--signing=[on,off,required]`

> Specify the SMB signing policy to use when connecting to a remote server. The keyword `on` enables negotiation of SMB signing, and `required` makes the capability mandatory. To disable client support entirely, even if SMB signing is supported by the server, set the parameter to `off`.

`-U`|`--user` *name*

> Specify the user name to use in the authentication request when connecting to a remote server. You can append the user's password to the login name by specifying a percent sign (%) and then the passphrase.

Connection options

`-i|--scope` *netbios_scope*

The NetBIOS scope value to be used when communicating with other NetBIOS hosts. You should never use this option unless absolutely required by the remote server.

`-n|--netbiosname` *name*

The calling name to be used in the NetBIOS session request. This is not needed for most network environments.

`-O|--socket-options` *option_list*

Define a list of socket options to be used in the client connection. The range of options will vary from system to system and is described fully in the manpage for the *setsockopt()* function call. This parameter is normally useful when testing performance and running benchmarks.

`-W|--workgroup` *name*

The list client's workgroup (or domain) name. This is useful when you need to specify a user's domain as part of the authentication requests.

---

eventlogadm

The *eventlogadm* command is used to manage Samba's EventLog *tdb* files and related settings. Its primary use is to write new EventLog entries. Unlike other Samba command-line tools, *eventlogadm* does not share any of the common options. Eventlogs are covered in Chapter 9.

Command synopsis

`eventlogadm [`*options*`]`

Options

`-d`

Enable the tool's debug output.

`-h`

Print command-line usage.

`-o write` *EventLogName*

Write a a log entry to the file *EventLogName.tdb* in Samba's *lock* directory. The logfile name must be listed in the eventlog list parameter in *smb.conf*.

`-o addsource` *EventLogName SourceName MessageFileDLL*

The Windows message file DLL location that will be downloaded by Windows clients when viewing Eventlog records.

findsmb

This Perl script reports information about systems on the subnet that respond to SMB name-query requests. The report includes the IP address, NetBIOS name, workgroup/domain, and operating system of each system.

The output from *findsmb* looks like this:

```
$ ./findsmb
                              *=DMB
                              +=LMB
IP ADDR         NAME      WORKGROUP/OS/VERSION
------------------------------------------------------------------------
192.168.1.46    FIR       [VALE] [Unix] [Samba 3.0.20b]
192.168.1.47    OAK      +[COLOR] [Unix] [Samba 3.0.14a]
192.168.1.74    MAPLE    *[VALE] [Unix] [Samba 3.0.22]
192.168.1.101   SPUD     *[AD] [Windows 5.0] [Windows 2000 LAN Manager]
```

The system with an asterisk (*) in front of its workgroup name is the domain master browser for the workgroup/domain, and the system with a plus sign (+) preceding its workgroup name is the local master browser.

Command synopsis

```
findsmb [options]
```

Options

-B

Specify the broadcast address when calling *nmblookup* to resolve master browsers and server names. If no subnet broadcast address is supplied, *findsmb* will look on the local subnet.

-d|-D

Enable debug messages in the *findsmb* code.

-r

Enable the root-only flag when calling *nmblookup*. This is useful when locating Windows 95 hosts on the network.

net

The *net* command is a program with a syntax similar to the MS-DOS/Windows command of the same name. It is used for performing various administrative functions related to Windows networking, which can be executed either locally or on a remote system.

This utility has the same general, authentication, and connection command-line options as many Samba tools.

Command synopsis

```
net [method] function [target_options] [misc_options]
```

The *function* argument is made up of one or more space-separated words. In Windows terminology, it is sometimes referred to as a function with options.

By default, the action is performed on the local system. The *target_options* argument can be used to specify a remote system (either by hostname or IP address), a domain, or a workgroup.

Depending on the function, the *method* argument can be optional, required, or disallowed. It specifies one of three methods for performing the operation specified by the rest of the command. It can be ads (Active Directory), rpc (Microsoft's DCE/ RPC), or rap (Microsoft's original SMB remote procedure call). To determine which methods (if any) can be used with a function, the *net help ads*, *net help rap*, and *net help rpc* commands can be used to list the functions for each method.

Chapter 11 contains more information on the *net* command as well as examples.

Target options

-S|--server *hostname*
: Specify the remote system using a hostname or NetBIOS name.

-I|--ipaddress *ip_address*
: Specify the remote system using its IP address.

-w|--workgroup *workgroup*
: Specify the name of the target domain or workgroup.

Miscellaneous options

-d|--debuglevel *level*
: Define Samba's log for displaying information debug messages.

-l|--long
: Long listing mode. This is provided for functions that print informational listings.

-n|--myname *name*
: The NetBIOS name for the client.

-p|--port *port*
: The port number to use when connecting to the server.

-P|--machine-pass
: Use the machine's trust account when connecting to remote servers.

-s|--configfile *configuration_file*
: The location of the Samba configuration file, overriding any compile time default location.

-U|--user *name*
: The user name to use in the authentication request when connecting to a remote server. You can append the user's password to the login name by specifying a percent sign (%) and then the passphrase.

-V|--version
: Print the Samba's version information.

-W|--workgroup *name*
: The list client's workgroup (or domain) name. This is useful when you need to specify a user's domain as part of the authentication requests.

RAP functions

domain
> Enumerate the list of known browsing domains and browse masters.

file [user|close|info]
> Enumerate all open files or ones opened by a specific user. You can also request the server to close a given file.

group [add|delete]
> The basic form of the group command allows you enumerate groups on the server as well as create new ones or remove existing ones.

groupmember
> Manage group membership.

password *username old_password new_password*
> Send a user password change request for *username*.

printq [list|delete]
> Enumerate jobs in a print queue or remove specific jobs.

server
> Enumerate hosts in the server's workgroup.

session [close|info]
> Enumerate open sessions on the server. You may also request additional information regarding a specific session or request that the server close the active session.

share
> Enumerate shares on the server similar to the *smbclient -L* command.

user [add|delete|rename|info]
> Basic user management functions such as enumerating, creating, removing, and renaming accounts.

validate username password
> Authenticate a username/password pair against the server's list of accounts.

RPC functions

abortshutdown
> Abort the shutdown of a remote server.

changetrustpw
> Change the machine's trust account password.

file [user|close]
> Enumerate all open files or ones opened by a specific user. You can also request the server to close a given file.

getsid
> Retrieve the domain SID from the remote server specified using the --server option and store the result in *secrets.tdb*. This is often used as part of the *net rpc vampire* process.

group [add|delete|members|addmem|delmem]
> The basic form of the group command allows you enumerate groups on the server as well as create new ones or remove existing ones. The membership-related subcommands can be used to list or modify the collection of users belonging to a group.

info
> Print information about the remote server and its domain.

join
> Join a Windows or Samba domain for use with `security = domain` configurations. If the *-U username%password* option is included, the specified username and password will be used as the administrative account required for authenticating with the PDC. If the -U option is not included, this function can be used only to join the computer to the domain after the computer account has been created using the Server Manager.

password *username new_password*
> Set the password for a user account. You must specify an account with administrative rights using the --user option in order to force the password change.

printer [list|driver|publish|migrate]
> Enumerate printers or drivers installed on the server. If the remote host is joined to an AD domain, you can also have the server publish the printer's information in the directory service. The final option allows you to migrate printers, drivers, or settings from the remote server to the local Samba host.

registry [enumerate|save|dump]
> Simple interface for viewing remote registry files as well as saving them to a local file. This is an experimental feature currently.

rights [list|grant|revoke]
> Manage the user privilege assignments on a server. You can enumerate the available rights and assignments. The grant and revoke subcommands allow you to add and remove assignments respectively. Chapter 5 discusses user rights in detail.

service [list|stop|start|pause|resume|status]
> Manage a server's collection of services. This includes listing installed services and their current state as well as toggling the state of running, paused. or stopped services. Chapter 9 covers the steps to setup service control on Samba hosts.

share [add|delete|allowedusers|migrate]
> Manage file shares on the server. This includes listing active shares as well as creating new ones and unsharing existing ones. You can also migrate shares and files from the remote server to the local Samba host. Share management is discussed in Chapters 9 and 11.

shutdown
> Shut down a server. This function accepts the -r, -f, -t, and -c miscellaneous options. The -r option (which can also be specified as --reboot) requests that the system reboot after shutting down. The -f option (which can also be specified as --force) forces a shutdown. The -t *timeout* option (which can also be specified as --timeout=*number*) specifies the number of seconds to wait before shutting down, and the -c *comment* option (which can also be specified as --comment=*string*) can be used to specify a message to the client user. On Windows, the comment appears in the Message area in the System Shutdown dialog box.

testjoin
> Validate the local host's machine trust account password in the domain.

trustdom [list|add|del|establish|revoke]

    Manage domain trust relationships on a Samba domain controller. Chapter 9 discusses the configuration details for establishing domain trusts.

user [add|delete|rename]

    Basic user management functions such as enumerating, creating, removing, and renaming accounts.

vampire

    Migrate user, group, and computer accounts from a Windows NT Primary Domain Controller onto a Samba PDC. Successfully running this command requires a large amount of prior server configuration. Chapter 9 covers the complete steps for migrating from a Windows domain to Samba.

ADS functions

changetrustpw

    Change the machine's trust account password.

group [add|delete]

    Enumerate groups on the server, as well as create new ones or remove existing ones.

info

    Print information about the Active Directory server.

join

    Join the local system to the Active Directory realm. This function must be used if your server is configured to make use of security = ads and Kerberos authentication.

keytab [create|add|flush]

    Manage a local Kerberos keytab file based on Samba's machine trust account password and domain membership. This incldues creating an initial keytab file from the information stored in *secrets.tdb* as well as adding new service principal names to the machine's account in AD. Chapter 10 explains how to use keytab files with Samba member servers in an AD environment.

leave

    Remove the local system from the Active Directory realm. Newer versions of *net* will disable the account rather than removing it.

lookup

    Send a CLDAP request to an AD domain controller and display the query results.

password *username@REALM*

    Change the Active Directory password for the user specified by *username@REALM*. The administrative account authentication information is specified with the -U option. The Active Directory realm must be supplied in all uppercase.

printer [search|info|publish|remove]

    Manage printer information stored in AD. This does not affect printers or print shares, but only the information about the printer stored in the directory services.

search *expr attrib*

    Perform a raw Active Directory search, using the standard LDAP search expression and attributes specified by the *expr* and *attrib* arguments, respectively.

status
> Print details about the Active Directory computer account of the system.

testjoin
> Validate the local host machine's trust account password in the domain.

user [add|delete|rename]
> Basic user management functions such as enumerating, creating, removing, and renaming accounts.

Miscellaneous functions

cache [add|set|del|flush|get|search|list]
> A simple database management tool for Samba's *gencache.tdb*. This can be helpful, for example, when tracking down name resolution errors caused by incorrect cached information.

getlocalsid [*name*]
> Print the machine's local SID stored in *secrets.tdb*. You may supply an optional domain name, in which case the SID for that name will be displayed instead.

groupmap [add|modify|delete]
> Manage Samba's group mapping table. You can establish new mapping records and update or remove existing ones. Samba's group mapping feature is discussed in Chapter 5.

help [*command*]
> Print the help text for a specific command. Not all commands have help text available.

idmap [dump|restore]
> Backup the idmap table to a text file or restore the table from a previous backup. The dump subcommand prints the table contexts to standard output.

lookup [host|ldap|kdc|master]
> Perform basic name resolution queries for determining the address of hostnames, directory servers, Kerberos KDCs, and local master browsers.

time [set|system|zone]
> Display the system time—in Unix *date* command format—on the target system. You can use the set and system subcommands to update the local host's clock.

setlocalsid
> Define the SID to store for the local machine in *secrets.tdb*.

nmblookup

The *nmblookup* program is a client program that allows command-line access to NetBIOS name service for resolving NetBIOS computer names into IP addresses. The program works by broadcasting its queries on the local subnet until a machine with the specified name responds. You can think of it as a Windows analog of *nslookup* or *dig*. This is useful for looking up regular computer names, as well as special-purpose names, such as __MSBROWSE__. If you wish to query for a particular type of NetBIOS name, add the NetBIOS type to the end of the name, using the format *netbios_name#dd*, where *dd* is the hexidecimal representation of the resource byte.

Command synopsis

```
nmblookup [options] netbios_name [netbios_name]
```

The *nmblookup* tool supports both the general and the connection option sets described in the beginning of this section.

Options

-A|--lookup-by-ip
: Interpret *netbios_name* as an IP address and does a node status query on it.

-B|--broadcast broadcast_address
: Send the query to the given broadcast address. The default is to send broadcast queries using all detected network interfaces.

-f|--flags
: Print the NetBIOS flags in the packet headers.

-M|--master-browser
: Search for a local master browser by looking up *netbios_name*<1d>. If *netbios_name* is specified as a dash (-), a lookup is done on the special name __ MSBROWSE __.

-R|--recursion
: Set the "recursion desired" bit in the packet. This causes the system that responds to try a WINS lookup and return the address and any other information the WINS server has saved.

-r|--root-port
: Use the root port of 137. This option exists as a bug workaround for Windows 95. This option might require the user to be superuser.

-S|--status
: Perform a node status query once the name query has returned an IP address. This returns all the resource types that the system knows about, including their numeric attributes.

-T|--translate
: Translate IP addresses into resolved names.

-U|--unicast unicast_address
: Perform a unicast query to the specified address. Used with -R to query WINS servers.

---

ntlm_auth

The *ntlm_auth* tool similar to a command-line version of the *pam_winbind* library and is provided for Unix daemons that require support for the NTLM challenge/response authentication. The most popular use of a *ntlm_auth* is in combination with the Squid Web Proxy server, although the tool has also been used in conjunction with PPP services, Apache authentication modules, and RADIUS servers, to name a few examples.

Command synopsis

```
ntlm_auth [options]
```

The *ntlm_auth* commands supports the general option set used by many Samba client tools and discussed earlier in this appendix.

Options

--challenge *hex_string*

> The NTLMSSP challenge, as a hexadecimal-encoded string.

--diagnostics

> Print additional information in order to help debug failures in the authentication process.

--domain *name*

> The user's domain name to use during authentication.

--helper-protocol *protocol_version*

> Use the standard input helper *protocol_version*. The list of currently valid protocol names is:

>> gss-spnego
>> gss-spnego-client
>> ntlm-server-1
>> ntlmssp-client-1
>> squid-2.4-basic
>> squid-2.5-basic
>> squid-2.5-ntlmssp

--lm-response *hex_string*

> The LanManager response string as a hexadecimal encoded string.

--nt-response *hex_string*

> The NT response string, as a hexadecimal encoded string.

--password passphrase

> The user's clear-text password to use in the authentication request.

--request-lm-key

> Request that the LanManager session key be displayed on standard output.

--request-nt-key

> Request that the NT session key be displayed on standard output.

--require-membership-of SID

> Verify that the user is a member of the domain group specified by the SID.

--username *name*

> The user's login name to use in the authentication request.

--workstation *name*

> The user's workstation name to use in the authentication request.

---

pdbedit

This program can be used to manage accounts that are held in a passdb module. Because this tool uses the passdb storage mechanisms directly and not MS-RPC, you must be the superuser to operate this tool.

Command synopsis

> pdbedit [*options*] *username*

The *pdbedit* utility supports the general option set common to many Samba client tools.

Options

`-a|--create`

Add the *username* to the SAM database. The command issues a prompt for the user's password.

`-b|--backend pwdb_name`

Specifiy the `passdb` backend name to use for the current operation, in place of the value define in *smb.conf*.

`-C|--value integer`

The value of an account policy. Refer to the `--account-policy` option for details on available policy names.

`-c|--account-control flags`

Define the account control flags for a user. The flags value must be a collection of one or more of the following types: N, D, H, L, or X. The account control flags must be enclosed using square brackets ([]). Discussions regarding the meaning of flags can be found in Chapter 5.

`-D|--drive drive_letter`

Set the Windows drive letter to which to map the user's home directory. The drive letter should be specified as a letter followed by a colon—e.g., H:.

`-e|--export pwdb_backend`

Export the user account database to another `passdb` format, written to the specified location. Used for migrating from one type of account database to another. The *pwdb_backend* argument is specified in the format of a valid passdb backend name, followed by a colon, then the location of the database. For example, to export the existing account database to an *smbpasswd* database in the file */etc/samba/smbpw*, *pwdb_backend* would be specified as `smbpasswd:/etc/samba/smbpw`.

`-f|--fullname full_name`

Set the full name of the user specified with the -u option.

`-h|--homedir unc`

Set the home directory path (as a UNC) for the user specified with the -u option.

`-I|--domain name`

Set the user's domain.

`-i|--import pwdb_backend`

A password database backend from which to retrieve account information, overriding the one specified by the `passdb backend` parameter in the Samba configuration file. This, along with the `--export` option, is useful for migrating user accounts from one type of account database to another. See the `--export` option regarding how to specify the *pwdb_backend* argument.

`-L|--list`

List the user accounts in the database. See also the `--verbose` option.

`-m|--machine`

Indicate that the account is a computer account rather than a user account. Used only with the -a option when creating the account.

-N|--account-desc *string*

Set the user's account description string.

-P|--account-policy *policy_name*

Define the policy to be modified by the *--value* parameter. Because the policy names contain whitespace, be sure to enclose the string in quotes. Valid policy names are as follows:

```
bad lockout attempt
disconnect time
lockout duration
maximum password age
min password length
minimum password age
password history
refuse machine password change
reset count minutes
user must logon to change password
```

-p|--profile *UNC_path*

Set the directory in which the user's profile is kept. The directory is specified as a UNC.

-r|--modify

Update an existing user rather than creating a new user.

-S|--script *UNC_path*

The UNC of the user's logon script.

-t|--password-from-stdin *passphrase*

Sets the user's password from standard input rather than prompting.

-U|--user-sid *SID*

Explicitly define the user's SID.

-u|--user *username*

The username of the account to add (with the -a option), delete (with the -x option), or modify.

-v|--verbose

Use verbose mode when listing accounts with the --list option. The account fields will be printed.

-w|--smbpasswd-style

Use the smbpasswd listing mode, for use with the --list option, which prints information in the same format as it would appear in an *smbpasswd* file.

-x|--delete

Delete the user (specified with the -u option) from the account database.

-Z|--logon-hours-reset

Reset a user's login hours acccount restrictions.

-z|--bad-password-count-reset

Reset a user's bad password count to 0. Frequently, you will need to unlock the account as well, unless the time specified by the "lockout duration" policy has elapsed.

profiles

The *profiles* program is a small utility for changing the SID in registry ACLs such as those found in user roaming profiles (*NTUSER.DAT*). This is useful when migrating user profiles from one domain to another.

Command synopsis

    profiles [options] filename

The *profiles* command supports the general option set common to many Samba client tools.

Options

-c|--change-sid *SID*
: The original SID that should be modified in access control entries.

-n|--new-sid *SID*
: The new SID that should replace any occurrences of the --change-sid value.

smbcacls

This program provides a way of remotely modifying Windows ACLs on files and directories stored on an SMB/CIFS share.

Command synopsis

    smbcacls //server/share filename [options]

The *smbcacls* tool supports the standard general and authentication options described earlier in this appendix.

Options

-a|--add *ACLs*
: Add one or more ACLs to the file or directory. Any ACLs already existing for the file or directory are unchanged.

-C|--chown *username*
: Change the owner of the file or directory. This is a shortcut for -M OWNER:*username*. The *username* argument can be given as a username or as the string format of a SID.

-D|--delete *ACLS*
: Delete the specified ACLs.

-G *groupname*
: Change the group of the file or directory. This is a shortcut for -M GROUP:*groupname*. The *groupname* argument can be given as a group name or as the string format of a SID.

-M *acls*
: Modify the *mask* of the ACLs specified. Refer to the following section, "Specifying ACLs" for details.

`--numeric`

> Don't resolve SIDs or access masks to their corresponding string representations.

`-S|--set ACLS`

> Set the specified ACLs, deleting any ACLs previously set on the file or directory. The ACLs must contain at least a revision, type, owner, and group.

`-t|--test-args`

> Validate the command-line arguments, but do not actually perform the requested modifications.

Specifying ACLs

In the previous options, the same format is always used when specifying ACLs. An ACL is made up of one or more Access Control Entries (ACEs), separated by either commas or escaped newlines. An ACE can be one of the following:

```
REVISION:revision_number
OWNER:username_or_SID
GROUP:group_name_or_SID
ACL:name_or_SID:type/flags/mask
```

The *revision_number* should always be 1. The OWNER and GROUP entries can be used to set the owner and group for the file or directory. The names can be the textual ones or the string representation of the SIDs.

The ACL entry specifies what access rights to apply to the file or directory. The *name_or_ SID* field specifies to which user or group the permissions apply and can be supplied either as a textual name or a SID. An ACE can be used to either allow or deny access. The *type* field is set to 1 to specify a permission to be allowed or 0 for specifying a permission to deny. The *mask* field is the name of the permission and is one of the following:

R   Read access.

W   Write access.

X   Execute permission.

D   Permission to delete.

P   Change permissions on the object.

O   Take ownership.

The following combined permissions can also be specified:

READ

> Equivalent to RX permissions

CHANGE

> Equivalent to RWXD permissions

FULL

> Equivalent to RWXDPO permissions

The *flags* field is for specifying how objects in directories are to inherit their default permissions from their parent directory. For files, *flags* is normally set to 0. For directories, *flags* is usually set to either 9 or 2.

smbclient

The *smbclient* program is the "Swiss Army knife" of the Samba suite. Initially developed as a testing tool, it has become a command shell capable of acting as a general-purpose Unix client, with a command set very similar to that of *ftp*. It offers the following set of functions:

- Interactive file transfer, similar to *ftp*
- Interactive printing to shared SMB printers
- Interactive tar format archiving
- Sending messages on the SMB network
- Batch mode tar format archiving
- Enumerating shares and workgroup contents on remote servers
- Debugging

Command synopsis

```
smbclient //server/share [password] [options]
```

It is possible to run *smbclient* noninteractively, for use in scripts, by specifying the -c option along with a list of commands to execute. Otherwise, *smbclient* runs in interactive mode, prompting for commands like this:

```
smb:\>
```

The backslash in the prompt is replaced by the current directory within the share as you change your working directory with *smbclient*'s cd command.

The *smbclient* command supports all three sets of command-line options (general, authentication, and connection) common to other Samba client tools.

Options

-b|--send-buffer *buffer_size*
> The size of the buffer used when transferring files. It defaults to 65,520 bytes and can be changed as a tuning measure. Generally, it should be quite large or set to match the size of the buffer on the remote system.

-c|--command *command_string*
> Pass a command string to the *smbclient* command interpreter. The argument consists of a semicolon-separated list of commands to be executed.

-D|--directory *init_dir*
> Upon starting up, causes *smbclient* to change its working directory to *init_dir* on the remote host.

-E|--stderr
> Send output from commands to stderr instead of stdout.

-g|--grepable
> When used in conjuction with the -L option, this parameter instructs *smbclient* to display share, server, and workgroup lists in a format that is easily parseable in shell scripts.

-I|--ip-address *IP_address*
> Set the IP address of the server to which the client connects.

-L|--list server
> List services (shares) offered by the server. This can be used as a quick way to test an SMB/CIFS server to see if it is working. If there is a name-service problem, use the -I option to specify the server.

-M|--message NetBIOS_name
> Allows you to send messages using the Windows messaging protocol. Once a connection is established, you can type your message, pressing Ctrl-D to end. The -U and -I options can be used to control the "From" and "To" parts of the message.

-m|--max-protocol level
> The maximum SMB/CIFS protocol dialoect that smbclient will advertise when negotiating a connnection with a remote server. Valid protocol names are:
>
> > NT1
> >
> > LANMAN2
> >
> > LANMAN1
> >
> > CORE
> >
> > COREPLUS

-p|--port port_number
> The port number used by *smbclient* to connect to the server.

-R|--name-resolve resolve_order
> Set the resolve order of the name servers. This option is similar to the resolve order configuration option and can take any of the four parameters lmhosts, host, wins, and bcast, in any order. If more than one parameter is specified, the argument is specified as a space-separated list. This option can be used to test name service by specifying only the name service to be tested.

-T|--tar command_string tarfile
> Run the tar archiver, which is *gtar* compatible. The tar file that is written to or read from is specified by *tarfile*. The two main commands are c (create) and x (extract), which can be followed by any of these options:
>
> a
> > Reset the archive attribute on files after they have been saved. See also the g option.
>
> b size
> > The block size for writing the tar file, in 512-byte units.
>
> g
> > Back up only files that have their archive bit set. See also the a option.
>
> I filename
> > Includes files and directories. This is the default behavior, so specifying this is redundant. To perform pattern matching, see also the r option.
>
> N filename
> > Back up only those files newer than *filename*.
>
> q
> > Suppress diagnostics.
>
> r
> > Perform regular expression matching, which can be used along with the I or X option to include or exclude files.
>
> X filename
> > Exclude specified files and directories.

Commands

?|help [*smbclient_command*]

    With no command specified, print a list of available commands. If a command is specified as an argument, a brief help message will be printed for it.

! *shell_command*

    Shell escape. Run the specified command in a Unix shell.

altname *filename*

    Cause *smbclient* to request from the server and then print the old-style, 8.3-format filename for the specified file.

archive *level*

    This controls the behavior in relation to the DOS archive bit when retrieving files. The available levels are:

    0   Ignore the archive bit entirely.

    1   Retrieve only files whose archive bit is set.

    2   Same as level 1 but resets the archive bit after the file copy.

    3   Same as level 0 but resets the archive bit after the file copy.

blocksize

    The blocksize to be used when writing *tar* files. The value must be between 0 and 65535.

cancel print_jobid [...]

    Cause *smbclient* to request the server to cancel one or more print jobs, as specified by the numeric job IDs provided as arguments. See also the queue command, which prints job ids.

case_sensitive

    Allows you to toggle case-sensitive and -insensitive filename lookups. The default is to match Windows behavior and use case-insensitive lookups.

cd [*directory*]

    With no argument, print the current working directory on the remote system. If a directory name is supplied as an argument, change the working directory on the remote system to that specified.

chmod *filename octal_mode*

    Requests that the server change the Unix file permissions on *filename* to *octal_mode*, specified in octal numeric format. Works only if the server supports CIFS Unix extensions.

chown filename UID GID

    Change the owner and group of the file specified by *filename* to those provided as decimal numeric arguments *uid* and *gid*. Works only if the server supports CIFS Unix extensions.

del *filename*

    Delete one or more files, as specified by the argument, from the current working directory. The argument can be a filename globbing pattern using the * and ? characters.

dir [*filename*]

    With no arguments, print a list of files and directories in the working directory on the server. If an argument is provided, only files and directories whose names match the argument will be listed. The argument can be a filename globbing pattern using the * and ? characters.

du
> Calculate the disk usage and free space available for the share.

exit
> Quit the *smbclient* program after terminating the SMB connection to the server. The q and quit commands are aliases for exit.

get *remote_file* [*local_file*]
> Copy the file specified by *remote_file* from the server to the local system. If no *local_ file* argument is specified, *smbclient* will name the local file the same as it is named on the server. If *local_file* is specified, it will be used as the name of the local copy. See also the *lowercase* command.

getfacl *filename*
> Display the POSIX ACL for *filename*. This operation is supported only if the remote server supports the CIFS Unix Extensions.

hardlink *source destination*
> A Windows hardlink from *destination* to *source*. Refer to the link command for creating Unix hard links.

history
> Display a list of recently executed *smbclient* commands.

lcd [*directory*]
> If no argument is provided, print the name of *smbclient*'s working directory on the local system. If a directory name is provided as an argument, changes *smbclient*'s working directory to the directory specified.

link *link_name filename*
> Create a hard link to *filename* and name it *link_name*. This command works only if the server supports CIFS Unix extensions.

listconnect
> Display all current SMB/CIFS connections held by the current smbclient session. This is really only of interest when connecting to MS-DFS root shares and following referrals.

lowercase
> Toggle the Boolean lowercasing setting. When this setting is on, names of files copied from the server with the *get* and *mget* commands will be changed to all lowercase. This is mainly used for accessing servers that report filenames in all uppercase only.

mask [*globbing_pattern*]
> Set the filename globbing pattern for use with the *mget* and *mput* commands when recursion is turned on. (When recursion is off, the setting has no effect.) Both *mget* and *mput* accept a globbing pattern as arguments; however, those patterns apply only to the current directory. This command specifies the pattern used for all subdirectories that are recursively traversed. The pattern stays in effect until it is changed with another *mask* command. To return the setting to its original default, specify a *globbing_pattern* of an asterisk (*), which matches all files. See also the *mget*, *mput*, and *recurse* commands.

mget *pattern*

> When recursion is turned off, copy files matching the file-globbing pattern, as specified by the argument, from the current working directory on the server to the local system. When recursion is on, the *pattern* argument is used to match directories in the current working directory, and the pattern specified by the *mask* command is used for matching files within each directory and all subdirectories. See also the *lowercase*, *mask*, and *recurse* commands.

mkdir

> Create a directory on the remote share.

more

> View a remote file using the local system's configured pager tool (e.g., the *more* command).

mput *pattern*

> When recursion is turned off, copy files matching the file-globbing pattern, as specified by the argument, from the current working directory on local system to the remote server. When recursion is on, the *pattern* argument is used to match directories in the current working directory, and the pattern specified by the *mask* command is used for matching files within each directory and all subdirectories. See also the *lowercase*, *mask*, and *recurse* commands.

newer *filename*

> Retrieve files with a timestamp newer than the one assigned to *filename*.

print *filename*

> Print the specified file. This command requires that *smbclient* be connected to a print share.

prompt

> Toggle the prompting mode. When prompting is on (the default), the *mget* and *mput* commands will interactively prompt the user for permission to transfer each file. The user can answer either y (yes) or n (no), followed by a newline, to this prompt. When prompting is off, all the files will be transferred with no prompts issued.

put *local_file* [*remote_file*]

> Copy the file specified by *local_file* from the local to the remote system. If no *remote_file* argument is specified, *smbclient* will name the remote file the same as it is named on the local system. If *remote_file* is specified, it will be used as the name of the remote copy. See also the *lowercase* command.

pwd

> Print the current working directory on the server.

queue

> Print information on the print queue on the server. This command requires that *smbclient* is connected to a print share.

recurse

> Toggle the recursion mode, which affects the *mget* and *mput* commands. When recursion is off (the default), the *mget* and *mput* commands will copy only files from the current working directory that match the file-globbing pattern specified as an argument to the command, and the pattern set by the *mask* command is ignored. When recursion is turned on, the *mget* and *mput* commands recursively traverse any directories that match the pattern specified as the argument to the command, and the pattern set by the *mask* command is used to match files in those directories.

rename *source destination*
> Rename the *source* file (or directory) to *destination*.

reput *filename* [*remote_filename*]
> Append a file from the local server to *filename* (or *remote_filename* if specified) on the remote server.

rmdir *directory*
> Requests that the server remove the specified directory.

setmode *filename attributes*
> Assign the specified MS-DOS file attributes on the specified file. The *attributes* argument has the format of a leading plus sign (+) or minus sign (-) either to set or to unset the attribute(s), respectively, followed by one or more of the characters r (read), s (system), h (hidden), or a (archive).

showconnect
> Display the active connenction for the current working directory. This command allows you to determine what server you are connected to after following a MS-DFS referral.

stat *filename*
> Perform a Unix *stat()* call on the remote *filename*. This call requires that the server support the CIFS Unix Extensions.

symlink *link_name filename*
> Request that the server create a symbolic link named *link_name* to *filename*. This command works only if the server supports Unix CIFS extensions. The server will not create a link that refers to a file not in the share to which *smbclient* is connected.

tar *cmd_str*
> Perform an archiving operation using the tar format. This is the interactive form of the -T command-line operation, and the *cmd_str* argument is specified in the same manner. See also the *tarmode* command.

blocksize *size*
> The block size, in units of 512 bytes, for files written by the *tar* command.

tarmode *mode* ...
> Specify how the *tar* command performs its archiving, including how it handles the archive attribute on files. Multiple *mode* arguments can be provided:
>
> full
>> All files will be included, regardless of whether their archive attribute is set. This is the default behavior.
>
> inc
>> Only files that have the archive attribute set will be included in the backup.
>
> reset
>> The archive attribute will be unset by *tar* after the file is included in the archive.
>
> noreset
>> The archive attribute will be left unchanged. This is the default.

hidden|nohidden
> Controls whether files with the hidden attribute set will be included in the archive. The default is to include files with the hidden bit set.

system|nosystem
> Determines whether files with the system attribute set will be included in the archive. The default is to include files with the system bit set.

verbose|noverbose
> If verbose mode is enabled (the default), file names will be printed as each one is included in the archive (when creating the archive) or is read from the archive (when extracting it).

volume
> Display the volume name of the share containing the current working directory. The volume name is dependent on the current connect when following MS-DFS referrals. Also refer to the showconnect command.

smbcontrol

The *smbcontrol* command sends control messages to running *smbd*, *nmbd*, or *winbindd* processes.

Command synopsis

> smbcontrol [*options*] *process message-type* [*parameters*]

smbcontrol supports the standard --version , --help, and the --configfile options described in the previous General Options section.

Options

-t|--timeout *seconds*
> The period before timing out while waiting for a response to a message.

Each *smbcontrol* command has up to three parts:

process
> The process or group of processes to which to send the message. If *process* is smbd or winbindd, all named processes will receive the message. If *process* is nmbd, only the main *nmbd* process (identified by Samba's *nmbd.pid* file) receives the message. If *process* is the numeric PID of a running process on the system, that process will receive the message.

message-type
> The type of message that is sent. For more information, see the section "smbcontrol message types" that follows.

parameters
> Additional parameters required by some messages.

smbcontrol message types

close-share *share_name*
> Close the connection to a share or shares. If *share_name* is specified as an asterisk (*), connections to all shares will be closed. To close a single connection, *share_name* is given as the name of a share, as specified in the Samba configuration file, not including the enclosing brackets. No message is printed if there is an error in specifying *share_name*.

debug *num*
> The debugging level. The *num* parameter specifies the level, which can be from 0 to 10.

debuglevel
> Print the current debugging level.

dmalloc-mark
> Instruct a process to remember a memory watermark. This option is of use only when the --enable-dmalloc option was included during the initial compilation.

dmalloc-log-changed
> Display the memory allocation statistics since the last dmalloc-mark command. This option is of use only when the --enable-dmalloc option was included during the initial compilation.

drvupgrade *driver_name*
> Send a notify message to *smbd* that *driver_name* has been changed so that the daemon can rebind driver initialization data to associated printers.

force-election
> Can be used only with *nmbd*, telling it to force a master browser election.

nodestatus
> Ask the *nmbd* daemon to perform a NetBIOS node status request.

ping *number*
> Sends *number* of pings and reports when they receive a reply or timeout. Used for connectivity testing.

profile *mode*
> This command controls profiling statistics collection. If *mode* is on, profile statistics will be collected. If *mode* is off, collection of statistics is turned off. If *mode* is specified as count, only counting statistics are collected (and not timing statistics). If *mode* is flush, the data set is cleared (initialized).

profilelevel
> Print the current profiling level.

pool-usage
> Dump the statistics for all current *talloc()* memory allocation.

printer-notify *printer_name*
> Send a notify message to *smbd* that *printer_name* has been changed so that the daemon can send a notification to any cliented monitoring that printer.

reload-config
> Instruct a daemon to reload its configuration information. This is an alternative to sending a process the HUP signal.

shutdown
> Ask a running process to gracefully terminate.

smbcquotas

The *smbcquotas* program provides a simple interface to query and set filesystem quotas on remote SMB/CIFS shares.

Command synopsis

```
smbcquotas //server/share [options]
```

The *smbcquotas* tool supports the standard general and authentication options described earlier in this appendix.

Options

-F|--fs
> Display filesystem quotas configured on the share.

-L|--list
> Display all user quotas configured on the share.

-n|--numeric
> Don't resolve SIDs or access masks to their corresponding string representations.

-S|--set *quota_string*
> Set the *quota_string* value for the SMB/CIFS share. The format of *quota_string* is covered in the Quota Settings section.

-t|--test-args
> Validate the command-line arguments but do not actually perform the requested modifications.

-u|--user *username*
> Display the quota settings for *username*.

-v|--verbose
> Increase the amount of information messages written to standard output.

Quota settings

Quota strings passed to the --set parameter can be in one of three forms. The first form is used to set a user quota policy. The username refers to the user whose quota is being set or modified. The *softlimit* and *hardlimit* values are given in bytes.

```
UQLIM:username/softlimit/hardlimit
```

The second type of quota string controls the filesystem quota setings. Once again the *softlimit* and *hardlimit* values are given in bytes.

```
FSQLIM:softlimit/hardlimit
```

The final format of the quota string defines overall quota behavior.

```
FSQFLAGS:flags
```

The *flags* argument is one of more of the following values, using the forward slash character (/) to delimit entries:

```
QUOTA_ENABLED
DENY_DISK
LOG_SOFTLIMIT
LOG_HARD_LIMIT
```

smbpasswd

The *smbpasswd* program provides the general function of managing encrypted passwords. How it works depends on whether it is run by the superuser or an ordinary user.

For the superuser, *smbpasswd* can be used to maintain Samba's passdb backend. It can add or delete users, change their passwords, and modify other attributes pertaining to the users that are held in (for example) an *smbpasswd* file, the *tdbsam* database, or an LDAP directory service using *ldapsam*.

When run by ordinary users, *smbpasswd* can be used only to update their encrypted passwords using the SMB/CIFS password change mechanisms. In this mode of operation, *smbpasswd* acts as a client to the Samba or Windows server.

Command synopsis

When run by the superuser:

```
smbpasswd [options] username
```

In this case, the username of the user whose passdb entry is to be modified is provided as the second argument.

Otherwise:

```
smbpasswd [options]
```

The *smbpasswd* command does not support any of the common Samba command-line parameters in order to ensure better backwards compatibility with older Samba releases.

Superuser-only options

-a *username*

> Add a user to the encrypted password file. The user must already exist in the system password file (*/etc/passwd*). If the user already exists in the passdb backend, the -a option changes the existing password.

-d *username*

> Disable a user in Samba's list of accounts. The user's entry in the file will remain, but will be marked with a flag disabling the user from authenticating.

-e *username*

> Enable a disabled user in the encrypted password file. This option overrides the effect of the -d option.

-m

> This option indicates that the account is a computer account rather than a user account. This older method of creating machine trust accounts in a Samba domain is strongly discouraged. Alternative methods of joining clients to a Samba domain are covered in Chapter 9.

-n

> Set the user's password to a null password. For the user to authenticate, the parameter null passwords = yes must exist in the [global] section of the Samba configuration file.

-R *resolve_order_list*

Set the resolve order of the name servers. This option is similar to the `resolve order` configuration option and can take any of the four parameters `lmhosts`, `host`, `wins`, and `bcast`, in any order. If more than one parameter is specified, the argument is specified as a space-separated list.

-w *password*

The password that goes with the value of the `ldap admin dn` Samba configuration file parameter.

-W

Same as -w, but prompts for the password rather than reading it in as a command-line parameter.

-x *username*

Delete the user from Samba's list of user accounts. This is a one-way operation, and all information associated with the entry is lost. To disable the account without deleting the user's entry in the file, see the -d option.

Other options

-c *filename*

Specifies the Samba configuration file, overriding the compiled default.

-D *debug_level*

The debug (also called logging) level. The level can range from 0 to 10. Debug level 0 logs only the most important messages; level 1 is normal; levels 3 and above are primarily for debugging and slow the program considerably.

-h

Print command-line usage information.

-r *NetBIOS_name*

Specify on which machine the password should change. If changing a Windows (or Samba) domain password, the remote system specified by *NetBIOS_name* must be the PDC for the domain. The user's username on the local system is used by default. See also the -U option for use when the user's Samba username is different from the local username.

-s

Cause *smbpasswd* not to prompt for passwords, but instead to read the old and new passwords from the standard input. This is useful when calling *smbpasswd* from a script.

-U *username*

Change the password for *username* on the remote system. This is to handle instances in which the remote username and local username are different. This option requires that -r also be used.

smbget

The *smbget* command is an SMB/CIFS variant of the Unix *wget* command. The tool is similar to *smbclient*'s get (or mget) command but makes use of the SMB URI syntax instead of UNC paths. Multiple file locations can be specified to be retrieved sequentially.

Command synopsis

```
smbget [options] SMB_URI [SMB_URI...]
```

Options

`-a|--guest`
Use an anonymous connection.

`-b|--blocksize size`
Define the blocksize to be *size* bytes for SMB/CIFS file transfers.

`-D|--dots`
Display progress dots during the file download.

`-d|--debuglevel level`
The verbosity of log messages to write to the console.

`-f|--rcfile filename`
Parse *smbget* options from the resource file *filename*.

`-n|--nonprompt`
Do not prompt for user interaction when downloading files or overwriting local files.

`-O|--stdout`
Write the retrieved file to standard output.

`-o|--outputfile filename`
Write the retrieved file to *filename*.

`-P|--keep-permissions`
Ensure that the local file has the same permission set as the original copy on the remote server.

`-p|--password passphrase`
Specify the password to send in the authentication request.

`-q|--quiet`
Write only minimal information messages during file downloads.

`-R|--recursive`
When the *SMB_URI* specifies a directory, recursively download files from the directory tree.

`-r|--resume`
Resume an incomplete file transfer.

`-u|--username name`
>   The login name to send in the authentication request.

`-w|--workgroup name`
>   The domain name to send in the authentication request.

`-v|--verbose`
>   Generate extra output to trace connection operations.

smbspool

The *smbspool* program provides the SMB/CIFS backend interface to the Common Unix Printing System. Although *smbspool* can be made to work with non-CUPS printing systems, it is recommend that you use *smbclient* instead in these environments.

Command synopsis

```
smbspool [DEVICE_URI] job-id user title copies options [filename]
```

The arguments for *smbspool*, as shown here, are those used in the CUPS printing system. The printer that the job is to be sent to is specified in the SMB URI format as the first argument or in the `DEVICE_URI` environment variable.

The *job* argument refers to the job number. The *user* argument is the name of the user who submitted the print job. The `title` argument is the name of the print job and must be supplied. It is used as the name of the remote print file. The *copies* argument is the number of copies that will be printed. This number is used only if the (optional) `filename` argument is supplied. Otherwise, only one copy is printed. The *options* argument, for specifying printing options, is ignored. The `filename` argument is used for specifying the name of the file to be printed. If it is not provided, the standard input will be used.

smbstatus

This program lists the current connections on a Samba server.

Command synopsis

```
smbstatus [options]
```

The *smbstatus* tool supports the set of general command line options previously described in this appendix.

Options

`-B|--byterange`
>   Produce information about byte range locks only.

`-b|--brief`
>   Cause *smbstatus* to produce brief output. This includes the version of Samba and auditing information about the users that are connected to the server.

`-L|--locks`
>   Print only the list of current file locks.

`-n|--numeric`
>   Do not convert Unix uids and gids to their associated names.

`-p|--processes`

Print only a list of smbd process IDs.

`-S|--shares`

Print only a list of shares and their connections.

`-u|--user` *username*

Limit the report to the activity of a single user.

`-v|--verbose`

Include additional information about current connections, locks, and processes.

smbtar

The *smbtar* program is a shell-script wrapper around *smbclient* for doing tar-format archiving operations. It is functionally very similar to the Unix *tar* program.

Command synopsis

    smbtar [*options*] [include|exclude *filenames*]

Options

`-a`

Reset (clears) the archive attribute on files after they are backed up. The default is to leave the archive attribute unchanged.

`-b` *blocksize*

The block size, in units of 512 bytes, for reading or writing the archive file. Defaults to 20, which results in a block size of 10,240 bytes.

`-d` *directory*

Changes the working directory on the remote system to *directory* before starting the restore or backup operation.

`-i`

Specify incremental mode; files are backed up only if they have the DOS archive attribute set. The archive attribute is reset (cleared) after each file is read. The default behavior is to ignore the archive bit and perform a full backup

`-l` *log_level*

The logging level. This corresponds to the `--debuglevel` option of *smbclient* and other Samba programs.

`-N` *filename*

Backs up only files newer than *filename*. For incremental backups.

`-p` *password*

The password to use to access a share. An alternative to using the *username%password* format with the `-u` option.

`-r`

Restore files to the share from the tar file.

`-s` *server*

The SMB server. See also the `-x` option.

-t *filename*

The file or Unix device to use as the archiving medium. The default is *tar.out* or the value of the TAPE environment variable, if it has been set.

-u *username*

The user account to use when connecting to the share. You can specify the password as well, in the format *username%password*. The username defaults to the user's Unix username.

-v

Operate in verbose mode, printing error messages and additional information that can be used in debugging and monitoring. Backup and restore operations will list each file as it is processed.

-x *share*

The name of the share on the server to which to connect. The default is backup. See also the -s option.

-X *file_list*

Exclude the specified files from the backup or restore operation.

smbtree

The *smbtree* program is similar to the *findsmb* Perl script, in that it enumerates workgroup contents. However, *smbtree* groups servers by workgroup and can includes a list of available shares on each server.

Command synopsis

    smbtree [options]

The *smbtree* command supports the general and authentication option sets common to many Samba client tools.

Options

-b|--broadcast

Broadcast requests for workgroup contents rather than attempting to query the master browser.

-D|--domains

Only enumerate workgroups names.

-S|--servers

Do not enumerate shares on servers. List only the workgroup names and the servers contained in each workgroup.

tdbbackup

The *tdbbackup* program validates a *tdb* file and creates a backup copy of the original database. This tool can be use to create backup copies while Samba is running. The structure-generated *tdb* file is guaranteed to be consistent, but if a Samba daemon possessed data cached in memory, the original *tdb* file itself may have been in a inconsistent state. Therefore, it is best to perform backups when the server is under a light load.

Command synopsis

```
tdbbackup [options] filename.tdb
```

Options

`-h`

Display a brief help listing.

`-s suffix`

Specify the suffix to append to backup files.

`-v`

Validate a *tdb* file. If file corruption is detected, you must restore it from a valid backup copy.

---

tdbdump

The *tdbdump* tool prints the contexts of a *tdb* file to standard output.

Command synopsis

```
tdbdump filename.tdb
```

---

tdbtool

The *tdbtool* program is an interactive utility for viewing and modifying *tdb* files. It should be viewed as a very low-level database management tool and used only as a last resort.

Command synopsis

```
tdbtool filename.tdb
```

After opening *filename.tdb*, you will be presented with a basic `tdb>` prompt. You can view the list of available commands by running the `help` command.

tdbtool commands

`create dbname`

Create a new *tdb* file named *dbname*.

`cdump`

Dump the *tdb* contents as a series of connection records.

`delete key`

Remove a record from the *tdb*.

`dump`

Dump the *tdb* contents as strings.

`erase`

Remove all records in the current open *tdb* file.

`freelist`

Display the database internal freelist structure.

`hexkeys`

Dump the database keys as hexadecimal strings.

info

    Print summary information about the *tdb* structure and records.

insert *key data*

    Add a new record to the *tdb*.

keys

    Dump the database keys as ASCII strings.

list

    Display the database's internal hashlist and freelist structures.

move *key newfilename*.tdb

    Move a record referenced by *key* in the current open *tdb* to *newfilename.tdb*.

open *dbname*

    Open an existing *tdb* filename *dbname*.

show *key*

    Display the record indexed by *key*.

store *key data*

    Replace an existing record in the *tdb*.

quit

    Exit the current tdbtool interactive session.

testparm

The *testparm* program checks a Samba configuration file for obvious errors.

Command synopsis

    testparm [*options*] [*filename*] [*hostname*] [*IP_addr*]

If the configuration file is not provided using the *filename* argument, then it defaults to the compile time location (e.g., */usr/local/samba/lib/smb.conf*). If the hostname and an IP address of a system are included, an extra check is made to ensure that the system is allowed to connect to each service defined in the configuration file. This is done by comparing the hostname and IP address to the definitions of the hosts allow and hosts deny parameters.

In addition to the following options, *testparm* also supports the standard --help, --usage, and --version arguments.

Options

-L|--server *server_name*

    Set the %L configuration variable to the specified server name.

--parameter-name *parameter_name*

    Print only the value of *parameter_name* to standard output.

-s|--suppress-prompt

    Disable the default behavior of prompting for the Enter key to be pressed before printing the list of configuration options for the server.

--section-name *share*

    Limit the parameter listing to the *smb.conf* section *share*.

`--show-all-parameters`

   Display a listing of all parameter names, type, and possible values. The output is formatted so that it can easily be parsed in shell scripts.

`-t|--encoding` *encoding_name*

   Print the *smb.conf* parameters and values using the specified character *encoding_name*.

`-v|--verbose`

   Enable verbose output that includes listing all *smb.conf* parameters, even if set to the default value. The default behavior is to provide a brief listing on only nondefault settings.

---

wbinfo

This program retrieves and prints information from the *winbindd* daemon, which must be running for *wbinfo* to function.

Command synopsis

```
wbinfo [options] [--domain=name]
```

Some command-line parameters allow you to limit the request to a specific domain defined by the `--domain` argument.

In addition to the following options, *wbinfo* also supports the standard `--help`, `--usage`, and `--version` arguments.

Options

`-A|--allocate-rid`

   Allocate a new RID from the `passdb` backend and print the assigned value.

`-a|--authenticate` *username%password*

   Check to see whether a user can authenticate through *winbindd* using the specified username and password. Any user may request the clear text authentication, but only the *root* user is able to test the challenge/response authentication mechanism.

`-D|--domain-info` *DOMAIN*

   Print information about the specified *DOMAIN* such as the domain SID, status of AD services, and realm name, if available.

`-G|--gid-to-sid` *gid*

   Convert the Unix gid to a Windows SID.

`-g|--domain-groups`

   Prints all groups that exist in Winbind's own domain as well as any trusted domains.

`--getdcname` *DOMAIN*

   Query a domain controller in Winbind's own domain for the name of a valid DC in the trusted *DOMAIN*.

`--get-auth-user`

   Print the currently defined *auth-user*, if one has been specified using the `--set-auth-user` option.

`-I|--WINS-by-ip` *ip_address*

   Send a request to the WINS server configured in *smb.conf* to convert the *ip_address* to a NetBIOS name.

`-m|--trusted-domains`

List all trusted domains known by *winbindd* included in the BUILTIN and local machine domains.

`-N|--WINS-by-name` *name*

Send a request to the WINS server configured in *smb.conf* to convert the *name* to an IP address.

`-n|--name-to-sid` *name*

Print the SID corresponding to the name specified. The argument can be specified as *DOMAIN/name* (or by using a character other than the slash, as defined by the Winbind separator character) to specify both the domain and the name. If the domain and separator are omitted, the value of the `workgroup` parameter in the Samba configuration file is used as the name of the domain.

`-p|--ping`

Send a simple ping request to *winbindd* to determine whether it is running.

`-r|--user-groups` *username*

Print the list of Unix group IDs to which the domain user belongs.

`-S|--sid-to-uid` *SID*

Convert the SID to a Unix uid and prints the result.

`-s|--sid-to-name` *SID*

Convert the specified SID to a user or group name.

`--separator`

Print the current `winbind separator` character.

`--set-auth-user` *username%password*

An alternative set of credentials to use when connecting to a domain controller. This option is normally not needed in current Samba releases.

`--sequence`

Print the current known sequence numbers for all trusted domains. This can be helpful in debugging problems since unavailable domains will be listed as `DISCONNECTED`.

`-t|--check-secret`

Request *winbindd* to validate the Samba's current machine trust account.

`-U|--uid-to-sid` *uid*

Convert the Unix uid to a Windows SID.

`-u|--domain-users`

Print all users that exist in Winbind's own domain, as well as any trusted domains.

`--user-domgroups` *SID*

List the SIDs of all domain groups to which the user belongs.

`--user-sids` *SID*

Retrieve a list of SIDs for all groups to which the user belongs, including domain local groups.

Downloading Samba with Subversion

In Chapter 2, we showed you how to download the latest stable version of Samba published by the Samba developers. For most purposes (including all production servers), this procedure is sufficient. However, sometime you might want to run a version of Samba that includes the latest bug fixes and features—maybe for research and testing purposes, or just to see what the Samba developers have been up to lately.

The Samba team keeps the latest Samba source code in a Subversion (SVN) repository. SVN is a freely available source configuration management system distributed under an Apache/BSD-style license. You can download the latest subversion release from *http://subversion.tigris.org*. The Samba team describes various ways to access its own SVN repositories at *http://devel.samba.org*.

Samba's SVN tree is broken up into multiple branches, one branch for each development effort. The current list of branches is as follows:

SAMBA_3_0
> This is the branch for all Samba 3.0 development. The code in the tree can undergo major changes between each 3.0.x release. If you want to watch (or participate in) the bleeding edge of Samba 3.0 development, this is the branch to obtain.

SAMBA_3_0_XX
> Each numeric 3.0 release (e.g., 3.0.23) will be assigned a branch for bug fixes (also know as *letter* releases). For example, the SAMBA_3_0_23 branch was created once version 3.0.23 was publicly available. Developers commit fixes to this tree for inclusion in the next bug fix release, such as 3.0.23a, 3.0.23b, and so on. This approach allows the more aggressive development to continue in the SAMBA_3_0 tree, making it easier to fix any minor, but important bugs in the current release code.

SAMBA_3_0_RELEASE

This branch contains the most recently released (or about to be released) version of Samba 3.0.

SAMBA_4_0

This is the research branch used for developing features under the guise of Samba 4. Refer to Chapter 1 for more information on Samba 4.

Once you have a working SVN client and have decided which branch to download, you can obtain the source tree with a single command. The following example downloads the current Samba 3.0 development tree to a local directory named *samba3*:

```
$ svn co svn://svnanon.samba.org/samba/branches/SAMBA_3_0 samba3
```

The resulting directory tree will have the same structure as the Samba source distribution described in Chapter 2, except with additional directories named *.svn* throughout the source tree. These directories are used by SVN to store information about each file in the source tree and how to update them.

Before following the steps outlined in Chapter 2 to compile Samba, build the *configure* script and related files by running the *autogen* command. You must have Autoconf version 2.53 or higher installed in order to perform this step.

```
$ cd samba3/source
$ ./autogen.sh
./autogen.sh: running script/mkversion.sh
./script/mkversion.sh: 'include/version.h' created for
  Samba("3.0.24pre1-SVN-build-17944")
./autogen.sh: running autoheader
./autogen.sh: running autoconf
Now run ./configure and then make.
```

You are now ready to build the Samba SVN tree, using the same procedures as you would for an official source release.

> You can also download the Samba SVN trees using anonymous *rsync* from *rsync://rsync.samba.org/ftp/unpacked/*.

The Samba developers typically update the Samba source code multiple times per day. Whenever you want to catch up to the latest changes, *cd* to the *samba3* directory and run the following command:

```
$ svn up
```

Each time you do this, you must reconfigure, recompile, and reinstall to update your installation, as we showed you in Chapter 2.

Configure Options

As we explained in Chapter 2, the *configure* program is run before the Samba source code is compiled to adapt the build process to the local architecture. At this stage, it is possible to specify options to customize Samba's behavior further and include or exclude features. Here is an example of specifying configure options:

```
$ ./configure --prefix=/opt/samba --with-acl-support
```

This example specification configures the Samba installation to install in */opt/samba* rather than the default of */usr/local/samba* and to include support for filesystem ACLs. We have picked these two configure options because they illustrate the usage of the two types of options that are included in versions up to Samba 3.0. The --with-acl-support option is a Boolean option, which can take a value of yes or no. If you want to be more explicit, you can specify --with-acl-support=yes. To turn an option off explicitly, you can also specify --without-*feature* rather than --with-*feature*=no.

Options such as --prefix are following by an equal sign (=) and one or more arguments. In this case, we are specifying a directory to be used as the software's install root.

The supported configure options vary from release to release. To get a list of the configure options for your release, use the following command:

```
$ ./configure --help
```

Table C-1 lists the *configure* options found in the 3.0.22 release.

Table C-1. Configuration options

Configuration option	Description
--enable-cups	Use the CUPS client libraries when communicating with *cupsd* to manage printers and print jobs.
--enable-debug	Build Samba to include debugging symbols for use with debuggers such as gdb.
--enable-developer	Enable additional compiler flags and other developer settings.

Table C-1. Configuration options (continued)

Configuration option	Description
`--enable-dmalloc`	Enable integration with the dmalloc memory debugging library.
`--enable-iprint`	Include support for the iPrint server libraries from Novell.
`--enable-pie`	Turn on support for Position Independent Executables (PIE) when compiling.
`--enable-socket-wrapper`	Replace basic network socket support with a local communication needed to run *make test*.
`--with-aio-support`	Support asynchronous disk I/O.
`--with-acl-support`	Support Unix filesystem ACLs.
`--with-ads`	Include support for Active Directory integratio (requires `--with-krb5` and `--with-ldap`).
`--with-afs`	Support clear-text logins to access Andrew Filesystem (AFS) mounts.
`--with-automount`	Support locating home directories in NIS automount maps.
`--with-cfenc=`*directory*	Use internal CoreFoundation encoding API when building on OS X/Darwin.
`--with-cifsmount`	Build the Linux CIFS filesystem mount helper utilities.
`--with-configdir=`*directory*	Location of configuration files.
`--with-dce-dfs`	Support clear-text logins to access DCE/DFS mounts.
`--with-fake-kaserver`	Include AFS Kerberos Authentication (KA) server support.
`--with-fhs`	Use FHS-compliant locations of files.
`--with-included-popt`	Use Samba's *popt( )* libraries rather than the system version.
`--with-krb5=`*base-dir*	Support Kerberos 5 (required for ADS support).
`--with-ldap`	Support communicating with LDAP directory services (required for ADS support).
`--with-libiconv=`*directory*	Specify the location of the iconv library.
`--with-libmsrpc`	Build the MS-RPC client library.
`--with-libsmbclient`	Build the SMB/CIFS client library.
`--with-libsmbsharemodes`	Build the share modes *tdb* library.
`--with-lockdir=`*directory*	Location of lock files.
`--with-logfilebase=`*directory*	Location of logfiles.
`--with-pam`	Enable PAM support in *smbd*.
`--with-pam_smbpass`	Build *pam_smbpass.so* PAM module.
`--with-piddir=`*directory*	Location of PID files.
`--with-privatedir=`*directory*	Location of *smbpasswd* file.
`--with-profiling-data`	Support gathering of profiling information.
`--with-quotas`	Support interaction with filesystem disk quotas.
`--with-readline=`*directory*	Enable support for the readline library.
`--with-sendfile-support`	Support *sendfile( )* system call.
`--with-smbmount`	Support *smbmount* and smbfs.

Table C-1. Configuration options (continued)

Configuration option	Description
`--with-smbtorture4-path=path`	Specify the location of the *smbtorture* tool from the SAMBA_4_0 SVN branch for use in *make test*.
`--with-spinlocks`	Use spinlocks instead of fcntl locks.
`--with-static-modules=modules` `--with-shared-modules=modules`	List plug-ins that should be linked statically into Samba or built as shared libraries.
`--with-swatdir=directory`	Location of SWAT files.
`--with-syslog`	Support syslog message logging.
`--with-sys-quotas`	Include support for Samba's filesystem quota abstraction layer.
`--with-utmp`	Support utmp file accounting.
`--with-vfs-afsacl`	Inlucde the AFS ACL Virtual Filesystem (VFS) plug-in.
`--with-winbind`	Build Winbind support.

Install Directory and Library Options

`--prefix=directory`

Define the install *root* directory used for the Samba daemons, client tools, configuration files, and libraries.

`--enable-pie`

Enable support for Position Independent Executables (PIE), if supported by the compiler.

`--with-cfenc=directory`

Enable support for special Unicode encodings when building on OS X/Darwin systems.

`--with-configdir=directory`

The directory in which Samba keeps its configuration file, usually called *smb.conf*.

`--with-fhs`

Adhere to the Filesystem Hierarchy Standard (FHS) when locating files. For details, see *http: //www.pathname.com/fhs*.

`--with-included-popt`

Include Samba's own support for parsing command-line options, instead of using the local system's *popt( )* C-library function.

`--with-krb5=base-dir`

Include support for Kerberos Version 5, specifying the base directory of the Kerberos distribution. This version of Kerberos is compatible with Windows 2000 and Windows Server 2003 Active Directory domains.

`--with-ldap`

> Include support for accessing LDAP directory services. This includes using the *ldapsam* `passdb` plug-in and integration with Active Directory. Currently, Samba supports only the OpenLDAP client libraries joining an AD domain.

`--with-libiconv=`*directory*

> A location for *iconv()* support. The *iconv()* function exists in the C library to perform conversion between different character sets. This option allows Samba's default method of determining the location of the *iconv()* library to be overridden. Ordinarily, the configuration process checks for support in the C library on the system and, if not found, uses code included in the Samba source tree. Using `--with-libiconv`, it is possible to specify explicitly where the support is located. The *include* files are assumed to be in *directory/include*, and library files are assumed to be in *directory/lib*.

`--with-lockdir=`*directory*

> The directory in which Samba keeps its database of information, including *tdb* files, *browse.dat* and *wins.dat*.

`--with-logfilebase=`*directory*

> The directory in which Samba keeps logfiles for the *smbd*, *nmbd*, and *winbindd* daemons.

`--with-piddir=`*directory*

> The directory in which Samba keeps the PID files for keeping track of the process IDs of the parent Samba daemons.

`--with-privatedir=`*directory*

> The directory in which Samba keeps the *smbpasswd*, *secrets.tdb,* and related files for authentication.

`--with-readline=`*directory*

> Location for *readline()* support. The readline function exists in the C library to accept a line of input from an interactive user and provide support for editing and history. Samba uses these functions in *smbclient* and *rpcclient*.

`--with-swatdir=`*directory*

> Where to install the HTML and images files for SWAT.

Developer Options

`--enable-debug`
`--enable-developer`
`--enable-dmalloc`

> These options are of primary use to Samba developers or when tracking down a bug in the Samba source code. The `--enable-debug` option provides the necessary symbols for use with debuggers such as *gdb*. The `--enable-developer` option is for adding additional compiler checks. And the `--enable-dmalloc` option support for the dmalloc runtime memory debugging tools.

`--enable-socket-wrapper`

> Include the internal socket wrapper libraries needed to support running a suite of regression tests driven by the *make test* command.

`--with-profiling-data`

> Include support for analyzing the execution time of Samba's internal code.

`--with-smbtorture4-path=`*path*

> Location of the *smbtorture* tool built from the the SAMBA_4_0 SVN branch. The Samba 4 version of this utility offers a much wider ranges of tests than the older one included in the Samba 3.0 releases.

Authentication Options

`--with-ads`

> This is a convenience option that enables both `--with-krb5` and `--with-ldap`. Both Kerberos 5 and LDAP support must be present on the system in order to support integration with Active Directory. More on building and configuring Samba in AD domains is discussed in Chapters 2 and 10.

`--with-afs`

> Include support for authenticating users who are accessing files on an Andrew Filesystem (AFS) mount thourgh Samba. This option requires that clear-text passwords be enabled on both the client and Samba server. Because it is not actively maintained, this feature may be removed in a future release. More details about users and authentication can be found in Chapter 5.

`--with-dce-dfs`

> Include support for authenticating users in a Distributed Computing Environment Distributed Filesystem (DCE/DFS) environment. This is a distributed filesystem included in some Unix variants and is not the same as Microsoft's Distributed Filesystem (MS-DFS). This option requires clear-text password functionality to be enabled on both the client and Samba server. Because it is not actively maintained, this feature may be removed in a future release. More details about users and authentication can be found in Chapter 5.

`--with-fake-kaserver`

> This option allows Samba to act as a Kerberos Authentication (KA) server when exporting AFS volumes.

`--with-pam`

> When this configure option is specified and the parameter obey pam restrictions in the Samba configuration file is set to yes, Samba obeys PAM's configuration regarding account and session management. More information on Samba's use of PAM is in Chapter 5.

--with-pam_smbpass

When this option is specified, the compilation process builds a PAM module called *pam_smbpass.so* and places it in the *source/bin* directory. This module allows applications outside of the Samba suite to authenticate users with Samba's configured `passdb` backend. For more information, see the *README* file in the *source/pam_smbpass* directory of the Samba distribution.

--with-winbind

Include Winbind support in Samba. This option is enabled automatically on systems that are known to support Winbind functionality. For more information on Winbind, see Chapter 10.

File Serving Features

--with-aio-support

Include experimental support for using the operating system's asynchronous disk I/O features. This is currently supported only on Linux platforms.

--with-acl-support

Include support for Unix filesystem access control lists (ACLs). The server must provide a filesystem ACL interface that is supported by Samba. See Chapter 6 for details.

--with-automount

Include support for the automounter, a feature often used in conjunction with NFS, to mount NFS shares automatically at the first attempt to access them. This feature is not actively maintained and may be removed in a future release.

--with-nisplus-home

Include support for locating the NIS+ server that is serving a particular user's home directory and telling the client to connect to it. Use `--with-automount` along with this option. This feature is not actively maintained and may be removed in a future release.

--with-quotas

Include integration with filesystem disk-quota support.

--with-sendfile-support

Check to see whether the Samba host operating system supports the *sendfile()* system call, which speeds up file transfers by copying data directly to and from kernel buffers, avoiding the overhead of copying to and from buffers in user space. If the operating system has the *sendfile()* system call, support is included in Samba for the `use sendfile` configuration file option.

--with-spinlocks

Use spin locks instead of the normal method of file locking that uses the *fcntl()* C-library function. Using this option results in a Samba installation that consumes much more CPU time on the host system. Use it only when absolutely necessary.

`--with-syslog`

Include support for syslog error logging. This option must be specified for the Samba configuration file parameters syslog and syslog only to work. This option is widely supported, but might not work correctly on all Samba host systems.

`--with-sys-quotas`

Include Samba's quota abstraction layer when integrating with filesystem quotes. Also refer to the `--with-quotas` option.

`--with-utmp`

Include support for user accounting in the system's *utmp* file. This option is necessary for the utmp and utmp directory Samba configuration file options to work. The option is widely supported, but might not work correctly on all Samba host systems.

`--with-vfs-afsacl`

Build a VFS module for interacting with AFS ACLs rather than using the default POSIX ACL mapping enabled by the `--with-acl-support` option.

Printing Options

`--enable-cups`

Include support for communicating with a CUPS server using the *libcups.so* library. The server must have the CUPS header files and development libraries installed for this feature. More about Samba, CUPS, and printing is presented in Chapter 7.

`--enable-iprint`

Include support for communicating with the Novell iPrint server. The server must have the iPrint header files and development libraries installed for this feature. More about Samba and printing is presented in Chapter 7.

Clients and Libraries

`--with-cifsmount`

Enable building the Linux *cifs* mount helper tools (*mount.cifs* and *umount.cifs*). You can find more information about the Linux *cifs* filesystem in Chapter 11.

`--with-libmsrpc`

Create the static and shared version (if supported on the platform) of a Remote Procedure Call (RPC) client library.

`--with-libsmbclient`

Create the static and shared version (if supported on the platform) of an SMB/CIFS client library.

`--with-libsmbsharemodes`

> Create the static and shared versions (if supported on the platform) of a library that allows file services outside of *smbd* to access Samba's share mode database. This option allows for integrating SMB/CIFS file locking with other file-sharing protocols, such as NetWare.

`--with-smbmount`

> Enable building the user-space utilities for mounting the Linux *smbfs* filesystem. Note that the *cifs* filesystem has made *smbfs* obselete.

`--with-static-modules=`*modules*
`--with-shared-modules=`*modules*

> Enable a list of plug-ins to be built as static features inside of Samba or as external share libraries. The primary use of these options is to build Winbind's *idmap_rid* and *idmap_ad* modules as shared libraries. More about Winbind and idmap backends can be found in Chapter 10.

Index

We'd like to hear your suggestions for improving our indexes. Send email to *index@oreilly.com*.

B

backends (CUPS modules), 212
    passdb, 125–131, 255
backup browser, 224, 227
backup domain controllers (BDCs), 24
backups, 323
bcast (name resolve order), 222
bind interfaces only option (smb.conf
        file), 103
broadcast address, 365
browse lists, 21, 223
browser
    backup, 227
    potential, 224
browser elections, 22, 224
browsing, 216, 223–229, 354–359
    a list of computers and shared resources,
        defined, 21
    anonymous, 318
    cross-subnet, 231
    server from the client, 359
    shared resource of a specific computer, 21
Browsing and Windows 95 Networking and
        CIFS/E Browser Protocol, 229
browsing configuration options, 233
browsing daemon, 373
browsing enhancements, 231
browsing, configuring Samba for, 229
BSD printing system, adding, 211
BSD Unix, 211–212
    automatically starting Samba
        daemons, 55
byte range locking, 152, 160

C

C$ share, 149
Can't copy service name, unable to copy to
        itself, 351
Can't find include file [name], 351
capturing network traffic, 340
case preservation, 154
case sensitivity, 154
check password script, 136
checking (message from configure script), 40
CIFS (Common Internet File System), 1
cifs mount helper tools, 417
CIFS Technical Reference from the Storage
        Network Industry Association, 310
clear-text passwords, 116
Client for Microsoft Networks, 63

commands, 375–408
    eventlogadm (see eventlogadm command)
    findsmb, 378
    net (see net command)
    nmblookup (see nmblookup command)
    ntlm_auth, 384
    options
        authentication, 376
        common, 375
        connection, 377
    pdbedit (see pdbedit)
    profiles, 388
    smbcacls, 388
    smbclient (see smbclient program)
    smbcontrol (see smbcontrol command)
    smbcquotas, 398
    smbget, 401
    smbpasswd (see smbpasswd)
    smbspool, 402
    smbstatus, 402
    smbtar, 403
    smbtree, 404
    tdbbackup, 404
    tdbdump, 405
    tdbtool (see tdbtool program)
    testparm (see testparm commands)
    wbinfo (see wbinfo command)
comment option (smb.conf file), 98
Common Internet File System (see CIFS)
comp.protocols.smb newsgroup, 369
compiling and installing Samba, 42–45
components, Windows, 62
Computer Management MMC plug-in, 262
config.log file, 40
config.status file, 43
configuration files, 43
configure options, 411–418
    bindir, 38
    datadir, 38
    enable-cups, 37, 411, 417
    enable-debug, 37, 411, 414
    enable-developer, 411, 414
    enable-dmalloc, 412, 414
    enable-iprint, 412, 417
    enable-pie, 412, 413
    enable-socket-wrapper, 412, 415
    libdir, 38
    localstatedir=directory, 38
    mandir, 38
    prefix, 38, 411
    prefix=directory, 413

relative identifier (RID), 24, 122
Remote Administration Protocol (RAP), 326
remote announce (browsing configuration
       options), 233
remote announce option, 232
   smb.conf file, 232
remote browse sync (browsing configuration
       options), 233
Remote Procedure Call (RPC), 272
Remote Procedure Call (RPC) client
       library, 417
Remote Registry Service, 264
remote server management, 261–270
   file shares, 261
   Performance Monitor, 268
   services, 264
rename user script, 246
require_membership_of=SID option (pam_
       windbind), 301
resolv.conf file, 219
RFC2307bis extensions, 129
RID (relative identifier), 122
root preexec, 183
rpcclient program, 30
rpm command (Unix), 33

S

SAM (Security Account Manager), 24
Samba
   advantages of using, 3
   as domain member server, 25
   common services, 2
   distribution, overview, 29
   downloading, 35
   introduction, 1–31
   simple network, 3
   web site, 31
   what is, 2
Samba 3.0, roles, 28
Samba backup domain (BDC)
   configuring, 252–254
       passdb recommendations, 253
Samba Primary Domain Controller (PDC)
   configuring, 235–252
       managing users and groups, 241–246
       setting up domain joins, 236–241
       system policies, 250
       user profiles, 246–250
   five minimum requirements, 235
Samba public GPG key, 35

Samba Web Administration Tool (see
       SWAT)
samba-vscan virus scanning plug-in, 181
search paths, setting, 45
secret key (Kerberos), 277
secrets.tdb, 414
section, 90
Security Descriptor Definition Language
       (SDDL), 266
security descriptors, 171
security levels, 112
security modes, 112–121
security tab in Explorer, 175
security, and printers, 205
SeMachineAccountPrivilege, 238
server announcements, 228
Server Manager (srvmgr.exe)
       application, 256
server scripts, executing, 182
server string option (smb.conf file), 96
service, 193
Service Location Protocol (SLP), 216
Service Ticket (Kerberos), 277
services, 330
session key (Kerberos), 277
session primitives, 17
session services (NBT)
   defined, 17
   tips, 18
set primary group script, 246
setuid binaries, 310
shares, 329
   ADMIN$, 149
   C$, 149
   PRINT$, 149
   special names, 148
sharing files, 4
sharing printers, 7
short preserve case, 156
SID (Windows security identifier), 122
SIDs (security identifiers), 24
SIGHUP signal, 374
SIGTERM (15) signal, 374
SMB networking, 217
SMB printer sharing in OS X, 196
SMB URI syntax, 371
smb.conf file, 46, 48–53, 80–111
   [homes], 90
   [printers] section, 90
   browsing, 233

About the Authors

Gerald (Jerry) Carter received his master's degree in computer science from Auburn University, where he continues to pursue his Ph.D. His involvement with Unix systems and network administration of Unix began in 1995, and he has been a member of the Samba development team since 1998. Jerry currently works for Hewlett-Packard, working on embedded printing appliances. He has published articles with various web-based magazines and teaches instructional courses as a consultant for several companies and conferences.

Jay Ts is a system administrator and programmer with many years of experience working with several versions of Unix and other operating systems. Nowadays, he works as an independent consultant out of his home in Sedona, Arizona.

Robert Eckstein has worked with Java since its first release. In a previous life, he was an editor for O'Reilly Media, Inc. and a programmer for Motorola's cellular technology division. He has authored, co-authored, or edited a number of books, including *Java Swing*, *Java Enterprise Best Practices*, *Using Samba*, *XML Pocket Reference*, and *Webmaster in a Nutshell*. In his spare time, he has been known to tinker with filmmaking and digital photography, as well as collect vintage video game consoles. He currently lives in Austin, Texas, with his wife, Michelle, his children, Lauren and Nathan, and their talking dog, Ginger.

Colophon

The animal on the cover of *Using Samba*, Third Edition, is an African ground hornbill (*Bucorvus cafer*). This type of bird is one of 50 hornbill species. The African ground hornbill is a medium- to large-size bird characterized by a bright red waddle under a very long beak, dark-colored body and wings, long eyelashes, and short legs. Like all hornbills, it has a casque, a large but lightweight growth on the top of its beak, which grows more folds as the bird ages. It is the only ground-dwelling species of hornbill, though it is able to fly when necessary. It lives in the grasslands of southern and eastern Africa and nests in the foliage of dense trees, not in nest holes in the ground as other hornbills do. Its diet includes mostly fruit, as well as large insects and small mammals. The African ground hornbill is considered sacred by many Africans, and, as such, this bird is part of many legends and superstitions.

The cover image is a 19th-century engraving from the Dover Pictorial Archive. The cover font is Adobe ITC Garamond. The text font is Linotype Birka; the heading font is Adobe Myriad Condensed; and the code font is LucasFont's TheSans Mono Condensed.

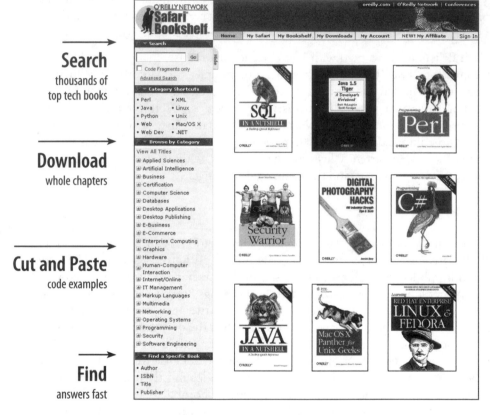